ALSO BY BILL SLOAN

Brotherhood of Heroes: The Marines at Peleliu, 1944—
The Bloodiest Battle of the Pacific War

Given Up for Dead: America's Heroic Stand at Wake Island

JFK: Breaking the Silence

JFK: The Last Dissenting Witness

Elvis, Hank, and Me: Making Musical History on the Louisiana Hayride
(with Horace Logan)

The Other Assassin (fiction)

The Mafia Candidate (fiction)

THE ULTIMATE

Bill Sloan

BATTLE

OKINAWA 1945 — THE LAST EPIC STRUGGLE OF WORLD WAR II

Simon & Schuster

New York London Toronto Sydney

Simon & Schuster
1230 Avenue of the Americas
New York, NY 10020

First Simon & Schuster hardcover edition October 2007

SIMON & SCHUSTER and colophon are registered trademarks
of Simon & Schuster, Inc.

For information about special discounts for bulk purchases,
please contact Simon & Schuster Special Sales at
1-800-456-6798 or business@simonandschuster.com

Designed by Davina Mock-Maniscalco

Maps by Paul J. Pugliese

Illustration credits can be found on page 403.

Manufactured in the United States of America

10   9   8   7   6   5   4   3   2   1

Library of Congress Cataloging-in-Publication Data
Sloan, Bill, date.
The ultimate battle : Okinawa 1945—the last epic struggle of World War II / Bill Sloan.
p. cm.
Includes bibliographical references and index.
1. World War, 1939–1945—Campaigns—Japan—Okinawa Island.
2. Civilian war casualties—Japan—Okinawa Island.
3. Okinawa Island (Japan)—History, Military. I. Title.

D767.99.O45S57 2007
940.54'252294—dc22   2007016871

ISBN-13: 978-0-7432-9246-7
ISBN-10:   0-7432-9246-4

To the memory of PFC Alfred E. "Al" Henderson, my late father-in-law, who fought at Okinawa with the 96th Recon Troop of the 96th "Deadeye" Division. After the war, like many other veterans who survived the battle, he never talked about what happened to him there. Now I can understand why.

Contents

Prologue: June 10, 1945   1

1. Building an "Iceberg"   9

2. "Like a Stroll in the Park"   30

3. Kids' Games, Pony Rides, and Barbecue   53

4. A Nasty Surprise on the Way South   67

5. A Divine and Deadly Wind   88

6. Death in the Hills, Death at Home   112

7. A Wall of Stone and Flame   135

8. Mud, Blood, and May-hem   151

9. Bitter Toll at Sugar Loaf   174

10. The Limits of Human Endurance   195

11. Divine Wind—Part II   216

12. The Crowded, Angry Skies   238

13. Collapse of the Shuri Line   255

14. The End of an Army   273

15. A Civilian Catastrophe   296

16. A Somber Victory   312

17. The Atomic Bomb—and Reprieve   331

Epilogue: Love Day Plus Sixty-two Years   353

Sources   365

Bibliography   377

Acknowledgments   383

Index   385

Maps

Okinawa 1945   32

Southern Okinawa   75

Major Action at Sea   95

Prologue

TANK COMMANDER Jack H. Armstrong was bleeding from both ears, addled by a concussion, and deafened by the shell that had just ripped a jagged eight-inch hole through the center of his Sherman tank, missing Armstrong by a foot or two at best.

The M4A1 Sherman was one of three tanks that had moved out ahead of infantry units of the First Marine Division this morning to scout enemy-infested Kunishi Ridge, the last remaining Japanese stronghold near the southern tip of Okinawa. When they'd come under intense artillery fire, the other two tanks managed to beat a hasty retreat, but Armstrong and his crew, grinding along in the lead, weren't so fortunate.

In the soundless void whirling around him, acting Sergeant Armstrong wondered if he was seriously wounded, maybe dying. Death was a constant companion these days for men of the First Marine Tank Battalion, and the expectation of being killed or maimed at any moment was as much a part of life as breathing. But now death felt especially close and intimate, and, as Armstrong squinted through the tank's smoldering innards at the young second lieutenant sprawled a few feet from him, he understood why.

The lieutenant, who'd come along on their mission strictly as an observer, was still writhing in agony, but it was obvious that he'd be dead soon. His belly was split wide open, and his intestines spilled out into his lap. His left forearm hung by a thin strand of mangled flesh. This was the lieutenant's first combat mission. It would also be his last.

The lieutenant's mouth moved, and Armstrong read the plea on his bloody lips without hearing them:

1

"Oh God, Mama, help me."

Armstrong turned to see Corporal Stephen Smith, the tank's driver, crawling toward him. As tank commander, it was Armstrong's responsibility to take charge of the situation.

He nodded toward the lieutenant. "I hate to move him, but let's try to get him outside," he told Smith, feeling the words vibrate in his throat. "If we take another hit, we're all dead."

Armstrong watched as the lieutenant pulled out his Ka-Bar knife and severed the thread of tissue that bound his ruined left arm to his body. When the arm fell away, its former owner dropped the knife and looked at Armstrong. "That might make it a little easier," he whispered.

With Armstrong attempting to hold the lieutenant's exposed organs in place, he and Smith half carried and half dragged him down through the escape hatch in the floor of the tank. Behind them, Private David Spoerke, the designated loader for the 75-millimeter cannon, moved to aid the Sherman's bow gunner and assistant driver, PFC Ben Okum, who was moaning and bleeding from wounds in his arm and leg.

It took what seemed like an hour for the five of them to make it to a nearby shell crater that was barely far enough away to keep them from being blown up with the disabled tank if it should explode. By the time they laid the lieutenant in the deepest part of the hole, his eyes were glazed and his face was grayish.

"Give me some morphine, and get out of here," he whispered. "They may open up on us again any second."

Armstrong's hearing was beginning to come back, and the lieutenant's words were faintly audible. "We can't leave you here like this," Armstrong said. "We'll try to get you a medic."

"Just go, Jack," the lieutenant said. "Don't waste your time."

Smith broke open one of the needle-equipped morphine packets that each Marine routinely carried and injected the dying man in the neck. Armstrong put some extra packets beside the lieutenant's right hand, and Spoerke tried to tie a belt around the stump of his left arm to slow the bleeding.

"Get moving," the lieutenant said. "That's an order."

The lieutenant was a new replacement who'd just joined the battalion as a platoon leader, and he'd been around only for a day or two. Armstrong couldn't even remember his name, but he seemed like a decent enough guy. He was a friendly, easygoing sort who got along well with the tank crews. He was also a helluva lot tougher than he looked.

Any man who can cut off his own arm with a Ka-Bar has to be one gritty SOB, Armstrong thought, *even if he's too deep in shock to know what he's doing.*

"Aye, sir," Armstrong said. "We'll send help back as soon as we can."

In his dazed condition, Armstrong almost forgot that he was under strict orders to destroy the gyrostabilizer unit on the tank's 75-millimeter gun to keep it from falling into enemy hands, so he had to stagger over to the Sherman, drop a grenade into the unit, and scramble back to safety.

Back at the crater, he took a last look at the lieutenant, who was silent and ashen but still appeared to be breathing. Then he bit his lip and turned to help Smith with the wounded gunner. As they stumbled back along the draw they'd come down a few minutes earlier, a burst of fire from Japanese rifles and automatic weapons kicked up dust inches from their heels. Armstrong took one brief glance over his shoulder at a hillside literally crawling with Japanese, each of them firing at the fleeing tankers. Then he ran for all he was worth, pulling Okum along by his good arm and thinking: *Those guys must be the worst shots in the Japanese army! How can all of them possibly be missing us?*

This was the third tank that had been blown out from under Armstrong in just over a month—the first by a volley of armor-piercing shells from a Japanese antitank gun, the second by a land mine. Four or five guys—both tank crewmen and members of the infantry fire team accompanying the tank—had been wounded in the blast from the land mine, at least two fatally, and Armstrong had lost a damned good driver to the antitank gun. But this third time seemed worse than the others. The image of the lieutenant lying in the shell hole haunted Armstrong, and he couldn't block it out of his mind.

Okum was dragging his bad leg behind him, and Armstrong was gasping for breath and wondering how much farther he could run when he spotted a rice paddy dead ahead. He pushed the driver over the bank into the shallow water and jumped in after him. Then both of them slogged desperately through the oozy, reeking mixture of mud and human excrement toward the safety of a rear area a half mile away.

⁓

A COUPLE OF HOURS LATER, his ears still ringing and his head pounding furiously, Armstrong made a distressing discovery: The shell that had doomed his tank hadn't come from enemy artillery. It had been fired from one of the First Marine Division's own 105-millimeter howitzers.

"We heard that General Buckner himself, commander of the U.S. Tenth Army, was directing the fire," Armstrong would recall long after the incident. "I understand he apologized to our battalion CO, Colonel Jeb Stuart, but that didn't make us feel a whole lot better."

His third close brush with death left Armstrong gun-shy. He'd always heard that every near miss brought a guy closer to the "big one." If that was true, the odds were bound to be catching up with him. If the third time was the charm, like they said, what about the fourth? Part of him chafed to get back into action, but he felt a surge of relief on learning that no replacement tank was immediately available. And when a fellow tank commander invited him to ride along on a mission to resupply a frontline rifle company, Jack said, "Thanks, but no thanks."

Each of Armstrong's three lost tanks had borne the same handpainted nickname—"Ticket to Tokyo." The name had a brash, bold ring to it that had appealed to all the guys in the original crew. They'd all had a hand in picking it, and they'd gotten a big chuckle the first time they'd seen it.

In those early days on Okinawa, most of Armstrong's buddies had kiddingly called him "Wheaties," for the breakfast cereal that sponsored a popular radio program called *Jack Armstrong, All-American Boy*. It had been typical of the wisecracking and bravado that characterized the First Marine Tank Battalion then. Before Okinawa, the Sherman tank had operated with near impunity throughout the Pacific theater, where the "sardine-can" enemy tanks were no match for it in armor or firepower. Not anymore, though. Now the Japanese had antitank weapons that could make a Sherman look like a hunk of Swiss cheese—and frequently did.

This was one reason why, in recent weeks, Armstrong's sense of humor had gradually gone dormant. Not many things seemed funny anymore, much less cute or clever. Living with death day after day and seeing your friends killed or crippled could make you old and grim before your time, and many of the guys who'd kidded "Wheaties" Armstrong about his heroic fictional namesake were gone now. His assistant driver and close friend, Corporal Alvin Tenbarge, had been blown apart in the land mine explosion, and Corporal Harlan Stephan, one of the best drivers in the battalion, had—like the young lieutenant—lost an arm to an armor-piercing shell. The difference was that Harlan was still alive, the last Armstrong had heard.

The casualty list grew longer each day, with the end of it nowhere in sight, and as nasty as Okinawa was, it was merely a warm-up, or so everyone believed. Next loomed an invasion of Japan itself, and every man in the First Marine Division who could still fire a weapon would be issued his own one-way ticket there.

We'll have a million casualties, maybe more, the rumor mill needled. *Eighty percent of us'll never make it back to the States in one piece. Make a joke out of that if you can.*

And yet, if he should be given a fourth tank to command, Armstrong knew it would bear exactly the same name as the first three. Plenty of other names were available—like "Sweet Mary" for a girl he'd known in Melbourne an eternity or two ago, or "Lone Star" for his native state of Texas, or "Jap Zapper" just for the hell of it. For that matter, there was no law that said a tank couldn't simply remain anonymous.

The last thing Jack wanted anymore was a ticket to Tokyo—or any place else in Japan. The only ticket he wanted now was one that would take him home alive to a quiet street in the Oak Cliff section of Dallas. But to give his next tank a different name would dishonor the men who'd bled and died in its predecessors.

Almost two and a half months earlier, just after the landing, the battalion had been supremely confident—cocky even. Despite all the hype and horror stories that had circulated beforehand, the Okinawa campaign started as smoothly and uneventfully as a training exercise. Except for the kamikazes bedeviling U.S. shipping, it looked as if the Japanese no longer had either the stomach or the heart for an all-out fight. In fact, it seemed at first that the American invaders might roll unimpeded down the entire sixty-mile length of Okinawa without ever getting their gun barrels hot.

During those first few days, it had seemed like a piece of cake. Then the cake had blown up in their faces.

⁓

OKINAWA was the last battle of the largest war since civilization began and the deadliest campaign of conquest ever undertaken by American arms. It rang down the curtain on one momentous era in the earth's political/military history and raised the curtain on another era even more momentous.

It started on April 1, 1945—which happened to be Easter Sunday as well as April Fool's Day—when tens of thousands of U.S. assault troops stepped ashore uncontested into an eerie silence. When it ended nearly three months later, the battle for Okinawa had claimed the lives of some 240,000 human beings, according to best available estimates.

Okinawa pitted the 541,000-member U.S. Tenth Army—including 183,000 combat troops—against the 110,000-man Japanese 32nd Army in a grinding struggle of attrition that lasted until June 21, 1945. It matched the greatest U.S. naval armada ever assembled against the best-organized, most determined corps of suicide fighters in history—the kamikazes.

Most of the ground fighting took place amid a picturesque country-side framed by hills and mountains and dotted with hundreds of farms and scores of small villages and towns where the bulk of Okinawa's civilian population lived. The number of civilians killed, many by their own hands, can only be estimated, but some authorities place the figure as high as 140,000—or nearly one in every three of the island's residents in 1945.

When the shooting finally stopped, the bodies of 107,539 Japanese soldiers were counted. U.S. losses totaled 12,274 dead and 36,707 wounded in combat. An additional 26,000 American servicemen were evacuated with so-called "nonbattle injuries," most of them neuropsychiatric disorders caused by constant, ceaseless stress—the highest number of any World War II battle.

In a very real sense, each American survivor of Okinawa now alive still carries his own personal scars from the ordeal. Some scars are as obvious as a missing limb, some as unobtrusive as a fragment from an enemy mortar shell buried deep in flesh or bone. Other scars may exist only in the mind yet can be traced to some of the most grievous wounds of all.

In a perverse sort of way, however, survivors of the battle also know that they owe a debt of gratitude to Okinawa and to what they suffered there. The toll they paid in blood and misery was the decisive factor in convincing President Harry S. Truman to unleash the awesome power of the atomic bomb. Without it, many of the U.S. assault troops who lived through Okinawa would have faced the ultimate horror: an invasion of Japan itself, months of block-by-block street fighting in Japanese cities, and projected American casualties of 1 million or more.

In the sixty-odd years since the Okinawa campaign ended, the United States has fought many other battles in many other parts of the world but none as massive, desperate, or brutal. Today's push-button warfare and weapons of incalculable destructive power have rendered many of the military concepts and tactics employed at Okinawa—as well as the vast legions of men required to activate them—as obsolete on the battlefield as spears, arrows, and stone catapults.

In view of this, it seems doubtful that another battle the likes of Okinawa will ever be fought between America's armed forces and anybody else's. Beyond being the last battle of World War II, Okinawa may one day be recalled as the last great human struggle of its size and scope ever waged on Planet Earth.

If so, Jack Armstrong and the scores of his U.S. Army, Navy, and Marine Corps comrades who tell their personal stories in the following pages may be the last human eyewitnesses to a spectacle as vast and soul-searing as was Okinawa in the spring of 1945.

They would tell you—to a man—that they fervently hope so.

CHAPTER ONE

Building an "Iceberg"

A s WITH MOST of the Japanese-held islands they assaulted in their long, brutal trek across the Pacific, virtually none of the GIs and Marines assigned to invade Okinawa had ever heard of the place until a few weeks before they landed there.

PFC Gene Sledge, a mortarman in K Company, Third Battalion, Fifth Marine Regiment (K/3/5), first saw the name when a friend showed him a *National Geographic* map of the Pacific and pointed to an island identified as Okinawa Shima. The very sight of it filled Sledge with foreboding. "Its closeness to Japan assured us of one thing beyond any doubt," he said. "Whatever else happened, the battle for Okinawa was bound to be bitter and bloody. The Japanese never sold any island cheaply, and the pattern of the war until then had shown that the battles became more vicious the closer we got to Japan."

"We were expecting the absolute worst at Okinawa," added PFC Bill Leyden, a fire team leader in K/3/5's First Rifle Platoon, who, like Sledge, had survived the holocaust of burning amtracks and dead and dying Marines on the beaches of Peleliu the previous September. "And everything the brass told us reinforced that expectation: We were gonna catch holy hell. It was gonna be the toughest landing of the war. We could expect 70 to 80 percent casualties on the beach, and so on."

As a raw replacement spoiling for his first taste of combat, Leyden had been in the first wave when he went ashore at Peleliu. Now, freshly recovered from a shrapnel wound that almost cost him his left eye—and one of just five combat-tested veterans in his platoon—he was quite satisfied to be in the fifteenth wave at Okinawa.

"I was older now—almost nineteen—and a little smarter, but not necessarily bolder," recalled the native New Yorker. "I'd figured out that I wasn't indestructible, after all."

THE HIGH-RANKING U.S. military leaders who began detailed planning for the Okinawa invasion in early October 1944 picked a seemingly odd code name for what would become the largest land-sea-air
assault in American history. For reasons best known to the admirals
and generals themselves, the coming fight for temperate, subtropical
Okinawa was labeled "Operation Iceberg."

Just what prompted this choice of names remains a mystery today,
even among survivors of the battle. Conceivably, Iceberg could have
been selected in hopes of misleading any enemy spies who came across
it. Almost everyone on both sides believed an American invasion of
Japan's homeland was just ahead, and some Japanese strategists had
long speculated that it might come by way of the Aleutian and Kurile
Islands—definitely iceberg country. In fact, thwarting such a U.S.
move had been a major motivation for Japan's seizure of Attu and
Kiska, the westernmost islands of the Aleutian chain, in 1942. On the
other hand, the Iceberg code name may have been merely a random
selection.

Whatever the rationale, the name seemed particularly incongruous
to Tech Sergeant Porter McLaughlin, a squad leader in an antitank platoon in the Army's Seventh Infantry Division. McLaughlin and his buddies had braved miles of oozy tundra, constant bone-chilling cold,
vicious arctic winds, and a fanatical enemy to reclaim Attu from its
Japanese captors in May 1943.

"A name like Iceberg would've fit Attu to a tee," said McLaughlin, an
Oregonian who had later been wounded at Kwajalein and also fought at
Leyte. "It was the wettest, coldest, most desolate place I've ever been, and
hundreds of our guys lost toes and feet to frostbite. But a more appropriate code name for Okinawa would've been 'Operation Inferno.'"

OKINAWA IS THE LARGEST ISLAND of the Ryukyus chain, which
curves west in a gradual arc stretching some 750 miles from just south
of Kyushu, the southernmost of Japan's home islands, nearly to Formosa, or Taiwan. It measures sixty miles long and up to eighteen miles
wide, but a narrow two-mile "waist"—the Ishikawa Isthmus—sepa-
rates the rugged, sparsely settled northern two-thirds of the island

from the southern third, where the vast majority of its 460,000 inhabitants were concentrated in the spring of 1945.

The quiet, simple Okinawan people held Japanese citizenship and were similar in appearance to the Japanese, yet of an ethnic stock that incorporated Mongol and Chinese influences and of smaller physical stature on average. The Japanese administrators who governed Okinawa generally looked down on the natives as rustic, peasant-class inferiors. Most lived in small villages or in the countryside, earning their living by farming and raising livestock. Below the isthmus, the gently rolling landscape of central Okinawa was dotted with neat farmsteads fringed with forests of banyan, bamboo, and pine and framed by steep ridges and deep ravines. Every acre of arable land was heavily cultivated in such food crops as sweet potatoes, sugar cane, beans, bananas, and rice. Pigs, goats, and chickens were also plentiful, as Marines and GIs with a taste for barbecue were quick to discover.

The island's capital and only true city was the port of Naha, population about 65,000 as of late 1944, before U.S. air strikes and naval shelling destroyed most of it and scattered its inhabitants. A few modern highways served the Naha area, but other Okinawan towns of consequence, including Shuri, Itoman, and Yonabaru, were connected only by primitive, unpaved roads more suited to ox carts than motor vehicles and virtually impassable during the rainy season.

Less than a century before its invasion by American forces, Okinawa had been a quasi-independent territory which maintained that status by paying hefty tributes to both China and Japan and had almost no contact with the outside world. But in 1853, Commodore Matthew Perry and his squadron of U.S. gunboats made a stop at Naha harbor en route to Yokohama to conclude a trade agreement with Japan's emperor.

Perry's visit and the Western influences that followed ignited momentous changes among the Japanese—including an aggressive thirst for territory that led to the annexation of Okinawa in 1879. Yet, prior to World War II, the lifestyle of the average Okinawan remained basically unchanged. At the time of the attack on Pearl Harbor, the largest island in the Ryukyus, known in the region as "the Great Loo Choo," was still virtually unknown in the West except among a few "geographers, historians, and maybe crossword puzzle fans," as one author put it.

By 1943, however, as the U.S. offensive against Japan intensified, Okinawa began drawing attention from America's highest-ranking military leaders, up to and including President Franklin Roosevelt. When FDR met in Cairo that year with British Prime Minister Winston Churchill and China's Marshal Chiang Kai-shek, decisions were reached that made Okinawa an increasingly likely target in the Allied grand strategy in the Pacific.

Until the early fall of 1944, however, the official strategic plan, known as Operation Causeway, called for an amphibious assault on Formosa, a target strongly favored by Admiral Ernest J. King, chief of naval operations, rather than Okinawa. The Formosa campaign was already penciled in for early 1945, and no one expected the tough-minded King—a man with a reputation for shaving with a blowtorch and chewing spikes for breakfast—to give up easily on his plan.

But Admiral Chester W. Nimitz, commander in chief of U.S. forces in the Pacific Ocean Area (CinCPOA), had become convinced that Operation Causeway should be scrapped or at least drastically altered. Although he originally supported an invasion of Formosa, Nimitz had grown to fear a disastrously high cost in casualties—up to 150,000 Americans killed or wounded. He also believed that Okinawa would serve as a better springboard for a direct assault on Japan because it was much closer to the home islands than Formosa. Finally, he concluded, control of Okinawa and Iwo Jima would cut off the Japanese from their chief oil supply sources in Burma, Borneo, and Sumatra, creating a severe fuel shortage for enemy ships and aircraft as the war entered its climactic phase.

The showdown between King and Nimitz came at a three-day meeting in San Francisco in early October 1944. At the time, the U.S. Joint Chiefs of Staff were deeply concerned that the prosecution of the war in the Pacific was behind schedule, and Nimitz's goal at the conference was to sell King on an altered strategy to speed matters up. The strategy called for abandoning the invasion of Formosa, which Nimitz was convinced was too strongly defended to be attacked successfully anytime soon. Instead, Nimitz would propose that Army General Douglas MacArthur's forces invade Luzon in the Philippines and that other Army and Marine units seize Iwo Jima and Okinawa.

Nimitz knew it was going to be a hard sell, so he prepared a strong, well-documented argument to support his case and brought along several key staff members to back him up. He was joined by Admiral Raymond A. Spruance, who shared command of the U.S. Pacific Battle Fleet with Admiral William F. "Bull" Halsey and who was on leave at nearby Monterey. Also accompanying Nimitz were Lieutenant General Simon

Bolivar Buckner, whose U.S. Tenth Army would draw the Okinawa amphibious assault assignment, and Lieutenant General Millard F. Harmon, overall commander of Air Force units in the Pacific area.

Both Nimitz and Buckner predicted ruinously high casualty rates in an invasion of Formosa, citing as evidence the 17,000 Americans killed and wounded in the fight for Saipan, where U.S. forces faced only 32,000 entrenched Japanese—a small fraction of the enemy force on Formosa. Based on these figures, Buckner estimated that American losses could exceed 150,000 men and seriously weaken U.S. resources in the Pacific.

King, as it turned out, had already seen a logistics report prepared for the Joint Chiefs that raised serious questions about the projected Formosa invasion, and Spruance had told King three months earlier that he supported an assault on Okinawa. Although King raised some tough questions and challenged parts of Nimitz's plan, he eventually agreed to cancel the Formosa operation in favor of Luzon, Iwo Jima, and Okinawa. Before the meeting adjourned, the grand scheme for the final phase of the Pacific war was in place, and tentative target dates were set for all three landings—December 20, 1944, for Luzon; January 20, 1945, for Iwo Jima; and March 1, 1945, for Okinawa—with the understanding that delay in the timetable might be necessary.

As the conference closed, both Nimitz and King still held out hope that a land battle for the Japanese homeland could be avoided and that the enemy could be battered into submission through massive, systematic air strikes against its cities. If not, however, the only remaining target for invasion after Okinawa would be Japan itself.

IN THE EARLY DAYS of the war, Okinawa had held a minimal—in fact, almost nonexistent—position in Tokyo's overall defensive strategy. As of late 1941, despite the fact that the Japanese fleet sometimes used Nakagusuku Bay on the east side of Okinawa as an anchorage, the only defense installations on the island consisted of a small naval station and airfield near Naha on the west coast and three artillery batteries manned by about 600 army troops.

Ironically, if the United States had invaded in late 1943, Okinawa probably would have fallen in a matter of hours, although Japanese air and naval forces assuredly would have made it difficult for American forces to hold the island. This situation remained unchanged until the spring of 1944, when the Imperial General Staff belatedly decided to arm the Ryukyus and base the 32nd Japanese Army on Okinawa. At the time, Tokyo still considered this a "rear area" mainly valuable for providing air support and a supply base for its forces in the Philippines and Marianas.

Even at this late date, a notable lack of urgency prevailed. It was June 29, 1944, before the 6,000 troops of the 44th Independent Brigade, the largest of the assigned Japanese army units, reached Okinawan waters aboard the troopship *Toyama Maru*—only to have it torpedoed beneath them by the U.S. submarine *Sturgeon*. The troopship sank like a rock, carrying more than 90 percent of the brigade—5,600 soldiers—to the bottom of the ocean. Then, as Imperial Headquarters scrambled to replace the lost brigade, the entire complexion of the Pacific war changed. Within days, American troops captured Saipan after a costly fight and broke through Japan's outer defensive perimeter in the Marianas. Far from being a relatively secure rear area, as Tokyo now realized, Okinawa stood directly in the path of the relentless U.S. march toward Japan proper.

Frantically, the Japanese rushed four infantry divisions and three independent brigades to Okinawa and other islands in the Ryukyus. They also assigned a tough new commander, Lieutenant General Mitsuru Ushijima, to take charge of the 32nd Army, replacing Lieutenant General Masao Watanabe, who was in failing health and incapable of directing a now-desperate campaign to fortify and hold Okinawa at all costs. Ushijima had served as an infantry commander in Burma in the early stages of the war and had later been appointed commandant of the Japanese Military Academy.

Considering that Ushijima, along with his chief of staff, Lieutenant General Isamu Cho, and his chief planning officer, Colonel Hiromichi Yahara, had barely nine months to prepare for what would be the greatest amphibious assault in American history, they did a remarkable job. They used the time to assemble a well-trained, well-armed 110,000-man fighting force, including 20,000 Okinawan conscripts, and to construct one of the most elaborate and impenetrable systems of natural and manmade defenses the world has ever seen.

While Operation Iceberg took shape on the American side, the Japanese were building their own veritable "iceberg" of coral and concrete within the ridges crisscrossing southern Okinawa. Like its oceanic counterparts, the deadliest portion of this iceberg lay hidden far below the surface—as tens of thousands of GIs and Marines would soon find out.

⸺

IN SOME RESPECTS, Ushijima, Cho, and Yahara represented one of the most effective and tactically brilliant teams of combat commanders ever put together by the Japanese army. But they were also a peculiar trio of opposites who frequently disagreed on strategy and whose personalities often clashed mercurially.

With bearing, mannerisms, and clipped mustache vaguely remindful of General John J. "Black Jack" Pershing, commander of the American Expeditionary Forces in World War I, Ushijima managed to exemplify both the finest in Samurai tradition and calm, dignified reserve. Always composed and never prone to excess, he remained above the sometimes heated give-and-take over critical issues, allowing members of his staff to thrash them out, then ratifying the decisions he deemed wisest. Yet he also took full responsibility for every order issued, ran an exceptionally well-ordered organization, and was held in the highest esteem by his officers and men.

Cho, by contrast, was an impetuous political extremist with a history of violence and skullduggery. In the early 1930s, as a member of a group of military hotheads who called themselves the Cherry Society, he had joined a plot to murder Japan's prime minister and replace him with a high-ranking general as dictator. At about this same time, he also advocated threatening the emperor at dagger's point, if necessary, to establish military rule in Japan. As an officer in virtually any other nation's army, Cho probably would have been executed for treason. But he had many admirers in the Japanese military—enough to be selected over a number of more experienced generals to become Ushijima's second in command. He was known for his hard-drinking, high-living, hard-driving style, and while his motives and methods may have been suspect in some quarters, no one ever questioned his personal courage or his ability to lead and inspire his soldiers.

Yahara, meanwhile, was Cho's direct opposite—a poised, deliberate intellectual whose aloof nature and unwillingness to pursue the failed tactics of banzai warfare made him unpopular with some of his peers but who was recognized as a planning genius even by those who disliked him. Despite the friction that often flared between them, Yahara and Cho also brought a rare kind of balance to Ushijima's staff. As one history of the battle for Okinawa noted: "Where Cho was impulsive, Yahara was deliberate; where Cho was almost mystically aggressive in the Samurai manner, Yahara was almost maddeningly rational."

It would fall to Yahara to design and fine-tune the strategy adopted by the 32nd Japanese Army in its defense of Okinawa. It was a strategy that flew in the face of every ingrained Samurai instinct that Cho held dear. But it was also a strategy that worked remarkably well.

Ushijima and his staff accurately guessed where the American landing would take place—on beaches near the village of Hagushi on the west side of the island just below the Ishikawa Isthmus. But under Yahara's plan, there would be no Japanese defense of the invasion beaches, no strongly fortified delaying points near the water's edge, and no reckless night-time counterattacks against the American beachhead. As Yahara, who had taken to heart the failure of such tactics at Peleliu and elsewhere, put it in one of his first directives to the 32nd Army: "Hand-to-hand combat with an enemy with superior firepower would be unsuccessful, especially at night."

Not only would the beaches and several miles of surrounding countryside be ceded to the invaders without resistance, but Okinawa's two largest and best military airfields, Yontan (aka Yomitan) and Kadena, also would be sacrificed because they were too close to the beaches to be held. Yahara's only concession was to position a major combat unit among rugged hills near enough to the airfields to keep them within range of Japanese mortars and artillery.

Three rugged ridge systems running roughly east and west across the southern third of Okinawa would form the core of Yahara's defense, and it was in these ridges that the bulk of the 32nd Army was put to work digging out intricate fortifications from which heavy artillery could strike any point in southern Okinawa and enlarging scores of natural caves into subterranean living quarters for thousands of men. Since the Okinawan hills had long served as a major artillery training center, the terrain was familiar to most Japanese gunners, and ranges and coordinates for many potential target areas were already well established. A network of caves beneath ancient Shuri Castle, which stood on one of the highest points on the island, would form the epicenter of the Japanese defenses and provide a secure haven for Ushijima and his staff that no American bomb or shell could penetrate.

Cho and others fumed over architect Yahara's meticulous strategy of static defense in depth. They branded it defeatist—and, in a sense, it was. Yahara had no illusions about his army's ability to hold the three ridge systems forever, and he was fully aware that the better-armed, better-equipped, more numerous Americans would eventually wear down the thinly stretched Japanese defenders. An integral part of his strategy was to hold each major defensive line as long as possible, then make an orderly withdrawal to the next line and repeat the process. Yahara knew full well that the 32nd Army would ultimately be destroyed, perhaps to the last man, and Okinawa would fall. But before it did, its defenders would exact a more fearful price in American blood than a thousand banzai charges could produce—a price possibly high enough to prevent an invasion of the Japanese homeland.

That, in the final analysis, was Yahara's only goal.

ON THE AMERICAN SIDE, meanwhile, Admiral Nimitz had picked some of his most capable and seasoned commanders to lead Operation Iceberg. Overseeing the long-range logistical planning for the operation was Nimitz's chief of staff, Rear Admiral Forrest Sherman. Admiral Raymond A. Spruance, whose Task Force 58 had scored the stunning victory at Midway in June 1942, turning the whole tide of the Pacific war in America's favor, was appointed Iceberg's officer in charge with the responsibility of protecting the invasion force before and during the battle. Placed in direct command of the amphibious forces was swashbuckling Vice Admiral Richmond Kelly Turner, whose fierce mannerisms were compared to those of a Celtic chieftain by historian Samuel Eliot Morison. Although his irascible nature irritated some of his peers, Turner had served with skill and distinction in similar roles in most of the major island campaigns in the Pacific, dating back to Guadalcanal.

Chosen to lead all ground forces of the U.S. Tenth Army—made up of four Army infantry divisions (the Seventh, 27th, 77th, and 96th) and three Marine divisions (the First, Second, and Sixth)—was Lieutenant General Simon Bolivar Buckner Jr., the handsome, forceful son and namesake of a Confederate Civil War general.

Although this would be his first experience in leading an entire army into combat, "Buck" Buckner was known as a "soldier's general" who preferred to spend his time at front-line positions rather than his own headquarters, and he was highly respected by his men. Tall and solidly built, with a mane of snow white hair, Buckner also looked the part of a "general's general," and he had the experience to back up his appearance. After serving in the Philippines during World War I, he was named commandant at West Point, and later oversaw the U.S. defensive buildup in Alaska and the Aleutians. He had been decorated for "distinguished and meritorious service" for his leadership in recapturing the islands of Attu and Kiska from the Japanese in 1942.

Heading the Marine contingent of the Tenth Army and serving as Buckner's second in command was Major General Roy S. Geiger, commander of the III Marine Amphibious Corps. Geiger was no stranger to ferocious, cave-busting combat, having been in overall charge of the bloody Peleliu campaign the previous September and October. As such, he had provided a much-needed voice of prudence and reason when other Marine officers were squandering lives in futile frontal assaults on a deeply entrenched enemy. One of the pioneers of Marine aviation, Geiger had also commanded the Corps' legendary "Cactus Air Force" at Guadalcanal.

Various historians and military observers have placed the total number of Tenth Army personnel at General Buckner's disposal on the eve of the Okinawa invasion at more than 541,000. But many of these were rear-echelon troops who would never hear a shot fired in anger during the battle, much less fire one themselves. The burden of solving the giant puzzle of Colonel Yahara's defenses and wresting Okinawa's high ground from General Ushijima's troops would rest on an amphibious assault force of just under 183,000 men.

Except for the 27th Infantry Division, which remained under-strength after suffering severe losses at Saipan, the other Army divisions had been enlarged from their usual strength of about 15,000 troops to almost 22,000 men each. The three reinforced Marine divisions averaged about 24,000 men apiece. All were seasoned fighting outfits, but each was heavily populated with new replacements untested in combat.

The 27th, a former New York National Guard unit counting only 16,143 men, was held in low regard by some U.S. commanders, who cited, in addition to its low numbers, inadequate training, inexperienced officers, and a subpar performance at Saipan, despite its high number of casualties. The fact that National Guard units were rarely sent into overseas combat also contributed to the decision to designate the 27th as a "floating reserve," whose primary projected role in the campaign would be to serve as an occupation garrison once the fighting was over.

Nevertheless, the 27th's commander, Major General George W. Griner, put his veterans and 2,700 new replacements through a rugged regimen of night maneuvers to get them as combat-ready as possible before embarking for Okinawa.

⌐

NEARLY SIX MONTHS before the first American ground troops landed on Okinawa, war had descended on the island from the skies, and its civilians had gotten their first bitter taste of the carnage and destruction they were destined to endure in the months ahead.

Early on the morning of October 10, 1944, only a week after the historic meeting between Admirals Nimitz and King in San Francisco, more than 1,000 Hellcat fighters, Helldiver bombers, and Avenger torpedo planes from Admiral Halsey's carriers struck the first major blow at Okinawa's defenses. In day-long raids, they ravaged Naha's port facilities, two major military airfields, and other targets with 500 tons of bombs and thousands of rockets.

According to Japanese records, ten transports, thirty merchant ships, a seaplane tender, a destroyer escort, two minesweepers, four midget submarines, six patrol boats, and eight antiaircraft boats were sunk in the harbor, along with countless small craft. Warehouses containing 300,000 bags of rice—a month's food supply for the 32nd Army—went up in flames, along with 5 million rounds of rifle and machine-gun ammunition and 10,500 rounds of small-bore artillery, mortar, and antitank ammunition.

Equally important by-products of the air strikes were thousands of aerial reconnaissance photos brought back by the planes. They enabled the Navy's mapmakers to create the first reasonably reliable scale maps of Okinawa, which would be useful to both infantry and artillery units once the battle at ground level began.

Tragically, the worst destruction and loss of life were inflicted on Okinawan civilians, who had no advance warning of the attacks and were blissfully unaware of any danger. Incendiary bombs dropped by the attacking planes set off uncontrollable wildfires that spread through the flimsy residential neighborhoods of Naha, destroying most of the city's buildings and killing more than 1,000 men, women, and children.

Fearsome as this toll was, however, it was barely a dribble in the deluge of civilian deaths yet to come.

———

FOR SEAMAN FIRST CLASS Lester Caffey, the battle for Okinawa began on March 23, 1945—eight full days before the first American troops set foot on the island. That was when Caffey's ship, the heavy cruiser *Wichita*, became the first major U.S. vessel to arrive and take up station a few miles off the west-side Hagushi invasion beaches. "The Old Witch," as she was pridefully known among her crew, was preceded only by the minesweeper *Starling*, which had cleared a safe pathway into the anchorage.

Caffey's job as a water tender in a fire room housing one of the eight giant boilers that powered the cruiser's engines was far from glamorous. But the strapping eighteen-year-old from the Hill Country of southwest Texas didn't mind the work—and he was good at it. Caffey had scored 398 out of a possible 400 on the required aptitude test to become a Navy fireman, and he'd volunteered for duty in the fire room.

When the big ship was traveling at cruising speed, there wasn't much for Caffey to do. But when it slowed down, he had to be prepared to reduce the flow of water to the boilers, and when its engines ramped up to flank speed of thirty-two knots, it was his responsibility to see that the boiler produced a steady 650 pounds of steam pressure.

Within the first hour of that first day, Caffey had found himself as busy as he'd ever been during nine-plus months in the Navy. One of the *Wichita*'s lookouts had spotted the periscope of a Japanese submarine and sounded the alarm. Moments later, loudspeakers crackled throughout the ship:

"General quarters! General quarters! Torpedo alert!"

Caffey raced for his battle station, stumbling and almost falling as the *Wichita*'s captain, Commander D. A. Spencer, ordered the engines to full speed and set the ship on a zigzag course.

The cruiser's overanxious gun crews opened fire almost immediately, hitting and sinking a nearby buoy by mistake. The sub, however, slipped away after firing a single torpedo at the *Wichita*.

"That torpedo came right past where I was standing," Caffey recalled many years later. "It couldn't have missed us by more than six feet. I saw the bubbles in the water."

Now, as the sun sank slowly in the West and nightfall approached on March 31—D-Day-minus-1—Caffey stared out over the cruiser's rail at the massive aggregation of some 1,500 ships that had joined the *Wichita* off Okinawa since that first day. The crew was still on alert, with lookouts posted fore and aft and gun crews at the ready. Since the sub scare, there'd been two kamikaze attacks and a nightly threat of incursions by enemy frogmen armed with everything from plastic explosives to knives.

Caffey's thoughts drifted halfway around the world to his family's farm in the mesquite and scrub cedar hills north of the town of Brady, population 5,002. In his mind's eye, he saw himself sitting in his dad's 1940 Chevrolet after church on a December Sunday and listening to a radio program called *The Old Fashioned Revival Hour* when a strident voice abruptly cut in above the strains of a hymn:

"We interrupt this program to bring you a special news bulletin from United Press. Planes, identified as Japanese, have attacked Pearl Harbor in the Hawaiian Islands, causing widespread damage and loss of life. Please stay tuned for further details as they become available. . . ."

Two and a half years later, on June 6, 1944—D-Day at Normandy—Les had enlisted in the Navy. He was barely three weeks out of high school, and his father, who already had two sons in the service, wasn't happy when he found out.

"But you've got a deferment," Les's father told his youngest son, "and the draft board told me you wouldn't be drafted because your farm work's vital to the national defense. Besides, I need you around here."

"Sorry, Dad," Les said, "but I just think it's time for me to go."

That had been six battle stars ago, and Caffey had never regretted his decision. He wondered if he'd still feel the same way by this time the next day.

⌐

ON MARCH 26, three days after the *Wichita*'s arrival, a dozen U.S. minesweepers began the nerve-wracking job of clearing Japanese mines from the waters around Okinawa—and suffered some of the first casualties of the campaign in the process.

"On March 24, we received a briefing at sea from three naval intelligence officers," recalled Lieutenant Commander Lewis Lacy, executive officer of the U.S.S. *Starling,* part of a group of four well-traveled minesweepers that included the *Skylark, Sheldrake,* and *Swallow.* "They told us, 'This is either going to be real easy or real tough, depending on whether the Japs use all their available suicide planes at Okinawa or save them for later. They've got 7,000 suicide planes available.'"

Although the *Starling* fired at two suiciders during the next few days and shot down one that narrowly missed hitting her, the greatest threat to the ship was from the mines it had come to collect. Lacy, a Texan from Fort Worth who'd spent two and a half years in the Pacific after graduating from midshipman school at Northwestern University in the same class with John F. Kennedy, soon learned how tough Okinawa would be.

On the minesweepers' first morning of action, as they worked their way shoreward from a depth of 150 feet, with the *Skylark* in the lead and the *Starling* following close behind, the *Skylark* struck two mines in rapid succession.

"After the second mine hit her, she sank in eight minutes," Lacy recalled. "She was the first American ship to go down at Okinawa, but we were able to rescue eighty-eight of her ninety-one crewmen. The other three men were lost, and several of those we rescued were badly hurt."

By March 30, the *Starling* had removed 603 mines—each of which was capable of blowing a landing craft to splinters—from the shallows that tens of thousands of invading U.S. troops would have to cross two days later.

⌒

As DARKNESS SETTLED over the sea around Okinawa on the evening of March 31, PFC Harry Bender Jr. felt more jumpy and apprehensive than he'd ever been in all his eighteen years. The closest thing to it, as far as he could remember, had been his first day of school in the fall of 1933.

"That first morning, my sister took me in the front door of the school and I walked straight out the back door without slowing down," he recalled. "I did the same thing every day for six weeks, and later, when I didn't get a report card because I'd never been to class, my parents got a little suspicious. Next thing I knew, I was enrolled in another school, and they were watching me like a hawk."

Now, as one of a bumper crop of untested replacements filling gaps in the ranks of K/3/5 left by the bloodletting at Peleliu, Bender would be facing his first combat the next morning. And for days he'd heard nothing from the company's veterans except how hellish the upcoming assault was going to be.

They say it'll be even worse than Peleliu, and we got the holy shit kicked out of us there, one of the old guys warned.

Yeah, I hear the Nips're waitin' for us behind a ten-foot concrete wall with machine guns every six feet, another chimed in.

By some accounts, it was a minor miracle that Bender had lived long enough to join the Marine Corps on his seventeenth birthday—much less to become the shortest rifleman in the First Platoon, standing just five feet four with his boondockers on.

As anyone who'd known Bender as a kid on the south side of Chicago could attest, he'd been, by his own description, "a royal pain in the ass," and the only rules he'd followed were his own. His natural penchant for trouble had continued into his teens, when he ran with a group of young street toughs. In fact, his enlistment in the Marines had resulted from an arrangement struck between Chicago juvenile authorities and Bender's father, Harry Sr., who happened to be chairman of the local draft board. It happened shortly after Harry Jr. and some friends "borrowed" a late-model car for a joyride through the Loop district.

"They gave me a choice," Bender acknowledged many years later. "I could either join the service or get hauled into juvenile court. The Marines sounded like a whole lot better deal than reform school."

Partly because of his short stature, Bender had always been a scrapper, and a tradition of combat also ran back through generations of his German-Irish family, whose members had fought in every American war dating back to the Revolution. His father, Harry Sr., a Marine in World War I, had been wounded in France while fighting in five of the six largest battles of that war involving American troops.

Because he was the only man in the first platoon who went to boot camp at San Diego—all the rest had undergone basic training at Parris Island, South Carolina—Bender picked up the nickname "Hollywood." And although he *did* bear a faint resemblance to a young Mickey Rooney, anyone who commented on his boyish appearance was asking for a faceful of knuckles.

Few things had frightened Harry Bender Jr. during his brief lifetime, but on that fateful evening, he was forced to admit that he was damned scared—more scared even than he'd been on that first day of school when he was six years old.

There would, after all, be no back door through which to escape when the First Platoon hit the beach the next morning.

⁓

FIRST LIEUTENANT Quentin "Monk" Meyer's final thoughts as he drifted toward asleep on the night of March 31 were about his fiancée, Francie Walton, and the letter he'd written her a few evenings earlier. He regretted not getting off another letter before the next day's landing. One reason he hadn't was a nagging worry that he'd conveyed too much about his own apprehensions to Francie already.

Several parts of that last letter kept sticking in his mind and making him slightly uneasy:

I had a nice dream the other night—the first one in a long time that was nice. I arrived home on a large ship with no one else aboard. I was at a big port, and down below you were standing all alone. . . .

Now Meyer wondered whether the "nice dream" had been so nice, after all. In retrospect, he sensed something somber and ominous about it, and it disturbed him that he couldn't recall how the dream ended.

As his family and close friends well knew, Monk Meyer's quiet, intense personality stood out in sharp contrast to the high-profile celebrity status he'd enjoyed—or, more correctly, tolerated—for much of his life.

By virtue of arriving in the world a few minutes before his twin brother, Cord, on November 10, 1920, Monk ranked as the eldest of four sons of well-to-do parents who divided their time between New Hampshire and New York City. Later, his mother gave birth to a second set of twins, Thomas and William, and when all four brothers ended up in the Marine Corps in 1944, the distinction had earned them front-page coverage in various U.S. newspapers.

By that time, however, Monk had already been famous around New England as a star halfback for Yale's 1942 football team and captain of its hockey team. Two years later at Peleliu, as a member of the newly formed Fourth Joint Assault Signal Company (JASCO in military jargon), he'd made what the press termed "the longest broken-field run of his career."

There had been no green grass or white stripes to mark that one. It was made through an area infested with hundreds of Japanese to reach the battered survivors of a company of Marines cut off from the rest of the First Marine Division, and it culminated with a 500-yard swim under heavy enemy fire. A short time later, Meyer retraced his route through the Japanese gauntlet to reach his own unit, then directed naval gunfire that helped break the siege of the trapped Marines. After the battle, Meyer's heroic dash earned him the Silver Star and a recommendation for the Navy Cross, and his photo again popped up in newspapers across the country.

Meyer himself would just as soon have had none of it, though. As he'd confided to Francie in that most recent letter:

I won't speak of the war. We think it and live it, and it bores me. It interests me only insofar as its length and its cost in good, young lives, but I know one thing for certain. In the next show, I'll do everything in my power to prevent the slaughter of my men. . . .

But then he'd slipped and written more about it anyway. Probably a lot more than he should have, he thought:

We've been busy shining our swords and girding our loins, both physical and mental. Armageddon is in the air!

As sleep closed over him, Meyer was still wishing he'd been a little less frank and dramatic about his feelings. He particularly wished he could retract that crack about Armageddon.

The last thing he wanted to do was make Francie worry.

⌒

EXCEPT FOR A FEW Army units assigned to seize several groups of islands off Okinawa's west coast, the rest of the 541,000 American assault troops and support personnel had little to do on March 31 but wait aboard their troop ships and LSTs and listen to the shuddering rumble of naval gunfire. The shelling had started almost a week earlier and continued, with brief intervals, ever since.

As the day wore on, tension ran high among GIs and Marines scheduled to hit the beaches the next morning. Men took showers, drew rations, exchanged their regular money for "invasion yen," checked their weapons and gear, and packed their kits. They received final orders from their unit commanders, who reminded them to get off the beaches and move inland as quickly as possible. They were warned about the ten-foot seawall that supposedly ran all the way around the island. It did nothing of the sort, as it turned out, and had been effectively pulverized by the pre-invasion shelling, but it was a primary source of worry among the troops.

As Army PFC Ellis Moore, a member of the 383rd Infantry Regiment of the 96th Division aboard LST 789, put it: "The Navy promised to knock that wall full of holes during their preliminary bombardment, but if they didn't, it was easy to picture us being picked off one by one by the Japs as we crawled over the top."

Everybody knew the next morning was going to be tough. According to word filtering down through the ranks, the assault units could expect to face the most viciously contested landing of the war. Reveille would come at 3:45 A.M., earlier yet for those who wanted to attend religious services. It was Easter Sunday, after all. It was also April Fool's Day. In the spirit of one occasion or the other—perhaps both—the top brass weren't calling tomorrow D-Day. It had been dubbed "Love Day" instead.

The men were advised to hit the sack soon after supper. "You'll need all the rest you can get," they were told. Most of them did so, but many had difficulty sleeping.

The prelude to Okinawa was over. The main event loomed just beyond tomorrow's dawn.

———

ON THE EVENING of March 30—Good Friday and Love-Day-minus-2—Gunner's Mate Third Class Hank Kalinofsky, captain of a twin-mount 40-millimeter antiaircraft battery on the rocket ship *LSM(R) 198*, had done something he knew no good Catholic boy should ever do: He'd eaten a huge turkey dinner and enjoyed every bite of it. Afterward, he felt an oppressive sense of having offended the Almighty.

I'm going to hell for sure, he thought. *But, man, that turkey was delicious!*

His attempts to rationalize his misdeed only caused his worries to deepen. Catholics were forbidden to eat meat even on ordinary Fridays, and to violate that rule on Good Friday itself, one of the holiest days of the year, surely had to rank among the most unforgivable of sins.

The events that followed did nothing to ease Kalinofsky's mind. The *LSM(R) 198* was one of a dozen rocket ships built especially for the Okinawa campaign. With the capability of firing 1,100 five-inch rockets within a span of about five minutes, each of the ships packed incredible firepower. They'd sailed together all the way from Charleston, South Carolina, to join the fight, but by Love-Day-minus-1, one of them, the *LSM(R) 197,* had already been destroyed by a kamikaze, and the suicide attacks were growing more frequent.

With most of their deck space taken up by 110 rocket launchers, their limited antiaircraft capability left the rocket ships highly vulnerable to the suiciders. As the man in charge of one of the *198*'s main AA weapons, Kalinofsky was as exposed to danger by kamikazes as any man on the ship. He tried not to dwell on that fact, but a worrisome question lingered in his mind:

Was this how God would choose to take His retribution against a gluttonous Good Friday sinner?

On Easter Sunday—Love Day at Okinawa—the twenty-four-year-old sailor from the coal-mining town of Edwardsville, Pennsylvania, was at his battle station before daybreak, still bothered by his transgression and the possible consequences. Someone handed Kalinofsky a sandwich, and he remembered telling himself: "I'm not likely to get another chance to eat for a long time. This will probably be breakfast and lunch and maybe dinner, too."

Then, suddenly, kamikazes were everywhere, streaking in low against the dawning sky, and Kalinofsky and the other gunners were throwing hundreds of rounds per minute at them. As he tried to hold his sandwich with one hand, the concussion from his twin-mount 40s jarred it from his grip, and he dropped it. In an instant, the sandwich was gone forever, probably into the sea. Kalinofsky felt a flash of chagrin, followed by a peculiar sense of relief.

Is this my only punishment for eating meat on Good Friday? he wondered. *Are we even now, God?*

Detecting no answer from above to his inquiries, he shut his mind to everything but the bucking twin 40s and the next approaching kamikaze.

As terrifying as they were to close-up observers like Kalinofsky, the suicide attacks that morning were actually scattered and sporadic compared to the kamikaze onslaught to be launched by the Japanese a few days later.

It would be the most massive suicide offensive the world has ever seen. Each day for weeks to come, Kalinofsky would wonder if his "sin" had truly been forgiven—or if his Maker had something far more terrible in store for him.

BECAUSE OF STRICT Navy orders to keep all ground troops confined below decks beneath locked hatches when air attacks were imminent,

Marine Tech Sergeant Walt McNeel didn't see a single kamikaze plane that morning. But he heard several, and each of them sounded as if it was headed straight for the hold of McNeel's troop ship. While there may have been sound reasoning behind the Navy's rule, it made many of the captives feel more helpless than if they'd been able to see the danger coming.

"We were trapped like a bunch of blind rats down there," said McNeel, who headed a repair crew for the Grumman F6F Hellcats of Marine night-fighter squadron VMF(N)-542. "It seemed ten times worse than being on deck and actually watching those planes come in."

The only word on what was happening outside had to be relayed by radio to squadron personnel by a Marine chaplain, who was allowed on the bridge, but usually, by the time the chaplain reported, the danger was past.

McNeel was a seasoned veteran whose older brother, Dave, a rifleman in the First Marines, had been killed at Peleliu and posthumously awarded a Silver Star. Walt himself had come under enemy fire more than once in the past—and fully expected to come under it again once the squadron went ashore—but he could never remember anything as terrifying as this.

The worst part of all, he thought, was that the brass estimated it would take a week or more to secure the Yontan airfield, where the squadron would be assigned. Until then, McNeel and the other ground crewmen would remain confined in the bowels of the ship, listening to the crackle of the chaplain's voice on the radio, and waiting. And wondering:

Will I live to set foot on dry land again, or will I die right here in this steel coffin?

⸻

ON LOVE DAY MORNING, one group of Marine infantrymen, angered and nervous because blowers used to circulate air in their ship's hold were turned off when electrical power was shifted to the antiaircraft batteries, started cursing and yelling at the sailors manning the locked hatches:

"We'll smother in this damned place! By God, let us out of here!"

"Sorry," the sailors replied, "we've got orders to keep this hatch dogged down."

PFC Gene Sledge, one of the Marines nearest the hatch, joined the uproar, and he and several others tried to loosen the clamps that held it shut. The sailors on the other side immediately retightened the clamps, but, as more desperate Marines threw themselves into the struggle, their combined efforts proved too much for the sailors.

"One of the sailors got pushed over and rolled across the deck," Sledge recalled. "In an instant, we were all outside breathing in the fresh air."

The only officer within sight, a young Navy ensign with a .45 automatic on his belt, tried in vain to corral the escapees. When the Marines ignored his shouted orders to return to their quarters, the ensign began threatening them with mass courts-martial. Finally, a friend of Sledge's spoke up:

"Sir, we're gonna hit that beach in a little while, and a lot of us may not be alive an hour from now. We'd rather take a chance on getting hit by a Jap plane out here than go back in there and smother to death."

The ensign glared at the man for a moment, then turned and fled toward the bridge. That was the last the Marines saw of him. A few minutes later, some of their own officers showed up.

"Grab your gear, and stand by to go down the nets," they said. "The boats are waiting."

It was almost a relief.

CHAPTER TWO

"Like a Stroll in the Park"

W HERE THE HELL are the Japs?"

It was a question repeated countless times on Love Day at Okinawa. By 8:30 A.M. on that Easter morning, April 1, 1945, when those in the first waves of the 183,000 U.S. Marine and U.S. Army troops in the assault echelon reached shore, they'd heard so many dire warnings repeated so often by their officers and NCOs that every man was expecting the worst experience of his life.

But with rare, isolated exceptions, men of the First and Sixth Marine Divisions, landing on the northernmost portions of the invasion beaches, stepped ashore into an eerie quiet, broken only by an occasional rifle shot or mortar round. Then they began moving cautiously inland with no evidence of organized enemy resistance.

Crewmen of the First Marine Tank Battalion's heavily armored Sherman tanks were among the first to reach shore and make the incredible discovery that their landing was unopposed.

When the landing craft carrying his Sherman reached Blue Beach Two, and Corporal Jack H. Armstrong got his first close-up look at what was happening ashore—or, more correctly, what *wasn't* happening—his reaction was confused astonishment.

There's got to be some mistake here, he thought. *Are we landing on the wrong island? If this is Okinawa, where's all the bodies and wrecked vehicles? Where's all the cannon fire and mortars?*

Armstrong's Sherman—bearing the self-confident nickname "Ticket to Tokyo"—rumbled onto the beach and negotiated a break in the seawall without difficulty or opposition. He wondered if the Japanese were playing some kind of devious April Fool's trick, but as tank commander, he knew he had no choice but to plunge ahead.

"I hate to sound superstitious," he told his driver, Corporal Harlan

Stephan, "but this is almost as scary as being shot at. You see any sign of the enemy?"

"I don't see a doggone thing," Stephan replied.

"Me neither," said Corporal Alvin Tenbarge, the assistant driver. "It's quiet as a church out there."

"Yeah," said Armstrong, "or maybe a graveyard."

Up and down the shoreline, other Shermans of the battalion were experiencing the same absence of resistance. Even so, when Armstrong's crew hurriedly climbed out to remove the tank's flotation pontoons and engine covers, the men couldn't shake the feeling that someone was sneaking up to attack them from behind. Armstrong kept glancing over his shoulder, and he noticed other crew members doing the same.

"Let's get rolling," Armstrong said. "I feel downright naked out here."

⌒

"THE LANDING'S UNOPPOSED! Looks like the Nips have taken a powder!"

Amtrack and Higgins boat crews quickly passed the word back to succeeding waves of assault troops streaming toward the beach. Many battle-hardened veterans reacted at first with guarded cynicism, then with shocked disbelief.

"We walked off our amtracks standing up," said PFC Bill Leyden, a fire team leader in the First Marine Division's K/3/5 who had witnessed a fearsome slaughter on the beach at Peleliu a few months earlier, where dozens of landing craft were destroyed before reaching shore. "It was the damnedest thing you ever saw. None of us could believe it."

"Man, I've had 'R-and-R' assignments tougher than this," remarked Sergeant R. V. Burgin, as he perched on the gunwale of the amtrack carrying his K/3/5 mortar squad toward shore. With two major battles under his belt, Burgin was recalling a pest hole of mud, rats, and rotten coconuts in the Russell Islands called Pavuvu, where the division had been sent to lick its wounds after a tough fight at Cape Gloucester on New Britain.

"If Hillbilly Jones was here, he'd probably be breakin' into song about now," said PFC George Sarrett, a fellow Texan sitting next to Burgin, referring to a musically talented young lieutenant named Ed Jones, killed by a sniper at Peleliu.

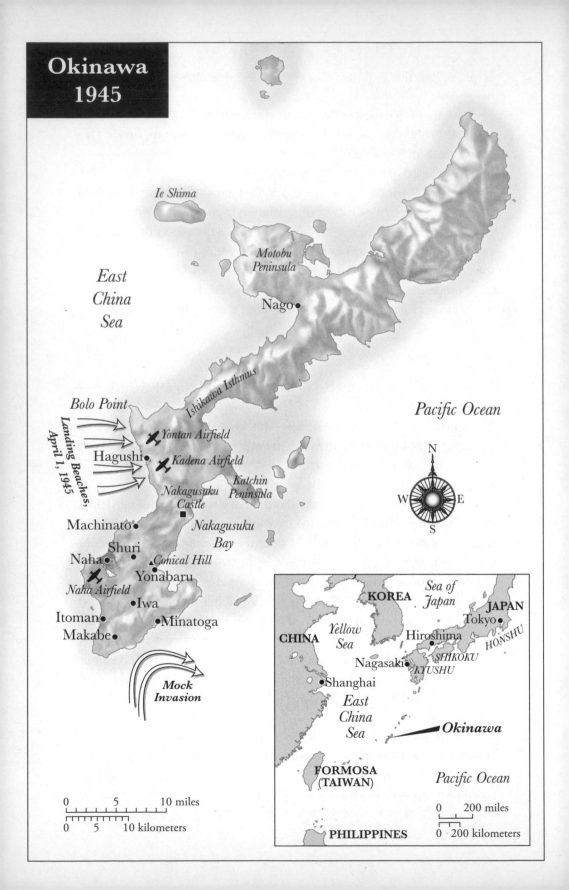

Okinawa
1945

Ie Shima

East China Sea

Motobu Peninsula

Nago

Ishikawa Isthmus

Bolo Point

Landing Beaches, April 1, 1945

Yontan Airfield

Hagushi

Kadena Airfield

Katchin Peninsula

Nakagusuku Castle

Pacific Ocean

N
W   E
S

Machinato

Nakagusuku Bay

Shuri

Naha   ▲*Conical Hill*

Yonabaru

Naha Airfield

Iwa

Itoman

Minatoga

Makabe

Mock Invasion

| 0 | 5 | 10 miles |
| 0 | 5 | 10 kilometers |

Sea of Japan

KOREA

JAPAN

CHINA

Yellow Sea

Tokyo

Hiroshima

Nagasaki

SHIKOKU

HONSHU

KYUSHU

Shanghai

East China Sea

Okinawa

FORMOSA (TAIWAN)

Pacific Ocean

| 0 | 200 miles |
| 0 | 200 kilometers |

PHILIPPINES

"Yeah, and he'd have everybody else singin' along, too," Burgin said. "You know the words to anything?"

"'Little Brown Jug,'" said Sarrett. "It's about the only thing I can carry a tune to."

"Well, let's hit it," Burgin said.

They started out tentatively and off-key, but after a few seconds, several other guys chimed in, and before long, a full chorus of robust voices was echoing across the calm water:

> *If I had a cow that gave such milk, I'd dress her in the finest silk,*
> *Feed her on the choicest hay, milk her fifty times a day.*
> *Ha-ha-ha! You and me! Little brown jug, how I love thee . . .*

YIELDING TO THE COAXING of his squad mates and joining the chorus, PFC Gene Sledge vividly recalled his own baptism of fire at Peleliu the previous September, and he marveled at how different today was. As the amtrack bumped against the beach, he could see thousands of men going unhurriedly about their business in dispersed combat formations while thousands more approached aboard hundreds of crowded landing craft.

When his amtrack was about fifty yards from the beach, Sledge had seen two Japanese mortar shells explode well to his left, sending up geysers of seawater but causing no damage. Sledge had tensed, expecting more rounds to follow, but those were the only enemy shells he saw fired that morning.

"We continued to look at the panorama around our amtrack with no thought of immediate danger as we came up out of the water," Sledge later recalled. "The tailgate banged down. We calmly picked up our gear and walked onto the beach."

Corporal Charles "Red" Womack, a squad leader in charge of three two-man flamethrower teams in Weapons Company, Third Battalion, Fifth Marines, literally couldn't believe his eyes as he crossed the beach. "We were expecting something every step," said the Peleliu veteran from McComb, Mississippi, "but nothing happened. There wasn't a sign of any Japs."

Much of the dreaded Okinawa seawall, which American troops had been led to believe would claim countless lives, had been pulverized by naval gunfire until it was little more than waist-high in many places and virtually nonexistent in others. The Marines scrambled across it easily without slowing down.

"On the part of the beach where I was, there was no sign of the wall," said Corporal Sterling Mace, a fire team leader in K/3/5's Third Platoon. "They'd told us we'd have to go over that wall on ladders, but it had been totally destroyed."

Like virtually all the veterans in the early waves, Mace proceeded quickly and stayed alert. Since losing his best buddy to a sniper's bullet on Peleliu, the twenty-year-old from Queens, New York, wasn't nearly as easygoing as he'd once been.

"You can't take anything for granted in a situation like this," he told PFC Bob Whitby, who was seeing his first action despite being an "old guy" of twenty-eight with a wife and twin daughters back home in Solon, Ohio. "The Nips are always full of tricks, and you can bet they've got something up their sleeves."

The only sign of the enemy they saw that morning, however, was the grisly remains of a squad of Japanese soldiers scattered around a yawning crater left by the fourteen-inch shell from a U.S. battleship that had killed them.

"The hole must've been twenty feet in diameter," Mace said, looking back on the sight from many years later, "and the bodies were all over the place. I started looking at their weapons, and for a second, I had a feeling of relief."

Look at the junk they've got for rifles, he thought. *Jeez, they look like something left over from the Civil War!*

Then the realization sank in on Mace. "These weren't old-fashioned long-barrel rifles," he said. "They were ordinary weapons, except for one thing—every one of their wooden stocks had been stripped cleanly away by the force of the blast."

As the platoon moved cautiously east, leaving the beach and the bodies behind, the skirmish line in which they'd started their advance seemed unnecessary, and they formed up in a column of fives to quicken their pace. Ahead of them lay green fields, garden plots lush with crops, a scattering of neat houses with tile roofs—and not a trace of other Japanese.

Damned pretty country, Mace thought. *Nothing at all like Peleliu.* He relaxed a little in spite of himself.

PFC Harry Bender, setting foot on enemy soil for the first time, was dismayed but heartened by the almost total absence of Japanese resistance. Some of the other replacements were starting to crack jokes about how easy the landing had been.

"What's so tough about this?" Bender heard one of them snort. "So far, it's like a stroll in the park."

"Just stay alert and don't get cocky," advised Sergeant Leonard "Hook" Ahner, Bender's squad leader. "You wouldn't want to die laughing."

The levity faded abruptly. Every guy in the First Platoon admired Ahner and held the lanky, laconic Hoosier from Huntington, Indiana, in the highest esteem. Bender, for one, wasn't nearly ready to take matters so lightly, anyway.

"What do you think this means?" Bender asked Leyden as they headed toward a pastoral tableau of rolling hills, cultivated fields, and stands of pine. The scene before them was so tranquil that it looked more like a painted backdrop for a movie than a real-life combat zone. "What're the Japs up to?"

"Who knows?" Leyden said. "But it makes me think back to something our drill instructor was always drumming into our heads in boot camp."

"What's that?" asked Bender.

" 'Anytime your attack's going too well, you'd better watch your ass. Chances are, you're walking into an ambush.' "

⁓

Ironically, while most of the beachhead was as quiet as a church, Love Day morning was a far different story for some 600 Army troops manning heavy artillery eight miles away on Keise Shima, a group of four tiny coral islets off Okinawa's west coast.

Two battalions of the 532nd Field Artillery had risked their lives five days earlier to set up two dozen 155-millimeter cannon on Keise Shima to support the U.S. landing. The first part of the morning was uneventful, but when the landing turned out to be unopposed, the big guns of the 532nd were assigned other targets.

"We fired between 300 and 400 rounds on D-Day," said PFC Ed K. Austin, "and for most of the time, we were also under return fire from the Japanese."

On March 28, the day Austin and his comrades had landed on

Keise Shima, they'd run into serious trouble from the get-go. Infantry units of the 77th Division had swept over the four islets the previous day to find them undefended, unoccupied, and apparently abandoned by the Japanese. Some thirty-six hours later, however, the enemy had abruptly changed his mind. By then, the infantry was gone and the artillerymen—with scant experience in close-quarter combat—were on their own.

The "long toms" of the 532nd were the largest-caliber land-based weapons in the Army's arsenal, and Keise Shima was ideally located to rain their fire on enemy beach defenses. Before the gun crews and equipment made it ashore, however, their LST became hopelessly hung up on a coral reef fifty yards offshore, stranding them in a highly vulnerable position.

"There we sat," said Austin, "with a shipload of shells and powder and no way to get them on land. We were stuck there for six or seven hours, but fortunately the Japs never fired a single shot at us during that time."

The guns themselves were lashed to small landing barges being towed by the LST, and, in Austin's words, the barges "went all cockeyed" when they hit the reef, making it impossible to unload them. In desperation, Austin and his mates eventually solved the problem by blowing holes in the barges with Thompson sub-machine guns and sinking them in shallow water, thereby stabilizing them sufficiently to manhandle the guns ashore.

However, the trouble was only beginning for the 532nd, a specialized "floating" regiment unattached to any of the Army or Marine divisions involved in the campaign. On the night of March 29, the Japanese—belatedly reconsidering their decision to give up Keise Shima without a fight—utilized a squadron of small boats to launch a fierce counterattack.

"We weren't in very good shape to play like infantry," recalled Austin, a strapping youngster from the high plains of West Texas. "We had four regular .50-caliber machine guns and one four-barrel quad-50 used mostly for antiaircraft. But the Japs overran the quad-50 and killed one of our guys. Luckily, another guy was able to put the gun on single-shot mode before he had to haul out of there. This meant it could only fire one round at a time instead of a steady stream. If the Japs had known how to fix it, they could've annihilated us."

Except for the machine guns, the only other usable weapons available to the American defenders were much despised .30-caliber Browning carbines known derisively as "peashooters" because of their inferiority to the M-1 rifle. The lightweight carbines were routinely issued to members of artillery units and mortar squads—who seldom had occasion to fire them in combat—because they were easier to carry for men encumbered with heavy ammo and other gear than the deadly accurate, semiautomatic M-1.

"With the help of Navy ships firing star shells, we held our positions all night," Austin said. "At dawn, the Japs jumped back in their little boats and pulled out—and then the Navy really clobbered them. I don't think any of them got away."

Before departing, however, the Japanese inflicted numerous casualties, and Love Day brought even greater losses.

"We were assigned to knock out a communications tower in the city of Naha," said Austin, "and when we began firing at it, the Japs started firing back. They already had our positions zeroed in and knew all the coordinates, so it was pretty tough for a while."

One Japanese heavy artillery round exploded in a gun pit housing the 532nd's headquarters company, killing everyone in it, including numerous officers. Another shell landed squarely in the middle of the gun pit containing Austin's gun crew, but it was a dud.

"Jap antiaircraft batteries were firing at us, too," Austin recalled, "but they were mostly a nuisance, and we kept shooting. Lots of times, we didn't know what we were shooting at. We just kept the shells flying."

⌒

ALL THE SPEARHEADING assault waves of the battle-hardened First Marine Division, which had started the U.S. offensive march across the Pacific at Guadalcanal in August 1942, were ashore intact in less than ten minutes. By 9:30 A.M. on Love Day, an hour after the division's amtracks plowed onto the Blue and Yellow Beaches, elements of the division's Seventh and Fifth Marine Regiments had passed effortlessly through the deserted village of Sobe, expected to be a hotspot of Japanese resistance, without sighting a single enemy soldier. The division's other infantry regiment, the First Marines, was being held in reserve.

"We advanced inland, and I neither heard nor saw any Japanese fire directed against us," PFC Gene Sledge recalled. "As we moved across the small fields and gardens onto higher elevations, I could see troops of the Sixth Marine Division heading toward the big Yontan airfield on our left."

After quickly securing the Green and Red Beaches at the north end of the beachhead, the Sixth Marine Division seized Yontan—one of the two most valuable military airbases on Okinawa—without firing a shot. By then, even cynical Peleliu veterans were beginning to feel more comfortable.

"Man, look at them pigs," said Sergeant Hook Ahner, nudging PFC Bill Leyden in the ribs and pointing toward a hog pen in an abandoned barnyard. "If things stay quiet, maybe we can have us some roast pork."

Leyden, who'd been born and raised in Brooklyn, frowned, then smiled uncertainly at his friend and squad leader. As a confirmed city boy, he had a hard time making the connection between the dirty, grunting animal in the pen and a plateful of pork chops.

"I'm sure it beats K-rations," Leyden said.

"Hey, listen," said Sergeant Ted "Tex" Barrow, a burly veteran from somewhere east of Dallas, "roast pig's some of the best eatin' you'll find anywhere."

"You guys're making me hungry," Leyden said. He unshouldered his pack and reached inside for one of the steak-and-egg sandwiches he'd constructed that morning from the untouched breakfasts of queasy replacements at his shipboard table.

Steak and eggs was the traditional "warrior's meal" served to Marine assault troops by Navy cooks before every amphibious landing, but many men facing their first combat could barely keep down a few sips of coffee, much less solid food. So after cleaning his own plate and securing a supply of bread, the enterprising Leyden had made the rounds of newcomers to the First Platoon, repeating the same question:

"You gonna eat that?"

Most shook their heads or mumbled something about not having much appetite.

"Well, hell, hand it here then," Leyden had told them. "Before this show's over, you'll learn to appreciate fresh meat and real eggs!"

⸺

NEAR THE CENTER of the beachhead and a hundred or so yards to the right of where PFC Gene Sledge, Sergeant R. V. Burgin, and the rest of the singers in the K/3/5 mortar section landed, a small river emptied into the sea. Identified on military maps as the Bishi Gawa, the stream formed the dividing line between the northern beaches occupied by the two Marine divisions and the southern half of the beachhead, where Army troops of the Seventh and 96th Divisions were simultaneously pouring ashore.

Like the Marines to the north, the GIs were encountering virtually zero resistance on the Purple, Orange, White, and Brown Beaches. At almost exactly 8:30 A.M. on Love Day, amphibious tanks of the 96th "Deadeye" Division roared through yawning cavities blown by Navy guns in the portion of the seawall along White Beach One. Moments later, infantry troops of the division's 381st and 383rd Regiments jumped off their amtracks and followed.

By the time they were joined a short time later by reserve troops of the 382nd Regiment, the beachhead was swarming with activity. Corporal Don Dencker of L Company, a mortar squad leader from Minneapolis, described the scene that confronted him as he disembarked:

"Amphibious trucks [known as "Ducks" or DUKWs] were bringing in supplies, and tank and artillery units were already ashore supporting the 381st Infantry. The Corps of Engineers beach party was unloading incoming supplies and generally maintaining order in the beach zone, which ran 500 yards or more inland."

Dencker had been concerned on the inbound trip aboard the amtrack because his unit was understrength, counting just 168 men instead of the 193 specified for an Army rifle company. The manpower shortage was caused by the diversion to Europe of promised new replacements to fill gaps left by the heavy casualty toll in the Battle of the Bulge.

When Dencker and his squad mates saw what was happening ashore, however, they were surprised and relieved. Numerous shell craters had been left by the Navy's preinvasion bombardment, but, otherwise, the busy beachhead bore no evidence of violent warfare. Having gone through weeks of hard fighting with the Deadeye division in the Philippines, Dencker was no stranger to combat, but he'd never encountered a situation to compare to this one.

"We could hear a limited amount of small-arms firing some distance inland," he said, "but nothing was in the sky except for a few of our planes flying protective cover."

Some of that firing likely came from the rifle company of Deadeyes led by Captain Alvin E. von Holle of Cincinnati, which was among the first American units to discover that Okinawa wasn't quite a total cake-walk, after all. The company had been approaching the foot of a ridge about two miles inland when enemy snipers opened fire from a small cave. Several of von Holle's men were wounded, and the rest scrambled for cover. As they did, they noticed a white flag flying from a tripod on a high point on the ridge. The flag apparently marked an abandoned enemy command post, which the snipers were now using as a hiding place.

The GIs returned the fire with BARs, tommy guns, and M-1s, quickly silencing the snipers, and von Holle took a close look at the first enemy bodies he'd seen since Leyte. Then he glanced up at the thirty-foot bamboo flagpole on the ridge and thought of the folded three-by-four-foot American flag he'd been carrying around for more than two years. He'd passed up various opportunities to raise the flag, but this one seemed too perfect to miss.

Von Holle pulled the flag out of his shirt, and, with the help of three of his men, Lieutenant James Redden, Sergeant Albert Janick, and PFC George Churchill, he ripped down the Japanese flag and replaced it with the Stars and Stripes. As they finished hoisting it to the top of the pole, civilian news correspondent Bill Land happened by to record the event for posterity.

"Half an hour later," Land wrote, "the men of the company were on their way . . . leaving the first American flag flying over Okinawa."

Whether it actually *was* the first may be open to debate—but it definitely wouldn't be the last.

A MILE OR SO NORTH of the flag-raising site, soldiers of the "Hourglass" Seventh Infantry Division were landing on the Purple and Orange Beaches, again without incident. By 9:30 A.M., they'd advanced to a railroad track roughly halfway between the beaches and Kadena airfield, and their tanks were across the seawall and moving steadily inland.

Like their Marine comrades, the Hourglass GIs were now grinning and elated by their unexpected good fortune. As one relieved Seventh Division rifleman expressed it on safely reaching the crest of a small hill: "I've already lived longer than I thought I would."

Yet he and his comrades couldn't help asking themselves that same nagging question:

"Where are the Japanese?"

At the moment, no one knew the answer.

⎯⎯

Six mornings earlier, PFC William Kottas and the other thirty members of his Army rifle platoon had had no reason to ask that question. They'd found more than enough Japanese to suit them when they'd landed on a craggy speck of land in the East China Sea and fired some of the first shots of the last and largest military operation of World War II.

At 8:30 A.M. on March 26, while most U.S. amphibious assault troops still languished aboard their ships, Kottas and his comrades from the 77th Division's 306th Infantry Regiment had grounded their three small boats on an island some fifteen miles west of Okinawa. Their objective was one of a group of nine islands known collectively as the Kerama Retto. None of the GIs knew this particular island's name at the time, but as they headed inland from a quiet beach, they quickly found out where the Japanese were—they were all around them.

Since dawn, twelve-inch shells from the 1912-vintage battleship *Arkansas* had blistered the Keramas relentlessly, and other Navy ships and carrier-based planes had joined the "softening-up" bombardment. From the sound and fury of it, Kottas caught himself thinking that any Japanese troops on the island must be either hiding in fear or already dead.

Then he heard a rustle in the thicket in front of him, and the twenty-four-year-old ex–farm boy from Nebraska froze in his tracks, his rifle poised with fixed bayonet.

"Whatsa matter?" whispered PFC Shorty Detore, Kottas's fire team buddy, crouching close beside him.

"Something in the brush," Kottas said. "Didn't you hear it?"

Detore, an Italian kid from New York City who was barely taller than the Browning automatic rifle he clutched, shook his head.

A split second later, three Japanese soldiers leaped out of the undergrowth. Detore raised his BAR and fired a pair of short bursts over Kottas's head as two of the soldiers ran toward them. The third Japanese was on top of Kottas before he could level his M-1, so he used his bayonet instead.

The Japanese were supposed to be exceptional bayonet fighters, and

Kottas had seen evidence of their deadly skill during combat on Leyte in the Philippines. But this time the wiry Nebraskan struck first, driving his blade to the hilt in the enemy soldier's abdomen just below the rib cage, then ripping upward with all the force he could muster.

The Japanese went down hard with a muffled, gagging scream, and blood gushed as Kottas tried to pull the bayonet out of the enemy soldier's body. When the bayonet refused to budge, he unfastened it from the rifle barrel and left it where it was. The Japanese clawed spasmodically at the blade and made gurgling sounds for a second or two. Then he stopped moving altogether.

Kottas heard Detore panting at his elbow. "You okay?"

"I think so," Kottas said. He stared for a moment at the man he'd just killed, then at the bullet-riddled bodies of the two other Japanese. No more than a minute later, as his rush of adrenaline ebbed, he began to shake uncontrollably.

⁓

BY MIDAFTERNOON, the small island—Kottas never did learn its name—had been secured. Meanwhile, other units of the 305th and 306th Infantry Regiments were running into stiffer resistance on other islands in the Kerama Retto. About 400 Japanese troops were on the island of Zamami; some 200 others occupied Aka Island, and about 75 Japanese held Geruma. Many were members of enemy Sea Raider Squadrons assigned to attack American ships with hundreds of small boats hidden around the islands.

Several companies of the 305th Infantry charged ashore at Aka and advanced quickly across the island, using grenades and satchel charges to blast Japanese defenders out of scattered earthworks. By 5:00 P.M. on March 26, they counted 58 enemy dead, and they had secured two-thirds of the island.

The going was tougher on Zamami, where the Japanese garrison remained in hiding all day, then attacked Company C of the 305th repeatedly between midnight and daybreak of March 27. With the help of two wounded buddies who passed him ammunition, PFC John D. Word used a dead comrade's BAR to single-handedly fight off three enemy attacks. Nearby, Sergeants John Galinsky and Patrick Gavin led a handful of other GIs in retaking a captured American machine gun and killing a half-dozen Japanese who were trying to turn the weapon on U.S. positions. By sunup, the surviving Japanese attackers had melted away, leaving twenty-seven dead behind.

About nine o'clock that same morning, William Kottas's platoon and the rest of the First and Second Battalions of the 306th Infantry hit a second target island just to the east. This one was Tokashiki, the largest landmass in the Keramas. It was also where Kottas's luck temporarily ran out.

It took until March 30 to complete the conquest of Tokashiki and send the surviving members of its 500-man garrison, most of whom were Korean labor conscripts, scattering into the brushy hills. Enemy resistance was mainly in the form of sporadic mortar fire that caused only a handful of American casualties. Among that handful, however, was Kottas, who took a chunk of shrapnel in the hip and another across the bridge of his nose when a mortar shell exploded a few yards away.

As he lay in an aid station awaiting evacuation to the hospital ship *Solace*, Kottas was more stunned and sickened by the carnage he'd witnessed among some of the 6,000 civilian inhabitants of the Keramas than by his own wounds.

"The Japs had told the civilians on those islands that we'd skin the men alive, butcher the babies, and rape the women," Kottas recalled many years later, "and, God help them, they believed it. They killed themselves by the hundreds."

By nightfall on March 30, D-Day for the largest military air, sea, and land operation ever conducted by America's military was still a day and a half away, but, in a very real sense, the battle for Okinawa had already been joined.

⁓

IN CONTRAST to the hard fighting in the Keramas, first-day casualties on Okinawa were nonexistent in many units, and incredibly low overall, considering that by nightfall on April 1, some 60,000 American troops were in secure control of all the west-side beaches and two major airfields. Some units had penetrated as much as three or four miles inland. The day's final casualty report showed 28 men killed, 104 wounded, and 27 missing, and many of these losses had resulted from accidents, so-called "friendly fire," or intentional self-inflicted wounds, rather than from hostile action.

Before the assault, military doctors and the Navy corpsmen and Army medics who assisted them had been warned repeatedly to be ready to treat the greatest number of dying and severely wounded Americans yet seen in any Pacific battle. To handle this bloody chore, a number of LSTs—large landing ships capable of transporting tanks and other mechanized equipment as well as men—had been designated as temporary floating hospitals. As soon as these LSTs disembarked their complements of tanks and amtracks, their tank decks were to be hurriedly cleared, cleaned, and outfitted with medical equipment and cots. Within minutes after the first waves of assault troops landed, small boats would begin ferrying the wounded back to the LSTs and tie up to specially rigged, pontoon-supported piers just outside the bow doors of the ships. But an hour passed, then another, and only a small trickle of wounded showed up. Some of the improvised hospital ships had no one at all to treat.

In *The Old Breed,* his classic history of the First Marine Division, author George McMillan cites the case of one anxiously waiting surgeon whose only patient on Love Day morning was a young Marine with a profusely bleeding finger.

"One of my buddies fired one and shot the top of my finger off," the Marine said.

Still expecting a heavy influx of more serious wounds, the surgeon told a corpsman to dress the Marine's finger and went to lunch. Later, the doctor came back out to the pier where the lone Marine was still waiting. He gazed once more toward shore, but there was still no sign of any other wounded.

"Come on," he finally told the man with the hurt pinkie, "let's go make you a new finger. You're very lucky that I've got the time to do it."

⁓

NOT ALL THE CASUALTIES occurred accidentally, however.

Shortly after Tech Sergeant Porter McLaughlin led his Seventh Division antitank platoon ashore, he heard two distinct rifle shots. When he ran to investigate, he found two men from Headquarters Company, Second Battalion, 32nd Infantry Regiment, writhing in pain on the ground.

"What happened here?" McLaughlin demanded.

"The damned fools shot each other, Mac," said Sergeant George Murphy, McLaughlin's best buddy and one of his squad leaders. "I swear to God they squared off and deliberately shot each other in the leg."

McLaughlin, a burly onetime amateur wrestler who had worked as a commercial fisherman before the war, immediately recognized one of the men as a habitual troublemaker with whom McLaughlin had tangled several times in the past. The guy had been court-martialed at least twice, once for slugging a noncommissioned officer and once for allegedly raping a Filipino girl. He'd threatened to kill McLaughlin one night until the platoon sergeant had jammed a .45 into the man's belly and caused him to have second thoughts.

As the two wounded men were being helped onto stretchers, Lieutenant John J. McQuillan, commander of E Company, to which McLaughlin's antitank platoon was attached, arrived on the scene and asked what was going on.

"They must've wanted out of the war pretty bad," Murphy said.

"As I hear it, they deliberately shot each other."

McQuillan stared at the wounded pair and shook his head. "When I think of all the good men we've lost in this outfit, these jerks make me sick," he said. "Get 'em outta here. I can't stand to look at 'em."

THE FIRST MARINE TANK BATTALION consisted of three companies, each made up of fifteen M4A2 and M4A1 Sherman tanks, fifteen five-man crews, several dozen reserve crewmen, mechanical and supply sections, and a headquarters company headed by Lieutenant Colonel A. J. "Jeb" Stuart, the battalion commander.

In the Okinawa landing, the battalion's thirty-ton tanks and their crews were spread out over a stretch of beach measuring a mile or more in length, and at certain points along that stretch, unknown hazards lurked. As a result, even as tank commander Jack Armstrong's "Ticket to Tokyo" advanced steadily inland accompanied by a fire team of Marine infantrymen, some of his fellow tankers were meeting disaster and death a short distance offshore on another part of Blue Beach Two.

Ironically, the villain wasn't the kind of sudden enemy attack that Armstrong feared but a bizarre oddity of nature: a series of yawning holes hidden beneath the surf that literally swallowed three Marine tanks and their crews when they were within a few feet of dry ground.

During a rare solemn moment many years later, the fatal incident was described in detail by Marine Private Howard O. Towry, a skinny eighth-grade dropout and reserve tank driver from Carrollton, Texas. Towry's prankishness and his uncanny talent for getting into trouble dated back to boot camp and had earned him a standing reputation as the battalion's biggest screwup. But the tragedy on the beach that day was no joking matter to him.

"The Army, which had a lot more experience with tanks than the Marine Corps, showed us how to install pontoons on our tanks that allowed them to travel safely through water as deep as the tank itself as long as the hatches were sealed," Towry recalled. "But these holes were so deep they put the tanks fifteen to eighteen feet below the surface, and the guys inside—especially those deep in the tank—couldn't get out. We never lost a person to enemy fire that day, but we lost all three tanks, and six of our men drowned. Those were the only casualties we had."

PFC Lloyd Binyarde, another Texan from the Rio Grande Valley town of McAllen, was the only man to escape alive from one of the three tanks, according to Towry. "He laid on his back and managed to kick the hatch open with his feet," Towry said. "The other four crewmen didn't make it."

These freakish deaths left a deep and searing impression on Towry, whose reaction was to adopt an even more devil-may-care attitude than he'd had before. That attitude intensified as the battle wore on and contributed mightily to his self-described status as a "wild, crazy, no-good little bugger."

"The way I looked at it," said Towry, "the odds were running out on me, just like they had for those guys who drowned, and since I didn't expect to make it home alive, I decided I'd have as much fun as I could before the damned war finished me off."

In the weeks to come, that's precisely what Private Towry did.

⌒

AN INTEGRAL FACET of Operation Iceberg—one that may have contributed to the lack of enemy response along the invasion beaches on Okinawa's west side—was an elaborate feint by troops of the Second Marine Division. This "mock invasion" was aimed at beaches on the southeast side of the island near the village of Minatoga and timed to coincide exactly with the actual assault. It definitely caught the attention of the Japanese, who believed until the last minute that it was real, although no naval bombardment preceded it.

Marines boarded seven waves of twenty-four LCVPs (landing craft, vehicles/personnel) each, and the first of them began bearing down on the Minatoga beaches at 8:00 A.M. But a half hour later, with four waves well beyond the line of departure, all the landing craft made a quick U-turn into a curtain of smoke and sped back to their ships.

American observers spotted only four Japanese artillery rounds fired at the LCVPs, and all fell harmlessly in open water. Enemy defenders had been ordered to hold their fire until the landing craft were actually ashore, but many apparently believed they had repelled a genuine amphibious assault.

To keep the Japanese confused and off balance, the Marines reboarded their LCVPs and prepared to repeat their ruse the following day. From all indications, this second "demonstration," as it was called, was similarly successful in that it kept two full divisions and one brigade of enemy troops well removed from the real action.

On the afternoon of Love-Day-plus-1, General Ushijima, overall commander of Japanese forces on Okinawa, issued an order that warned: "On the Minatoga front, the enemy's plans cannot be disregarded. The Army will use the 62nd Division to hold the main line of position over a long period; it will use its main strength to annihilate the enemy who plans new landings."

The most serious threat to the Minatoga feints came from kamikaze "hell-birds" flying from the Japanese home island of Kyushu, but heavy U.S. air strikes had vastly diminished the number of enemy planes available for such missions by that time. The worst attack occurred near daybreak on Love Day off the Minatoga beaches when a suicide pilot crashed his plane into the port side of *LST 884*, triggering a roaring fire and exploding stores of ammunition just as troops were being loaded into landing craft. Another suicider struck the transport U.S.S. *Hinsdale* at about the same time.

Ironically, these kamikaze attacks on the demonstration forces accounted for a large percentage of Love Day casualties. Sixteen Marines were reported killed or missing, and thirty-seven were listed as wounded.

The stricken transport and LST remained afloat but dead in the water. They were among the first U.S. vessels to be towed to a soon-to-be-crowded "cemetery of ships" in the Kerama Rhetto.

⌒

CORPORAL DAN LAWLER felt tense and fidgety, and, despite the pleasant coolness of Love Day afternoon, beads of sweat dotted his forehead as he crossed the sprawling Yontan airfield with the other nineteen Marines of K/3/5's .30-caliber machine gun section.

The Japanese had made no serious attempt to defend Yontan, their largest air base on Okinawa, against the rapidly advancing Americans, and, in fact, Lawler had neither seen nor heard any sign of the enemy since coming ashore that morning. But he couldn't help thinking back to another afternoon, seven and a half months earlier, when he'd started across another Japanese airfield at Peleliu and never reached the other side.

As a nineteen-year-old ammo handler from Hudson Falls, New York, Lawler had been in the first wave to reach the Peleliu beaches, where the scene was like something out of hell itself. All he could see and hear were earth-shaking explosions and screaming, wounded, dying men. But the next afternoon had been even worse. That was when the entire Fifth Regiment of the First Marine Division had been ordered to storm unprotected into merciless enemy fire to seize the Peleliu airfield.

There'd been plenty of reason to sweat that day. The temperature was around 110 degrees when the charge started at 1:00 P.M., and it was close to a half mile across the field with almost no cover along the way.

Just stay as low as you can, don't bunch up, and run like hell, a senior NCO advised. *With luck, most of you guys'll probably make it.*

Lawler had tried to do exactly as he was told, but with two boxes of .30-caliber ammo weighing him down, it was tough going. He'd been about halfway across when he heard the inbound enemy artillery shell coming. It hit within a few feet of him and sent him sprawling with a broken right arm, three broken fingers, and shrapnel wounds in his back. The struggle for Peleliu had been less than thirty hours old, but for Lawler, the battle was over. He'd spent weeks in a hospital at Guadalcanal before he was able to return to his unit—just in time to make the Okinawa trip.

Now Lawler shook himself, wiping his face with his shirtsleeve and trying to squeeze the images of Peleliu out of his mind. As he glanced toward his marching comrades, his eyes met those of Sergeant Alex "Hurricane" Henson, a squad leader from Kentucky and a Marine since December 1940, who had picked up his nickname as a member of the company boxing team.

"You look kinda pale, buddy," Henson said. "You feel okay?'"

"Yeah, I'm all right," Lawler replied. "I was just thinking how different this is from the last time I crossed a Jap airfield."

"Yeah, I know," Henson said. "I was there, remember?"

"This one's been so easy it makes me jumpy," Lawler said.

"Maybe it's good to stay a little jumpy," Henson told him. "Regardless of what it may look like, this one ain't over yet—not by a damned sight."

About dusk that same afternoon, Seabees with bulldozers were clearing wrecked enemy planes from Yontan's parking aprons and taxiways, as well as a squadron of cloth-and-wood dummies built by the Japanese. Marines bivouacked at the edge of the field were heating their rations over small fires when they heard the drone of an engine and were surprised to see a lone aircraft coming in low for a landing.

They were even more surprised when they saw the dark red "meatballs" on the wings of the plane and recognized it as a Japanese Zero.

The Marines grabbed for their weapons as the plane made a flawless landing. The pilot eased to a stop, unhurriedly removed his parachute, climbed out of the cockpit, and jumped down to the tarmac. Clearly unaware that he'd landed on enemy territory, he began walking nonchalantly toward the Marines, then froze in his tracks and reached instinctively for his pistol.

The Japanese aviator was too far away—and it was too dark—for anyone to see his expression as volleys of shots from multiple American rifles cut him down. But in the instant between his realization of what he'd done and his death, a look of utter dismay must have crossed his face.

"It never fails," one Marine was heard to remark wryly as he and several armed comrades clustered around the pilot's body. "There's always some poor bastard who doesn't get the word."

⟶

As DARKNESS DESCENDED on Love Day evening, one small group of Marines and sailors from the Fourth Joint Assault Signal Company (JASCO), commanded by Lieutenant Quentin "Monk" Meyer, found themselves alone—and apparently forgotten—on a pitch-black sea filled with hidden perils. After leaving their LST early that morning, they'd been told to stand by and wait for landing orders. But that had been almost twelve hours ago, and they were still marooned aboard their open Higgins boat a mile or more from shore.

The function of JASCO units, which had first become operational in mid-1944, was to operate in close proximity to enemy lines, locate

Japanese troop concentrations and artillery and mortar positions, then report their locations to gunners on Navy ships. It was dangerous work that had earned Meyer a Silver Star at Peleliu for helping break a Japanese stranglehold on a surrounded company of Marines. But that high-risk mission had been no more nerve-wracking for Meyer than waiting aboard the small boat through the night of Love Day and the interminable hours of the next morning for sneak attacks by Japanese frogmen and suicide boats.

"We were supposed to go ashore with the Third Battalion, First Marines," recalled Private Gil Quintanilla, one of nine rifleman-scouts armed with tommy guns and assigned to protect JASCO radio operators. "But after we boarded the Higgins boat, I think something went wrong, and battalion headquarters just lost track of us."

It was an example of the kind of logistical problems that inevitably develop when 60,000 men and thousands of tons of equipment and supplies must be transported from ships to hostile shores in a single day under full combat conditions. In all likelihood, since the landings elicited virtually no enemy response and the location of major enemy troop concentrations and fortifications was unknown, there was little for a JASCO unit to do ashore.

Under the circumstances, it probably seemed reasonable to delay landing the unit until it could be given some useful assignment. But instead of being sent back to the LST to await developments, Meyer and his men were left bobbing in the East China Sea—and keeping watch for human sharks—from 8:00 A.M. on Love Day until after 9:00 A.M. the following morning.

"It wasn't bitterly cold, but the temperature dropped to around fifty degrees overnight, and all of us were soaking wet and chilled to the bone," said Quintanilla. "None of us got any sleep, either, because we had to keep a constant sharp eye out for Jap frogmen with satchel explosives and knives in their teeth."

Shivering in the darkness, Meyer and Quintanilla tried to maintain casual conversation to help them stay alert.

"You know, Quint," Meyer mentioned at one point, "I'm from New Hampshire, where they have at least ten feet of snow every winter, but I can't ever remember being this cold."

"Well, if *you're* cold, just imagine how I feel," Quintanilla muttered through chattering teeth. "I'm from Tucson, Arizona, where they don't even know what snow looks like."

No sunrise had ever been greeted with more appreciation by the men of the Fourth JASCO than the one that brightened the eastern sky above Okinawa on the morning of April 2, 1945.

FOR DALLAS-BORN Corporal Elliot Burnett, a veteran member of Headquarters Company, 11th Marines, the only bit of Love Day excitement had come when he and a buddy were buzzed by a Japanese Zero as they hauled a cartload of equipment for the artillery regiment's command post. The rest of the day had been uneventful, and, by nightfall, Burnett still hadn't seen a trace of the enemy at ground level.

"Our area was so quiet and peaceful that first night that one of our staff officers, a captain, decided to string his jungle hammock between two trees and sleep outside," Burnett recalled. "But sometime during the night, a lone Jap soldier wandered through the area and bumped right into the captain's hammock. All at once, we heard this bloodcurdling scream, followed by the sound of running footsteps. We all grabbed for our weapons, but there wasn't a shot fired. By then, the Jap had vanished."

ALL TOLD, Love Day had lived up to its name for most of the American troops now controlling an eight-mile-long beachhead stretching, at some points, nearly halfway across Okinawa's midsection. The weather was clear, the temperatures moderate, the countryside pretty and peaceful. The sandy soil was easily dug for foxholes and gun pits. Notably absent were the jungle foliage and tangled vines of the tropics, replaced by stands of fragrant pines gracing gentle hillsides. Many men helped themselves to fresh fruits and vegetables growing along their line of march. PFC Gene Sledge and his fellow Marine mortarmen actually saw Easter lilies in full bloom that Easter Sunday.

Of the few enemy soldiers encountered by U.S. Army and Marine assault troops the first day, almost all were teenage Okinawan conscripts left behind to defend the Yontan and Kadena airfields while the rest of Japan's 32nd Army withdrew to elaborate defensive positions in the hills. These lightly trained Okinawan youngsters, reluctant fighters at best, tended to flee at the first sound of American gunfire.

With the "stroll in the park" continuing on the second day, First Marine Division commander Major General Pedro del Valle appeared plainly puzzled as he addressed U.S. media representatives at a press conference. "I don't know where the Japs are, and I can't offer you any good reason why they let us come ashore so easily," he said. "We're pushing on across the island as fast as we can move the men and equipment."

Major General Lemuel Shepherd, del Valle's counterpart in the Sixth Marine Division, admitted, however, that his own bewilderment was tempered by relief. "There was a lot of glory on Iwo," Shepherd remarked after setting up his command post inland from a quiet beach, "but I'll take it this way."

General Roy Geiger, commander of the Marines' III Amphibious Corps, was as elated as he was confused. "Don't ask me why we haven't had more opposition," he told a *New York Times* correspondent. "I don't understand it . . . [but] now we're in a position to work over the Jap forces at our leisure at the least possible loss to ourselves."

Meanwhile, Vice Admiral Richmond Kelley Turner, commander of the vast naval armada that had brought the Tenth Army to Okinawa, reported to his boss, Admiral Chester Nimitz: "I may be crazy, but it looks like the Japanese have quit the war, at least in this sector."

The reply from Pacific Fleet headquarters in Hawaii was succinct, sarcastic, and extremely prophetic: "Delete all after 'crazy.'"

CHAPTER THREE

Kids' Games, Pony Rides, and Barbecue

WHILE AN INVISIBLE ENEMY waited patiently in his intricate lair of interconnected caves and tunnels, Love Day's stroll in the park escalated into a frolicsome lark for many Americans during the next several days.

With its beachhead secure, the various components of the U.S. Tenth Army's assault force moved off in divergent directions. The First Marine Division headed toward the east coast of Okinawa while the Sixth Marine Division geared up for a thrust into the lightly settled northern half of the island. The Seventh and 96th Infantry Divisions also marched east on a route that kept them south of the First Marine Division as the Army units prepared to make a sharp right turn toward suspected enemy positions in the southern ridges.

Meanwhile, troops of the 77th Infantry Division were still occupying the Kerama Retto and other westward islands seized prior to the main invasion. The Second Marine Division was in reserve following its Love Day feint at Okinawa's southern beaches, and the 27th Infantry Division remained aboard ships offshore, also in reserve.

As more and more rear-echelon troops arrived on the bustling beachhead, souvenir hunting, unauthorized excursions into the lush countryside, petty thievery, and just plain silliness reached epidemic proportions.

⁓

"WE HAD A BALL for most of the first thirty days," recalled Private Howard Towry, the self-confessed "worst screwup" in the First Marine Tank Battalion. "The First and Sixth Marine Divisions went looking north and east for somebody to fight, but they didn't find any Japs to speak of. Meanwhile, a bunch of us were back on the beach, just riding around and acting stupid. We were hunting souvenirs, killing chickens, shooting pigs, and just having fun."

The situation was tailor-made for enhancing Towry's unenviable reputation for getting in trouble, and he lost no time making the most of it. He and two buddies, Privates George Ziperski from Milwaukee and Floyd Ramsey from Pinkneyville, Illinois, caught three spirited Okinawan ponies and raced one another around the countryside, raiding untended chicken coops and pigpens as they went. "We'd shoot a chicken or two, or maybe even a pig, and take them back to camp and barbecue them," said Towry. "We were eating dang well there for a while."

Unfortunately for Towry and his mates, Lieutenant Colonel Austin C. Shofner, provost marshal of the First Marine Division and commander of its military police group, also took a shine to the ponies and decided they were better suited for MPs and officers than for goof-off buck privates. "He said it didn't look like we were gonna be doing any fighting for a while, so he was gonna organize an officers' stable," Towry said.

"All enlisted men are ordered to turn in any horses in their possession immediately," the posted order decreed. "Enlisted men will no longer be allowed to keep a horse or ride one."

To hell with that, thought Towry. *I got me a real pretty horse, and I ain't about to give him up.*

Towry, Ziperski, and Ramsey managed to hide their ponies overnight, and the next morning, they set off on another foraging expedition. A few hours later, they were galloping along a dirt road, carrying a bag of chickens and another of eggs, when a jeep approached. In its rear seat was none other than Colonel Shofner himself.

Towry cringed, feeling the officer's eyes boring into him as the jeep roared past, then jerked to a stop at an MP checkpoint about 200 yards up the road.

Uh-oh! he thought. *We're in big trouble now!*

After hurriedly concealing their contraband chickens and eggs in a roadside ditch, the three miscreants rode over to the checkpoint, where Towry offered a lame excuse in hopes of getting them off the hook.

"We were just trying to get us some food before we turned our horses in, Colonel," he said.

The hard-nosed Shofner, a former battalion commander known throughout the division as "Shifty" and famed for escaping the Japanese-occupied Philippines in time to command a battalion of the Fifth

Marines at Peleliu and be wounded there, was unimpressed. "Shut up and dismount," he snapped. "Don't speak till you're spoken to. All I want from you is your name, rank, and serial number."

Towry and company meekly complied and watched their horses being led away. After a dressing-down by the colonel, they were allowed to return to their unit, but the next morning, they were picked up by a squad of MPs and taken to an improvised stockade.

"It was nothing but a big sweet potato patch with barbed wire strung around it—no tents, no foxholes, no nothing," Towry recalled. "That afternoon, some Japanese planes came in to strafe the beach and the airfield, and there we were with bullets knocking sparks off the fence and nowhere to run and no place to hide."

When the planes returned the next day, the prisoners were allowed to take cover in a dugout just outside the enclosure. The rest of the time, Towry whiled away the hours by digging sweet potatoes with his bare hands. He ate some of them raw and threw others at passing Okinawan civilians who paused to stare, point, and occasionally laugh at the incarcerated Marines.

After three days of this, Towry and his buddies were summoned before a panel of officers to hear the charges against them. Fortunately, the colonel in charge of the hearing was someone other than Shofner, but he was also a tough, no-nonsense type. The three errant Marines faced seven charges in all, including, in Towry's words, "being outside our assigned area without a pass, improper uniforms, no steel helmets, no gas masks, riding a forbidden horse, and some other stuff."

"Why were you riding the horses when you'd been ordered not to?" the colonel demanded.

There was only silence from Ziperski and Ramsey, but Towry spoke up. It wasn't the wisest move he ever made. "Well, sir, I'm from Texas," he said with a disarming grin, "and I reckon I'm just real fond of horses."

The colonel glared at him for a moment, then shook his head. "Okay, Tex, I'm going to let you go," he said, "but I want to tell you something, and by God you'd better pay attention."

"Yes, sir. I'm listening, sir."

"If I ever—repeat *ever*—catch you making trouble again, I'll put your ass back in that sweet potato patch until the damned war's over and everybody else has gone home! Is that clear?"

Less than an hour later, a chastened Towry was making his way back toward his battalion's bivouac area—on foot, of course—when a Japanese Zero zoomed low over the beach on a strafing run. Along with everyone else around him, Towry hit the deck as machine gun bullets peppered the nearby sand, then watched as the plane pulled up and circled back for another pass.

Towry had never been under fire from the air before, and he couldn't understand why none of the men around him were firing back at the Zero, which was less than fifty feet off the ground.

Well, by damn, he told himself, *if nobody else is gonna shoot at that son of a bitch, I will. Next time he flies over, I'm gonna get me that plane.*

He rolled over onto his back, raised his M-1, and waited until the Zero was directly above him. Then he ripped off an eight-round clip of ammo at the attacking plane.

"I shot way behind him, and I must've missed him by half a mile," Towry recalled many years later, "and the next thing I know, some great big sergeant's grabbing me by my shirt, lifting me straight up in the air, and shaking me like a rag doll."

"What the hell you think you doin', boy?" the sergeant yelled.

"Well, what does it look like?" Towry yelled back. "I'm trying to shoot down that Jap plane."

"You dumb little bastard," the sergeant said, "don't you know what Condition Red control is?"

"No, I never heard of it."

"It means you can't hit that damn plane with a rifle, and you ain't supposed to try," the sergeant told him. "There's a Corsair up there that'll take care of that Zero, and it don't need no help from you. I got a good mind to send you down to the colonel and tell him to throw you in the brig."

Oh, no! Towry thought. *Not again!*

⁓

Towry wasn't the only horse lover among the Americans on Okinawa—although he was surely among the unluckiest—and there were plenty of horses to love.

In addition to plow horses and draft animals used for farmwork, trained cavalry horses were also in abundance on the island, the site of a principal training center for mounted units of the Japanese army before the war. Many were handsome, spirited steeds, and one in particular quickly caught the eye of Marine Sergeant Alex Henson, a squad leader in K/3/5's machine-gun section, who had grown up in the heart of thoroughbred country south of Lexington, Kentucky.

"Not long after we landed, I spotted one of the prettiest horses I ever saw walking along the beach," Henson said. "He was solid white and wearing a wooden saddle, and he had a minor flesh wound in his hip. I went over and caught him easily and doctored the wound. Then I spent the rest of the day riding him all over the beach. I had a great time."

That evening, Henson tied the horse to a barbed wire fence for safekeeping. But when he went back the next morning, the horse tried to bite him. "I figured his hip must be hurting him, so I let him go," Henson said. "I never saw him again, but I've often wondered what happened to him. He was one beautiful animal."

MARINE PFC ORLIE UHLS, a youngster of German descent, had grown up on a large farm in southern Illinois and was well acquainted with horses and most other kinds of livestock. He was also one of the few men in K/3/5's Third Rifle Platoon with intimate knowledge of how to kill, dress, and butcher a hog.

After commandeering a good horse for himself, Uhls rounded up another one for his friend, Corporal Sterling Mace, the wisecracking twenty-year-old from New York City who'd never been closer to a hog killing than a slab of bacon in a meat market in his native Queens.

"Hey, Mace, let's go boar hunting," Uhls suggested on the morning of Love-plus-2.

Mace frowned at his buddy. "You gotta be kidding," he said. "How we gonna do that?"

"Easy," said Uhls. "We ride around till we find us a good-sized hog, then we shoot that sucker. I'll handle the rest."

Uhls was as good as his word. Within an hour, he, Mace, and Sergeant Ted "Tex" Barrow, a veteran hog killer from rural Texas who volunteered to go along, hauled a fierce-looking, but very dead, black boar back into camp.

When the boar was dressed out, it didn't look nearly as big to Mace as it had alive. It didn't look all that appetizing, either. Uhls butchered it as if he'd done the same thing a hundred times before, deftly cutting it into chunks small enough to roast over an open fire. As the meat sizzled in the flames, a dozen or so other Marines were drawn by its smell.

"An hour or so later, there was nothing left of that hog except some well-gnawed bones," Mace recalled later. "All I got was one lousy pork chop."

⌒

Sergeant Leonard "Hook" Ahner, whose nickname was prompted by his eagle-beak nose, had had roast pork on his mind since his first afternoon ashore, and the longer he thought about it, the more his mouth watered. When he heard from his friend Tex Barrow that the guys in K/3/5's Third Platoon had just barbecued a full-grown boar—and eaten it all without letting Ahner know—the veteran First Platoon squad leader was fit to be tied.

"Okay, that does it!" Ahner told his buddies, PFCs Bill Leyden and Pete Fouts. "I can't believe those guys cooked that meat on sticks over an open fire like they were having a doggone weenie roast. Tomorrow morning, we're gonna go out and find ourselves a hog of our own. Then I'm gonna show you people what *real* roast pork tastes like."

Ahner was also as good as his word. In an hour of foraging, he, Leyden, and Fouts located a fat, young hog—considerably larger than the one Uhls had bagged—on an otherwise deserted farm. Ahner dispatched the animal with a single shot from his .45, and the three of them hung it over a sturdy pole and carried it back to camp. There the hog was gutted, scalded, and scraped according to Ahner's directions, then wrapped in wet burlap and cooked for several hours in a pit of hot coals.

That evening, few First Platoon riflemen bothered to open their C-rations. All were invited to join Ahner and his accomplices in eating "high on the hog."

Even Leyden, Mace's fellow New Yorker, had to admit that he'd seldom smelled anything more delectable than the pork when it was removed from the pit and unwrapped. Despite his original doubts, he ate all he could hold, and in years to come, he'd recall the evening as one of the most enjoyable interludes he ever spent on what was supposed to be a battlefield. But the occasion would also be seared into his memory as a portent of the terror and tragedy ahead.

Early the next morning, L-Day-plus-4, K/3/5 was ordered to move out, but there was still a lot of meat left, and Ahner had no intention of leaving it behind. "Let's figure a way to carry it, and we'll finish it up tonight," he said. "It's too good to waste."

One Marine managed to locate a pot large enough to hold the cache of pork, and others fashioned a pole that allowed two men to carry the pot on their shoulders. Ahner himself took the leading end of the pole while someone else grabbed the other end. Then the platoon set out along a narrow dirt road, bantering and joking back and forth as they marched.

"Several guys took turns carrying the back end of the pole," Leyden said, "but Hook refused to let anybody relieve him on the front end. That was just the way he was."

It had been Ahner who had calmed Leyden's jangled nerves on the way to the beach with the first wave at Peleliu, when shells were bursting all around their amtrack and seventeen-year-old Leyden feared his resolve might desert him. Both had been wounded at Peleliu and spent time in the same Navy hospital on New Caledonia, and Ahner's wry humor, coolheaded savvy, and quiet courage had sustained Leyden more times than he could count over the year they'd spent together.

"He never seemed tired or down," Leyden said. "He was always upbeat and optimistic, always doing more than his share. He was my idol, my mentor, and the best damned friend I ever had."

The platoon had gone about two miles down the road when a sharp, flat, popping sound suddenly echoed among the men. Every Marine within earshot, veteran and newcomer alike, instantly recognized the "pop" as the ominous sound of an igniting hand grenade with its pin dislodged.

Nobody could tell at first where the sound originated, but its meaning was clear: Within five seconds or less, the grenade would explode.

"Grenade!" someone shouted. "Hit the deck!"

For a tiny fragment of a second, Leyden's eyes met Ahner's, and Leyden realized with terrible clarity what was about to happen. The errant grenade—one of two that every Marine rifleman carried in combat—was in a pouch on Ahner's left hip.

Leyden knew from Hook's expression that the same realization had struck him. As the men around him dived for cover, Ahner dropped the pole and whirled away from them. He threw himself to the side of the road, positioning his body to smother the grenade and shield his comrades from the blast.

From all indications, Ahner died instantly. Two other Marines suffered superficial lacerations from grenade fragments, but if not for Ahner's quick thinking and final act of selflessness, up to a half-dozen men might have been killed. Similar heroism had been recognized with posthumous Medals of Honor when Marines jumped on grenades thrown by enemy soldiers, but Ahner's sacrifice would be officially listed as an accident.

The whole platoon stood dazed as Lieutenant Tom "Stumpy" Stanley, the company commander, knelt beside Ahner's smoking corpse and shook his head. Many of the men wept. Some shuffled off alone, trying to collect themselves. Several took out their own grenades and hurled them away, cursing. No one knew for certain what had caused the grenade's firing pin to dislodge, but each man present knew it could just as easily have happened to him.

"We also knew that a man's first instinct would be to unbuckle his belt and fling it away from him to save himself," Leyden said. "But typical of Hook, he thought of the rest of us first."

Stretcher bearers came and carried the body away. "Get ready to move out," Lieutenant Stanley said quietly.

As he wiped his face on his sleeve and turned to rejoin the platoon, Leyden reached down and picked up the Thompson submachine gun Ahner had dropped just before the explosion. He dusted it off, hugged it to his chest, and followed the rest of the platoon down the road.

It was much later before anyone thought about the pot of meat that had fallen to the ground in the frenzied seconds after the grenade popped, then left behind by the roadside. It didn't matter. No one in the platoon had any appetite left for roast pork.

⁓

THE RANGE OF REACTIONS of the Okinawan people to the American strangers represented a peculiar paradox. Some, like those encountered early on in the Kerama Retto by troops of the 77th Infantry Division, were terrified to the point of taking their own lives and those of their families for fear of what unspeakable atrocities the invaders would commit against them. At the opposite extreme, many others were eager to make friends with the Americans.

As Marine Sergeant Alex Henson of K/3/5's machine-gun section recalled: "The civilians we saw during those early days were usually shy at first, but most of them were friendly and helpful. Despite the fact that we were disrupting their lives, they gave us the impression that they weren't sorry we were there."

The Okinawans' reasons for this reaction gradually became apparent to Marines and GIs when they noticed that the only civilians they encountered were women, children, and elderly men. Every able-bodied young Okinawan male had been conscripted by the Japanese to serve—often with great reluctance—either as laborers or soldiers.

Henson and his buddies got acquainted with one family in particular—an older man with two daughters in their early twenties—who lived in a farmhouse about a mile from the American lines and went out of their way to welcome the Marines.

"The first time we went over there, we were just scrounging around for something to eat, and this guy brought us out some eggs," Henson said. "While we were in that area, about a week and a half, we went to their house pretty often, and they always treated us real well. We would've gone more often, except that the Okinawan farms were absolutely alive with fleas. Some of the outbuildings were black with them."

⁓

WHILE THEIR UNINVITED American guests pillaged their vegetable gardens, stole their chickens, slaughtered their pigs, and trotted away on their horses, a large percentage of civilians took refuge in the hundreds of ancestral tombs that were prominent and unique features of the island's landscape.

Until they were either coaxed or forced out into the open by Marines and GIs, countless civilian families hid inside these large burial vaults. The oldest of the tombs were natural caves, but the more recent ones were sturdy aboveground structures of stone and concrete carved into the hillsides. Usually, they were either shaped like small houses or of a rounded "turtleback" design. Even the poorest farm families built the finest tombs they could afford, tended them with great care, and used them not only as places for burials and ceremonies honoring the dead but also as centers of family life, holiday celebrations, and even picnics.

In the simple, insular world of the Okinawan farmers, the dead were held in high reverence and their bodies subjected to a series of rituals rooted in antiquity. Three years after death, the bones of the deceased were carefully washed, then stored in ceramic urns within the tomb for thirty-three more years, at which time a final memorial service was held to symbolically set their spirits free. Rural Okinawan culture never glorified death or the sacrifice of human life by warriors for nationalistic causes as did the Japanese.

The gentle beauty of the tombs and the attitude underlying them were generally overlooked by Japan's 32nd Army, but its troops had been quick to recognize the tombs' value as underground fortifications. Likewise, battle-savvy Marines and GIs learned early on not to bypass the tombs without making sure they weren't occupied by Japanese soldiers.

AS HE HIKED UP a rolling hillside ahead of his men, Army Platoon Sergeant Porter McLaughlin paused a few paces from a tomb beside the rutted dirt road they were following. He raised his hand and motioned the unit to halt.

"Has anybody checked that thing out?" he asked Sergeant George Murphy, jerking a thumb toward the tomb.

Murphy shrugged. "A bunch of our infantry's been along this way, but I'm not sure."

"I think I heard somebody talking in there," McLaughlin said. "Let's take a look."

He and Murphy crept close to the tomb's entrance, which was partially blocked by a large rock, and listened intently for a moment. Sure enough, McLaughlin heard soft but distinct voices coming from the tomb's dark interior.

"Sounds like a little kid," he whispered, "but cover me, anyway." Then he cupped his hands and yelled: "Whoever's in there, come on out! We don't want to hurt you. Everything's okay."

McLaughlin relaxed a bit as the face of a small boy slowly emerged from behind the rock. The boy quickly ducked back out of sight, then just as quickly reappeared in the timeless child's game of peekaboo. He looked to be eight or nine years old.

McLaughlin dug a K-ration candy bar out of his pocket and showed it to the boy. "Come on out, and you can have this, okay?"

McLaughlin heard a rustle of movement behind the boy as he stepped into the sunlight, reaching for the candy. Then other faces—lots of them—began materializing in the tomb's entrance.

They came forth warily, one by one—about two dozen people in all. Most were women, some with babies in their arms, and other young children, but there were also three or four old men. When the Okinawans realized that the soldiers weren't going to shoot or bayonet them, many began to smile, bow, and chatter.

After the civilians were all out, Corporal Lloyd Scoles, a gunner on one of the platoon's 37-millimeter weapons, ventured inside with his carbine to make sure the tomb was empty. He came back out in a hurry, brushing and swatting at himself with both hands.

"Jesus, that place is swarming with fleas," he said. "There must be a million of 'em. How the hell did those people stand it?"

"How long you figure they've been hiding in there?" Murphy wondered.

"God knows," said McLaughlin. "Let's see if we can round up some more K-rations. Those kids all look hungry."

BECAUSE THE FIRST MARINE DIVISION had already endured the hardest fighting and heaviest casualties of the Pacific war, it had been given a relatively easy mission in the opening phase of the Okinawa campaign. As its first objective, the Old Breed was to advance across the island's narrow waist all the way to its eastern shore and conduct general mopping-up operations in central Okinawa. The First would then secure the so-called Eastern Islands on the far side of Chimu Wan Bay to prevent any Japanese attempt to base troops on these islands that might threaten U.S. forces from the rear.

Planners had expected it to take the First about two weeks to fight its way to Okinawa's east coast, wiping out remaining pockets of enemy resistance en route. But since the advance was unopposed—and there was no mopping-up to do—the virtually unbloodied division crossed the island in just four days, with only occasional enemy contact along the way.

One exception to the general calm in which the First Marine Division operated occurred in the area where its Seventh Marines was joined to a line formed by the Fourth Marines of the Sixth Division. On the night of April 2, several hundred Japanese infiltrators came calling, striking especially hard at the portion of the line held by the Seventh's E Company, Second Battalion.

"The Japs got between two of our defensive perimeters and got our guys shooting at each other in the confusion," recalled Corporal Melvin Grant, a twenty-year-old flamethrower operator attached to E Company.

As the sun went down on April 2, the company was told to dig in, and Melvin, whose younger brother, PFC Scott Grant, was also on Okinawa with the Sixth Marine Division, found a small ditch that was "just deep enough for my flamethrower." But just as he was settling in, a sergeant came by and told him he'd have to move about fifty yards down the line. Grant, being the ninth of sixteen children born on his parents' hardscrabble Oklahoma farm, was used to being shuffled around, so he took the inconvenience in stride. Later, he'd have reason to be eternally grateful for his eviction.

"Two company cooks who took over my little ditch were stabbed to death by infiltrators that night," Grant said, "and they also killed two other Marines in our company. The Japs tried to trick our men by speaking English, and sometimes it worked, especially with men who hadn't been in combat before."

An hour or so after midnight and a short distance from Grant's foxhole, a Marine sergeant heard a voice in the darkness a few feet away.

"How'd you make out, Joe?" it asked quietly.

The English was perfect, but the accent wasn't. The sergeant raised his .45 and fired five times, riddling a Japanese infiltrator clutching a bayonet. "I made out fine, you bastard," the shooter said calmly.

When the sun came up the next morning, it revealed seventy-one dead Japanese. E Company's casualties were four dead and a dozen wounded.

⸺

By April 5 (L-plus-4), all three infantry regiments of the First Marine Division had units comfortably bivouacked in two-man pup tents near the shore of Chimu Wan Bay, where its troops, except for being slightly weary from climbing hills, were still very much in relaxation mode. Until the very end of April, most of the Old Breed would continue to enjoy what amounted to a monthlong vacation from the war.

"It was more like maneuvers than combat," said PFC Gene Sledge, whose mortar squad kept its guns stowed rather than set them up needlessly. "We didn't even dig foxholes."

"If the Japs had been close enough to see how we were acting during those early days," added Sledge's K/3/5 comrade, Corporal Sterling Mace, "they might've been able to chase us back into the sea with one good-sized counterattack."

Meanwhile, the newly formed Sixth Marine Division—sometimes referred to as "the New Breed"—was seeing its first action as a unit, although it incorporated hundreds of battle-hardened veterans transferred from other divisions. The Sixth had been handed the more demanding task of clearing scattered enemy forces from northern Okinawa. In getting this job done, its men would travel farther, face stiffer resistance, and absorb considerably more casualties in April than their counterparts in the First, particularly during a costly weeklong fight against Japanese entrenched in the heights of the Motobu Peninsula. Yet in general, even for the Sixth, April would be a veritable cakewalk compared to what other Marines had faced at Guadalcanal, Tarawa, Peleliu, and Iwo Jima.

For Army troops of the 96th and Seventh Divisions, however, the period of playful leisure, easy duty, and next to no contact with the enemy was destined to last only a few days—hardly more than a long weekend, in fact. The two divisions accomplished all their assigned objectives for the first ten days in just seventy-two hours. They raced across the island with the Hourglass Seventh anchoring the left (north) leg of the advance, and the Deadeyes of the 96th spearheading the right (south) leg of the drive.

As these coordinated troop movements were completed without a trace of organized opposition, rampant speculation continued among the GIs about where—and why—the Japanese were hiding. There was also spirited debate over whether they'd fight when they were found.

"By now, I'm sure our intelligence knew the Jap defenders were concentrated in the southern end of the island," said Corporal Don Dencker of the 96th, "but at our level, we were completely in the dark. Later it became apparent that the Japanese in the high ground to the south were watching our every move and patiently waiting for us to advance against their well-prepared positions."

Late on the afternoon of April 3, Major General John R. Hodge, commander of the Army's 24th Corps, issued orders to launch a full-scale drive to the south. He handed the Deadeyes of the 96th the mission of capturing a dominating stretch of high ground on the west side of the line identified on maps as the Urasoe-Mura Escarpment. The Hourglass Seventh's assignment was to seize an equally dominating mass called Hill 178 on the east side of the line.

No one from Hodge on down to the lowliest private could foresee what lay ahead—that both divisions would be stopped cold before reaching either objective, then hurled back with staggering losses.

As Dencker had surmised, military intelligence and the commanders of the U.S. Tenth Army did by now have a good idea of where the Japanese were concentrated. The problem was that nobody on the American side had yet grasped either the enemy's intentions or his capabilities, much less the scope and complexity of the defensive juggernaut created by Japanese General Ushijima and his architect, Colonel Yahara.

Hodge himself had no inkling that he was sending his best, most experienced infantry regiments against the outer works of Ushijima's main line of defense in the ridges around Shuri Castle. So elated was Hodge by the pace of his troops' advance thus far that he held high hopes of them sweeping quickly through the high ground, capturing the port of Naha, and wrapping up the Okinawa campaign in short order.

On April 4, with optimism matching that of their commanding general, the Seventh and 96th Divisions wheeled south toward the nearest of the saw-tooth ridges that crisscrossed southern Okinawa.

The idyllic interlude that had begun on Love Day with jubilant Deadeyes picking and eating ripe tomatoes along their line of march was about to end with sudden, savage fury.

The beginning of the end came on April 4–5, as they unknowingly approached one of the most formidable keystones of General Ushijima's Naha-Shuri-Yonabaru Line—a rather ordinary-looking chunk of rock known as Kakazu Ridge.

As the official history of the 96th would later note: "The honeymoon was over."

CHAPTER FOUR

A Nasty Surprise on the Way South

ON THE MORNING of April 4 (L-plus-3), the Third Platoon of the 96th Recon Troop, a mechanized cavalry/reconnaissance unit, was on the move long before first light. Its assignment: to reconnoiter road conditions and enemy troop disposition ahead of the advancing Third Battalion of the 383rd Infantry Regiment, alerting 96th Division intelligence by radio of any Japanese activity, hazardous road conditions, or other obstacles encountered along its route.

Some of the platoon's three dozen officers and men yawned as they piled into vehicles sandbagged for protection against road mines and bristling with armament. Then, silent and watchful, they headed south past the town of Chatan. Division headquarters wanted them a full hour ahead of the 383rd by the time the infantrymen jumped off at 6:00 A.M., allowing enough lead time to keep the main force from stumbling unawares into trouble.

Known as "the eyes and ears" of the 96th Division, the recon troop was roughly half the size of a regular rifle company, counting about 110 enlisted men in its ranks. Its three platoons of about thirty men each were often assigned to separate areas where their mobility, observation skills, and communications training were most sorely needed. They hadn't seen much action since coming ashore, but all that was about to change.

As the convoy proceeded slowly down Okinawa's Route 1 with its headlights turned off in the predawn darkness, it was led by a pair of veteran scouts, Corporals LaMont Clark and Eric Lane, who moved out ahead of the vehicles on foot to check the roadway for mines. The rest of the men were packed into four jeeps, two half-tracks, and an M-8 armored car nicknamed the "Reluctant Virgin." Most of them had been on similar missions in the past, and they weren't expecting this one to be much different from the others.

They were wrong. Before the morning was half over, this patrol would take them as close as men could come to hell on Earth.

⌐

AROUND 5:00 A.M., the little caravan reached the village of Mashiki, where the road forked, and Captain Robert O'Neill, the troop CO, ordered a halt to consult his sketchy maps.

To the left, although there was too little light to see it clearly, a strip of high ground called Cactus Ridge zigzagged toward the main mass of Kakazu Ridge and the deep gorge fronting it. A stone's throw to the patrol's right was Okinawa's coastal plain and western shore. Angling off to the left was a rough, winding secondary road that appeared to follow a north-south ridge in the general direction of the town of Uchitomari, which was less than a half mile away, according to the maps. The question was: Should they stay on the main route, one of the island's better thoroughfares, or venture onto this uninviting byway?

In addition to Captain O'Neill, several other officers had accompanied the patrol, including Lieutenants William Kramer, Fred Messer, and Ralph Watt, and the senior NCO on the trip was Staff Sergeant Leonard Hawks. Behind the steering wheel of the armored car was PFC Rudolph Pizio, a muscular Italian kid from Havertown, Pennsylvania. Seated beside him was the M-8's commander, Corporal John M. Cain, a lanky, bespectacled youngster from Wisconsin, whose scholarly appearance belied an inner toughness earned in the jungles of the Philippines.

O'Neill decided they should check out the side road, which was little more than a cow trail, and the officers got out of their jeeps to wait while Cain and Pizio drove on. Soon, however, a pair of short stone walls bracketed the road so tightly on either side that the Reluctant Virgin was unable to squeeze between them. The M-8 was a bulky six-wheeler and the only vehicle in the group mounting a 37-millimeter antitank weapon as well as .30- and .50-caliber machine guns. The two half-tracks carried two machine guns apiece but no cannon, and each of the jeeps had a single .30-caliber mounted between the front seats and positioned to fire above the windshield.

"Turn the car around, and go on back to the village," Cain told Pizio. "I'll walk up to the top of the ridge and have a look."

As he began his climb, Cain noted a lingering hint of chill in the morning air—nothing at all like the sticky heat of Leyte, where a man could break a sweat just by drawing a breath. In a minute or two, he reached the crest of the hill and pushed his way through a dense stand of brush. Cain had grown up in the woods of northern Wisconsin, and he was totally comfortable in rough country, but when he peered cautiously down the other side of the hill, he felt his throat constrict.

Below, he saw dozens of enemy soldiers moving around in the growing light. They were hauling equipment and supplies, working on gun emplacements, and chattering among themselves. For a panicky second or two, Cain imagined that all of them were staring directly at him, but then he realized they hadn't spotted him yet.

Retreating quickly to where Pizio was still trying—without success—to turn the armored car around on the impassable road, Cain gasped out his discovery: "The other side of the ridge is alive with Japs! Back the car down the hill and get out of here, but be as quiet as you can about it."

Cain veered past the armored car and raced back to the village on foot, arriving well ahead of Pizio. Captain O'Neill and Lieutenants Kramer, Messer, and Watt, along with the crews of the two half-tracks and a fourth lieutenant who'd recently joined the troop as a replacement and whose name Cain couldn't recall, were standing calmly beside the road.

Cain ran up to O'Neill. "Looks like this is where the trouble starts today, Captain," he panted.

O'Neill frowned. "What do you mean? What trouble?"

"Well, I can tell you there's at least 150 Japs up on that ridge looking right at us," Cain said. "This place is about to be crawling with them. I figure they're going to set up their main defensive line along here because the ridge runs right up to the ocean on this side and apparently most of the way across the island on the other."

"Well, hell," said the newly arrived lieutenant, "take your M-8 and the half-tracks up there and open fire on the bastards before they get dug in."

Cain stared at the unfamiliar lieutenant for a moment, then shook his head. He knew he could be court-martialed for disobeying a superior officer's direct command, but at the moment, he had too much else on his mind to care.

"I've got a feeling plenty of them are already dug in, and there's no way I'm putting my M-8 out in front," he said. "We'll take heavy casualties if we run our vehicles out there. I'm willing to take my whole point unit up on the ridge dismounted. Then if we draw fire, it'll be scattered, and we'll have a chance. We'll have our radios with us, and once we locate the Jap positions, we can get the information back to division G-2. Otherwise, the infantry coming up behind us is in for a nasty surprise."

"Damn it, Corporal," the lieutenant fumed, "I'm giving you an order."

Trying hard to stifle his anger, Cain turned to Lieutenant Messer, a respected veteran from Texas who'd been through the North Africa campaign before joining the 96th and winning a battlefield commission for his performance at Leyte.

"What do you think, sir?" he asked Messer. "What would you do if you were in my shoes?"

"I'd do exactly what you said you'd do, son," Messer replied, giving the other lieutenant a withering look.

"Okay, let's knock it off and hop to it," said Captain O'Neill. "We're wasting time here." He turned to Corporal August Ward. "You take your half-track out front, Ward. Cain, you follow up in the M-8, and the other half-track will follow you."

Cain had no choice but to obey his captain's command, but he felt sick in his gut as he and Ward started back to their vehicles. Ward was one of his closest buddies in the outfit, and the only way the assignment he'd just been handed could be much tougher was if the captain had told him to walk to the top of the ridge and throw rocks at the Japanese. He wondered if the two of them would see each other alive again after the ride they were about to take.

"Listen, Augie," Cain said, "I want to give you a little advice. You and I both know your half-track's bound to get hit out there. When it does, get your men the hell out of it as fast as you can, you hear? Just bail out over the side, and get away from the damn thing. Otherwise, you're all dead meat."

Ward, a husky blond Virginian, smiled tightly. "I'll try to remember that," he said.

Cain pulled off his binoculars and handed them to his friend. "Here, you may need these," he said. Then he turned and ran to the M-8, where his crewmen, PFCs Pizio, Charlie Kubitz, and John Shutes, were waiting. Kubitz was already in the turret.

"Get division G-2 on the radio," Cain told Shutes, the radio operator. "Tell 'em to stand by and be ready. We may not have a chance to tell them anything twice."

WARD'S HALF-TRACK lurched forward, and Cain pulled in about twenty-five yards behind it. They descended a slight grade, bypassing the walls that had stopped the M-8 before, then following the single-lane dirt road to the top of the ridge. Cain held his breath as they started down the other side. There was no sign of enemy activity as he watched the lead half-track reach flat—and disturbingly open—ground at the bottom. Off to his left, he noticed a suspicious knoll that instantly worried him.

If we're going to get hit by anything like antitank guns, it'll come from right there, he thought, *and if there's anyplace to hide around here, I don't see it.*

Cain was starting to feel dizzy from trying to keep his right eye on Ward's half-track and his left eye on the base of the knoll. Then he spotted a mound of dirt with tall, wheatlike grass growing on top of it. Beside it was a six-foot-deep gully. The sight sent relief surging through him.

Boy, if we have to take cover, Cain told himself, *this is as good a place as we'll find to do it.*

The thought had barely formed in his mind, and he was only about ten yards from the gully, when he saw a flash and a puff of smoke. A millisecond later, an armor-piercing shell ripped through the undersection of Ward's half-track.

In the ringing instant of silence that followed, as the half-track lumbered to a dead stop, Cain screamed at Pizio: "Go for the gully, Rudy! Get in the damn gully!"

Then at Ward: "Get out of there, Augie! Get everybody out of there!"

As he yelled, Cain grabbed a 37-millimeter round and jammed it into the breech of the M-8's cannon, not knowing where to aim but determined to be ready if a target presented itself. He knew there had to be an enemy pillbox somewhere close.

The silence ended with a roar of antitank, mortar, machine-gun, and sniper fire that seemed to erupt from everywhere at once. The Japanese had planned and executed their coordinated attack well, positioning their powerful 47-millimeter antitank guns—capable of penetrating the armor on an M-8 or a Sherman tank from up to 400 yards—to command the whole valley. Then they'd waited to fire until the American patrol was exposed from front and rear.

Just as a second enemy round struck Ward's immobilized half-track,

Cain realized the shell had come from a camouflaged pillbox on the knoll above the M-8. But when Kubitz, the gunner, tried to open fire, he was unable to sight in on the pillbox because the high grass around it blocked his field of vision.

When the third round hit the half-track, instantly engulfing the bed of the open vehicle in flame, Cain saw two human bodies blown out of it. They hurtled several feet into the air, then hit the ground on the back side of the half-track. Cain thought one of them was PFC Gene Pisarski, and he was sure the other one was Augie Ward.

"Left, left!" Cain bawled at Kubitz, who was slightly hard of hearing. "Left and down! You're on him now! Fire!"

The armored car shook with the recoil of the 37-millimeter, and a cloud of smoke and dust issued from the damaged pillbox. Now that Kubitz had the range, he poured a series of high-explosive rounds into the enemy position, and Cain leaped to the .30-caliber machine gun.

"I'm opening up with the .30," he shouted. "Just watch my tracers, and direct your fire where they are!"

As the machine gun chattered, Cain cursed himself silently for giving Ward his binoculars. Now Ward was out of action and seriously hurt, his body lying fifteen feet from Cain and squarely behind the ruined half-track, and Cain needed the glasses desperately. With them, he could've spotted the aperture in the side of the pillbox and directed Kubitz's fire directly into it.

Then, to Cain's dismay, he saw the still-blazing half-track start to move. Jolted by repeated direct hits, it began rolling slowly backward down the incline up which it had come moments earlier. As it lumbered past only a few feet away, Cain saw blood literally pouring out of it. The body of PFC Kyle C. Riley, its radio operator, hung over the side of it, the chest cavity blown open and the torn remains of Riley's heart and lungs glistening red against the olive-drab metal.

Cain watched in helpless horror as the left rear track of the vehicle passed directly over Ward's body. He squeezed his eyes shut and bit his tongue to keep from screaming.

After running over Ward, the runaway derelict continued to gather speed until it reached the bottom of the incline, where, incredibly, its momentum began carrying it up the other side. From the armored car, Cain could see Captain O'Neill and Lieutenants Kramer and Messer walking toward the half-track as if they were coming to greet it. A couple of wounded men dragged themselves out of the vehicle seconds before a fourth round struck it, blowing apart most of its rear end and bringing it to a final, shuddering halt. All three officers went down when the blast hit, and there was no way to tell if they were dead or alive.

The second half-track, meanwhile, was making a desperate attempt to head back north out of harm's way. Just as it turned broadside in the road, a Japanese shell crashed into it, and the driver struggled out, staggered a few feet, then fell.

As machine-gun and small-arms fire rattled like hailstones off the Reluctant Virgin's armored hide, there was no sign of the four jeeps and their occupants. Their speed and maneuverability might have allowed them to escape, but Cain had his doubts.

A shout from Kubitz broke into Cain's dazed thought patterns: "We're all out of high-explosive ammo for the 37."

"There's some canister down below," Cain said. "Use it, and just raise your elevation a little." Then he hollered across to Pizio: "Hey, Rudy, get me G-2 on the radio in a hurry."

"Roger," Rudy said. Seconds later, he handed Cain the mike.

"We've been ambushed down here," Cain said. "This big ridge in front of us is heavily fortified, and the ridge to our left is loaded with Jap troops and God knows how many antitank guns. We've lost two half-tracks, and I've got at least five or six men down. We need artillery in here in a hurry and any other help we can get."

"I'll switch you over to artillery so you can give them your coordinates," G-2 replied. "I think we've got some tanks in the area, and I'll see if I can get you some air support down there, too."

Cain winced as more volleys of small-arms fire peppered the armored car. He glanced at his watch. It was barely 8:00 A.M., but it felt like midnight.

⁓

FROM HIS REGIMENTAL HEADQUARTERS several thousand yards away, Colonel Edwin T. May, commander of the 383rd Infantry, had spent considerable time studying Kakazu Ridge through binoculars and on maps, and he'd reached the conclusion that it didn't look all that difficult. The Urasoe-Mura Escarpment about three-quarters of a mile farther south appeared to be a much more formidable natural barrier, and it seemed more likely that the Japanese would concentrate their main defenses there, rather than on Kakazu.

The seizure of Kakazu itself, May believed, would be a mere preliminary to an assault on the Urasoe-Mura heights, and General John Hodge, commander of the 24th Corps, seemed to concur.

It was an understandable conclusion, particularly since neither commander realized at the time that the maps supporting it were inadequate and short of detail. But for the infantrymen of May's regiment, it would prove a grievous mistake. May had no inkling that he was about to attack the strongest Japanese defensive positions on Okinawa.

As Corporal Cain had noticed, an entire system of hogback ridges formed a jagged barrier that ran all the way from 1,000-yard-long Kakazu to the coastal plain on the island's west side, where it was anchored by two smaller hills designated as Kakazu West. The projected line of attack by the 383rd placed Kakazu proper on the left flank of May's regiment and Kakazu West on its right flank.

What neither May nor Hodge—much less any of the Deadeye dogfaces in the assault force—could know was that Kakazu's defenders, commanded by Colonel Munetatsu Hara, had been laboring for months on a maze of interconnected subterranean fortifications and tunnels. Mutually supporting artillery and mortar positions had been carved up to 150 feet deep into solid rock, impervious to the largest shells and bombs in the U.S. arsenal and camouflaged to the point of invisibility, even from a few yards away.

Further complicating the approach to Kakazu was a yawning gorge that fronted it from end to end, making armored support for attacking infantry impossible. The gorge formed a gigantic natural tank trap that no tracked vehicle could cross, and any attempt by tanks to attack either flank of the ridge would expose them to merciless, interlacing fields of Japanese artillery and mortar fire.

Along the northern face of the ridgeline, Colonel Hara's troops had also established a network of forward positions, utilizing the Okinawan tombs where possible and constructing concrete pillboxes where no tombs existed. But Hara placed most of his infantry and all his mortars on the southern reverse side of the ridge, where they were virtually impervious to any type of enfilading fire.

Because none of this was known to American commanders, even sobering early reports of unexpected enemy strength and "stiffening resistance" along the approaches to Kakazu, like those radioed back to division headquarters by the 96th Recon platoon, aroused little concern.

Colonel May, known as a warrior of the "old school," stood firm in

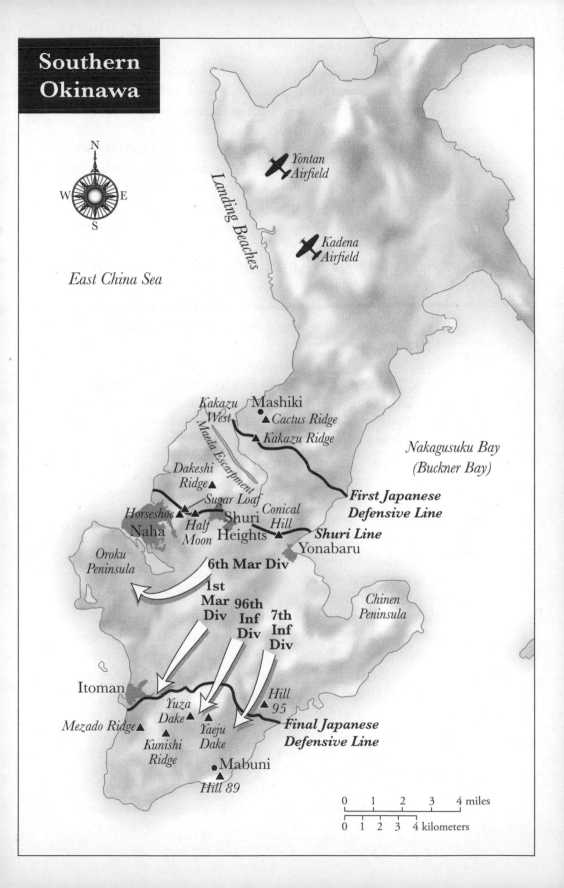

Southern Okinawa

N
W E
S

East China Sea

Landing Beaches

Yontan
Airfield

Kadena
Airfield

*Kakazu
West*

Mashiki
▲ *Cactus Ridge*
▲ *Kakazu Ridge*

Maeda Escarpment

*Dakeshi
Ridge* ▲

Sugar Loaf
Horseshoe ▲▲▲ Shuri
Naha *Half* Heights
Moon

*Conical
Hill*
▲

***First Japanese
Defensive Line***

Shuri Line

Yonabaru

*Nakagusuku Bay
(Buckner Bay)*

*Oroku
Peninsula*

6th Mar Div

**1st
Mar
Div**

**96th
Inf
Div**

**7th
Inf
Div**

*Chinen
Peninsula*

Itoman

*Yuza
Dake* ▲

Mezado Ridge ▲

*Kunishi
Ridge* ▲

*Yaeju
Dake* ▲

▲ *Hill
95*

***Final Japanese
Defensive Line***

● *Mabuni*

Hill 89

0 1 2 3 4 miles

0 1 2 3 4 kilometers

his belief that the best and quickest way to breach an enemy line was by frontal assault. But, based on early reports from patrols probing the enemy's forward positions, division headquarters urged caution for the moment, and May agreed to postpone his all-out attack.

Instead of assaulting Kakazu on April 5, as May had initially envisioned, the 383rd would be allowed a few extra days to solidify its perimeter and scout enemy positions more thoroughly. Although impatient at the delay, May and his battalion commanders would use the interval to study the situation, assess reconnaissance reports, and fine-tune their plans.

Before daylight on April 9, they decided, four rifle companies of the 383rd would storm Kakazu Ridge and Kakazu West simultaneously, with two other companies on call if needed and one full battalion in ready reserve. To gain surprise, there would be no advance bombardment by artillery or planes.

May fully expected both objectives to be secured by his Deadeyes by the following morning. But he grossly underestimated the strength of Colonel Hara's forces, as well as their ability to inflict costly damage on the thinly spread troops of the 383rd during the five-day interval before they were scheduled to storm Kakazu.

BY ABOUT 10:00 A.M. on April 4, slightly more than two hours after the 96th Recon's Third Platoon had met disaster, a brief artillery barrage directed by Corporal Cain had silenced the Japanese antitank weapons, mortars, and machine guns, at least for the moment. Two carrier-based Marine Corsairs had also zoomed in low to blast the enemy positions with salvoes of rockets.

After that, a lull fell over the ridge. Now and then, scattered small-arms rounds still pinged off the M-8 armored car, but for the most part it was quiet, and the platoon's haggard survivors had their first chance to catch their breath, attend their wounded, and assess their losses.

While Cain stayed on the radio with division, pleading for more artillery and air, Kubitz, Pizio, and Shutes—along with Corporal Clark and several others—dashed out to check on injured comrades and to try to move them to the relative safety of the gully where the Reluctant Virgin rested.

"Take a look at Augie Ward, and see if there's anything you can do for him," Cain said grimly as his crew climbed out of the M-8. "If he's still breathing, try to make him as comfortable as you can."

Deep within, Cain was certain that Ward—already wounded and motionless before his own half-track had backed over him—was either dead or dying. From three or four arms' lengths away, Cain had seen both the left rear track and left front wheel of the ten-ton vehicle pass directly over Ward's abdomen. Common sense said there was no way anyone could live through that, but Cain couldn't stand it until he knew for sure.

The minutes dragged by while he sat there alone, clutching the radio and sinking into what was probably a mild state of shock. When Corporal LaMont Clark appeared beside him, Cain was only dimly aware of his presence. He later remembered wondering where Clark had come from, apparently forgetting that he'd been scouting the roadway on foot all the way from Chatan.

"See if you can find some medics and send them this way," Cain mumbled. "We're shot to hell and in bad shape down here."

The next thing he remembered with any clarity was when Rudy Pizio climbed down through the hatch with a grin on his face.

"I still can't believe it, but Augie's alive," he said. "I don't even think he's hurt too bad."

Cain frowned. "Are you putting me on?"

"I'm serious," Rudy said. "He had these two canteens, one on each hip, and he was lying in soft mud. Somehow the canteens held up the track and the wheel, and they pushed him down into the mud instead of cutting him in half."

A close friend and frequent sparring partner of Ward's back in happier times, Corporal Clark had been among the first to reach the injured man, and he was totally awed by the lack of damage to Ward's vital organs. "He was skinned up and bruised pretty good," Clark recalled later, "but otherwise he was okay. It was a damned miracle, as far as I could see."

It was also a rare speck of good news amid a mountain of disaster. Two members of the platoon—PFCs Riley and James Crouch—were dead, and at least five others were seriously wounded, including Lieutenants Messer and Kramer. Both half-tracks were total wipeouts, along with three of the four jeeps.

One of the jeeps, driven by PFC Alfred E. Henderson, a tall, rail-thin Arkansan from Pine Bluff, had been hit in the rear end by a mortar round, causing its gas tank to explode. Henderson had managed to jump from the vehicle barely scathed, but the gunner in the backseat had been severely wounded.

Worse, the remnants of the patrol were now stranded alone in enemy territory with only infrequent artillery support and an occasional Corsair to hold the Japanese at bay.

Moments after Kubitz and Shutes had returned to the M-8 from tending to the wounded, and Kubitz had resumed his position in the gun turret, a ferocious new volley of Japanese automatic-weapons fire ricocheted off the armored car. Several rounds ripped open a ten-pound tin of coffee that someone had lashed to the top of the turret. Coffee grounds flew in all directions and filtered down in little trickles on Kubitz's head and shoulders.

The gunner ducked and covered his head until the firing eased off. Then he reached up and wiped at the grounds streaming off his helmet. "Coffee anyone?" he inquired.

For a second, the tension eased, and everybody laughed.

 —◦

IT WAS CLOSE to noon when the pinned-down recon survivors spotted the first infantry units of the 383rd entering the village of Mashiki. At first, it was a cause for jubilation since it meant that help was finally close at hand, especially for a half-dozen wounded men who'd lain for hours without medical attention.

Almost immediately, however, a fire fight broke out, and the American infantrymen took cover in the village, still too far away to provide any relief for Cain and his comrades.

By now, continued enemy shelling had increased the earlier toll among the platoon. The Japanese gunners had concentrated their fire on the two disabled half-tracks until they succeeded in hitting their fuel tanks, causing both to explode in bright-orange fireballs and wounding several additional men.

As the crew of the Reluctant Virgin watched from the gully, three Sherman tanks, part of Company C of the 763rd Tank Battalion, started out from the village. Oblivious to the concealed 47-millimeter enemy tank-busters lurking ahead, they started up the same path taken that morning by the recon patrol, and passed within a few feet of the two burned-out half-tracks. The first two tanks were buttoned up, but the

third one had its hatch wide open, and the tank commander was survey-
ing the road ahead. On the route the Shermans were following, they
would pass within ten feet of the M-8—if they got that far.

What in God's name do you guys think you're doing? Cain thought.
You're driving straight into a trap.

He grabbed for the radio, but by the time he reached division G-2,
the two buttoned-up tanks had already been hit and halted in their
tracks. The third Sherman was almost side by side with the M-8, and its
commander had just closed his hatch, when it was struck squarely by a
high-explosive shell.

"There was a good-sized explosion inside the tank," Cain recalled
later, "and immediately the hatches opened up, and flames came gushing
out. That tank had bought it."

The radio operator and two other crewmen bailed out of the Sherman through one of the upper hatches. Then the radio operator ran
back, opened the other topside hatch, and dragged his critically burned
commander out of the inferno inside.

"I'm watching three tanks being destroyed," Cain shouted into his
microphone, "and one of them's probably got fatalities. These pillboxes
are still tearing us apart. We've got to have more artillery in here."

Despite being hit, the first two tanks had managed to continue on
down the road toward Uchitomari. Cain had a clear view of them until
they reached the outskirts of the town, where Japanese 155-millimeter
howitzers found and destroyed both.

Throwing down the microphone, Cain climbed out of the M-8 and
darted through enemy rifle fire to try to help the stricken crewmen of the
third tank. When he reached the spot where the Sherman's radio operator was sprawled beside the tank commander, Cain's despair only deepened. The radioman's burns didn't look too bad, but the tank
commander—whom Cain recognized as a guy he'd stopped to talk with
along the road the day before—had literally been roasted alive.

"The only skin that wasn't burned off of him was in his shoes," Cain
said, "and his flesh was hanging off in gobs all over him. I took my shirt
off and covered him with it, and I held him in my arms for about an
hour. There was nothing else I could do."

Amazingly, the young tanker was still conscious and talking. "I'd sure
hate for my folks to have to see me like this," he whispered. "I'm so dang
messed up, I don't think they could stand it."

"They'd want to see you, no matter what," Cain said.

"Yeah, maybe so," the tanker responded quietly, "but it'd just be too hard on them. It'd hurt 'em too much. I think it's better for me to go ahead and die."

Cain tried to think of something else reassuring to say, but he couldn't. Before long, the burned man lapsed into shock. After that, he didn't talk anymore.

MEANWHILE, Corporal Clark, who'd been only a short distance from the two other tanks when they were hit, and who was the nearest foot soldier to the scene, crawled under the blazing Shermans to claw away the mud that held their escape hatches shut and free their trapped crews.

"I was able to get six of the guys out, but, God, they were all terribly burned and screaming in pain, and I didn't have a damned thing to give them," Clark said. "So I ran back [to the 383rd's lines] to find a medic, but the medics were all shot up, too, and none of them could come with me. One did give me his medical bag, though, and I took it back and gave some morphine shots to the guys that were burned."

It was only afterward that Clark noticed his right arm was bleeding from deeply embedded shell fragments.

A SHORT DISTANCE east of where Clark and Cain huddled with the wounded tankers near Okinawa's west coast, troops of the Hourglass Seventh Infantry Division were advancing on a line parallel to the 96th. In fact, the two divisions were so close together that some units of the Seventh's 32nd and 184th Regiments passed through elements of the 96th in the process. Thus far, however, the Seventh had drawn no more than token opposition as it pressed southward while the 96th was catching hell.

Optimism ran high among the Hourglass GIs until midafternoon on April 4, when the Second Battalion of the 184th was halted by heavy rifle and automatic weapons fire from the heights of Castle Hill, named for the ruins of an ancient castle at its peak. When Lieutenant Colonel Delbert Bjork, the battalion commander, ordered his Company E to assault the hill, it was met near the top by volleys of small-arms fire and thrown back. Both the company commander, Captain Wilburt Byrne, and his executive officer were killed.

As the official Seventh Division history noted: "[F]or the first time, opposing enemy strength was of more than nuisance value." It would remain so for the next two and a half months. For the men of the Seventh, like their comrades in the 96th, the honeymoon was, indeed, over.

That evening, under occasional sniper, mortar, and artillery fire, Platoon Sergeant Porter McLaughlin's antitank unit, along with the rest of the Second Battalion, 32nd Infantry, set up its first "serious" defensive perimeter of the campaign north of the town of Ouki.

In contrast to their comrades in the 184th, the men of Colonel Mickey Finn's 32nd had advanced briskly through the flatlands along the east coast, facing no fortified heights to assault and meeting only scattered resistance. Only orders from division headquarters to keep their right flank tied in with the line of the 184th prevented them from covering more ground. But after manhandling their 37-millimeter antitank guns for miles across the island, then south for more miles (jeeps were supposed to be available for such long hauls, but they seldom were), the men were tired and edgy as they gulped their C-rations and dug in for the night.

All three of the platoon's 37s were positioned on the perimeter, loaded with antipersonnel canister rounds, and pointing south. If the Japanese should pull a banzai charge like those the platoon's veterans had fought off at Attu and Kwajalein, the "pea-shooters" would be ready. McLaughlin and his squad leaders, Sergeants George Murphy, John Knorr, and Louie Vissio, bedded down a few yards to the rear of one of the guns, determined that they'd be ready, too.

In its march across the Pacific, the platoon had seen several of its 37s wrecked or blown to pieces, but this particular gun had traveled thousands of miles and come through three major battles with only a scratch or two. McLaughlin had nicknamed it "Galloping Gertie" in honor of his aunt, Gertrude LaWear, who'd taken three-year-old Porter to raise after his mother's death. He still wrote Aunt Gertie at least once a week, and she'd gotten a huge kick out of it when he told her what they'd named the gun.

"Looks like the 184th found the Nips, all right," said Murphy. "I wonder if they've got anything planned for us tonight?"

Knorr shook his head. "It's their artillery that worries me. They've got a helluva lot of it, and they know how to use it. Nothing scares the new guys like their first artillery barrage. You always gotta ask yourself, 'When that next round comes in, which way do I jump to make it miss me? Or do I just hunker down where I am and not jump at all?' New guys don't know the answers yet."

"Yeah, and some of 'em never get a chance to learn," said "Pruneface" Vissio—so christened by his buddies not because his face was wrinkled and purple but because his family owned a prune farm in California.

"Incoming artillery scares the hell out of everybody, not just the new guys," said McLaughlin. "It scares the hell out of *me*, for Christ sake, and I've been getting shot at for over two years. They say every close one that misses you raises the odds that the next one won't. I'll take an enemy I can see anytime over some jerk trying to kill me from a mile or two away."

Murphy eyed several Sherman tanks drawn up next to Galloping Gertie, their machine guns and 75-millimeter howitzers pointing southward into the gathering twilight.

"I'll tell you one thing," he said quietly. "I'd sure hate to be a Jap trying to penetrate these lines tonight."

⁓

SEVERAL HOURS LATER, an antsy young machine gunner on one of the Shermans guarding the 32nd Infantry's perimeter heard suspicious noises in the darkness beyond the end of his gun barrel. He hesitated for a moment, holding his breath, then opened fire with his .30-caliber weapon.

Amid the silence that followed, the gunner soon detected another faint sound. Sometimes, it ebbed away to nothing, only to come back louder after a brief interval. When the gunner realized what it was, an agonizing chill seeped through him, from his toenails to the roots of his hair.

It was the sound of a baby crying.

When it was light enough to see, the sound was still audible at times, and some of the men, Porter McLaughlin among them, went out to check. They found two young women and a small boy, all dead of multiple bullet wounds. Lying nearby was a little girl about two years old, shot through the groin but still alive.

"She was one of the most beautiful children I ever saw," recalled McLaughlin some sixty years later. "We carried her back to an aid station, where a medic examined her and told us she couldn't make it. He gave her a shot of morphine to relieve her suffering, and she died a few minutes later. It tore me up for weeks afterward. Once in a while, it still does."

By sunrise that same morning, April 5, the Japanese had abandoned their Castle Hill positions, but they'd merely withdrawn to a much stronger system of fortifications a short distance away, where four separate ridges converged from four different directions on a bulky, mound-shaped hill. This central mass of high ground rose 475 feet above sea level and was capped by a sheer, forty-foot shaft of coral known simply as "the Pinnacle."

Like all other major enemy strongholds in the ridges, the Pinnacle was defended by an extensive network of caves, pillboxes, machine-gun nests, and rifle pits, some carved deep inside the hill and others arranged in layers among the slopes below. All were well camouflaged on the outside and connected by subterranean tunnels to an underground command center concealed beneath two less prominent coral outcroppings just to the west. The Pinnacle's weakness was that it was isolated from other fortified heights, meaning that its defenders could expect no outside help in the event of an all-out assault.

Beginning early on April 5 (L-plus-4), Major General Archibald Arnold, commander of the Seventh Division, ordered a series of attacks against the Pinnacle by several battalions of both the 184th and 32nd Infantry Regiments.

The advance would continue, but from this point on, every yard gained would be purchased with the blood of Hourglass GIs.

Corporal Don Dencker and his Deadeye comrades in L Company, Third Battalion, 381st Infantry Regiment, had been placed in reserve for the division's southward thrust. Consequently, their honeymoon lasted for more than a day after the 96th Recon platoon's nightmare began near Uchitomari. But it ended at precisely 1:00 P.M. on April 5, when the first Japanese shells came roaring in.

Out ahead of Dencker's outfit, the First Battalion of the 381st had already been under enemy fire for some time and was stymied at the foot of a small hill called Clay Ridge. But L Company, leading the advance of the Third Battalion, had moved to within 500 yards of the front lines without drawing the attention of Japanese gunners concealed in the high ground. When orders came to set up a defensive perimeter, the proximity of the exploding shells motivated Dencker and his foxhole mate, PFC Ernie Zimmer, to dig as fast and deep as they could in the time allotted.

Now, with round after round from 75-millimeter enemy howitzers battering the company area, they cowered as far down in their hole as possible, wishing they'd dug even deeper. Dirt and rock kicked up by the blasts showered down on them as they held their breath and winced at the shriek of incoming ordnance, interspersed with the screams of wounded men and frantic cries of "Medic! Medic!"

When the shelling tapered off after about fifteen minutes, Dencker peered cautiously over the edge of the foxhole. The first thing he saw was the mangled body of his buddy, PFC Tony Sak, who'd often shared a foxhole with Dencker during the fighting at Leyte. Sak had been caught in the open when the shelling started, and a round had hit within a few feet of him. He was a mass of shredded flesh and broken bones, and one glance told Dencker that his friend was mortally wounded, but Sak was still crying out in agony.

"Oh, God, help me," he moaned. "Somebody help me."

The medics were all occupied with other badly wounded men—including Captain James A. Fitzpatrick, the company commander, who would be evacuated moments later. But Corporal Earl Sonnenberg, one of the company cooks, rushed out while shells were still exploding a few yards away and dragged Sak back to his foxhole. It was a courageous but pointless gesture. The wounded man was dead by the time Sonnenberg got him to cover.

"Why the hell did you do that, Earl?" somebody asked. "Tony was done for, and you damn near got yourself killed, too."

"I had to do it, man," Sonnenberg said. "I mean, Lord, he was from Wisconsin, just like me."

Something about the way Sonnenberg said it made his explanation sound perfectly logical.

⌐

THE MORNING of April 6 (L-plus-5) broke on three U.S. infantry regiments stalemated well short of the main Kakazu–Kakazu West ridgeline. In the 96th Division zone, the 383rd Infantry was still trying to gain control of Cactus Ridge, the same long, low hill on which the 96th Recon's Third Platoon had almost been wiped out.

Cactus was located a good three-quarters of a mile north of Kakazu, and its capture was essential if the drive south was to continue. But after briefly occupying the crest of Cactus the previous afternoon, troops of the 383rd had been driven back down its slopes and were now bogged down at about the same spot where the 96th Recon survivors had finally been relieved two days earlier.

In the Seventh Division sector to the east, meanwhile, the First Battalion of Colonel Bernard W. Green's 184th Infantry still had its hands full attempting to seize two key points of high ground. Although the Japanese had quit Castle Hill itself, the medieval ruins of Nakagusuku Castle atop it were still defended by troops embedded on nearby slopes behind twenty-foot-thick terraced walls. The forty-foot-tall Pinnacle, meanwhile, was held by about 100 well-dug-in Japanese troops armed with ten machine guns and seven 50-millimeter knee mortars. The Japanese commander on the Pinnacle, Lieutenant Senji Tanigawa, was under orders not to retreat.

Identified by some historians as the promontory where Commodore Perry's expedition had raised the American flag in 1853, the Pinnacle posed a significant menace to U.S. troop and supply movements along Okinawa's Route 13. It also dominated a vast expanse of the coastal plain on the island's east side.

Between them, the Pinnacle and Castle Hill commanded an imposing view across the entire east-west width of Okinawa and gave the enemy visibility as far north as Yontan airfield and south to the end of the island. Before the Americans could approach, much less directly attack, the main Kakazu–Kakazu West ridgeline—or take advantage of this superb visibility themselves—these two heights, like Cactus Ridge, had to be taken.

Of the four Army regiments spearheading the southward drive, only the 32nd Infantry was still able to gain appreciable ground in its advance down Okinawa's east coast during the period of April 4–7. But resistance gradually stiffened there, too, and until a breakthrough could be achieved by the 184th, the 32nd would have to hang back to protect the other regiment's flank.

The breakthrough came on April 6–7 when, after repeated assaults, repeated failures, and inordinately heavy American casualties, considering the size of these small strongpoints, both the Pinnacle and Castle Hill finally fell.

On the morning of April 6, troops of Colonel Daniel C. Maybury's First Battalion, 184th Infantry, finally routed the Japanese from their warren of caves and spider holes in the Pinnacle, killing all but about twenty of the defenders.

The night before, Colonel Yukio Uchiyama, commanding Japanese forces defending Nakagusuku Castle, had elected to withdraw his troops. But enemy riflemen and gunners kept Castle Hill in their sights from neighboring high ground, preventing the Americans from securing the hill for another forty-eight hours.

Cactus Ridge, where the battle for Okinawa had been fully joined for the first time on April 4, proved a much tougher nut to crack, mainly because, like Kakazu and Kakazu West beyond it, it was part of an entire system of high ground and was impossible to flank. A series of man-made barriers, including mines, an antitank ditch, and barbed wire entanglements, also protected its entire 1,500-foot length.

A deluge of enemy mortar rounds and machine-gun fire made getting within effective rifle range of the ridge itself a major challenge for the men of the 383rd's Second Battalion, commanded by Major Prosser Clark. It took most of one day to get there, but they did it. Then, on the morning of April 6, two full companies of riflemen charged the crest in World War I style to finish the job.

"We stood up in waves, firing everything we had and throwing grenades by the dozen," said Staff Sergeant Francis Rall of Company E. "I guess that was too much for the Nips."

Clark's battalion killed 150 enemy soldiers and knocked out at least fifteen pillboxes and numerous mortar positions—the same ones that had played havoc with American tanks and armored half-tracks two days earlier. And when the Japanese defenders tried to counterattack that night, they were beaten back with an additional 58 soldiers lost.

Japanese artillery pounded Cactus for the rest of the night, and fighting would continue in the area until mid-April, much of it only a few score yards from the line formed up by the 383rd the day John Cain's platoon was ambushed nearby. But by April 7, the ridge crest was in American hands for keeps, and Colonel May considered it secure enough to move his headquarters there.

Cain, incidentally, had returned to his bivouac area on the evening of April 4 half expecting to face a court-martial over some harsh words he'd exchanged with Captain O'Neill after finally extricating the Reluctant Virgin from the ambush site. Instead, he got an apology from a contrite O'Neill, a promotion to sergeant, and a recommendation for a Silver Star.

"I feel bad about what happened," the captain told Cain. "We should've listened to you when you said there was a better way to handle the situation. If we had, we probably wouldn't have had so many casualties, so much loss of life."

On May 6, 1945, while the heaviest fighting of the Okinawa campaign raged a short distance away, Cain's medal was pinned on his muddy uniform shirt by Major General James Bradley, commander of the 96th Infantry Division.

"I was just glad we were able to get warnings out to our infantry heading into that area, in particular the 383rd," Cain said later. "I had a lot of buddies in those companies."

In testimony to the vagaries of war, Corporal Clark received scant recognition for his own heroic actions during the ambush. Although awarded a Bronze Star for gallantry under fire, Cain's fellow Wisconsin native never received the actual decoration. As of early 2006, he was also still waiting for a long-promised Purple Heart, a memento of the shrapnel wound in his right arm, where he continues to carry several pieces of a Japanese shell.

ON THE EVENING of April 8, Colonel Eddy May conferred one last time with General Hodge, commander of the Army's 24th Corps, concerning the attacks planned for the next morning. May's newly established command post on Cactus Ridge, where the meeting took place, was a mere 800 yards from the principal target of May's regiment— Kakazu Ridge.

The preliminary skirmishing was over. The main attack would start before dawn on April 9. It would last longer than May had ever dreamed, and before it was over, those 800 yards would feel like 800 miles.

CHAPTER FIVE

A Divine and Deadly Wind

B EFORE LATE 1944, few Westerners had ever heard the word "kamikaze," and fewer still knew its original meaning. Translated literally from the Japanese, the term means "Divine Wind," and it owns a revered place in Japanese history and spiritual folklore. Its origin can be traced back to 1281, when Chinese emperor Kublai Khan, son of Mongol conqueror Genghis Khan, dispatched a mighty naval armada to invade and seize Japan's home islands.

No man-made force available to Nippon at the time could possibly have thwarted Khan, whose victory seemed assured until a monstrous typhoon off the Japanese coast destroyed many of his ships and scattered the rest. The people of Japan interpreted the great storm as evidence of heavenly protection and credited their salvation to this Divine Wind.

Six and a half centuries later, in the closing days of World War II, with total defeat closing in around the Japanese military, some of its leaders clung to the belief that history could repeat itself. In a desperate effort to halt another foreign invasion, they devised a modern version of the Divine Wind—powered not by the gods of nature but by thousands of young Japanese zealots eager to sacrifice themselves for their emperor.

The result was the largest coordinated suicide operation the world has ever seen. The Divine Wind that reached its full fury at Okinawa not only ranks among the most relentless aerial assaults in the history of warfare, it also stands as history's largest mass air operation in which no attacking plane or pilot was expected to return from a mission.

Thus, while two U.S. Army divisions received their baptism of fire on the drive into southern Okinawa, and two Marine divisions scoured the rest of the island with little or no enemy contact, the armada of ships supporting the ground campaign and the Navy's Task Force 58 were enduring daily doses of mayhem from above.

To the tens of thousands of American sailors who faced the aerial onslaught of the kamikazes—as well as thousands of rear-echelon Marine and Army troops confined aboard sitting-duck transports and LSTs during the early stages of the battle—it meant ongoing terror and tragedy. For the U.S. Pacific Fleet and its commanders, it posed the greatest threat—and caused the heaviest damage and gravest casualties to Navy personnel—since the attack on Pearl Harbor.

Much of the rest of the world viewed Japan's suicide campaign as the war's ultimate example of inhuman military tactics, but to the Japanese high command, it was the noblest and most sacred of crusades. Tokyo's last remaining hope of securing a negotiated peace with America and her Allies, and of sparing the Japanese people a scorched-earth fight to the death on their home soil, rode on the wings of the Divine Wind.

THE FIRST RECORDED kamikaze-style attack against a major American warship was carried out in the Philippines five and a half months before the Okinawa invasion. On October 15, 1944, off Leyte, Japanese Rear Admiral Masafumi Arima tried to crash-dive the aircraft carrier *Franklin*, only to be shot down short of his target by Navy fighters. This sacrificial act by a high-ranking officer of the Imperial Navy was, however, widely publicized in Japan, where it was falsely reported that Arima had succeeded in hitting the carrier. The incident—and the fabrications surrounding it—served to light the fuse for Japan's full, unwavering commitment to suicide warfare.

A mere ten days after Arima tried to sink the *Franklin*, the first operational kamikaze unit—small though it was—was flying one-way missions against other U.S. ships in the Philippines. Over the coming weeks, hundreds of fanatically patriotic young Japanese airmen flocked to become kamikaze pilots.

One early volunteer for the suicide missions expressed his feelings about his fate in a farewell letter to his parents, dictated to a friend who held the paper against the fuselage of the twenty-three-year-old pilot's plane as he prepared for his final takeoff:

> Words cannot express my gratitude to you. It is my
> hope that this last act of striking a blow at the enemy will
> serve to repay in small measure the wonderful things you
> have done for me. Mother . . . I do not mind if you

weep . . . but please realize that my death is for the best,
and do not feel bitter about it. . . .

    This is my last day. The destiny of our homeland
hinges on the decisive battle in the seas to the south,
where I shall fall like a blossom from a radiant cherry
tree. . . .

The seeds from which a highly organized kamikaze campaign quickly sprouted were sown on October 19, 1944, in the dusty Filipino town of Mabalacat. At a meeting that day between Vice Admiral Takijiro Ohnishi, newly appointed commander of Japanese naval air forces in the Philippines, and officers of Japan's 201st Air Group, the concept of mass suicide bombing was first endorsed as a necessary tool for victory.

    Admiral Ohnishi was grim-faced as the meeting opened.

    "As you know, the war situation is grave," he began. "The appearance of strong American forces in Leyte Gulf has been confirmed. The fate of the empire depends upon the outcome of the *Sho* Operation."

    The admiral referred to a master offensive-defensive plan, completed the previous July after Japan's main Pacific defense line had been breached by U.S. forces. Under the *Sho* plan, the site of the next American offensive—regardless of where it might come—would be designated as the "theater of decisive battle," and all available Japanese forces would be rushed there to stop the Americans at all costs. The plan had been activated the previous day, October 18, and the Philippines had been declared the "decisive battle" area.

    Listening to the admiral was Commander Rikihei Inoguchi, senior staff officer of the First Air Fleet, recently sent from Manila to advise the 201st Air Group. Inoguchi was all too aware that fewer than 100 operational Japanese warplanes remained in the Philippines area. All the rest had been destroyed or disabled by relentless American attacks, and the nearest others were on Formosa, so the question in Inoguchi's mind was obvious: What could he and his fellow fliers possibly do to check the enemy offensive with such painfully inadequate resources?

    The next words out of Ohnishi's mouth made Inoguchi wonder if the admiral had read his mind.

    "In my opinion," Ohnishi said, "there is only one way of assuring that our meager strength will be effective to a maximum degree. That is to organize suicide attack units composed of Zero fighters armed with 250-kilogram bombs, with each plane to crash-dive into an enemy carrier." He paused, studying the men around him. "What do you think?"

A lengthy silence followed. Most of the officers were aware that the practice of "body-crashing" had already been used by Japanese fighter pilots during air-to-air combat with American bombers, and that more than a few fliers had urged using the same tactics against U.S. carriers.

As Inoguchi later explained as coauthor of *The Divine Wind,* a postwar book published in the United States, the kamikaze concept became more understandable in view of the heavy odds faced by Japanese fliers in 1944. Their chances of coming back alive from any sortie against U.S. carriers, he wrote, "was very slim, regardless of the attack method employed," and kamikaze tactics heightened their odds of causing maximum pain and damage to the enemy.

Inoguchi's friend, Commander Asaichi Tamai, executive officer of the 201st Air Group, finally broke the silence. "Just how effective would it be," Tamai asked a fellow staff officer, "for a plane carrying a 250-kilogram bomb to smash bodily into a carrier's flight deck?"

"The chances of scoring a direct hit would be much greater than by conventional bombing," the other officer replied. "It would probably take several days to repair the damage to the flight deck."

After brief discussion and another long pause, Tamai asked for a few minutes to think over the matter and left the room with an aide.

"I share completely the opinions expressed by the admiral," Tamai said when he returned. "The 201st Air Group will carry out his proposal. May I ask that you leave to us the organization of our crash-dive unit?"

Admiral Ohnishi nodded silently, but his expression clearly revealed his inner feelings. As author Inoguchi described it: "His face bore a look of relief, coupled with a shadow of sorrow."

⟞⟝

ADJOURNMENT of the historic meeting at Mabalacat was followed within hours by the creation within the 201st Air Group of a special attack corps of twenty-six fighter planes and pilots. Picked by Tamai to command the unit was Lieutenant Yukio Seki, a young graduate of Japan's Naval Academy, a recent bridegroom, and a survivor of numerous combat missions in the Marianas. At Seki's suggestion and with Tamai's approval, it was to be called the Shimpu Attack Unit ("shimpu" being another way of reading the Japanese characters for "kamikaze").

On the morning of October 20, 1944, soon after Admiral Ohnishi gave his approval, a posted notice ordered by Tamai announced the unit's creation—and, in no uncertain terms, its goals and purpose:

"The 201st Air Group will organize a special attack corps and will destroy or disable, if possible by 25 October, the enemy carrier forces in the waters east of the Philippines...."

The announcement proved chillingly prophetic. At 10:45 A.M. on October 25, the U.S. escort carrier *St. Lo,* cruising east of Leyte, was attacked and sunk by a Japanese pilot who deliberately crashed his plane into the ship. A few hours later, Imperial Headquarters in Tokyo officially announced the formation of the Kamikaze Special Attack Corps.

On the same day the *St. Lo* went down, several hundred other suicide attacks were aimed at American ships. Although only a quarter of them scored hits, mainly on smaller vessels with inadequate antiaircraft firepower, the attacks unnerved American sailors and inspired the Japanese high command to make the suicide raids an integral part of Tokyo's *Sho* strategy.

In all, 1,228 Japanese suicide planes, almost all of them ferried from widely scattered parts of the empire, struck at U.S. ships during the Philippines campaign, sinking 34 vessels and damaging 288, with heavy loss of life. But this was only a warm-up to the havoc to be wreaked by the kamikazes at Okinawa when it became the *Sho* Operation's next "theater of decisive battle."

FROM THE MOMENT the U.S. invasion armada began gathering in the Ryukyus during the last two weeks in March, kamikazes appeared frequently over the waters around Okinawa. Ironically, one of the first major Okinawa-bound American ships to feel the sting of Japanese bombs—although these were dropped by a regular bomber, not a kamikaze—was the same carrier *Franklin* that had been Admiral Arima's initial target five months earlier.

Shortly after 7:00 A.M. on March 19 (L-minus-12), a Japanese Judy dive-bomber, flying from the southernmost Japanese home island of Kyushu, broke out of low clouds and released two 550-pound bombs from barely 100 feet above the *Franklin*. Both penetrated the carrier's wooden flight deck, killing scores of sailors and airmen on impact and setting off disastrous fires in the hangar deck below, where two dozen planes were being fueled and loaded with bombs, rockets, and ammo.

The blasts knocked the *Franklin*'s skipper, Captain Leslie Gehres, to the deck of the navigation bridge. By the time he managed to regain his feet, he saw a "sheet of flame" roar out from under the starboard side of the flight deck, swallowing up the starboard batteries and spreading rapidly aft.

Simultaneously, a huge column of flame and black smoke boiled up the carrier's forward elevator well, and to try to clear it, Gehres ordered his helmsman to swing the ship to the right. When he did, however, thick, oily smoke from the fires below enveloped the entire island superstructure of the ship. Suddenly realizing that a second bomb had struck the *Franklin*, Gehres ordered another swing back to the left, clearing the smoke, but the carrier was in deep trouble.

As the heat rose in the blazing hangar deck, dozens of bombs and twelve-inch "Tiny Tim" rockets mounted on the burning planes began to detonate, touching off scores of secondary explosions that shook the ship and spewed igniting missiles in all directions. "Some screamed by the bridge to starboard, some to port, and some straight up the flight deck," recalled Commander Joe Taylor, the *Franklin*'s executive officer, who was caught in the middle of the conflagration. "Each time one went off, the fire fighting crews instinctively hit the deck." Many firemen were killed and injured, and Taylor himself narrowly escaped by crawling across the splintered flight deck to the bridge.

Meanwhile, some seamen sought refuge on the ship's stern, only to find themselves trapped there. Among the more fortunate ones was Machinist's Mate Louis A. Vallina, who was standing on the fantail when a terrific explosion blew him off the ship like a human projectile.

"I landed so far out in the water I didn't have to worry about being sucked under," Vallina said. But without a life belt, he was still in danger of drowning until a good-sized piece of the *Franklin*'s flight deck floated by. Vallina grabbed the splintery chunk of wood, and a short time later, a destroyer picked him up, along with several other sailors who'd also been blown overboard.

Engulfed in a gigantic inferno fed by exploding planes and ordnance, the *Franklin* appeared doomed. But Captain Gehres refused to abandon ship, and thanks to courageous fire crews who fought the blazes until afternoon, the carrier survived—barely. More than a quarter of the men aboard her did not, however. The final toll showed 724 killed and 1,428 wounded—three men out of every four in the big flattop's crew.

During the same series of attacks that ravaged the *Franklin*, Admiral

Raymond Spruance's Task Force 58 was targeted by a total of 193 Japanese planes, including 69 kamikazes. The carrier *Wasp* was also disabled, and two other U.S. carriers suffered less serious damage.

At 6:55 A.M. on March 27, as American warships bombarded the Okinawa invasion beaches in preparation for the main landing, a kamikaze crashed into the stern of the light cruiser *Biloxi.* Minutes later, two others struck the battleship *Nevada* and the minesweeper *Dorsey* almost simultaneously. Another plane hit the destroyer *O'Brien,* and yet another kamikaze made a bee line for the destroyer *Laffey* but was downed just short of the ship.

The next day, an LST ("long, slow target" in Navy jargon) was also hit by a suicide bomber. And on March 31, four kamikazes descended on the heavy cruiser *Indianapolis*—Admiral Spruance's own flagship. One of them managed to scrape the cruiser with its wing and plant a bomb in an oil bunker before being shot down. Nine seamen were killed, twenty more wounded, and Spruance was forced to transfer his headquarters to the battleship *New Mexico.*

The toll convinced Admiral Matome Ugaki, commander of Japan's Fifth Air Fleet, and his chief of staff, Rear Admiral Toshiyuki Yokoi, that concentrated aerial suicide attacks against Task Force 58 might delay or even prevent the Okinawa landing. Toward that end, Yokoi, who had received complete leeway to orchestrate the navy's phase of these attacks as he deemed best, decided to intensify the role of the kamikazes beyond anything the U.S. Navy had seen before.

The starting date for the most intensive phase of the kamikaze campaign, code-named TEN-Go, was set for April 6. (The timing would undoubtedly have been better if TEN-Go had started before or during the American landing, but collecting the necessary planes was a slow process.) As it was, the operation would incorporate every plane of every type that could be scraped together by the Japanese military, but heavy U.S. raids on enemy airfields left the number well short of the 4,085 aircraft originally specified for the suicide operation in a joint army-navy agreement.

Admiral Yokoi's plan was to tie up the ships of Spruance's Task Force 58 with a series of attacks while the main kamikaze force struck the beachhead. He intentionally delayed most of his planes' takeoff until noon or later in hopes of catching many U.S. fighter patrols refueling on carrier decks or at Kadena and Yontan airfields.

The plan looked good on paper, but Spruance's carrier task group

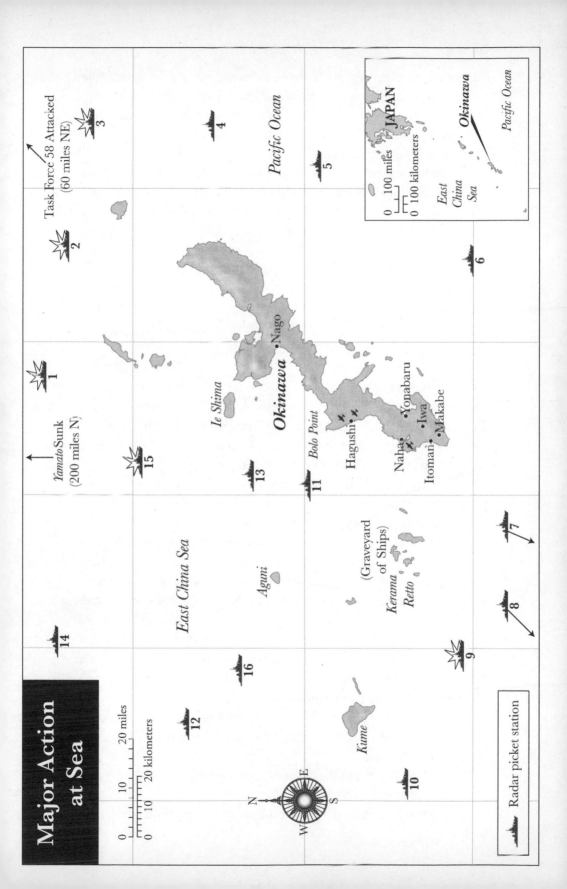

Major Action at Sea

Yamato Sunk
(200 miles N)

Task Force 58 Attacked
(60 miles NE)

Pacific Ocean

Okinawa

Nago

Ie Shima

Bolo Point

Hagushi

Naha

Yonabaru
Iwa
Makabe

Itoman

East China Sea

Aguni

(Graveyard
of Ships)

*Kerama
Retto*

Kume

→ Radar picket station

0   10   20 miles
0   10   20 kilometers

N
W — E
S

Inset map

*East
China
Sea*

JAPAN

Okinawa

Pacific Ocean

0   100 miles
0   100 kilometers

had long before instituted a policy of continuous sunup-to-sundown aerial patrols, so there was no chance of the suiciders slipping past them unchallenged. In addition, broken Japanese codes had already alerted U.S. intelligence to expect a full-scale kamikaze blitz as soon as the enemy could assemble enough planes.

In the fanciful phraseology of the flower-loving Japanese, the all-out campaign of suicide bombing had been designated "Kikusui Number One." Translated to English, Kikusui means "Floating Chrysanthemums." The attached numeral merely indicated that subsequent attack phases could be expected—unless Kikusui Number One succeeded in devastating the U.S. naval force at Okinawa and forcing it to withdraw.

The twentieth-century version of the Divine Wind was about to reach gale force.

AT SUNRISE ON APRIL 6, the skies above Okinawa were generally overcast, and a chill northeasterly wind was whipping up waves offshore. A phalanx of U.S. destroyers continued to screen the bombardment group's battleships and cruisers as they steamed slowly along both sides of the island, awaiting target assignments.

It was the time of day when kamikazes often made their appearance, but on this particular morning, the cloud-layered skies were strangely quiet. The only early-morning attack planned by Admiral Yokoi had been by a hodgepodge collection of twenty-nine navy planes against U.S. shipping off the west-side Hagushi beaches. But the attackers were hampered by bad weather and accomplished nothing of consequence. As the sun rose higher, tension mounted among Navy gun crews on constant high alert, but a conspicuous absence of enemy air activity continued.

"Considering where we were, it had been a rather routine day," Commander Julian Becton, captain of the destroyer *Laffey,* would recall later. "This situation continued through the midday meal and into the afternoon, but then all hell broke loose."

At a quarter past high noon, as the carrier *Bennington* was launching its sixth patrol of the day, the first of Admiral Ugaki's suicide planes were detected by lookouts.

"Red alert! Red alert!" the carrier's loudspeakers blared. "Enemy aircraft approaching! Air attack imminent!"

Immediately, a destroyer on the *Bennington*'s port quarter opened fire with its five-inch batteries and every 20- and 40-millimeter antiair-craft mount it could bring to bear. Soon, the weapons of a half-dozen ships forming a protective ring around the carrier were blazing in a continuous roar.

Meanwhile, at 12:20 P.M., the *Bennington*'s sister carrier, the *Hornet,* hurriedly launched eight Grumman Hellcats, which streaked south to intercept and destroy two Judy dive-bombers and three Zero fighters. The *Bennington*'s own Hellcats also came to its defense, downing at least twenty-five bogies by late afternoon, and a single pilot from the light carrier *Belleau Wood,* Ensign Carl Foster, was credited with six kills.

The *Bennington*'s closest call came around 1:00 P.M. when a determined suicide pilot aimed his Judy bomber at the carrier's flight deck from astern. The plane exploded in a ball of flame a scant twenty yards from the ship, peppering the fantail with its fragments and temporarily disabling the rudder. It was a near miss that came breathlessly close to fulfilling Admiral Ugaki's fervent hope of putting an American carrier out of action, but the damage was quickly repaired, and the *Bennington* remained fully operational.

⁓

Gunner's Mate Hank Kalinofsky had worried for days about his "unpardonable sin" of eating a forbidden turkey dinner on Good Friday, the holiest of fasting days in the Catholic Church. Yet the dark mood that descended on him following the turkey episode was based on more than vague fears of divine retribution. There was also a nagging feeling that his luck in general was turning sour—or perhaps running out entirely.

After spending his first two years of service dodging Nazi U-boats and dive-bombers in the Atlantic aboard the destroyer-escort *McNulty,* Kalinofsky had been less than overjoyed to find himself at Okinawa as a 20-millimeter gunner on the rocket ship *LSM(R) 198,* a vessel too small even to have a proper name (albeit packing tremendous firepower for its size). And the fighting in Europe was as good as over now, at least where the Navy was concerned, while the biggest battle of the Pacific war was exploding all around Kalinofsky and the *198.*

Adding to his malaise was the loss of a sister rocket ship, the *LSM(R) 197,* sunk by a kamikaze on March 26, long before this newest flurry of attacks. But several days earlier, when he'd received word that the

McNulty, too, was now at Okinawa and that one of its gunners had been killed in action, Hank's mood and attitude had begun to change.

The dead guy had been a seaman of Hank's same rank assigned to the very 20-millimeter gun that Hank had once manned on the *McNulty.* The more Kalinofsky thought about the irony of the situation, the more he pondered its meaning:

Is this the same fellow who replaced me? What if it'd been me standing there behind that 20, instead of him, when the bomb hit? Was it fate, or God's will—or what?

In the days since, Kalinofsky had come to spend more time counting his blessings than cursing his bad luck. He decided he was actually fortunate to be on one of the Navy's inconspicuous "small boys" instead of one of the bigger ships that Japanese pilots always went after first. The *197* may have been short on respect and amenities, but one of its greatest assets was being able to lose itself among the carriers, cruisers, and destroyers that towered over it when the kamikazes swooped down.

Gradually, an eerie sense of calm took hold of Kalinofsky's consciousness. Sometimes he could almost imagine an invisible protective shield covering him. Other times, he relied on pure fatalism to keep his nerves under control during the suicide attacks.

They're going to keep coming at us until one of two things happens, he'd tell himself firmly. *Either we blow them out of the sky, or they won't stop till they get us; it's that simple.*

That same identical thought flashed through Kalinofsky's mind on the afternoon of April 6, when he looked up and saw the Baka bomb coming straight at him.

He made a valiant effort to get the damned thing in his gunsights, but there was no time to fire. The Baka—a dynamite-laden glider whose doom was assured the instant it was launched and whose only goal was to take as many Americans with it as possible—was too close. It was close enough for Hank to see every facial feature of the Japanese pilot who sat astride the flying bomb, guiding it toward destruction with a crude sort of joystick.

Kalinofsky held his breath and watched the Baka hit the water no more than twenty feet off the *197*'s port bow. The bomb had missed its mark because the rocket ship, following the standard zigzag course prescribed during air attacks, had "zigged" at precisely the right moment— and, of course, because it was such a small target.

As the bomb vanished under the waves with its passenger, it flung a geyser of seawater high in the air, and a couple of quarts of it splashed over Hank's head, running down his face and drenching his uniform. That was how close it had come.

God must've forgiven me about the turkey, he thought. *If I was supposed to die out here, I'm pretty sure I'd be dead already.*

⁓

TO THIS DAY, the exact number of Japanese planes involved remains uncertain, but Kikusui Number One's daylong succession of suicide attacks on April 6 was concentrated in three main areas.

Drawn from several airfields on the nearest Japanese home island of Kyushu, 120 enemy aircraft, about half of them suiciders, were directed to hit two task groups of Task Force 58, operating approximately 100 miles northeast of Okinawa. Half the Japanese planes, however, couldn't locate their targets, so they continued to Okinawa to attack random targets. Among those who did find the U.S. task force were the planes that attacked the carrier *Bennington* late that morning. Most were shot down by Navy fighters before they could inflict any damage.

Other primary outlying targets were the U.S. destroyers *Bush, Colhoun,* and *Cassin Young,* assigned respectively to Radar Picket Stations One, Two, and Three, located along an arc some forty miles north of Okinawa as part of an early-warning radar network scanning the skies for Japanese planes. These attacks were led by 104 late-model Zero fighters flown by some of Japan's best surviving navy pilots, whose mission was to engage defending U.S. carrier planes long enough for the conventional and suicide bombers to reach their targets.

The bombers themselves were a mixture of about 230 old and new, large and small aircraft. About a fourth of them were forced to abort soon after taking off from scattered enemy bases because of mechanical problems. But the rest, including 180 kamikazes, were all that three isolated American destroyers could cope with—and more.

The *Bush,* manning Picket Station One, was the first to feel the suiciders' wrath. At 2:55 P.M., a Judy dive-bomber streaked in at wave-top level through a hail of fire from the destroyer's five-inch and 20- and 40-millimeter guns, slamming into the side of the vessel squarely amidships. Simultaneously, its bomb exploded on deck, causing massive damage topside and destroying the forward engine room below, knocking out both boilers and leaving the *Bush* dead in the water.

"Help! Help! Anyone on this circuit, help!" the *Bush*'s radio operator screamed into his voice transmitter.

A squadron of Navy fighters responded quickly, temporarily driving the other kamikazes away, but the rescuers were soon forced to return to their carrier for fuel and ammo. By now, numerous fires had broken out aboard the *Bush*, and Commander Rollin Westholm, the skipper, had all available fire crews trying to subdue them. Totally without power, the *Bush* wallowed helplessly in the sea while a dozen or more Vals and Zeroes circled like vultures just out of range of the burning destroyer's remaining guns.

Meanwhile, a dozen other enemy planes zoomed east to attack the *Cassin Young* at Station Three, inexplicably bypassing the *Colhoun* at Station Two en route, although skies had cleared, and visibility was rated as unlimited that afternoon. With no defensive action needed for the *Colhoun*'s own protection, Commander George R. Wilson swung his ship back to the west in response to the *Bush*'s calls for help.

When Wilson reached Station One around 4:30 P.M., he found two small gunboats screening the disabled *Bush* as their gun crews kept wary eyes on the enemy planes hovering nearby. Then, as Wilson attempted to position his own ship between the *Bush* and her attackers, four Zeroes came roaring after the *Colhoun*.

The first pilot released a bomb that missed, then splashed his plane between the two destroyers, but the other three Zeroes came on together to bracket the *Colhoun* fore and aft. Accurate work by Wilson's gunners, along with the captain's own deft maneuvering of his ship, staved off two of the planes—but the third Zero was a killer. It crashed the *Colhoun* astern, destroying two 40-millimeter mounts and their crews even as its bomb and engine tore through the deck into the after fire room, blowing out the boiler and killing everyone in the vicinity.

Fire crews sprang to work on the ensuing fires, and, unlike the *Bush*, Wilson's ship was still able to limp along at fifteen knots on one engine. The determined suiciders were far from finished, however. Almost immediately, two Val dive-bombers and a Zero swooped down, using the same style of coordinated attack as the first three kamikazes—and with equal success.

The two destroyers' five-inch guns and AA batteries sent both Vals plunging harmlessly into the water, but the speedier Zero eluded their fire long enough to crash the *Colhoun*'s forward fire room, wrecking its other engine and leaving Wilson's destroyer in the same powerless predicament as the ship it had tried to save.

Fifteen minutes later, a third trio of enemy planes showed up to finish the job. Again, two lumbering old Vals were led by a Zero, but this time, it was the Zero that was blown out of the sky and the Vals that did the damage, crashing both wounded destroyers. One grazed the upper works of the *Colhoun*, then released a bomb that ripped a three-foot gash in the ship's hull below the water line. The other crashed into the *Bush* amidships, almost cutting the ship in half.

After another short lull, three Kate bombers brought still more torment to the smoldering, sinking remains of the two destroyers. One crashed the wardroom of the *Bush*, where a score or more wounded sailors lay, adding to an already fearful loss of life.

Ensign F. R. Chapman, piloting a Hellcat off the *Hornet*, arrived on the scene in time to send the other two Kates blazing into the East China Sea. But Chapman's heroics were too late to save the *Bush* and *Colhoun*.

The *Bush* went down first, at 6:30 P.M., as its captain and surviving crewmen clung to rafts and floater nets nearby. The *Colhoun* followed later that night, about two hours after Commander Wilson ordered the final members of a salvage crew to abandon ship.

Ninety-four officers and men died aboard the *Bush*. The death toll on the *Colhoun* stood at thirty-five.

⁀

THE LARGEST, most dangerous phase of Kikusui Number One came late on April 6, just as Ensign Ben McDonald, a gunnery officer aboard the heavy cruiser *Wichita*, was allowing himself to relax a little.

From his battle station aft, McDonald had spent the whole afternoon watching the aerial pyrotechnics from a distance as scores of kamikazes zoomed down on Task Force 58, to be met by withering gunfire from hundreds of U.S. ships and planes.

At age nineteen, McDonald was the youngest—and, in his own words, the "greenist"—ensign on board the *Wichita*, where he'd been assigned in February 1945, a few months removed from the University of Texas in Austin.

He still had to grin a little when he remembered his first encounter with Captain J. J. Mahoney, the *Wichita*'s skipper, shortly after McDonald had ascended a Jacob's ladder from a whale boat and set foot on the venerable cruiser for the first time.

"Welcome aboard, Mr. McDonald," the captain said. "After what we've been through, we can use some new blood. What's your specialty, son?"

"Well, sir," said McDonald, "I was trained in communications in cadet school."

The captain's reply caused the fledgling ensign to pale slightly. "Good," Mahoney said, "you should make a fine gunnery officer. I'm putting you in charge of all our aft 40s and 20s, plus machine guns. You're going to be a very busy young man. Carry on."

McDonald had been busy, all right. In his new job, he was responsible for four "tubs" of four 40-millimeter guns each, four 20-millimeter AA batteries, and a half-dozen .50-caliber machine guns, all located on the Old Witch's fantail. These weapons were part of the cruiser's main line of defense against air attacks, and, since arriving in Okinawan waters, they'd had to be manned constantly for up to seventy-two hours at a stretch. "Busy" was a gross understatement.

So far, most of the day's action had been well removed from the *Wichita,* and McDonald was grateful to have gotten safely through the morning and most of the afternoon. But the Witch had already survived more than one encounter with suicide planes, suicide boats—even suicide frogmen—and he had no doubt that more lay ahead.

When the attacks came, McDonald knew that he and his gun crews would be in the thick of them and squarely in harm's way. There was no more inviting target than the fantail of a big ship, and "watching the Old Witch's ass" was their whole reason for being there.

Still, as the afternoon passed and the sun began to settle behind the clouds in the western sky, even the men standing at their 20-millimeter guns, where they'd been for most of the day, allowed themselves to ease off a bit.

In a half hour or so, McDonald told himself, *it'll be too dark for a kamikaze to spot a target, even one as big as the Witch.*

He had no inkling of how close he and his men would come to death within that brief span of time.

⁓

THE DECREPIT old Zeke came out of nowhere through a break in the clouds on the *Wichita*'s port quarter, and it was right on top of the cruiser before anyone spotted it. At the second McDonald first saw it, it was gliding straight for the bridge at an altitude of less than 100 feet.

"Bogie to port!" he shouted into the intercom. "Fire! Fire!"

The port-side aft batteries and machine guns opened at once, but the Zeke was already so close that, in the words of Seaman First Class Les Caffey, an unwilling observer from the fantail, "It looked like it was going to fly down our throats."

Pandemonium swept the afterdeck as dozens of sailors caught topside, including Caffey and several buddies taking a break from the boiler room, scrambled for cover and ran for their battle stations.

"We were sitting on the fantail playing pinochle," Caffey recalled, "when we looked up, and there he was. Then we heard this god-awful explosion and thought we were dead for sure, but it was only one of our five-inch guns going off."

The Zeke was roughly 100 yards from the ship when fire from one of McDonald's 20-millimeters blasted away part of its tail, causing the plane to veer drunkenly off course as its pilot released a 500-pound bomb. The bomb missed the *Wichita* by perhaps fifty feet, by McDonald's estimate, as the Zeke crashed into the sea. But as it made its last dive, one of the plane's wings struck a glancing blow to the cruiser's deck not far from where Caffey and his mates had been playing cards moments before.

Eleven sailors were injured, but all survived. The Old Witch herself was hardly scratched.

⁓

NIGHTFALL finally brought an end to the carnage and gave widely scattered U.S. naval units a chance to assess their own damage and learn what had happened to their comrades elsewhere.

The *Bush* and *Colhoun* were among three U.S. destroyers sunk and eight others knocked out of the war with heavy damage on the opening day of Kikusui Number One. The *Emmons*, a destroyer-minesweeper, was also lost, and its sister ship, the *Rodman*, barely survived. Other battered destroyers, including the *Hyman, Morris, Mullany, Leutze,* and *Newcomb,* were towed to the growing graveyard of ships in the Kerama Retto and never returned to the campaign.

Support vessels lost off Okinawa's Hagushi beaches included *LST-447* and two ammunition-loaded transports, the *Hobbs Victory* and *Logan Victory.*

The actual toll to U.S. shipping and Navy personnel was disastrous enough without any exaggeration, but the Japanese, as usual, padded the figures shamelessly. Admiral Ugaki's headquarters first claimed two battleships, seven other warships, and five transports sunk, later adding three cruisers and eight destroyers to the total.

April 6 had been a costly, harrowing day for the Pacific Fleet, and the respite offered by darkness would be brief and fitful. Additional waves of suicide bombers would bring more of the same the next day as Kikusui Number One continued unabated.

⟶

HORRIFIC AS IT WAS, the toll on Navy personnel and ships on April 6–7 could have been far worse if not for a series of little-known events that began nearly two weeks earlier in the Kerama Retto when U.S. forces nullified a significant Japanese threat to the 1,500 American ships supporting the invasion. The islands off Okinawa's west coast were pockmarked with dozens of natural caves in which the Japanese had hidden hundreds of small plywood motorboats intended for what amounted to suicide missions against U.S. shipping.

The terrain of the Keramas, characterized by sharp cliffs rising abruptly to heights of up to 600 feet above their many inlets, made it next to impossible to attack the boats or their hiding places effectively from the air. This was why the job of finding and destroying the boats had fallen to units of the Army's 77th Infantry Division and heavily armed, shallow-draft Navy vessels capable of moving in close to shore to direct cannon fire at the boats.

The threat posed by these Japanese "Q-boats" was primitive by standards of modern warfare, but it was extremely real—and it might have gone undetected much longer if not for the pilots of two U.S. Piper Cub reconnaissance planes. During a low flight over the islands on March 26, they'd spotted numerous odd structures that aroused suspicion.

"All the islands had these railroad tracks leading from the water to caves," said Lieutenant John Kriegsman, one of the pilots. "There were dozens of them with nothing else visible. We couldn't figure out what that meant."

Not long after Kriegsman radioed his findings to division headquarters, Navy ships sank three prowling Q-boats and captured a fourth, and the U.S. command quickly fitted together the pieces of the puzzle: The caves were sanctuaries for the boats, and the railroad tracks were their launching ramps.

Each boat was capable of carrying a 264-pound depth charge, timed to explode within five seconds of being rolled overboard beside an American ship. Because the Q-boats were slow, unarmored, and shoddily built, their crews faced overwhelming odds of being killed on their missions, either by their own explosives or by American fire, but they did have a slightly better mathematical chance of survival than the pilots who flew Japanese kamikaze planes.

Thanks to the discovery by the two Navy fliers and quick action by naval units and troops of the 77th Infantry, virtually none of the suicide boats ever reached their intended targets. Army infantry units located and scuttled many of them, and a squadron of Navy LCIs (landing craft, infantry), converted to gunboats equipped with Army mortars, .50-caliber machine guns, and 20- and 40-millimeter cannon, blasted hundreds more to splinters.

St. Louis–born Gunner's Mate Don Brockman, who had interrupted his freshman year at the University of Missouri to join the Navy in February 1944, manned one of two .50-caliber machine guns aboard *LCI(M) 660* and played an active role in the destruction.

"We went into the Keramas more than a week before the invasion and shot the hell out of those suicide boats," Brockman recalled later. "We had four 20-millimeter guns that were especially effective against them. It looked like the Japs had 1,000 boats stashed out there, and we sank all of them we saw—except for one that we took onboard and used later as a mail boat."

By the end of their campaign in the Keramas, the 77th Division had counted 291 of the boats destroyed by its own troops. Overall, only a handful escaped, and they would have no appreciable impact on the coming battle.

One facet of the largest, most pervasive campaign of suicide warfare in the annals of human conflict had been effectively eliminated. But if the Q-boats had been available on April 6, the Navy would have faced a menace from the sea that matched the one from the air—especially during the nighttime hours.

To the U.S. Navy, however, gaining control of the Keramas had far greater significance than nullifying the Q-boat threat. Equally important during the weeks ahead would be the excellent protected deep-water anchorage provided by the islands. Over the next three months, scores of Navy ships would find their way to the Kerama Retto for repairs, refitting, or abandonment after being damaged in kamikaze air attacks.

Some of the first of these were the tragic product of Kikusui Number One. But the suicide attackers might have claimed dozens more ships—and hundreds more human casualties—if the Q-boats had remained operational.

⌒

THE LARGEST and most auspicious of the Japanese "chrysanthemums" that floated toward Okinawa that early April didn't come by air but by sea. This 863-foot-long kamikaze weighed 69,000 tons, and its name was *Yamato*, an ancient word that literally means "Japan." It was the grandest battleship ever built, and its deliberately planned one-way voyage to certain destruction was the grandest Japanese sacrificial gesture of the war.

It was hoped in Tokyo that the doomed voyage of the *Yamato* would serve two purposes: (1) to divert as many U.S. fighter planes as possible from the aerial kamikazes, allowing more suicide planes to reach their Okinawa targets, and (2) to give the world's mightiest battleship one last chance to engage American warships that were no match for her awesome firepower.

The *Yamato* carried nine monstrous 18.1-inch guns in three triple turrets. The most massive weapons ever placed aboard a ship, each could hurl a 3,220-pound shell a distance of almost thirty miles. U.S. battleships mounted nothing larger than sixteen-inchers, with a range of just over twenty miles, and some of the older dreadnoughts were limited to twelve-inchers. The *Yamato's*, 100 antiaircraft batteries, with guns ranging up to 5 miles, formidable provided aerial defense.

Despite her outer skin of sixteen-inch-thick armor, the *Yamato* was as graceful as she was powerful, and her uniquely designed series of waterproof compartments made her as hard to sink as any ship could be. Her sweeping foredeck, swept-back funnel, and shapely hull gave her a sleek profile that belied her size and bore no resemblance to the bulky "pagoda look" that characterized most Japanese capital ships. Historian Samuel Eliot Morison described her as "singularly beautiful," while the U.S. Naval Institute called her "the mightiest engine of destruction afloat." Both were right, but the *Yamato* was more than that. She was a symbolic source of pride to the Japanese navy and the entire Japanese nation.

Yet during a three-year-long game of hide-and-seek with the U.S. Pacific Fleet, the *Yamato* had made scant direct contribution to Japan's war effort. Although present at Midway and other major battles, she'd rarely fired her huge guns at an enemy target. Now, perhaps, her swan song would afford her that opportunity—if not to rain doom on outclassed American warships, at least to run aground on Okinawa and use her long rifles to pulverize the U.S. beachhead and the Kadena and Yontan airfields.

The officers and men aboard the *Yamato* and her escorts were under no illusions about their chances of returning alive from the mission. Shortly before sailing, Captain Tameichi Hara, skipper of the light cruiser *Yahagi,* part of the task force screening the *Yamato,* addressed his crewmen:

> As you know, hundreds of our comrades have flown bomb-laden planes on one-way missions against the enemy. Thousands more . . . are standing by at every airfield. Hundreds . . . are ready in submarines to man one-way torpedoes. Thousands of others will drive explosive torpedo boats or crawl the bottom of the sea to fasten explosive charges against enemy ships. Our job in this mission is part of the same pattern. [It] appears suicidal, and it is. But I wish to emphasize that suicide is not the objective. The objective is victory.

By the time she slipped from her moorings in Tokuyama Bay on the west side of Kyushu, it was already 3:20 P.M. on April 6, and the queenly *Yamato* was many sailing hours too late to accomplish the first part of her mission. If she were to divert U.S. aircraft from intercepting Japanese suicide planes, it would have to be the second day's kamikaze fliers who benefited since all the first day's flights were already en route to their targets and visible on U.S. radar screens.

It didn't really matter. Naval code experts at Pearl Harbor, working with coded Japanese radio messages, had learned days earlier of Tokyo's bizarre plans for the *Yamato.* By 8:00 P.M. on April 6, when the superbattleship, accompanied by the *Yahagi* and eight destroyers, passed through Bungo Strait into the Pacific, the U.S. submarines *Threadfin* and *Hackleback* were posted in the strait, watching and reporting the passage to Task Force 58.

Alerted by the subs, Vice Admiral Marc Mitscher, commanding TF

58's carrier group, dispatched eight large and four light carriers north to launch two strong attack forces—386 aircraft in all—at dawn on April 7. The first group, including most of Mitscher's available Hellcat fighters, was to intercept the Japanese suicide planes bound for Okinawa.

The mission of the other group, composed mainly of Helldiver dive-bombers and Avenger torpedo planes, with a dozen or so Hellcats flying cover, was to find and sink the *Yamato* while she was still more than 200 miles from the Hagushi beachhead.

AT 10:30 A.M. on April 7, a shorthanded squadron of eleven Helldivers—normal complement fifteen planes—roared off the flight deck of the carrier *Bennington* and streaked north through inclement weather toward a point southwest of Kyushu. Each plane in the squadron, led by Commander Hugh Wood, carried two 1,000-pound bombs, eight five-inch rockets, and a full stock of ammo for their two wing-mounted 20-millimeter cannon—all earmarked for the *Yamato*.

At the controls of one Helldiver was Lieutenant (j.g.) Francis Ferry, a section leader and veteran of more than thirty combat missions, including the first massive raid on Tokyo by 1,200 U.S. planes the previous February. But despite his experience, Ferry had a special reason to be sweaty-palmed with excitement at the prospect of hunting down the *Yamato*. Less than three weeks earlier, on March 19, he'd been among eight Navy fliers who had a crack at the giant battleship as she lay in Kuri harbor off Japan's main island of Honshu—only to come up empty. One Helldiver and its two crewmen had been lost in the attack, and Ferry himself had been lucky to get his severely damaged plane back to the *Bennington*.

Now the native Nebraskan was getting a second chance at the same target, and this time he was determined to make the most of it.

The foul weather and generally bad flying conditions seemed to be working in the *Yamato*'s favor that morning, however. Latest radar trackings placed the battleship about 120 miles southwest of the southern tip of Kyushu, but visibility was down to five miles, and the junction of the East China Sea and the western Pacific Ocean was a big place. Under the overcast skies, the *Yamato* and her entourage could be difficult to spot.

Wood, the squadron leader, told his pilots to expect to sight the target around noon, but conditions continued to worsen as the squadron bore north. Intermittent showers splashed the planes' windshields, and several lost their way or were forced to divert. Only four of the eleven Helldivers that had taken off from the *Bennington* were able to reach the target area—not a good sign, Ferry figured, when you were coming up against the greatest concentration of AA firepower afloat.

Fortunately, however, Ferry's squadron had plenty of help. A total of about 280 U.S. carrier aircraft were now converging on the *Yamato,* and Navy flying boats were shadowing the prey and guiding the attackers to their target. The carrier pilots were encouraged when, roughly seventy-five miles from the target area, the persistent clouds began to break up and skies started to clear.

The four planes in Ferry's group were flying at about 6,000 feet, and the eyes of their crews were fixed on the sea ahead and below, when Wood's radio man broke the silence:

"I've got a contact, sir. Twenty-five miles."

"Have contact and will investigate," Wood told the *Bennington,* nosing his plane down.

Ferry and his gunner/radio operator, nineteen-year-old Airman Second Class Fred Warner, caught their first glimpse of *Yamato* and company at virtually the same instant.

"There she is, sir," Warner said. "I can see her plain as day."

"We've got contact, too, Woody," Ferry told Wood.

Now the radio crackled with other messages confirming contact and the carriers' staccato responses.

"Take the big boy!" ordered Commander E. G. Konrad, strike chief aboard the *Bennington.*

"Dive-bombers, take on the battleship," echoed the group air commander aboard the *Hornet.* "Let's get the big bastard!"

"Start your dive at glide angle," Wood instructed his three remaining pilots, "and follow me!"

All four planes dove on the *Yamato* from 3,000 feet with Wood leading the way, Ferry right behind him, and Ferry's wingman, Lieutenant (j.g.) Edward Sieber, next. The fourth pilot, Lieutenant (j.g.) Richard Cory, was unable to stay in formation as the planes made the sharp turn through clouds to hit the *Yamato,* so he aimed for the cruiser instead.

Just above 500 feet, Ferry dumped both his bombs and fired all his rockets at once. As he did, he got a clear kaleidoscopic view of the *Yamato* and the action bursting around her.

He saw the graceful battleship trying to hide beneath a rain cloud, and moving very slowly in comparison to the Helldiver's screaming speed . . . then one of his own 1,000-pounders exploding in a ball of fire just aft of the *Yamato*'s island and near its third 18.1-inch turret . . . the bombs dropped by Lieutenant Harry McCrae of the *Bennington* hitting the sea short of the battleship . . . Sieber's plane pulling out of its dive surrounded by purple puffs of ack-ack . . . a seemingly endless chain of other U.S. planes wheeling and swooping over the Japanese flotilla . . .

"I had a gun camera mounted on my plane, so I circled the battleship and took some pictures," Ferry recalled. "I thought I observed three separate bombs hit the *Yamato*, one of them penetrating a magazine area and starting a major fire. All three of us [Wood, Sieber, and Ferry] were credited with hits, and Wood got the Navy Cross for leading the attack."

It took three waves of American bombers and torpedo planes, in attacks covering more than an hour, to put the mighty *Yamato* under. In addition to at least three bombs that hit home, the behemoth was blasted by no less than eleven torpedoes.

"Dozens of Navy fliers deserve a share of the credit for sinking the *Yamato*," Ferry observed decades after the fact. "It was a group effort if there ever was one, and there are many valid stories to tell besides my own."

A second attack wave by planes from the *Bunker Hill, Essex,* and *Bataan* closely followed the first, inflicting multiple torpedo hits that left the *Yamato* listing dangerously to port and starting to flood. By the time the third and final wave arrived at 2:00 P.M., many of the battleship's guns had been silenced, allowing attackers to peck away at her ravaged port side with little opposing fire.

The list to port rapidly worsened. Men and weaponry slid off the tilting decks into the sea. Admiral Seiichi Ito, realizing his ship was about to capsize, left the bridge and went to his cabin to await the end.

At 2:20 P.M., some 240 nautical miles from the Hagushi beaches that were her intended target, the *Yamato* rolled over and vanished under the waves. Even after she was no longer visible, blasts from detonating ammunition still wracked her steel innards and spewed flames high in the air above her grave.

The cruiser *Yahagi* and four destroyers from the *Yamato*'s screening force were also sunk. The other four destroyers, two of them badly damaged, managed to pluck a few survivors out of the water before slipping away. Behind them, they left an estimated 3,700 to 4,250 dead Japanese sailors—almost 3,000 of them on the *Yamato*.

American losses totaled twelve airmen killed or missing and ten U.S. planes shot down.

The *Yamato*'s grotesque mission had ended in utter disaster, but it did little or nothing to diminish Japan's commitment to suicide warfare. Within hours, orders were issued in Tokyo by Combined Fleet Headquarters to prepare for Kikusui Operation Number Two.

CHAPTER SIX

Death in the Hills, Death at Home

A S THE OKINAWA CAMPAIGN moved into its second week, the terror endured by U.S. sailors on ships offshore and by the Army's Seventh and 96th Infantry Divisions on land stood in stark contrast to the ongoing lull enjoyed by many of the Marines on the island.

During the period of April 7–10, while the Navy battled back against the Divine Wind, and GI infantrymen made their first charges into the nightmare of Kakazu Ridge, the First Marine Division remained virtually on "shore leave" just a few miles away.

After crossing the island and securing the east coast of Okinawa without firing a shot in anger, the men of K Company, Third Battalion, Fifth Marine Regiment (K/3/5) passed their days patrolling the area and talking in disbelief about the lack of fighting. They found no sign of the enemy other than an occasional Japanese corpse, and their evenings were spent fighting nothing more menacing than boredom.

"We spent a lot of time loafing around and brewing 'jungle juice' out of raisins and grain alcohol we borrowed from the medics," recalled Sergeant R. V. Burgin. "Some nights we'd have a big sing-along, like we used to have on Pavuvu with our lost buddy, Lieutenant Hillbilly Jones."

Two or three Marines had managed to get string instruments ashore, and although they weren't among the world's most accomplished musicians, they managed to make plenty of noise when fueled by enough jungle juice. The songs they played and sang ranged from solemn hymns like "The Old Rugged Cross" to such rowdy ballads as "Take Me Back to Tulsa" and folk favorites like "Birmingham Jail" and "Wabash Cannonball," and the jungle juice sometimes flowed late into the night. George McMillan, author of The Old Breed, recounted one such session that ended when a participant, on the point of passing out after downing almost a full canteen of the potent concoction, was still pleading: "Play me another! Play me another!"

"Can't play no more, man," replied the equally inebriated guitarist. "Ain't got but two strings left!"

Also providing some diversion were numerous Okinawan children, whose wide-eyed shyness was quickly overcome by Marines' smiles and K-ration chocolate bars.

When K/3/5 was assigned to land on one of the islands off Okinawa's east coast to make sure that no enemy troops were skulking there, they found no Japanese soldiers but roughly 100 civilians.

"They went up into the hills and hid from us at first," said PFC Harry Bender, "but gradually they wandered out and made friends, especially the little ones."

As PFC Bill Leyden tried to keep his mind off the recent grenade accident that had claimed the life of his friend and squad leader, Sergeant Leonard Ahner, he spent the better part of several days playing the role of drill instructor to a group of small boys armed with sticks. "I showed them how to stand at attention, and the ones who did it right got a piece of candy," Leyden recalled.

"He did a good job of it, too, considering the only way he could communicate with the kids was with gestures," added Bender. "Before he was done, he had them doing close-order drills and marching about as well as I could."

Leyden and other friendly Marines endeared themselves to the children to such an extent that many wore long faces when K/3/5 departed. "They stood on the beach and waved as we shoved off in our boats," said Bender. "It kind of gave you a lump in your throat and made you hope the war would somehow bypass these kids."

Not every effort to combat boredom was quite so constructive or well received, however. One K/3/5 Marine went to considerable effort to shake the explosive powder out of a grenade, intending to toss it among a group of comrades as a trick—perhaps not realizing how deeply many of his buddies had been affected by Ahner's death. But the prankster unintentionally left enough powder behind to cause a resounding *bang* when the grenade went off. "Nobody got hurt," said Bender, "but the guy wasn't too popular after that, to say the least."

EVEN IN THE UNEVENTFUL neverland where K/3/5 drifted, there were occasional ugly reminders that Americans were dying just the distance of a few rifle shots away. One came in a report that the unit's counterpart in another regiment—K Company, Third Battalion, Seventh Marines—had suffered the division's first serious losses in a Japanese ambush. The enemy had opened fire from both sides as K/3/7 moved along a pathway through dense woods, killing three Marines and wounding twenty-seven.

A few days later, K/3/5 was assigned to patrol the same area where the ambush occurred, and the scene of the fighting, littered with enemy corpses and bloodstained American equipment and uniforms, left a deep impression on PFC Gene Sledge.

"The scene was like . . . a page of a history book," Sledge would write later. "The Marines had suffered losses, but they had inflicted worse on the attacking Japanese. We saw no Marine dead; all had been removed when the relief troops had come in and aided K/3/7 to withdraw."

But Sledge, Sergeant Burgin, and other members of their mortar section did find plenty of what Sledge called the "flotsam of battle"—empty machine-gun ammo boxes, clips for M-1 rifles, spent carbine shells, discarded dungaree jackets and leggings, bloody dressings, and large red-brown spots where the dried blood of Marines covered the ground. Lying on both sides of the path were about twenty dead Japanese.

"We knew that blood could've been ours just as easy as not," Burgin said. "Seeing it got us back on our toes, I can tell you."

⌒

THE SIXTH MARINE Division's advance across the Ishikawa Isthmus and into lightly populated northern Okinawa, meanwhile, had met with only slightly more resistance than the Old Breed's thrust to the east coast.

Like their First Division comrades, the men of the Sixth had covered ground at a far more rapid pace than either division commander General Lemuel Shepherd or III Marine Amphibious Corps commander General Roy Geiger had expected. By nightfall on April 5, all of their L-plus-15 objectives had been gained in a third of the time originally allotted.

At first, the terrain was rolling, grassy land with scattered trees and the rugged mountains farther north forming a distant backdrop. The houses and farms along the way were deserted for the most part, and two of the division's three assault regiments—the 22nd and 29th Marines—

encountered only occasional small groups of Japanese soldiers, who offered token resistance before melting away.

The other assault regiment, the Fourth Marines, made up largely of
former Marine Raiders, elite commandos with heavy combat experience
who had been incorporated into regular regiments, was bloodied early,
however. On its second day ashore, the regiment's L Company, Third
Battalion, was caught in a firefight that cost it two dozen killed and
wounded in one rifle platoon, while leaving 150 enemy soldiers dead.
The regiment's First Battalion reported killing another 250 Japanese as it
drove into the town of Ishikawa on the eastern coast.

Otherwise, it was mostly smooth and rapid sailing for the division.
Indeed, one of the biggest problems faced by the Sixth in the early going
was trying to move its troops as fast as the lack of opposition permitted.
Every available piece of mechanized equipment was pressed into service
to transport infantry, but the vehicles were frequently forced to wait
while the Sixth Engineer Battalion rebuilt key highway bridges destroyed
by the Japanese.

Initially, the light resistance led General Shepherd to conclude that
the enemy had no strongly held positions in the north. If this were the
case, he theorized, then a single infantry regiment—the 29th Marines—
might be able to overrun the wild, mountainous Motobu Peninsula
without assistance.

But reports from division intelligence and reconnaissance units indicated that most of the Japanese north of the isthmus had moved into
the high ground on Motobu, which jutted west about a dozen miles
into the East China Sea, and these warnings soon changed Shepherd's
mind. The most advantageous spot for a defense in depth was Mount
Yaetake, a 1,200-foot peak near the center of the peninsula—which was
precisely where more than 2,000 Japanese troops under Colonel Takehido Udo had taken up strong positions in a warren of ridges and caves.

Udo's force included two full battalions of well-trained infantry, an
artillery unit with 150- and 75-millimeter weapons, a naval unit with two
6.1-inch coastal guns capable of hitting targets up to ten miles away, plus
150 additional naval personnel and two companies of Okinawan conscripts. He also had an ample supply of mortars, light and heavy machine
guns, and 20- and 25-millimeter AA weapons modified for ground warfare. In an area with virtually no roads worth the name, the Japanese had
another important asset—a large herd of horses for moving equipment
and supplies.

General Shepherd knew none of these specifics, only that an enemy force of some size (Shepherd underestimated it at about two companies) was hiding somewhere in Motobu's tangled, mountainous wilderness. But by April 7, the intelligence and recon reports had convinced him to take a much more deliberate approach than originally planned. It was a decision that may well have saved the 29th Marines from annihilation.

As of the morning of April 8 (L-plus-7), Shepherd's revised scheme of attack shaped up like this: The 22nd Marines were deployed all the way across the main body of Okinawa, blocking off the rest of the desolate north against any Japanese incursion from that direction. The 22nd was also covering the rear of the 29th, which remained in the forefront of the drive onto the peninsula, located about a third of the way up the northern part of the island. Most of the Fourth Marines, meanwhile, was in ready reserve near the village of Ora, except for a few companies that had hooked up with units of the 22nd to probe Japanese strength on Motobu.

Things went well enough at first. Before noon on April 8, the Second Battalion of the 29th seized an abandoned Japanese PT boat and midget submarine base on the coast of the peninsula without opposition. But late that afternoon, the First Battalion ran into heavy enemy fire near the town of Itomi and was forced to dig in, and the next day, the Second Battalion also came under attack as it advanced along an inland road between Itomi and a village called Togushi.

Patrols and probes sent out over the next two days by all three battalions of the 29th met sharp resistance, proving once and for all to Shepherd and the regiment's New Zealand–born commander, Colonel Victor Bleasdale, that the crest of Mount Yaetake was held by a formidable enemy force. If Colonel Udo's defenders were to be dislodged from their mountain fastness, the 29th would need major help from the rest of the division. It was also clear that Motobu could never be secured as long as the enemy held the peak.

If there was any good news for the Sixth Marine Division, it was that, unlike Kakazu Ridge to the south, where the configuration of enemy defenses defied any attempt to flank them, Udo's smaller force on Mount Yaetake *could* be flanked. The bad news was that the combined efforts of all three of the division's infantry regiments would be needed for the job, and losses could run high.

While Shepherd devised a two-pronged pincer movement designed to bring the Japanese positions under intensive pressure from two directions, U.S. planes and artillery were called in to pound the mountaintop for a couple of days.

At 8:00 a.m. on April 14, the Marines stormed Mount Yaetake simultaneously from east and west. Two battalions of the Fourth Marines, plus one battalion of the 29th, formed the western assault force, while the other two battalions of the 29th charged the mountain's heavily forested base from the opposite side. The Marines on the west managed to gain the crest of a 700-foot ridge adjoining Yaetake's main mass, but the east side attack sputtered from the start and soon stalled, with heavy Japanese fire keeping the attackers bogged down for the next two days.

Even on the western prong of the assault, the advance was painfully slow and continuously harassed by small teams of Japanese armed with Nambu light machine guns who hid in the thick undergrowth until Marines moved past, then struck from behind in shoot-and-run attacks. After a short burst from an invisible machine gun killed Major Bernard W. Green, commander of the First Battalion, Fourth Marines, one of Green's staff officers described the Japanese as "a phantom enemy."

"Jesus, they've all got Nambus," said one Marine, crouching in the brush and searching in vain for something to shoot at, "but where the hell are they?"

Only occasional bloodstains on the ground or in the brush gave evidence that some of the Marines' return fire was finding its mark. Uncharacteristically, the Japanese were apparently taking their dead with them, since only a few enemy bodies were found.

At the end of a harrowing day, units advancing from the west dug in facing two heavily fortified ridges, designated as Hill 200 and Green Hill, both of which would have to be taken before the Marines could attack the western slope of Mount Yaetake itself.

By noon on April 15, the Japanese run-and-shoot tactics had been augmented by a concealed 75-millimeter gun that fired from the mouth of a large cave. The gun seemed impervious to Navy shells, Marine artillery, 500-pound aerial bombs, and canisters of napalm because its crew, after firing several rounds, would pull the weapon deep inside the cave, then wheel it back out after a few minutes to fire again.

The next morning, Lieutenant William H. Carson's Company C of the Fourth Marines took more than fifty casualties driving to the top of the hill before the gun was finally silenced, but they won the crest and held it despite their thin ranks and a shortage of ammunition.

Corporal Richard E. "Dick" Bush, a rifle squad leader from

Waukegan, Illinois, was in the forefront of the assault as he led his men up the face of Yaetake through a storm of enemy fire. Bush's squad was the first to break through the enemy's outer perimeter, then sweep over the ridge and drive into the core of the Japanese defenses.

"We've got 'em on the run!" Bush yelled, rallying his men as they routed enemy defenders from their entrenched positions. "Don't let up now!"

At that instant, an enemy machine gun opened fire, cutting Bush's legs from under him, and he fell to the coral, bleeding profusely from wounds in both thighs and unable to move.

"Corpsman! Corpsman!" Bush heard somebody screaming just before he blacked out.

A short time later, as he lay semiconscious in an aid station with four other men from his company, all of them badly hurt, Bush heard something small and hard strike the ground beside him. He managed to rouse himself enough to glance toward the sound and saw a Japanese grenade lying inches from his right hand.

Instinctively, he grabbed the grenade, rolling toward it and smothering it against his body as it exploded.

For a long time after that, Bush remembered nothing else. But he miraculously survived to wear the Medal of Honor he was awarded for saving the lives of his four wounded comrades.

PFC PAULIE DE MEIS may have been the youngest Marine in the Corps when he lied about his age to enlist at age fifteen in the spring of 1943. Eager to avoid a date with juvenile authorities in his native Brooklyn, where he was in major trouble for running numbers and horse bets, Paulie had already tried—and failed—to get into the Coast Guard, Navy, and Army. The Marines were his last resort.

"There wasn't a line of guys waiting to join the Marines, like there was at the other recruiting offices," de Meis recalled. "I found out why pretty damned quick."

While serving with the First Marine Raider Brigade at Guam— where he was bayoneted in the gut by a Japanese soldier, then lay all night under the soldier's body after killing him with a .45—Paulie had picked up the nickname "Bazooka Kid" because he *was* a kid and he carried a bazooka. But he was an "old man" of seventeen on the morning of April

16, 1945, when he charged up Mount Yaetake with K Company, Fourth Marines.

A little more than halfway up the slope, his bazooka was blown out of his hands by a mortar blast that also put two ugly holes in his belly, not far from where the bayonet had sliced into him.

"I knew that flamethrower and bazooka guys had the highest mortality rate of anybody in the Corps," de Meis recalled later, "so it didn't surprise me much to get hit, but it did seem kind of strange to get it in the gut again."

As he lay beside his ruined weapon, clutching his stomach with both hands and watching streams of blood dribble through his fingers, two perplexing questions kept running through his mind:

Would I be better off in jail back in Brooklyn? And who the hell says lightning never strikes twice in the same place?

BEFORE NIGHTFALL on April 16, as Paulie de Meis and Dick Bush lay within a few feet of each other in the same field hospital, two other companies of the Fourth Marines—E and F—were digging in near the summit of Green Hill, after gaining 900 yards through murderous fire.

Determined to maintain pressure on the enemy, General Shepherd ordered a final attack by his western forces the next morning. But because many men in the Fourth and 29th Marines were weary to the point of exhaustion, he ordered units of the 22nd Marines to move in from the south and bolster the assault by hitting Colonel Udo's flank.

On April 17, after almost a week of constant combat, capped off by fierce hand-to-hand fighting between Marines and scores of bayonet-wielding Japanese, Shepherd's men secured the crest of Mount Yaetake and both Hill 200 and Green Hill as well. They found 347 Japanese bodies covering the hilltops and dozens more in trenches and dugouts. At least 100 defenders were killed by 14-inch shells from the battleship *Tennessee.*

Sporadic, isolated fighting continued until April 19, when the Marines counted more than 2,000 enemy bodies—all but a handful of Colonel Udo's force. A few Japanese troops, along with Udo himself, managed to slip off the peninsula and escape into the wilds of northern Okinawa, but Mount Yaetake and the rest of Motobu were firmly in American hands. The victory, however, came at a hefty price for the Sixth

Marine Division, which counted 213 men killed or missing and 757 wounded.

"[I]t was as difficult as I can conceive an operation to be," said Colonel Alan Shapley, commander of the Fourth Marines, who had also commanded the Marine detachment aboard the ill-fated battleship *Arizona* at Pearl Harbor, where he earned a Silver Star for heroism. "It was an uphill fight all the way."

Undeniably, the battle for Mount Yaetake had been anything but a picnic. Even so, the Army troops of the 96th and Seventh Infantry Divisions, now stymied and suffering several miles to the south along Kakazu Ridge, might well have taken issue with Shapley's comment if they'd heard it.

IT WAS WITH considerable reluctance that Colonel Eddy May, commander of the 96th Division's 383rd Infantry, delayed his regiment's all-out assault on Kakazu Ridge and Kakazu West until the morning of April 9. But as May counted his 326 dead and wounded following the assault's collapse, he surely had ample reason to wish that he'd canceled it altogether.

The attack on the two ridges started with considerable promise in the predawn darkness, with May withholding any advance artillery fire to achieve surprise. By daybreak, lead platoons in three of the four advancing companies had climbed almost to the top of the two peaks while encountering only a few enemy pickets, which they bayoneted. Colonel Hara's defenders still seemed unsuspecting, but the situation was too good to last.

An hour after jump-off, as Sergeant Alvin Becker of L Company reached the crest of the northernmost of two knolls atop Kakazu West, he spotted a Japanese soldier on the other knoll. Becker waved reassuringly to him, and the soldier waved back. Then Becker blasted him with his BAR, and in the sergeant's words, "All hell started popping."

Only then did the Deadeyes realize that the reverse slope of Kakazu West was honeycombed with Japanese fortifications that no one had known were there until this moment.

Though the truth was slow to penetrate the division command structure, May's infantrymen never had a realistic chance of holding either piece of high ground. Only two rifle companies (with a third in reserve) were sent against each ridge, where they were met and thrown back by massive enemy firepower from deeply entrenched Japanese on the reverse slopes.

Rightly sensing that the American force facing him was too small to hold the high ground, Colonel Hara, the Japanese commander, mounted four furious counterattacks on both contested ridges. Hara's troops suffered heavy casualties—some inflicted as they charged through their own mortar fire—but they stopped the Americans in their tracks and came perilously close to overrunning the Deadeyes' lines.

Only L Company of the 383rd made it to the top of Kakazu West, while I Company, the other attacking unit, was pinned down near the foot of the northern slope. Leading the climb to the crest was L Company's CO, First Lieutenant Willard F. "Hoss" Mitchell, a powerfully built former college football star at Mississippi State.

Mitchell's Deadeyes adored their commander, and they fought hard for "Cap'n Hoss," but they were soon forced into a defensive perimeter in a shallow saddle between the two highest points on Kakazu West. With enemy grenades, mortar shells, and TNT satchel charges crashing down around them, they knew they could expect no help up top from I Company. It was also clear that enemy machine guns covering the open slopes below made retreat as dangerous an option as staying where they were.

The saddle was barely deep enough to shelter Mitchell and his men, provided they remained in a prone position, hugging its coral floor. Yet if they could also remain patient, Mitchell reasoned, they might deal the Japanese substantial misery if they tried to charge the saddle and exposed themselves to fire. When the Japanese did exactly that, L Company's riflemen were ready and waiting.

"The charging Japanese came within three feet of us and threw satchel charges that looked as big as boxes of apples," recalled Sergeant Marshall W. Weaver years later, still amazed that he survived.

"Come on, you lardtails!" Mitchell boomed, using his pet name for his riflemen while hurling grenades as fast as he could pull the pins. "Remember, you're with the Hoss—and the Hoss has God on his side! Now get after those sons of bitches!"

After spotting a 320-millimeter Japanese spigot mortar a short distance away that was capable of wiping out the whole company with one of its huge shells, PFC Joseph Solch took his CO at his word. He, Mitchell, and several others charged the mortar position, killing all nine members of its crew. Moments later, Solch fired his BAR from the hip in a squatting position, emptying three clips at attacking enemy soldiers and sending an entire company of Japanese scrambling for cover.

But by about 4:00 P.M., most of Mitchell's men were wounded, and with the saddle under withering fire from three directions, the situation was growing more desperate by the minute.

"We're out of machine-gun ammo, and I don't know if we can hold off another charge, even with God's help," Mitchell told Lieutenant Bill Curran. "We'd better call for some smoke shells and get the hell out."

When the smoke-screened retreat down the slope was over, seventeen of Mitchell's men were dead or missing. Thirty-seven others had serious wounds and had to be carried from the hill, and, among the survivors, only three men escaped without injuries of some type. But L Company had also exacted a high price from the Japanese, who left 165 bodies in tangled piles around the saddle. In recognition of the gallant stand by Cap'n Hoss and his lardtails, the company would receive the first Presidential Unit Citation awarded on Okinawa.

Fierce fighting also raged that afternoon on adjacent Kakazu Ridge, where Captain Jack Royster's A Company and First Lieutenant Dave Belman's C Company were driven back from the crest after suffering nearly 50 percent casualties. Captain John van Vulpen's B Company was sent to attempt a rescue, but it got only as far as a deep gorge at the foot of the northern slope before it was also pinned down.

At this point, Lieutenant Colonel Byron F. King, commanding the First Battalion of the 383rd, pleaded with Colonel May to let his besieged A and C Companies withdraw.

"We are in a serious predicament," he radioed May. "There are only fifty men left on the ridge, and an estimated battalion of Japs are moving up for counterattack."

But May was undeterred and adamant.

"I'm sending G Company to reinforce you," he told King. "Hold the hill at all costs. You'll lose just as many men if you try to withdraw, and you'll lose the high ground, too. If you're jumpy, have the executive officer take over."

But Captain Royster, in tremendous pain from shrapnel wounds to the face, could still see with far greater clarity than either King or May that his men were caught between the proverbial "rock and a hard place." One more enemy counterattack was almost certain to overrun his position, yet to retreat down Kakazu's coverless slope under mortar and artillery fire would be akin to suicide. Without bothering to contact May or

King, he radioed the 88th Chemical Mortar Battalion and, like Hoss Mitchell, asked for smoke shells.

After waiting for more than an hour because of high winds that kept blowing the smoke back in their faces, the trapped Deadeyes atop the ridge inched their way downhill on their bellies through another smoke-screen, dragging and carrying as many of their wounded as they could.

PFC Edward Moskala, a BAR man from Chicago, who had already knocked out two enemy machine guns with grenades and his automatic weapon, volunteered to cover the retreat as a rear guard. He was the last able-bodied man to reach safety below, but when he learned that a wounded buddy was still on the hill, Moskala went back for him. Then he went back a second time to try to get another wounded man out—and this time he didn't return.

According to his surviving comrades, Moskala single-handedly killed at least twenty-five Japanese during his two rescue missions. For his self-sacrificing courage, he was posthumously awarded the Medal of Honor.

Colonel May's men had been soundly repulsed, but their defeat was actually much less disastrous than it could have been. While the 383rd's losses totaled 70 dead or missing and 256 wounded, reasonable estimates placed enemy dead and wounded at close to 600—a remarkable toll considering that the Japanese fought from formidable fixed positions against GIs crossing open ground. In the end, the counterattacks ordered by Colonel Hara had proved more damaging to his own troops than to the Americans.

UNFORTUNATELY FOR THE DEADEYES, however, Brigadier General Claudius Easley, a tough, impetuous Texas A&M graduate from Waco who served as the division's assistant commander, didn't wait to learn the full extent of the 383rd's defeat before personally organizing a second, much larger assault on Kakazu.

Described by Easley as a "powerhouse" attack with no attempt to take the enemy by surprise, this assault was spearheaded by four infantry battalions—about 3,000 men—backed by most of the division's 105- and 155-millimeter artillery, along with coordinated air strikes and naval bombardment by the battleship *New York*. The yawning gorge at the base of the ridge precluded the use of tanks, so the infantrymen would have no covering armor.

When the assault jumped off at 7:15 A.M. on April 10, Colonel Hara's defenders, safe and invisible in their steel-reinforced underground fortifications—and utterly untouched by the rain of American bombs and shells preceding the attack—were waiting with rifles, grenades, machine guns, mortars, and field pieces.

This time, it would be the Second and Third Battalions of the 383rd leading the attack across the gorge against the main ridge. (An angry May had by now relieved Colonel King of command of the beat-up First Battalion, which was so depleted that it was considered unfit for further immediate combat.) Meanwhile, fresh troops of the First and Second Battalions of Colonel Michael E. Halloran's 381st Infantry were sent to tackle Kakazu West.

The results of this second attack can be summed up in a few unhappy words: More men. Different lineup. Same disheartening results.

For two days, General Easley's Deadeyes threw themselves at the Kakazu ridgeline. Just after 8:00 A.M. on April 10, two companies of Lieutenant Colonel Russell Graybill's Second Battalion of the 381st crossed the gorge and moved up the northern face of Kakazu West with their skirmish line under a ferocious enemy mortar barrage and raked by a pair of heavy machine guns.

Staff Sergeants Arvil Brewer and Robert Kulp led a five-man charge that knocked out the two machine guns with grenades and killed their crews. By 9:30 A.M., Companies E and F of the 381st again held the saddle where Lieutenant Hoss Mitchell and his lardtails had made their stand the day before—and found themselves in much the same predicament until Graybill sent G Company to reinforce them, allowing them to hang on.

Meanwhile, the Second and Third Battalions of the 383rd were caught up in a dismal repeat of what Colonel May's First Battalion had suffered on Kakazu proper twenty-four hours earlier. This time, the Second Battalion never even made it to the ridge but was pinned down crossing the gorge by a hail of mortar fire that sometimes reached a rate of sixty rounds per minute. The Third Battalion got to the main ridge, but suffered heavy losses, and, just after 1:00 P.M., Lieutenant Colonel Edward Stare, the battalion commander, radioed that he was short of men and the Japanese were counterattacking.

To complicate matters, rain began falling at noon and continued for hours. That night, Stare's men were stymied below the crest of Kakazu, while the two battalions on Kakazu West huddled in their holes under canvas shelter halves being pounded by heavy Japanese artillery fire from the heights of Shuri several miles away. The Japanese also put their massive spigot mortars into action, and, although they were woefully inaccurate, they created havoc. When one errant 674-pound round struck an unoccupied hill, it sent a landslide crashing down on a cave housing an aid station of the 381st, killing thirteen men and wounding nine.

It took two more days of hopeless stalemate before General Easley finally concluded that Kakazu was too tough a nut to be cracked by the 96th Division alone.

On the morning of April 12, after another round of heavy but ineffective air strikes, Easley ordered a final assault on Kakazu Ridge by Lieutenant Colonel John Cassidy's First Battalion of the 381st. Like all the rest, the attack was beaten back—with a loss of forty-five more Deadeyes.

East of Kakazu, the 382nd Infantry was meeting similar failure against another stubborn crag called Tombstone Ridge. When the regiment's advance was stopped cold, its men were forced to set up a defensive perimeter to consolidate their position and guard against Japanese attacks from the rear. Like those on the reverse slopes of Kakazu and Kakazu West, the interwoven defenses on Tombstone were simply too strong.

The only significant American advance achieved between April 9 and 12 was by troops of the Seventh Infantry Division, who gained up to 1,000 yards during that period before being stalled themselves north of Hill 178, a peak used as a key observation point for Japanese artillery.

"We blew the hell out of the place before we went up, but it didn't do much good," said PFC Francis Lambert, a Chicago native who'd already been through battles at Attu and Kwajalein. "We stormed the hill at daybreak and got thrown back. Then they brought up a tank for support, but the Japs knocked it out and chased us back down again. All I remember is enemy fire coming from all directions at once."

Total casualties in the 96th and Seventh Divisions during the three-day series of attacks stood at 2,880, including almost 700 killed or missing. Enemy losses were officially estimated at 5,750, but that figure was probably too high by at least one-third.

The bloody futility of the battle left Major General James "Jim" Bradley, commander of the 96th, shaken and heartsick. As the casualty count mounted, he was also alarmed at the decline in his division's combat strength, but for the moment, he had no choice but to leave his infantry in position along the Kakazu ridgeline to meet whatever the Japanese might throw at them next.

And while virtually every Deadeye in the division's three infantry regiments was missing a wounded buddy or mourning a dead one, they were about to learn that their country had also lost its commander in chief.

Franklin D. Roosevelt, the only president that most of the young men on Okinawa had ever known, was dead.

⁓

SHAKEN BY DAYS of kamikaze attacks, many of the men aboard Navy ships were sitting down to breakfast on the morning of April 13 when shipboard loudspeakers began blaring out the distressing news:

"Attention, all hands! President Roosevelt is dead! Repeat, our supreme commander, President Roosevelt, is dead!"

For thousands of soldiers, sailors, and Marines at Okinawa—like the general public at home—the announcement struck like a lightning bolt. Although his health had been failing for months, protective national media had concealed Roosevelt's physical decline, just as his totally paralyzed legs had been kept a closely guarded secret for more than twelve years. So when "the Chief" suffered a fatal stroke at Warm Springs, Georgia, on April 12 while having his portrait painted by noted artist Elizabeth Shoumatoff, the news flash stunned the world.

With the possible exception of Abraham Lincoln, no wartime president in America's history had been held in higher regard by the rank and file of its armed forces or more closely identified with the war effort. While he had his share of political foes, FDR had become an inspirational father figure to millions of younger Americans, especially those serving their country in faraway places.

"One of our saddest days on Okinawa was the day we learned President Roosevelt had died," said Corporal Jack Armstrong, the Marine tank commander. "I saw grown men cry unashamedly because we loved that old man."

A common early reaction, before grief and reality settled in, was disbelief. "I thought the report was Jap propaganda," said Sergeant Major Walter L. Snyder of the First Marine Division. Many others were also skeptical until Admiral Richmond Kelly Turner confirmed the news in a special message to Navy personnel. Then the sorrow spread and deepened, underscored by fear and uncertainty about what was going to happen next.

"Not the least bit interested in politics while we were fighting for our lives, we were saddened nonetheless," said Marine mortarman Gene Sledge. "We were also curious and a bit apprehensive about how FDR's successor, Harry S. Truman, would handle the war. We . . . didn't want someone in the White House who would prolong it one day longer than necessary."

Some of Sledge's K/3/5 comrades were less deeply touched, however. "I didn't have time to worry about some politician in Washington," said PFC Bill Leyden. "All my concern was for the guys around me—the buddies I depended on. They were the only thing that mattered."

Many ground units across Okinawa, particularly those in rear areas, and most ships offshore held special memorial services that were generally well attended. Even many front-line troops, with enemy artillery rounds whistling overhead, paused for a few moments to pay a quiet tribute. The 96th Division newsletter, the *Deadeye Dispatch*, expressed the feelings of many in a special edition:

"We have lost . . . a man whom every soldier has felt to be his friend—a personal friend—one who has cared for the soldier's needs and protected his future."

Not every man in the 96th shared those sentiments, of course. As PFC Don Dencker of L Company, 382nd Infantry, looked back on April 13, 1945, nearly sixty years later, his most troubling recollections weren't related to FDR's death but to the long list of casualties suffered by the company on that date.

"It was a bad day because of Japanese bombardment," Dencker said. "PFC Oscar Jenkins of the Third Platoon was killed, and ten other men from the company were evacuated with wounds that day. Because we were involved in a deadly struggle, and our immediate concerns overshadowed a tragic event for our country, I heard only a few expressions of regret. I felt that FDR's death was certainly sad and untimely, but I also felt that it had absolutely no effect on my own situation."

Even the Japanese, however, felt moved to offer a tribute of sorts in a propaganda leaflet dropped on American positions facing Kakazu Ridge.

"We must express our deep regret over the death of President Roosevelt," it said. "The 'American Tragedy' is now raised here on Okinawa with his death."

Clearly, the Japanese intended to compound that tragedy if they could. Even before the announcement of FDR's passing reached Okinawa, General Ushijima's troops were launching a strong series of counterattacks in hopes of shattering the thin American lines before Kakazu and decimating the battle-weary 96th Division.

For a dozen days, Ushijima had held firmly to a strategy of forcing the Americans to come to him, and it had paid major dividends. His troops had inflicted heavy losses on the enemy while sustaining little damage to their own defensive perimeter. But for General Cho, Ushijima's hotheaded chief of staff, the passive strategy was almost unbearable. Now, with the U.S. assault stopped cold in the ridges and American forces seriously weakened, Cho convinced Ushijima that the time was ripe for a Japanese counteroffensive.

It was the preoffensive bombardment by Ushijima's artillery and mortars that had dealt misery to Don Dencker's company of the 382nd Infantry on the night of April 12 and the morning of April 13. The barrage that hit the 96th Division sector was the heaviest yet launched by the Japanese in the Pacific war, with more than 1,000 rounds falling on the 381st Infantry, 1,200 on the disheveled 383rd, and a comparable number on the 382nd.

According to Cho's plan, six battalions of Japanese troops would slip through American lines across most of the front. Three battalions would attack the Seventh Division on the east, and three more would hit the 96th on the west. Cho foresaw his troops breaking through the thin U.S. front and penetrating rear areas to within four miles of Kadena airfield, where they would take cover in tombs, then emerge in daylight to rout U.S. rear-echelon units. He conjectured that American artillery and planes would be powerless to intervene in the resulting chaos, in which opposing troops would be clashing hand to hand, and the two forward U.S. divisions would be forced into disorderly retreat.

Because of a tenacious American response and countless individual acts of heroism by Deadeyes and Hourglass GIs, it didn't work out that way. This time, it was Japanese troops who were charging well-defended U.S. fortifications and suffering ruinous casualties.

Infantrymen of First Lieutenant Julius Anderson's Company A of the 381st, clinging by their fingernails just below the crest of Kakazu, fought off two determined Japanese counterattacks, enabled by the courage and fortitude of Tech Sergeant Alfred C. "Chief" Robertson, a half-Sioux Indian.

Using every kind of weapon at his disposal—including a BAR, an

M-1, grenades, a bayonet, and a trench knife—Robertson single-handedly took out two Japanese machine guns and killed twenty-eight enemy soldiers. Then, crawling to the crest of the ridge with a radio, he directed mortar fire that destroyed several close-in enemy positions. He was awarded a Silver Star.

Meanwhile, a mortar squad of the 381st led by Staff Sergeant Beauford T. "Snuffy" Anderson of Beloit, Wisconsin, had taken cover in a tomb near the northwest corner of the draw between Kakazu and Kakazu West. When Anderson heard the Japanese attackers coming, he ordered the squad into the rear of the tomb. Then he moved out onto a rocky ledge above the enemy soldiers and bombarded them with all the grenades he could find. After also emptying his carbine, he ran back into the depths of the tomb and began grabbing up mortar shells, the only remaining weapons at his disposal.

Twisting the shells from their casings, jerking out the safety pins, and smashing the rounds against a rock to activate the firing mechanism, Anderson hurled fifteen of the missiles into the draw like footballs, while the screams of the enemy soldiers below faded to faint moans. When the sun came up, the bodies of twenty-five dead Japanese covered the draw, along with seven knee mortars and four machine guns that the attackers had never had a chance to use. Anderson's impromptu one-man barrage earned him a Medal of Honor.

These and countless other episodes of personal heroism caused General Cho's plan to fail miserably. By the morning of April 14, the Japanese counteroffensive had burned itself out, but American forces were too exhausted and beaten up to take advantage of the situation, so the standoff along the Kakazu ridgeline continued without much change.

Long after the grief and distraction related to President Roosevelt's death faded away, the debilitating struggle for Kakazu would grind on. Yet days would pass with almost no discernible movement, except for replacing depleted American units with fresh, unbloodied ones.

On April 14, the battered 383rd Infantry Regiment, which had borne the brunt of both the fruitless assaults of April 9–10 and the ill-fated Japanese counterattacks, was relieved by troops of the 27th Infantry Division. Otherwise, each passing day seemed to be a carbon copy of the one that went before. The American lines remained in the same positions, harassed by the same daily enemy artillery fire and unable to dislodge the strong Japanese positions on the ridges' reverse slopes.

EVEN AS THE BLOODY IMPASSE at Kakazu continued, troops of the First Marine Division's Seventh Marines were running into more unexpected trouble in a supposedly peaceful area well to the north. On April 14, slightly more than a week after the regiment's Company K had suffered heavy losses in an ambush by a Japanese patrol, a similar fate befell another Seventh Marines company, E/2/7.

Within a half-hour period, the company suffered twenty-nine killed and wounded—a casualty rate of almost one per minute. One of the first men hit was PFC Americo "Moe" Milonni, an Italian teenager from Rochester, New York, who vividly recalled the attack sixty-one years later. It occurred exactly a year and two days after Milonni's enlistment in the Marine Corps.

"We were advancing along a trail up the side of this mountain, and my lieutenant told me to keep an eye on the trail because somebody had spotted some Japs moving our way," Milonni said. "As I sat there watching, I saw two Japs coming toward me, and I shot one, but they were in tall grass, and I missed the other one. I knew he was trying to circle around behind me, but I couldn't see him for the grass."

Behind him, Milonni heard one of his buddies yell: "Look out! They're coming up the trail!"

At almost that same instant, Milonni felt a rifle bullet tear into his chest, knocking him backward about fifteen feet. "All I knew was I couldn't breathe," he said. "I didn't know the bullet had gone through my lung, and I was bleeding internally. Fortunately, a couple of buddies got to me in a hurry and helped me out. They put sulfa powder on my wound and propped me up so I could breathe better. They kept me company and told me I was gonna be okay."

One of those buddies was PFC Melvin Grant, who recalled how Milonni was, in turn, trying to help a wounded sergeant, even as Milonni himself was literally "drowning in his own blood."

In the midst of a fierce firefight, two stretcher bearers loaded Milonni onto a stretcher and tried to take him to an aid station. But within a few yards, one bearer was struck by enemy fire, and Milonni was also hit again, this time in the buttocks.

Some two hours later, when the firing eased off, Milonni finally received treatment at a battalion aid station, and, by the end of the day, he was in a Navy hospital on Saipan.

"They had to stick a needle in my chest cavity to draw out the blood," he recalled, "but I tried to treat the wound in my butt myself because I was ashamed to let the nurses see my ass. I was just a stupid eighteen-year-old kid!"

GENERAL HODGE, commander of the U.S. 24th Corps, was convinced that one principal reason for his troops' lack of progress against the Kakazu ridgeline was a shortage of ammunition for his heavy artillery—a direct result of kamikaze attacks that had sunk two ammo-laden transports off the Hagushi beaches.

Despite the stalemate at Kakazu and heavy losses to the 96th and Seventh Divisions, General Buckner, the Tenth Army commander and Hodge's immediate superior, was generally satisfied with the overall state of the campaign thus far. He took comfort in the fact that the Sixth Marine Division was in almost full control of the northern two-thirds of Okinawa, and the Army's 77th Division was quickly stamping out remaining enemy resistance on the strategic island of Ie Shima, some four miles west of the Motobu Peninsula in the East China Sea.

With these positives in mind, Buckner, too, believed that massive artillery strikes could hold the key to victory in the south, and he was willing to wait until enough ammo was available to support a "juggernaut" offensive, the likes of which had never been seen before in the Pacific.

Replacements were rushed in to fill the gaps in the ranks of the Seventh and 96th, and once the conquest of Ie Shima was complete, Buckner planned to transport the entire 77th to the main island as a ready reserve, capable of taking over front-line positions in six hours or less.

By April 18, the needed ammunition had arrived, and, in anticipation of the coming assault, set for the next morning, Buckner moved his headquarters from the cruiser *Eldorado* to a site near the village of Uchi, a couple of miles southwest of Kadena airfield.

Hodge made no bones about the difficulty of the task ahead. "It's going to be really tough," he told dozens of reporters at a press briefing. "There are 65,000 to 70,000 fighting Japs holed up ... and I see no way to get them out but to blast them out yard by yard."

A big part of this blasting, Hodge hoped, would come from massed artillery—so much of it that, in the words of one artilleryman, "After we get done, our infantry can *walk* into Shuri."

At 6:00 A.M. on April 19, twenty-seven battalions of Army and Marine artillery, manning weapons ranging from 105-millimeter cannon to huge eight-inch howitzers, opened fire on Japanese positions in the Kakazu ridgeline and the Urasoe-Mura Escarpment beyond. For the next twenty minutes, thousands of shells poured down on enemy areas in the biggest bombardment of the Pacific war. Then the barrage moved 500 yards ahead for ten minutes while the infantry feinted an attack, then returned to its earlier range with shells timed to explode just off the ground to inflict maximum damage on enemy troops in the open.

The sound and fury of the barrage was earthshaking, but its effect on the Japanese was minimal at best. Brigadier General Josef Sheetz, who commanded the artillery, later expressed doubt that his guns had killed even one enemy soldier for every 100 rounds of the 19,000 fired that morning.

None of the Army commanders realized it at the time, but because of the artillery's ineffectiveness, the massive infantry attacks that followed were doomed to failure from the outset. When Seventh Division troops assaulted two outcroppings called Skyline Ridge and Ouki Hill, two battalions of Colonel Mickey Finn's 32nd Infantry advanced smartly for 500 yards before being mauled and pinned down by enemy mortars, machine guns, and artillery.

Tech Sergeant Porter McLaughlin, whose antitank platoon was firing armor-piercing shells at Japanese caves in support of one of Finn's battalions, watched the rout from about 400 yards away.

"For the first time in the war, our infantry had tank-mounted flamethrowers providing cover for them that morning," McLaughlin recalled, "but our kids still couldn't make any headway."

McLaughlin and his men were down below, watching A Company trying to storm up the side of the barren hill. The Americans were almost to the top when the Japanese swarmed over the ridge and threw them back. "We found out later that the Japs turned one of our flamethrowers on some of our wounded," McLaughlin said. "It gave us a terribly sick and hopeless feeling."

In the 96th Division zone, where the objectives included Tombstone Ridge and other hills in the Tanabaru-Nishibaru ridgeline, the situation was much the same. Corporal Don Dencker's Company L, Third Battalion, 382nd Infantry, came under heavy artillery fire while backing up the First Battalion in what mortar man Dencker termed "an unpleasant symphony of noise" from Japanese 150-millimeter guns.

"By early afternoon, the First Battalion was stopped after taking the northern half of Tombstone," Dencker recalled. "Our company advanced cautiously on the east flank beyond the First Battalion, and about 2:30 P.M., our Second Platoon ran into an enemy machine-gun pillbox on the east edge of our advance."

The pillbox was destroyed and its machine gun silenced, but not before Platoon Sergeant Tom Loter and PFC Robert Hake were killed and two other members of the platoon mortally wounded.

Such tragic scenes repeated themselves all over the 96th's sector on April 19 as the Deadeyes netted only negligible gains but lost more men to casualties than on any other day of the campaign. The newly inserted 27th Division, meanwhile, had no better luck in its sector opposite Kakazu Ridge than the Deadeyes had had there ten days earlier, even though the 27th's infantry was supported by thirty Shermans of the 164th Tank Battalion. Twenty-two of the tanks were destroyed or disabled by Japanese 47-millimeter guns and suicide squads with satchel charges. It was the greatest one-day loss of U.S. armor in the Okinawa campaign.

"We could hear the radio messages from the tanks of the 164th as they were being decimated," said Lieutenant Bob Green, a tanker attached to the 96th Division. "It was heartrending to listen to their agonized pleas for assistance as they became cut off, isolated, and under constant attack."

April 20 was another bad day for American forces. Don Dencker's Company L was hit particularly hard, suffering thirty-five battle casualties, including ten men killed in action or dead of wounds. Among the KIAs were two of Dencker's close friends, Staff Sergeant Alvin Engan and Sergeant Bob Heuer. Lieutenant Bob Glassman, the company's weapons platoon leader and commander of Dencker's mortar squad, was grievously wounded.

"By the end of that day, our strength had been reduced to 101 men from the 168 who'd landed on April 1," Dencker recalled.

On April 21, 22, and 23, the attacks continued, and some gains were registered. Colonel Finn's 32nd Infantry managed to clear Skyline Ridge, thanks in large measure to the heroics of Sergeant Theodore McDonald, who single-handedly overpowered and killed a Japanese machine-gun crew, then threw their weapon and a knee mortar to a group of GIs on an embankment below him. Troops of the 32nd also finally wrested Hill 178 from the Japanese, who left behind caves filled with some 400 bodies.

Led by the indomitable Lieutenant Hoss Mitchell and his L Company lardtails, now bolstered by a large crop of replacements, 96th Division troops also took and held most of Tanabaru and Nishibaru ridges after a three-and-a-half-hour slugfest with Japanese on the reverse slopes. U.S. losses, however, were staggering—118 killed or missing and 660 wounded.

By the morning of April 24, elements of all three Army divisions facing Kakazu were set to launch what they hoped would be one final coordinated attack against the ridgeline that had frustrated them for fifteen straight days. But General Ushijima, realizing that his position had become untenable, had one last trick to play. The evening before, under cover of darkness, Ushijima's forces had quietly relinquished their positions on Kakazu and Kakazu West as part of an orderly general withdrawal to their next main system of defensive fortifications—the Naha-Shuri-Yonabaru Line.

The battle for the Kakazu ridgeline was indisputably an American victory because, with their pullback, the Japanese yielded considerable ground. But the price at which that ground had been purchased was dear and devastating, and the withdrawal was carried out precisely as Colonel Hara, Ushijima's master strategist, had planned. The labyrinth of deep defensive positions now confronting U.S. troops in the enemy-held heights around Shuri would make the Kakazu ridgeline look like an anthill.

Still, the beleaguered, bone-weary GIs were more than willing to accept any small favors the wily Japanese commander might send their way. As the 96th Division's official history would later note, Ushijima's withdrawal from Kakazu was received by the Deadeyes like "manna from heaven."

CHAPTER SEVEN

A Wall of Stone and Flame

WHEN THOUSANDS of armed and desperate men spend hour after hour, day after day, killing and maiming one another in fighting that drags on for weeks, logic, rational thought—and sanity itself—are frequently among the casualties. Incongruity tends to become standard procedure. The bizarre is increasingly commonplace. The most grotesque sights and sounds disguise themselves as natural aspects of life. Men routinely do and endure things they'd consider intolerable under normal circumstances.

So it was during the spring of 1945 in the ridges of southern Okinawa.

ON A CLEAR Sunday morning in late April, Tech Sergeant Porter McLaughlin was trying to compose a letter to his aunt Gertrude, but his mind kept wandering, and he found it hard to concentrate. Every minute or two, an enemy artillery shell whistled overhead, and Porter inevitably paused to listen until he was sure the round wasn't landing anywhere near. Then he'd glance back to what he'd written and try to refocus:

"Dear Gert, It's a beautiful day with blue skies and only a few clouds, and it's hard to imagine a war's going on till you hear the guns blasting. . . ."

After a dozen days of nonstop combat with the Seventh Division's 32nd Infantry, now stalled at a place called Conical Hill, McLaughlin's antitank platoon—which had spent far more time lately using flamethrowers than its usual 37-millimeter guns—had finally been pulled off the line for a little rest. But even back in rear areas like this one, there was rarely a night when Japanese infiltrators didn't come calling.

The previous night had been typical. Three hours before dawn, PFC

Christian Rupp, in a foxhole behind one of the 37s and about twenty feet from McLaughlin, heard a noise in darkness.

"I think somebody's out there," Rupp whispered to his foxhole partner, but the other man was sound asleep.

Rupp, who drew occasional jibes from buddies who claimed he was "a little on the slow side," hadn't lacked for a speedy decision and fast action in this case. He sprang forward and grabbed the lanyard of the primed and loaded 37. He waited for about five seconds, staring into the curtain of darkness but still not seeing anything. Then he heard the noise again, and he fired.

The Japanese infiltrator was only inches from the muzzle of the gun when Rupp's round literally tore him in half. The memory of the incident kept distracting McLaughlin from his letter writing, but then he'd squeeze it out of his mind and try again:

"You know, Gert, it's strange what a guy thinks about sometimes out here. Right now, I'd give just about anything for some tunafish and mayonnaise the way you used to make it. Funny, huh? Think you could mail me some?"

McLaughlin had finished the letter and was lying in the sun eating a chunk of recently delivered fresh bread, the first he'd had in at least two weeks, when a jeep pulled up and a young Navy officer in freshly laundered khakis climbed out of it.

The officer stepped gingerly past the mangled body of the Japanese infiltrator, still lying where Rupp's shot in the dark had blown it.

"Do they get that close very often?" the officer asked, his eyes wide as he indicated the corpse.

"Sometimes," McLaughlin said. "This one got too close for his own good."

"Are you Porter McLaughlin?"

Porter frowned, certain that he'd never seen the man before and wondering how he knew his name. "That's right. What can I do for you?"

"I'm Lieutenant R. E. Harris, and I'm your uncle by marriage," the visitor said. "I'm on the troopship U.S.S. *Bingham,* and I just got a chance to come ashore, so I dropped by to say hello. Hey, you don't know where I can find some of that Okinawan lacquerware everybody's talking about, do you? I'd sure like to get some for souvenirs."

As the triviality of the moment sank in on McLaughlin, he almost laughed out loud. It was hard to believe that he and his "uncle"—who wasn't married to Gert but to Porter's aunt Ysleta, whom he hadn't seen

in years—were part of the same huge military operation. It was almost as if they were two different species of creatures from two different planets.

Finally, he managed a smile and nodded. "Yeah, what's left of a village is down at the bottom of this hill. You might be able to find a few pieces there that aren't broken." Hunting for lacquerware in violated tombs and shelled-out houses wasn't exactly Porter's idea of a good time, but it certainly wasn't the most unpleasant thing he'd done recently, either. "Come on, I'll show you."

By the time McLaughlin and Harris got back from the village with three intact pieces of lacquerware, the platoon was having its first mail call since moving south. Among the handful of letters Porter received was one from the State of California, threatening him with immediate arrest for several unpaid traffic tickets.

"Get a load of this," he said, showing the letter to Captain John J. McQuillan, the CO of Company E. "Looks like I'm in big trouble now."

"Give me that thing," McQuillan said. He grabbed the letter, scribbled "Deceased" across the front of the envelope, and handed it back to Porter. "Just have the mail guy return it to the sender," the captain instructed. "I guarantee they won't bother you again."

⌒

While the Seventh and 96th Divisions were throwing their infantry regiments into the slaughter around Kakazu Ridge, the Army's 77th Division was fighting a little-known engagement against Japanese forces on the island of Ie Shima off Okinawa's northwest coast. In one of the peculiarities of large, complex campaigns, the most noted combat correspondent of World War II had chosen to cover the obscure action on Ie Shima rather than the bloody torment at Kakazu.

The tell-it-like-it-is, foxhole-level reporting of Ernie Pyle had made him a celebrity in his own right, a household name across the nation, and a hero to many of the men he wrote about. As the author of two runaway bestsellers on the war in Europe and the most widely read newspaper columnist in America, he was held in high esteem by men of all ranks and all branches of the service. Unlike some war correspondents who preferred hobnobbing with generals and admirals, Pyle had no qualms about getting down in the dirt, sweat, and blood where enlisted men lived to tell their stories, and they respected him for it. It had, in fact, been a suggestion in a Pyle column that persuaded Congress to pass leg-

islation in May 1944—nicknamed "the Ernie Pyle Bill"—authorizing 50 percent more pay for servicemen in actual combat than for those working as office clerks and "living comfortably in a hotel in Rio de Janeiro."

Ordinary "grunts" also tended to remember any chance encounter with the man they called "the GI's friend." Sixty-one years after the fact, Marine Lance Corporal Melvin Grant still held fond memories of a momentary Love Day contact with Pyle on the Hagushi beachhead.

"'Hey, flamethrower, look here!' he yelled, and when I turned, he or somebody with him shot a photo of me," Grant recalled. "I knew it was him because I recognized him from pictures I'd seen."

Teenage K/3/5 machine gunner Dan Lawler, on the other hand, was initially puzzled when he saw Pyle industriously scribbling notes on a pad during a visit in the First Marine Division area.

"What're you doing, old man—writing a book?" Lawler quipped as he ambled past.

"Matter of fact, I am," Pyle replied. "You want to be in it?"

When the scribbler's identity suddenly dawned on the youthful Marine, Lawler grinned, and his face turned red. "Sure, I'd be honored," he said, shaking Pyle's hand.

"He stayed with us for several days, and he was a helluva nice guy," Lawler recalled decades later. "I'll never forget him."

The legendary journalist's arrival on Ie Shima on April 17 (L-plus-16), after spending time with the First and Sixth Marine Divisions, was cause for jubilation among the GIs of the 77th. They'd spent the entire campaign thus far clearing enemy resistance on small dots of land west of the main island and had yet to set foot on Okinawa proper. But someone important was finally coming to their isolated back corner of the war, and they appreciated Pyle all the more when reports circulated that he'd left a sickbed on a Navy ship to come to Ie Shima. Maybe now America's press would pay some overdue attention to a fight that was turning out to be much tougher than expected.

At the outset of the campaign, General Buckner had planned to bypass Ie Shima until his Tenth Army was securely in control of Okinawa itself. But when the Japanese failed to mount a serious defense of the north, Buckner moved up the Ie Shima landing and handed the assignment to Major General Andrew Bruce's 77th.

The enemy commander on Ie Shima, Major Masashi Igawa, had at his disposal only a battalion of regulars—930 men—from Japan's 44th Brigade, but he'd done an amazing job of supplementing this small force

with support personnel from noncombat units, Okinawan conscripts, and even civilians. Igawa had also utilized every weapon of every size and shape on Ie Shima, from 75-millimeter field pieces and machine guns stripped from junked aircraft down to sharpened bamboo spears, ensuring that each of his 3,500-member garrison was armed with *something*.

Like other Japanese commanders in the Okinawa campaign, Igawa concentrated his forces in deeply dug positions on the highest point of ground available—a 578-foot hill on the island's east end called Iegusugu Yama—and in concrete pillboxes buried under houses in adjacent Ie Town.

Three solid days of intense naval bombardment, led by the fourteen-inch batteries of the battleship *Texas,* preceded the landing on the morning of April 16 by two regiments of the 77th, Colonel Joseph Coolidge's 305th Infantry and Colonel Aubrey Smith's 306th.

For most of the day, the advance went well with few casualties reported, and the 306th had little trouble seizing the island's only airfield. But after nightfall, Major Igawa's troops launched a vicious counterattack in which human kamikazes armed with live mortar shells rushed American lines and blew themselves up. One GI suffered a broken arm when he was struck by a blown-off human leg from one of the suicide bombers.

On April 17, the day Ernie Pyle arrived, Japanese resistance stiffened sharply and heavy fighting raged into the evening from Ie Town and the beach along a strip of high ground that would come to be known as Bloody Ridge. As the star of Scripps-Howard News Service and United Features Syndicate, the forty-five-year-old journalist had by this time witnessed more front-line fighting than most of the infantrymen he was joining. He'd covered the invasions of North Africa, Sicily, Italy, and finally Normandy. Now, with the war about to end in Europe, he'd come halfway around the world to the Pacific because, as Pyle himself put it, "There's a war on, and I'm a part of it."

That afternoon, Pyle got a close-up view of the action from an observation post near the front, where he sweated out a brief mortar barrage that sent several other newsmen scurrying to the rear. Early on the morning of April 18, Pyle signed autographs for a group of GIs lined up outside the 305th command post and talked briefly with General Bruce. But the writer was eager to get to the front, and Colonel Coolidge offered him a ride in his jeep, along with two members of the regimental staff and the driver. The jeep pulled in behind three trucks and a military police jeep, then passed through a bivouac area where two infantry battalions were finishing breakfast and packing their gear to move into the line.

As the small convoy approached a road junction, an enemy machine gun chattered from somewhere. The jeep swerved crazily as two of its tires were shot out, and the radiator spewed steam from another bullet hole. As the vehicle jerked to a stop, all five occupants jumped clear, taking cover in ditches on both sides of the road.

"Ernie and I, on the right side of the jeep, landed in the ditch away from the line of fire," Coolidge recalled later. "The others, we hoped, had found shelter on the left side of the road. I had seen Barnes, our driver, jumping to the left. Ernie and I were quite safe; the ditch dropped off three feet from the side of the road."

After Pyle assured the colonel that he was okay, Coolidge cautioned him to stay down while he called out to other members of the party to determine their condition. All reported they were safe.

Then came another brief burst from the machine gun, and Coolidge ducked back down as one round kicked dust in his face and ricocheted over his head. When Coolidge turned to look, Pyle was lying on his back with his hands on his chest, holding a knitted cap that he always kept with him. The colonel saw no blood, and it wasn't until he noticed a neat, round hole in Pyle's left temple that he realized the writer had been fatally hit.

Pyle was buried in the 77th Division cemetery on Ie Shima in a casket hastily constructed from packing crates. By the time the simple funeral took place, the Japanese machine-gun sniper responsible had been hunted down and killed with grenades by an infantry patrol from the 305th.

At the site of his death, division GIs erected a wooden marker which read: "On this spot, the 77th Division lost a buddy, Ernie Pyle, 18 April 1945." It was later replaced by a pyramid-shaped concrete monument with a brass plaque bearing the same inscription.

The next day, because of the death of its renowned visitor, the 77th Division's all-but-overlooked fight on Ie Shima was front-page news all over the United States. President Harry Truman, in the White House for less than a week, suggested a special Congressional Medal of Honor be struck in Pyle's honor. Hollywood joined wholeheartedly in the mourning, mainly to promote the release of *Ernie Pyle's Story of GI Joe,* a new blockbuster movie based on Pyle's wartime writings and experiences.

Found on Pyle's body—probably the last thing he'd written before his death—was a rough draft of a column intended for release when the war in Europe ended. It read in part:

> [T]here are many of the living who have had burned into their brains forever the unnatural sight of cold dead men scattered over the hillsides and in the ditches along the high rows of hedge throughout the world.
>
> Dead men by mass production—in one country after another—month after month and year after year. Dead men in winter and dead men in summer.
>
> Dead men in such familiar promiscuity that they become monotonous. Dead men in such monstrous infinity that you come almost to hate them. . . .

Now Ernie Pyle himself had joined the ranks of those of whom he wrote.

To THE SOUTH, on Okinawa itself, in the days immediately following the enemy's abandonment of Kakazu and Kakazu West, there was little time for rejoicing by the "victorious" GIs. Even if there had been, few of them had either the strength or motivation to do much celebrating.

On April 24, freed of the onerous chore of mounting another assault on the ridgeline that had been their nemesis for so long, troops of the Seventh and 96th Divisions found the strength to surge ahead up to 1,000 yards by the end of the day. On the left side of the advance, the Seventh drove south from Skyline Ridge and Hill 178 toward a new objective, a jutting mass of rock known as Conical Hill. In the center, the 96th worked its way close to the Urasoe-Mura Escarpment while staying joined to the Seventh's western flank.

Only the less-experienced 27th Division was prevented from advancing by a stubborn pocket of resistance and the fact that the west end of its lines was within shouting distance of the new Japanese defensive perimeter on the escarpment.

On April 25–26, however, the whole 24th Corps came to another dead standstill with the massive outcropping of Urasoe-Mura frowning down on them from a few hundred yards away. As the battle for it pro-

gressed, this rugged expanse of high ground was more commonly referred to by U.S. commanders as the Maeda Escarpment because of the
nearby town of Maeda, and ordinary GIs called it various names, including Hacksaw Ridge, Sawtooth Ridge, and simply "that big son of a bitch."
By whatever name it was known, however, the escarpment represented a
logistical nightmare as intricate as any ever devised by military planners.

The 500-foot-high plateau was a formidable enough barrier when
viewed only from its exterior. It stretched about 4,200 yards from east to
west, with the last fifty or sixty feet below its crest consisting of a sheer
wall of rock that could be scaled only with ladders or other special gear.
The crest itself was a narrow, jagged ribbon of rock, ranging in width
from as little as twenty yards to about fifty yards and zeroed in over its
entire length by crisscrossing enemy fields of fire.

The east end of the escarpment was anchored by Conical Hill, Kochi
Ridge, and a jutting spire called Needle Rock that towered above everything else. Anchoring the western end was a cleverly designed Japanese
defense zone containing scores of small positions embedded in a maze of
low coral and limestone ridges known to U.S. map readers as "Item
Pocket." Overall, it was, as the 96th Division's official history phrased it,
"an obstacle calculated to chill the blood of the most hardened infantryman."

As intimidating as the escarpment appeared from the outside, the
biggest part of the nightmare lay concealed deep within its impenetrable
walls. There, thousands of Japanese troops occupied what amounted to a
gigantic subterranean fortress, compared by some historians to an "underground battleship."

Carved into the escarpment was a vast system of caves, many large
enough to hold entire companies of men and connected to one another
by a network of tunnels. Smaller passageways led to gun ports and firing
apertures hollowed into both sides of the ridgeline. Just beyond the escarpment was the town of Maeda, where the Japanese had converted a
group of concrete school buildings into fortified blockhouses. Lower hills
farther south were also dotted with enemy artillery, mortar, and machine-gun emplacements with their guns trained on the top and forward
slopes of the escarpment.

Despite their bitter experiences at Kakazu, many U.S. field commanders still failed to grasp the size, complexity, and sophistication of
the Japanese defenses now facing them. On April 25, General Easley, assistant commander of the 96th, came up to a regimental command post

near the Deadeyes' front lines to study the east end of the escarpment through binoculars. His basic conclusion: Lots of artillery would be needed.

Yet, by now, there was overwhelming evidence that artillery was virtually impotent against this type of defense. Just days earlier, the heaviest artillery barrage yet seen in the Pacific had failed to dent the Japanese defenses at Kakazu, and the fortified bastions along the Maeda Escarpment were even deeper and more nearly impregnable. On April 26, after the usual pounding by Navy guns, Army artillery, and air strikes, Deadeye riflemen briefly occupied the top of the escarpment, but murderous fire from enemy troops and weapons untouched by U.S. bombs and shells immediately chased the GIs back down the northern slope.

The next day, April 27, a high-risk exploratory mission by Captain Louis Reuter Jr., a company commander in the 381st Infantry, led to a startling discovery. Reuter and two enlisted men who accompanied him proved once and for all how extensive and complex the Japanese defensive positions actually were. When the trio found a cave opening on the northern face of the escarpment, they ventured cautiously inside and felt their way along until they saw a shaft of light coming from an opening far above.

The light revealed at least three levels below the Americans' vantage point, and Reuter could hear voices speaking Japanese. As the group crept back toward the cave's entrance, they found another tunnel leading off to their right, and by crawling a short distance in that direction, they reached a room with an observation slit cut through the rock to the outside. Binoculars and a telescope lay on the floor nearby. When Reuter peered through the slit, he could see every major road used by 96th Division troops, and his field of vision stretched as far north as the Hagushi beaches.

The interior of the escarpment, the captain realized, was literally a honeycomb of defensive fortifications and observation posts from which the enemy could see every move the Americans made for miles around—and which no amount of U.S. bombardment was likely to destroy or seriously damage.

Now the three Army divisions facing the escarpment at least had a clear idea of what they were up against. As one 381st Infantry Deadeye put it after being driven off its top as one of thirty-five unwounded survivors out of a company of 160 men: "We were squatting right on the lid of a vast fortress and didn't know it."

U.S. military intelligence, meanwhile, was beginning to speak in terms of enemy "circles of defense." Although the circles were nowhere near concentric, each represented a solid, ingeniously crafted line of fortifications. The first circle had been anchored by Kakazu Ridge and Kakazu West. The wall-like Maeda Escarpment, now blocking the Americans' path and backed by concentrated heavy artillery in the mountain fastness of the so-called Shuri Defense Zone, was the linchpin of the second circle.

Less obvious at the moment was that a third circle of defense was prepared and ready for a last stand by General Ushijima's forces in a system of high ground near the southern tip of Okinawa, anchored by Kunishi Ridge. General Buckner and his staff still believed that, once the escarpment and the Shuri heights were captured, Japanese resistance would collapse, and the battle would be over.

In a psychological sense, it was just as well for the Marines and GIs on the front lines that their commanders hadn't yet guessed the truth.

⌒

IN THE THREE-PLUS WEEKS since the 96th Recon Troop had become one of the first American units to be bloodied by the enemy, its men had rarely enjoyed sleep, rest, or any respite from battle. The troop's mechanized armor was of little use against the heavily entrenched Japanese positions around Kakazu, and the type of small patrols it had used to feel out the enemy on Leyte were hardly feasible. But its three platoons had seen plenty of action, often splitting up and going in three different directions to serve as riflemen/scouts for various infantry regiments—and occasionally even other divisions.

On April 26, however, all three platoons were given the same unsavory assignment: to relieve the Seventh Division Recon Troop and fill a critical gap in the line along the Maeda Escarpment between the Third Battalion of the 383rd Infantry on the east and units of the Seventh Division on the west.

The men left their vehicles at what they judged to be a safe distance to the rear before taking up defensive positions as infantry just below the crest of a low hill. The area was considered a hot spot, a favorite target for Japanese artillery and mortars, but it did possess one saving advantage: A split in the escarpment created a slight defile that offered a measure of protection for the troop's two-man foxholes.

"They shelled us unmercifully for four straight nights," said Tech Five Bill Strain, a native Oklahoman and designated BAR man in the Second Platoon. "Thank God we were on the backside of the crest, where this fault line dropped two or three additional feet, giving us less exposure to the hellacious enemy fire."

After almost a month of lugging his sixteen-pound BAR wherever he went, Strain thought his arms must be at least an inch longer than they'd been on Love Day. To free himself of the heavy weapon at night, he'd adopted a routine of laying it on the edge of the foxhole with the breach toward him and the magazine facing outward. That way, he could grab it and fire almost instantly if Japanese infiltrators showed up, as they often did.

"The Jap artillery didn't fire much during the daytime," Strain said. "They were afraid if they did our spotter planes would pinpoint their locations, but they really poured it on at night."

On the second night, April 27–28, more than 100 rounds of 150-millimeter enemy shells pounded the Second Platoon area, severely damaging two of its supposedly safe trucks but miraculously causing no casualties among the men. During the barrage, however, a chunk of shrapnel struck Strain's BAR, neatly splitting its magazine in half along with every round inside it. Other shell fragments went into the breach of the weapon, causing it to shoot up Strain's web belt and all the spare magazines it contained. The belt was only inches away from Strain, yet he somehow emerged unscathed.

The nighttime bombardments were as frustrating as they were terrifying because there was no way to retaliate against the enemy artillery. But when they abated, enemy soldiers often moved in close to try to overrun the Deadeyes' positions. On the third night, Strain and his foxhole buddy, PFC George "Bill" Allen, got their chance to fight back when infiltrators attacked with grenades.

"The problem was, with my BAR destroyed, the only weapon I had left was a .45 automatic sent to me by my dad," Strain said. "I gave it quite a workout that night."

The Japanese attackers were also plagued by a problem—one that doubtlessly saved many American lives in the course of the Pacific war. Unlike U.S. grenades, the Japanese versions didn't have a spring-loaded striking mechanism to ignite them. Before it would explode, an enemy grenade had to be triggered by a sharp blow, usually against the helmet of the soldier carrying it, but it frequently refused to ignite on the first try.

"Allen and I could hear the sound of those grenades being slammed against the Japs' helmets, followed by a lot of cursing in Japanese," Strain said, "so we just fired at the sound of the swearing, and it worked pretty well. We could understand their anger, but we didn't have a damned bit of sympathy for them."

Finally, on the morning of April 30, all three 96th Recon platoons were withdrawn from the "shooting gallery" where they'd weathered everything the Japanese could throw at them for close to 100 hours, and Strain and his comrades were moved to the rear for a ten-day breather. For his role in the troop's ordeal, Strain was awarded a Bronze Star.

⌐

WITH THE OKINAWA CAMPAIGN now almost a month old, pressure was mounting throughout the U.S. command structure for faster progress. The pressure started at the top with Admiral Nimitz, who was impatient to wind up the campaign so that the entire island could be used as a staging base for the all-out assault on Japan. Nimitz was also disturbed by the heavy toll being taken on Navy ships by the kamikazes—disturbed enough to come to Okinawa in person with his staff to warn General Buckner that the present pace of the campaign was unacceptable.

Nimitz's message was made clear to Admiral Turner, overall commander of U.S. amphibious forces, who, in turn, prodded Buckner to either get his Tenth Army in high gear and keep it there or yield his command to someone who could. The ultimatum caused Buckner to pass the pressure down to his division and regimental commanders.

"Brigadier General Easley now became the man delegated to getting and keeping elements of the 96th Division moving forward," recalled Lieutenant Bob Green, whose 763rd Tank Battalion was seeing its once-invincible Shermans ripped apart like tinfoil by Japanese 47-millimeter guns. "Most of the Maeda Escarpment was in the 96th's sector, and it was the immediate problem holding up the advance of our ground troops."

According to Green, Easley became obsessed with developing a plan to flank enemy positions on the escarpment's reverse slopes. Many of the infantrymen didn't realize how much pressure Easley was under to get the front line moving, Green said. "It seemed to them that he was trying to get them all killed, and it reached the point where they hated to see him coming."

Not all the pressure on Buckner came from above, however. Many of his major subordinates further down the chain of command differed sharply with the Tenth Army commander over how the campaign was being run, and several proposed broad changes in strategy and tactics to break the stalemate in the south.

At the same time, Buckner was confronting what he viewed as serious personnel problems. The ranks of General Hodge's 24th Corps had been thinned drastically by casualties, and although replacements were on the way, they were slow in arriving. Furthermore, ammo for the artillery was still in less-than-plentiful supply after the kamikaze sinking of the two munitions ships.

Speculation continues today about Buckner's seeming reluctance to bring the First and Sixth Marine Divisions, still basically idle but only a few miles from the main combat zone, into the action much earlier than he did. Some observers blame the delay on Buckner's desire to see his own Army troops earn credit for the victory at Okinawa, and this may well have been a factor.

By April 25, the 77th Infantry Division had secured Ie Shima, and Buckner can hardly be faulted for bringing it to southern Okinawa as quickly as possible to relieve the badly bruised 381st and 383rd regiments of the 96th, whose men had taken more casualties and seen more front-line combat than anyone else. The Deadeyes had killed an estimated 2,500 Japanese since starting their new offensive against the Maeda Escarpment, but their own losses had been grievous, and they'd failed to gain much ground in any part of their zone. On April 29, the 77th's 307th Infantry relieved the 381st, and the 383rd was pulled off the line the next day.

Meanwhile, the First Marine Division, arguably the most experienced combat division in the U.S. armed forces—and certainly among the freshest at this point—began its relief of the hard-hit 27th Division on April 30–May 1. But the Sixth Marine Division—70 percent of whose troops were seasoned combat veterans—would remain in limbo until May 7, when it was finally moved onto the line to take over the extreme western flank.

To complicate matters, several of Buckner's division commanders outspokenly favored making a second landing behind the Shuri Line in southern Okinawa to outflank General Ushijima's defensive stronghold. By April 22, Major General Andrew Bruce, commander of the 77th, was urging Buckner to let his division land on the southern coast near Minatoga and establish a second beachhead. Bruce's division had successfully executed a similar maneuver at Leyte, and he was convinced it could repeat that success on Okinawa. Buckner rejected the idea, citing difficult reef conditions at Minatoga, inadequate beaches, and various logistical problems, including the continuing shortage of ammunition.

Students of military tactics still debate the merits of Bruce's strategy, but both General Pedro del Valle, commander of the First Marine Division, and General Lemuel Shepherd, commanding the Sixth Marine Division, reportedly favored the idea of a second landing. Shepherd, in particular, stated after the war that he repeatedly urged Buckner to use the Second Marine Division, sitting in reserve and completely idle, for such a landing. By late April, however, with the diversionary tactics for which the Second Marine Division had been brought to Okinawa complete, the division had returned to Saipan, and bringing it back would have involved tremendous effort, expense, and delay.

In the end, Buckner turned down all plans for a second amphibious assault. Rightly or wrongly, he was convinced that any landing on the southeast coast would be extremely costly to his forces—in his words "another Anzio [referring to the bloody U.S. landing in Italy in 1943], but worse."

In Buckner's view, it was far more vital to relieve his beaten-down infantry divisions with fresh troops so that the Tenth Army could continue to exert maximum pressure against the main Japanese defensive line.

⌒

ALTHOUGH THE 27TH DIVISION'S original projected role was to serve as the postbattle occupation force for Okinawa, not as a frontline combat unit, it had acquitted itself well. Major General George W. Griner, commander of the New York National Guard division, had trained his troops hard, but after heavy action at Makin, Eniwetok, and Saipan, they arrived at Okinawa shorthanded, with only about 16,000 men, compared to 22,000 to 24,000 for the other engaged U.S. divisions.

Then the prolonged fight for Item Pocket, which was basically over by April 27, had drained the understrength division so severely that it could do little but cling to a defensive perimeter during the final days of the month. When units of the First Marine Division moved in to relieve the 27th on May 1, the GIs were an exhausted, hollow-eyed lot as they filed off the line past the incoming Marines.

"Shortly, a column of men approached us on the other side of the road," recalled PFC Gene Sledge of K/3/5. "Their tragic expressions revealed where they had been. They were dead beat, dirty, and grisly. . . . I hadn't seen such faces since Peleliu."

Except for an occasional nod or grunt, there were few attempts at communication between the Army and Marine troops as the two columns passed each other.

"The Army guys were so beat up and wiped out, I don't know if they had the strength to talk," said Corporal Sterling Mace of K/3/5's Third Platoon. "And for sure, none of us who were replacing them felt like saying, 'Well, so long, guys. Have a nice life'—not when we were heading into the same shit they were leaving."

Once in a while, though, two pairs of eyes met, and a man felt moved to speak to another.

"It's hell up there, Marine," one tight-faced GI muttered to Sledge as he shambled past.

"I know," Sledge responded, a bit miffed that the GI might think he was a "boot." "I was at Peleliu."

The GI stared blankly at him and stumbled on.

"Keep your five-pace interval!" an officer warned the Marines. "Get off the road, stay in dispersed order, and don't bunch up!"

As the company started at double-time across an open field, Japanese artillery and mortars opened fire as if on cue. The thunder of their explosions shook the ground, and craters blossomed in all directions, vomiting up geysers of dirt and rock. Suddenly, everybody was running and dodging at once, the Marines in one direction and the GIs of the 27th in the other.

The pop and chatter of enemy rifle and machine-gun fire joined the roar of larger shells. The metallic twang of 50-millimeter knee mortars brought puffs of smoke erupting from the ground like dirty gray flowers. Canister shot from 47-millimeter antitank weapons, designed to cut men to ribbons, whined across the field. Shells from 150-millimeter howitzers rumbled out of the sky, blasting craters ten feet wide.

"Corpsman! Corpsman!" the anguished cries came. "Stretcher bearer!"

"Use your smoke grenades!" someone to the rear yelled. "For God's sake, make smoke before they chew us to pieces!"

As Sledge raced for his life up the gentle slope of the ridge, he saw shock and naked fear in the faces of the men around him. For once, his always-talkative friend and squad mate, Corporal Merriel "Snafu" Shelton, was too busy running to utter a word. Even crusty Sergeant R. V. Burgin, a three-campaign veteran and the senior noncom in the K/3/5 mortar section, wore an expression of stunned dismay.

"Hit the deck, and dig, damn it, dig!" Burgin howled as they threw themselves to the dirt.

Sledge described the scene as "an appalling chaos" and a "bedlam of racket and confusion." Making the shelling infinitely worse was the abrupt jolt of leaving the tranquil countryside of the past month and plunging, in the space of a few moments, into the deadliest storm of fire and steel that any man in K/3/5 had yet witnessed.

As he and Snafu Shelton hurriedly gouged out a pit for their 60-millimeter mortar, Sledge wondered what had happened to the haggard 27th Division GI who had spoken to him as they passed. Sledge could still hear the man's plaintive words. He would remember them for the rest of his life:

"It's hell up there, Marine."

The soldier's warning had been prophetic. Seconds later, the very hell of which the GI spoke had erupted again, and he and his comrades had been caught in the middle of it, along with K/3/5. Concerned as he was for himself, Sledge couldn't help feeling sorry for the battle-worn scarecrows of the 27th, whose only wish was to keep from being killed during the last few critical moments before they reached safety.

If that one particular GI had made it out alive, Sledge thought, the hell was probably all over for him. Rumor had it that the 27th Division was being sent to the uneventful west coast of northern Okinawa to rest, recuperate, and guard against the unlikely possibility of an enemy counterlanding. In other words, the GI and his mates would soon be experiencing the same easy, nonthreatening life that the First Marine Division had enjoyed for the past month.

For Sledge, Shelton, Burgin, Mace, and other members of K/3/5, however, the worst of Okinawa's hell was just beginning.

4

5

6

Early on, Marines and GIs advanced rapidly past
Okinawan farms (top) with no signs of the enemy
and few shots fired. Army General Simon Buckner
(above left) and Marine General Roy Geiger (right,
same photo), commanding the assault force, were
amazed by the lack of opposition, but Japanese
Generals Mitsuru Ushijima (above right) and
Isamu Cho (below right) had prepared a nasty
surprise as the invaders attempted to move south.

7

1

2

On Love Day—April 1, 1945—with the battleship *Tennessee* blazing away in the background (top), a landing craft heads for Okinawa's invasion beaches and a major surprise: the beaches were undefended. A day later, supplies poured ashore unimpeded (above), and many American troops found time to "adopt" Okinawan ponies (left).

3

8

9

Abandoned Japanese
fortifications (top) were found
in many of the sacred family
tombs that dotted the
Okinawan landscape. Small
suicide boats intended for
attacks against U.S. ships
(above) were seized and
destroyed by U.S. forces on
lightly defended offshore
islands. Other "souvenirs" left
behind by an invisible enemy
included bombs hidden in
cabbage plants (right).

10

GIs of H Company, 382nd Infantry (top left), struggle toward Kakazu Ridge, site of Okinawa's first bloody impasse, where 96th Division troops under General Claudius Easley (upper right) and Colonel Eddy May (middle right) suffered heavy losses. Members of the 96th Recon Troop (lower left), were among the first U.S. soldiers to collide with strong Japanese forces on April 4. Corporal John Cain (lower right) received a Silver Star for his life-saving heroism that day.

17

16

18

19

Surviving "lardtails" of Company L, 383rd Infantry, sprawl exhausted (top left) after being driven from the crest of Kakazu Ridge. Meanwhile, troops of the Seventh Infantry Division (center), including the anti-tank platoon led by Sergeants Porter McLaughlin (top photo, upper right) and George Murphy (lower photo, upper right), were also caught up in fierce fighting. Even the smallest Japanese caves (left) could spell big trouble.

20

21

22

23

24

Acting Sergeant Jack Armstrong (top right and second from left, top left) commanded a Sherman tank called "Ticket to Tokyo" until it was blown out from under him, killing its driver, Corporal Alvin Tenbarge (standing, top left photo). Armstrong and his fellow tankers provided vital support for front-line infantry of the First Marine Division (center) by blasting enemy gun positions like the one at left.

25

26

Beginning in early May, torrential rains turned the battlefield into a huge quagmire and continued day after day during Okinawa's bloodiest month. The downpours flooded bivouac areas (top), bogged down all types of equipment (above), and made it next to impossible to dig foxholes. There was, however, no shortage of water for shaving.

27

28

29

30

A Japanese "Oscar" suicide plane (top inset) closes in on the U.S. destroyer *Laffey* (top) during mass kamikaze attacks on April 16, 1945. Two other suiciders left a yawning hole in the hangar deck of the carrier *Bunker Hill* (above) killing or wounding 650 seamen. When the Japanese super battleship *Yamato* was attacked and sunk by U.S. dive-bombers and torpedo planes (right), 90 percent of her 2,767-man crew perished with her.

31

33

32

34

35

The destroyer *Hugh Hadley* (top, inset) became Okinawa's champion kamikaze killer on May 11, when its gunners (top) downed 23 Japanese planes, bringing its total kills to 25. Lieutenant Doug Aitken (above, wearing cap), along with other crewmen and the *Hadley*'s skipper, Commander Joe Mullaney (above right), managed to keep their crippled ship afloat. The carrier *Enterprise* (in distance, right), flagship of Admiral Marc Mitscher, also survived three direct kamikaze hits on the same day.

36

Tracer bullets crisscross the skies above Okinawa's Yontan Airfield (left), where a Japanese "Sally" bomber filled with guerilla raiders (center photo) crash-landed to attack U.S. planes on the night of May 24. The raiders damaged nine aircraft before the last of them was killed (below). Marine Sergeants C. J. Haines and Walt McNeel (bottom inset) show off a "scoreboard" of enemy planes shot down by their Yontan-based night fighter squadron.

37

38

39

40

41

42

43

44

45

46

Marine flyers scramble to their planes (top left) as enemy "bogies" approach. Yontan-based night-fighter pilots scoring radar-assisted "kills" included (left to right, center) Lieutenants Arthur Arceneaux, Frank O'Hara, and Herbert Groff. Lieutenant Fred Hilliard (top right) was lost after downing a Japanese Zero. Above, wrecked Japanese planes litter the area around the airfield.

Sugar Loaf Hill (top) didn't look like much from a distance, but it was a major linchpin of the Shuri Line. Among the Marines bloodied while charging its slopes were (left, top to bottom) PFC Ray Schlinder, Corporal Walt Rutkowski, and Major Henry Courtney, who was posthumously awarded the Medal of Honor. Other Marines battled their way up Wana Ridge (center), where medics and stretcher bearers (above) faced a flood of wounded.

Flame-throwers like the one (below) operated by Corporal Melvin Grant (as his assistant, Private Ricky Cuerton, covers him) were vital in cracking the Shuri Line. Only after Marine riflemen battled snipers amid the ruins of Shuri Town (bottom) and charged enemy positions across mercilessly open ground could the Stars and Stripes be hoisted above shell-battered Shuri Castle (left).

53

54

55

57

56

Caught between two armies, Okinawa's civilians suffered a calamitous tragedy that claimed an estimated 150,000 innocent lives. As fleeing refugees lined the island's roads (top), U.S. troops did their best to help the aged and infirm (above and right), and provide care for small children. But piles of human bones (bottom) remained after the battle as grisly evidence of mass civilian suicides triggered by unfounded fears of Americans.

58

59

60

Corporal Dan Lawler (right), a Marine machine gunner, collected numerous personal photographs (left and below) from the bodies of Okinawan and Japanese soldiers, many of whom Lawler had killed himself. But his most haunting souvenir (above) was found on a wall in a shelled-out girls' school where many of the pictured students and faculty had died violently a short time earlier.

62

61

63

64

65

66

The end of the Okinawa struggle brought a broad spectrum of emotions to American fighting men. Framed by a massive shell hole in the wall of a demolished theater (top), a lone Marine surveys the ravaged capital city of Naha. Among rows of white crosses (below), Tenth Army GIs and Marines mourned their commander, General Buckner, who was killed in action on June 18, but three days later, they celebrated on Hill 89 (right) near where Japanese Generals Ushijima and Cho committed hara-kiri.

67

68

CHAPTER EIGHT

Mud, Blood, and May-hem

A S OF MAY 1 (L-plus-30), the weary GIs of the Seventh Division's three infantry regiments had been in continuous combat for nearly four weeks. But unlike their equally battle-worn comrades in the 27th and 96th Divisions, who had been pulled off the line at the end of April and sent to rear areas for rest and recuperation, the Seventh's infantrymen had remained at the front with no firm word on when they might expect relief.

Whether advancing, retreating, or huddled in their foxholes, they were pounded day and night by Japanese artillery and mortar fire. Now and then, they'd get a brief respite from the shelling, and, for lengthy intervals, the firing would be only sporadic. But it was impossible to relax because each man knew the next enemy round that roared overhead could be the "big one."

Only overwhelming exhaustion made sleep possible, and enemy infiltrators haunted the nights. Meals were almost always K-rations, gulped between firefights and during bombardments. Uniforms, unchanged for nearly a month, were stiff with sweat and dirt, frequently mixed with blood, urine, and feces. For men under fire, the procedures of civilized hygiene were strictly low priority. Men saw their buddies riddled with bullets and blown to bits by bursting shells every day, so why should they care if someone saw them soil or wet their pants?

When unrelenting misery and stress drag on, day after day and with no end in sight, every passing hour pushes each man closer to his personal breaking point. Add torrential rains and endless mud to this evil milieu, as did the arrival of May, and the psychological burdens weigh even heavier.

Under such oppressive conditions, even good soldiers can crack—and many of them did in May 1945 in the ridges of southern Okinawa.

AFTER ALMOST A MONTH on the move, Army Tech Sergeant Porter McLaughlin's antitank platoon had parked two of its 37-millimeter guns, but the third gun was still being kept close at hand for use as a giant sniper rifle. There were no Japanese tanks to be found, and the 37s' short range made them useless against targets more than a few hundred yards away, but they provided an effective response to dug-in enemy machine-gun and small-arms positions.

For the most part, McLaughlin's unit had been functioning since mid-April as a regular rifle platoon in the Seventh Division's 32nd Regiment, Second Battalion. Along with flamethrowers, BARs, M-1s, and grenades, the remaining antitank gun had seen extensive action during mopping-up operations against bypassed Japanese caves.

"We were taking a lot of artillery fire wherever we went," McLaughlin said. "The Japs knew the place like the palms of their hands, and they had every crossroads and grove of trees zeroed in."

By this time, many men had the eerie feeling that the enemy gunners were watching them every second. As one member of the platoon told McLaughlin: "I'm starting to think the damned Japs have a shell with the name of each guy here engraved on it."

If it were true, the enemy missile bearing the name of PFC Adrian Henry, a handsome, sandy-haired twenty-year-old recent replacement from Niagara Falls, New York, came screaming in just as McLaughlin led the platoon into a small, shell-blasted village. McLaughlin's trained ear heard the round coming a few seconds before it hit.

"Incoming mail!" he shouted. "Take cover!"

A driving rainstorm had struck a short time earlier, leaving the soldiers wading through slippery, ankle-deep mud in soaked uniforms. McLaughlin hit the boggy ground, sliding on his stomach through the mire. Then he watched, as if in slow motion, as Henry ducked behind a free-standing wall—all that remained of a shelled-out farmhouse—while another GI did a belly flop in the mud on the opposite side of the wall.

An instant later, the shell hit on Henry's side of the barrier, demolishing what was left of the wall and killing the young soldier instantly. McLaughlin saw his body hurled into the air by the force of the blast, then fall back into the mud like a worn-out rag doll.

Nearby, the second GI—Porter couldn't remember his name, but most guys in the outfit called him "the Indian" because he was part Navajo—pulled himself from under a pile of debris and stumbled to his feet. Shaking his head but seemingly unhurt, he staggered over to Henry's body, stooped beside it, and carefully removed a .45 automatic from the dead man's web belt.

Though dazed by the blast, McLaughlin immediately recognized the pistol as the Indian shoved it under his own belt and lurched away. PFCs didn't usually carry .45s, but this one had been Henry's most treasured possession, a gift from his father, who'd carried the weapon across France in World War I.

"Hey, what're you doin'?" McLaughlin yelled hoarsely.

The Indian seemed not to hear. He sprang back to his feet, cast a wild-eyed glance toward McLaughlin, then darted through the mud back in the direction from which the platoon had come.

McLaughlin had always respected the Indian as a good man and a dependable soldier—never the type to steal a dead comrade's pistol and run away with it—and he couldn't understand what he was seeing.

Then McLaughlin heard another incoming shell, and he sensed that this one was going to hit about as close as the other one had. He fell back into the mud, covering his head with both arms. As the shell exploded a dozen yards away, something hot and heavy hit him in the back, knocking the wind out of him.

For a second, McLaughlin thought the shell had had his name on it, but when he managed to sit up, he realized he'd merely been blindsided by a chunk of steaming mud the size of a basketball. The force of the explosion had torn it from the ground and slammed it squarely between his shoulder blades. A few feet away, he noticed a blown-off human foot lying in the mud almost within arm's reach. Another shell exploded nearby, quickly followed by another.

"You okay, Mac?" he heard his buddy, Sergeant John Knorr, asking.

"Yeah, let's get out of here," McLaughlin croaked, struggling to his feet. "The Japs've got our range for sure."

As he made his way toward the edge of the village, he looked around for the GI who'd taken Henry's .45, but "the Indian" was gone. Porter never saw him or the pistol again, but he learned later at battalion head-quarters that the runaway had been diagnosed with battle fatigue and sent to a psychiatric unit.

"The battalion CO wanted to court-martial him," McLaughlin said, "but the docs said he was shell-shocked and didn't even know where he was. He was totally out of his head."

Before May was half over, the Indian's malady would become epidemic.

UNTOLD NUMBERS of historians, journalists, and military observers—not to mention thousands of ordinary enlisted men who suffered through it—have attempted to describe conditions and events that prevailed in southern Okinawa during May 1945. But none has fully succeeded in capturing the unmitigated horror of that time and place—a horror that defies not only human verbal skills but human imagination as well.

Words, no matter how graphic, inevitably fall short. Even tears, curses, and other emotional eruptions can't convey the total impact of what happened there. Maybe this is why so many Okinawa veterans have chosen to take their memories of that awful month to the grave rather than try to explain the horror to friends and families.

Ironically, half a world away in the European Theater of Operations, it was the best of times. On May 8, after nearly six years, millions of deaths, and incalculable destruction, the war in Europe ended. Nazi Germany surrendered. Adolf Hitler committed suicide. Back home in the States, millions of Americans poured into the streets to celebrate VE—"Victory in Europe"—Day. And from Paris to Panama and London to Luzon, most of the 8 million men and women in the U.S. armed services joined the revelry. Navy ships off the Hagushi beachhead fired thousands of rounds to mark the event, creating such an uproar that many troops ashore thought the Japanese were launching a counterinvasion.

But for American ground forces at Okinawa, it was unquestionably the worst of times. Mourning, misery, and terror were the order of each day. May 1945 would rank among the deadliest months in the history of the U.S. military, and the higher the casualty count soared, the more the reports of peace in Europe resembled a taunting fantasy.

As K/3/5's PFC Gene Sledge put it: "We were resigned only to the fact that the Japanese would fight to total extinction on Okinawa, as they had elsewhere, and that Japan would have to be invaded with the same gruesome prospects. Nazi Germany might as well have been on the moon."

APRIL 29 was Emperor Hirohito's birthday and the most notable holiday on the Japanese calendar. That evening, General Ushijima called his staff together for a meeting in the spacious cave 100 feet below Shuri Castle that housed the headquarters of Japan's 32nd Army.

Ushijima himself took no part in the heated discussion that dominated the meeting, preferring to let each staff officer have his say concerning the current combat situation. Much of the talking was done by General Cho, Ushijima's fiery—and increasingly impatient—chief of staff.

"We must mount a massive counterattack while we still have the strength!" Cho stormed. "In a few more weeks, attrition will have eaten away at our forces, and we will be too weak to take the offensive. We must strike now and destroy the Americans, even at the risk of losing our whole army. Better we should all die fighting than to keep slipping passively toward sure defeat!"

Cho's ringing call for offensive action fell, for the most part, on receptive ears. Of all the officers present, only Colonel Yahara, the mastermind of Japanese defensive strategy on Okinawa, rose to speak in opposition.

"It is a stark reality that the enemy has penetrated the Shuri Defense Zone by up to two kilometers in one month of fighting," Yahara admitted. "But it is also true that on no other invaded island have our forces held out for so long with major elements intact. The Americans have suffered great losses, and the 32nd Army is still strong enough to offer prolonged resistance. But it would be folly to attack, because to break through the American lines on the high ground would demand much greater forces than we possess.

"Therefore, the army must continue its current operations," Yahara concluded, "calmly recognizing its final destiny, for annihilation is inevitable, no matter what is done."

A few of his more conservative fellow officers shared Yahara's view, but most showed no enthusiasm for the colonel's grim projections. Cho, on the other hand, offered an audacious, detailed plan to smash the American front, annihilate four U.S. divisions, and uphold the honor of the 32nd Army. Just after midnight on April 30, with passions fueled by large quantities of sake, Cho's plan was approved by a resounding majority of the officers, along with a recommendation to launch the main attack before daylight on May 4.

Clearly, Cho had spent a great deal of time working out the details of his plan: Japan's 24th Division was to seize the eastern end of the Maeda Escarpment and the town of Maeda, gaining control of Highway 5. Then the 44th Brigade would drive to the west coast and cut off the First and Sixth Marine Divisions. With help from the 62nd Division, the 44th Brigade would wipe out the Marines even as the 24th Division was re-capturing the escarpment. On the east side of the island, meanwhile, two Japanese infantry regiments would attack the U.S. Seventh Division from high ground around Conical Hill.

Cho considered the area near the town of Maeda the key to the en-tire offensive, so he assigned extra infantry and two companies of light and medium tanks to bolster the attack there. He also arranged for a preattack barrage by heavy artillery and even managed to line up air sup-port, a rarity for Japanese ground troops at Okinawa. On the evening of May 3, Japanese bombers would attack both Yontan and Kadena airfields as well as rear areas of the U.S. Tenth Army, and on the morning of May 4, coinciding with the first phase of the offensive, a major kamikaze at-tack would be directed at U.S. ships offshore.

Within three or four days, Cho believed, his forces could drive the Americans back some three and a half miles to an east-west line running all the way across the island and through the town of Futema, headquar-ters of the U.S. 96th Division (which Cho erroneously identified as Gen-eral Buckner's headquarters). At that point, Cho concluded, even if the line couldn't be held by surviving Japanese troops, the Imperial Army would at least have preserved its honor—something it could never do by hiding in holes and waiting to die.

When the recommendation was presented to Ushijima, he ratified it with a swiftness that must have stunned Yahara and with almost no dis-cussion—except to express his own personal willingness to fight to the end in one final desperate bid for victory. A short time later, official or-ders were issued for what would be the Japanese army's last—and blood-iest—offensive of the war.

As the orders made their way down the chain of command to indi-vidual units of the spearheading Japanese 24th Division, their intent was clear and their wording straight to the point:

"Display a combined strength. Each soldier will kill at least one American devil."

EXCEPT FOR OCCASIONAL SHOWERS, the whole month of April had been characterized by clear, generally pleasant weather. But the arrival of May signaled an abrupt—and unwelcome—change. Torrential rains began to fall almost as soon as the calendar turned and continued for most of the month.

"It has rained all day here today," wrote PFC Alfred "Al" Henderson of the 96th Recon Troop in a letter dated May 2 to his wife, Gladys, back in Pine Bluff, Arkansas. "Sure be glad when the sun comes out and stays out. It is really muddy and cold. If this keeps up, we will need overcoats."

And it *did* keep up, day after day after day, with only occasional respites. Henderson was fortunate that his platoon had just been pulled off the front lines and sent to a rear area for a few days to guard a hospital and rest. Instead of muddy foxholes, he and his buddies had three-man tents, comfortable cots, clean blankets, and three hot meals a day. "What a treat!" Henderson wrote, "and the chow's really good, too."

For Marines and GIs at the front, meanwhile, the effects of the daily downpours were much more miserable—and dangerous.

"Every morning, there was six inches of water in our foxholes, and the rain just went on and on," said PFC Harry Bender of K/3/5's First Platoon. "Pretty soon, the mud was shin-deep, and the hills were so slippery you could hardly stand up when they ordered you to advance. The Japs rigged a kind of booby trap by burying grenades in the mud with only their plungers sticking up, so if you stepped on one of them, it'd explode. You had to watch out for them constantly."

⟶

ALONG THE LINE where K and L Companies of the First Marines' Third Battalion replaced the beat-up GIs of the 27th Division on May 1, there was no respite from the enemy artillery fire. Brief interludes of nail-biting quiet were inevitably shattered by the rumble of incoming ordnance, particularly from one huge 150-millimeter battery that the Japanese rolled in and out of a cave on railroad tracks..

After forty-eight hours of this, Sergeant George Peto, an "old man" of twenty-two from Akron, Ohio, and a Marine since the summer of '41, felt as if he'd been under fire for a solid month. "At first, we were confident that we could move against the Japs," Peto recalled decades later, "but we were badly mistaken. All we could do was hunker down while they pounded the hell out of us."

Peto was no stranger to tough combat conditions. His mortar section had been instrumental in rescuing eighteen survivors out of a First

Marines company of 235 from a besieged coral knob called "the Point" on Peleliu. In three major campaigns, Peto had had more close calls than he could count. Just hours before, a six-inch shell had blasted the observation post where he was directing 81-millimeter mortar fire. Peto had been knocked off his feet, showered with debris, and had his phone ripped from his hand.

"Damn, we thought sure you were dead," one of his fellow mortarmen told Peto when the dirt-covered sergeant staggered out of the ravaged observation post. But except for a few bruises and scratches, Peto was unhurt. So far, nothing the enemy had thrown at him in more than two years had hit home.

The same couldn't be said about Peto's closest friend, Corporal Henry Rucker of Gaffney, South Carolina. Rucker had been severely wounded by a Japanese machine gun at Peleliu, then spent months in a hospital only to have the misfortune of recovering in time for Okinawa.

"I called him the 'hard luck kid' because if Rucker didn't have bad luck, I guess you could say he wouldn't have had any luck at all," Peto said. "But from the first day we met, when we were both fresh out of boot camp at Parris Island, we formed an instant friendship that grew stronger as time went by."

Around midday on May 3, during a momentary lull in the shelling, Peto paused on his way to his new observation post beside a group of seven Marines who were bunched close together among some rocks. His best buddy Rucker was among them.

"You guys better get out of that huddle and put some space between yourselves," Peto said. "One shell from that Jap 150 could take you all out in the blink of an eye."

"Aw, don't worry about it," Rucker responded. "We'll be all right. Just watch yourself in that OP. You're the one who damned near bought it the other day."

Peto shrugged. "Okay, but don't say I didn't warn you."

As he walked on, Peto thought how nice it would be to be back in Melbourne, where he and Rucker had spent so many carefree weekend liberties together while they were camped near the Australian city in '43. They'd both found more-or-less steady girlfriends in Melbourne, and the woman Rucker was dating managed a fancy restaurant where they could always get a great meal for no charge. After a second, the memory burst like a bubble and was gone.

Peto had gone only a couple dozen steps when he heard the enemy shell coming. It sounded like a freight train, and Peto hit the deck just as it exploded. A moment later, he glanced back toward where Rucker and the other Marines had been, but all he could see was smoke and flying debris. Then the smoke cleared and he saw the bodies scattered like bundles of old clothes on the ground. He felt his guts go numb as he realized one of them was Rucker.

"Corpsman!" Peto screamed. He stumbled back toward where his buddy lay, but before he got close enough to see Rucker, Peto's lieutenant caught him by the shoulder and held him back.

"You don't want to see this, George," the lieutenant said. "Just let the medics handle it."

Two of the seven Marines had been killed instantly, and Rucker was near death with a gaping wound in his abdomen, one arm a mutilated stump, and shrapnel wounds over his entire body. A few feet away, one of PFC Charles Kelly's legs dangled by a thin string of flesh, which a corpsman severed before Kelly was loaded onto a stretcher. Three other men were seriously wounded.

"Gimme my damn leg," Kelly groaned. "I ain't leavin' here without my damn leg!" The corpsman obliged by placing the leg on the stretcher beside Kelly.

"Cut my stomach open," Rucker pleaded as another corpsman worked over him. "I'm burning up inside. I can't stand the pressure." The corpsman cut off Rucker's cartridge belt instead, which relieved his pain a little.

"I don't see how he can make it," the medic said, "but let's get him out of here."

The "hard-luck kid" surprised everybody in the outfit by clinging to life until the next morning, when he died aboard a hospital ship.

—⁀—

At 4:30 A.M. on May 4, a massive Japanese artillery barrage roared out of the wet darkness along the Maeda Escarpment, signaling the start of the great counteroffensive designed by General Cho and approved by General Ushijima. Within the next thirty minutes, some 8,000 rounds would hammer the Seventh Division zone along the east coast, and another 4,000 would pound the 77th Division area on the Seventh's right.

Several hours before the big guns fired their first salvoes, however, the enemy offensive had already gotten off to an ominous beginning.

Around midnight, two Japanese engineer/shipping regiments attempted landings on the east and west coasts of Okinawa, using the remnants of the enemy's suicide motorboat fleet. But Navy ships and Army guard units spotted the east coast attackers while they were still on the water, killing almost all of them before they ever reached shore. The west coast attackers managed to land but were wiped out almost to a man by troops of the First Marine and 96th Infantry Divisions. In all, about 1,000 Japanese were killed.

Meanwhile, trouble for troops of the Seventh and 77th Divisions had started as early as 3:00 A.M., when GIs heard Japanese voices and the clatter of moving tanks as a large group of infiltrators tried to slip past their lines. A platoon-sized force of riflemen and an undetermined number of tanks made it through, only to be trapped behind American lines and cut to pieces.

By 7:30 A.M., just three hours after the opening artillery barrage, the momentum of the Japanese offensive had all but dissolved. Violent fighting continued all day and through the night of May 4–5, but the Japanese were no more able to dislodge the Americans from their well-entrenched positions than the Americans had been when the situation was reversed.

The outcomes of numerous small, ferocious engagements help explain why the offensive collapsed.

   • A five-man artillery observation team, led by PFC Richard Hammond and positioned on a hilltop beneath a rocky knob to fill a gap in U.S. lines between the 306th Infantry's First and Third Battalions, fought off repeated charges by scores of screaming Japanese. Private Joseph Zinfini was killed by an enemy bullet to the head, and Hammond and all three of his other comrades were seriously wounded, but they held on until a patrol from the 306th routed the attackers. The fleeing Japanese left more than 100 bodies behind against American losses of one killed and four wounded.
   • Captain Edward S. Robbins and his shorthanded E Company of the 306th were dug in on a hill east of Highway 5 when a large force of Japanese attacked out of the darkness at 4:40 A.M. on May 5. Fifteen minutes later, the enemy was in retreat, and Robbins's company was counterattacking along with several other companies. At day's end, more than

800 enemy dead were counted, and six Japanese tanks had been destroyed.

• At first light on May 5, Lieutenant Richard Mc-Cracken, commanding A Company of the Seventh Division's 184th Infantry, was observing from a position that allowed him an extended view of the flats along the east coast, when he spotted a target that left him almost speech-less: By McCracken's estimate, about 2,000 enemy soldiers were congregated in plain sight in a wide-open area at the foot of a hill known as Y2 Ridge, on top of which was the First Battalion command post.

Unable to contact artillery directly, McCracken called Colonel Daniel Maybury, his battalion commander. "Sir! Sir!" McCracken gasped. "There's Japs all over the place down there. There must be two battalions of them, and they're all sitting ducks!"

"Great!" Maybury replied, equally excited. "For once, we've finally got them outside their damned caves and in the open."

"Yes, sir," said McCracken, "but we need to move fast on this. A bunch of these Japs are right at the base of your hill and no more than 100 yards from where you're sitting."

"Oh, no," Maybury argued, "that's a patrol from Company K down there."

"I don't know who the hell it is," said McCracken, "but there's a lot of them, and they've got two field pieces pointed right at your CP."

Maybury cursed and rang off to call in mortar and ar-tillery fire. In the meantime, two U.S. tanks showed up and opened fire on the Japanese manning the two 75-millimeter guns. By late morning, both Japanese battalions, trapped in the open without cover while waiting for transportation, had lost well over half their men and most of their officers.

Early on that second morning, a tearful General Ushijima, who had watched the debacle unfold from a vantage point atop the Shuri heights, told Colonel Yahara the offensive was at an end, and that, henceforth, he would defer to Yahara's judgment on the best use of his remaining troops. By afternoon, even General Cho was forced to admit that his offensive was a disastrous failure, and at 6:00 P.M., Ushijima ordered his army to resume its defensive positions.

Cho's offensive had left the 32nd Army with more than 6,000 dead and most of its tanks destroyed, but American losses also ran high. The First Marine Division reported 649 killed, wounded, or missing in the two days of fighting, and the Seventh and 77th Infantry Divisions listed a combined total of 687 casualties for the same period.

It was, and would remain, Ushijima's only serious tactical mistake of the campaign, but it had cost the Japanese defenders dearly. As the U.S. Army's official history of the Okinawa campaign bluntly expressed it: "Over-ambitiously conceived and ineptly executed, the offensive was a colossal blunder."

For the First Marine Division, the contrast between the last days of April and the first days of May could hardly have been more pronounced. The pure shock of the change was comparable to being kicked out of paradise into the deepest, hottest depths of perdition. In the words of George McMillan, author of *The Old Breed*, it required "some severe readjustments."

K/3/5 had recorded its first combat death of the campaign on the afternoon of May 1. Corporal Howard Nease, renowned as the man who treated his comrades to all the purloined turkey from the officers' mess that they could eat on New Year's Eve 1944 at the rest-camp island of Pavuvu, was killed by shrapnel as the company ran through artillery fire to relieve the Army's 106th Infantry.

Then, at 9:00 A.M. on May 2, in a driving rainstorm, K/3/5's three rifle platoons jumped off with the rest of the Third Battalion, Fifth Marines, to assault the same ridges that had held the GIs of the 106th at bay for days—and with the same disheartening results.

PFC Gene Sledge prayed for the charging rifle platoons as he watched from his mortar position. "The riflemen hardly got out of their foxholes when a storm of enemy fire from our front and left flank forced them back," Sledge recalled. "The same thing was happening to the battalions on our right and left."

"We hadn't gone but about 100 yards when they hit us with a deluge of mortar fire," said PFC Bill Leyden, leading a fire team in the First Platoon. "There must've been a thousand Jap knee mortars up there."

Four men from K/3/5—Sergeant John P. Heeb and PFCs Harman Baur, Cecil Stout, and Marion Westbrook—were killed that day. Eight others were wounded, including First Lieutenant Bucky Pearson, commander of the First Platoon. Sledge and three of his fellow mortarmen answered an urgent call for stretcher bearers to carry critically injured Marines out of the line of fire.

Gunnery Sergeant Hank Boyes, winner of a Silver Star at Peleliu for directing the destruction of a major Japanese pillbox, guided his men to safety through a cut in the ridgeline, then threw smoke grenades to cover their retreat as a firestorm of machine gun, mortar, and small arms fire roared around him.

Boyes was the last man to make it through the crossfire in the cut. When he got back to the company lines, he had a bullet hole through his dungaree cap, another through his pants leg, and he was bleeding from knee mortar fragments in his leg.

"You need to get to an aid station, Hank," somebody told him. "Want me to call a corpsman?"

"Forget it," Boyes said. "I'll take care of it myself, and I'm staying right here."

May 3 was a repeat of the same action with a similarly grim outcome for K/3/5: Privates Wilburn L. Beasley and Jay W. Whitaker were killed and ten others wounded. (Lieutenant Pearson returned to duty after four days, but all the other wounded except Boyes were evacuated.)

After less than sixty hours of combat, the company had lost twenty-four men—10 percent of its total strength.

Then, on May 4, came the big Japanese counteroffensive. One of its primary objectives was to isolate and destroy the First Marine Division.

—⁊

MARINE CORPORAL JACK ARMSTRONG, commander of a Sherman tank that had recently become the only one in Armstrong's platoon equipped with a flamethrower for cave busting, woke up with a bad feeling on the morning of May 4. As it turned out, the feeling was amply justified.

"The tank-mounted flamethrower was a terrific weapon and a lot more effective than the handheld kind," Armstrong said, "but that big cylinder of napalm that went with it made me nervous. I figured if a Jap shell hit that thing, we'd all be deep-fried in a matter of seconds. I felt the same way about the gasoline-powered tanks the Army used, and I was really thankful that ours was a diesel."

Armstrong had plenty of company in these sentiments. As his fellow Marine tank commander and fellow Texan Corporal Floyd Cockerham put it: "The Marine high command deserves credit for refusing to accept gasoline-powered tanks. The twin-engine diesels we had were just right. They had a top speed of thirty-five miles per hour, which was good considering their size, and we never lost a single one to an in-tank explosion."

Until five days earlier, when it was ordered to the front to support the First Marine Division's three infantry regiments, the First Marine Tank Battalion had been living the proverbial "life of Riley" in the quiet countryside north of the combat zone (as the irrepressible Private Howard Towry could attest). But as a veteran of Cape Gloucester and Peleliu, Armstrong had known the good times couldn't last forever. In fact, he considered it a miracle that the battalion hadn't been thrown into the fighting much earlier.

After seeing so many of their own tanks destroyed or disabled in the fight for Kakazu Ridge, Army brass had been trying for the past two weeks to get their hands on the Marines' unblemished Shermans. Only strong objections by General Roy Geiger, overall Marine Corps commander at Okinawa, coupled with a direct appeal to General Buckner, had kept the battalion from being transferred to Army control.

Armstrong was glad that he and his crew were able to partner with a five-man fire team of Marine infantry. Every Sherman in the platoon had its own assigned fire team, and although they changed from time to time, the infantrymen and tankers felt a strong sense of kinship and mutual support.

"Our fire team saved our bacon more than once when Japs tried to hit us with TNT or Molotov cocktails," Armstrong said.

The foot soldiers got a kick out of Armstrong's having nicknamed his tank "Ticket to Tokyo." They also liked hitching a ride on the Sherman's deck when there were no enemy snipers around, but they balked at riding inside.

"I feel trapped in there, man," one of them told Armstrong, "like I'm in a damned steel coffin. It scares the hell out of me."

"That's funny," Jack retorted. "What scares me is walking around outside with no protection, like you guys do. I feel a whole lot safer down in the guts of this tank."

On the afternoon of May 4, the "Ticket to Tokyo" rumbled through a draw between two ridges on its way back to friendly ground after a tank-infantry firefight with the attacking Japanese. Armstrong was in his usual position at the right rear of the tank's turret, keeping a wary eye out for enemy suicide squads from what was called the "fighting compartment basket."

Immediately in front of Armstrong in the "basket" was PFC Ben Okum, the assistant driver/machine gunner, and on Okum's left was Private David Spoerke, the loader on the Sherman's 75-millimeter cannon and, at eighteen, the youngest man in the crew. Corporal Harlan Stefan, the driver, was at the controls in the left front hull of the tank, and beside him in the right front hull was Corporal Alvin Tenbarge, the gunner on the 75.

The five of them had been together since Cape Gloucester, and they'd made it through the biggest tank battle of the Pacific war on Peleliu without a scratch. Armstrong sometimes wondered if they'd all been born under the same lucky star. It seemed unlikely, since Stefan, Tenbarge, and Okum were from Michigan, while Armstrong was from Texas and Spoerke was from Wisconsin.

After that day, he'd never have cause to wonder about it again.

⁓

THEY WERE ALMOST CLEAR of the draw when three Japanese 47-millimeter armor-piercing shells roared out of nowhere within seconds of one another. The first round blew a gaping hole through the front of the Sherman squarely between where Stefan and Tenbarge were sitting.

Droplets of blood spattered Armstrong's goggles and dribbled down his face. He thought he heard a muffled scream from up front. Then the second and third shells hit, drowning out everything else and flinging shards of shrapnel past Armstrong's head. The tank ground to a standstill.

In the thunderous silence that followed, Armstrong wiped the blood from his face with his gloved hand and tried to stand up. "Harlan!" he yelled, barely able to hear his own voice for the ringing in his ears. "Are you okay?"

"Oh, God, I think he's dead," Spoerke mumbled in the smoky gloom. Then the tank lurched abruptly forward, throwing Armstrong backward.

"Gotta get away," he heard Stefan groan as the tank gathered speed. "Gotta get out of here."

At least he's alive, Armstrong thought, *but he's bound to be hurt.*

When the Sherman stopped again, it was past the draw and sheltered by a hill from the Japanese gun, and Armstrong finally managed to squeeze between Spoerke and Okum to get a look at Stefan. What he saw shook him from the roots of his hair to the soles of his feet, but it also made it clear that he'd just witnessed a miracle.

"Only God knows how Harlan was able to drive that tank out of danger," Armstrong recalled many years later. "His left arm was completely gone. The first shell had blown it off just below the elbow, and by the time I reached him, he looked like he'd lost a gallon of blood. The driver's seat was full of it, and it was still gushing from the stump, but somehow he'd driven us to a relatively safe area with just one arm. Otherwise, we'd have all been dead."

Armstrong looked over his shoulder at Okum, who was staring wide-eyed at Stefan. "For Christ's sake, get a tourniquet on him before he bleeds to death," Armstrong said, then shouted back at Spoerke: "Davey, go out through the turret and see if you can find a corpsman."

"You gotta get these other guys out of here, Jack," Stefan whispered. He was already going into shock from loss of blood, but the rest of the crew was still his main concern. "Check on Tenbarge. I think he's bought it."

I must be in shock myself, Armstrong thought. Until that moment, he'd been so totally focused on Stefan that he'd forgotten about Tenbarge. Now he turned to look at the gunner, but, in the gloom, all he could see was a still, dark form. When he reached out to feel for wounds, his hand plunged wrist-deep into a yawning, blood-filled cavity where Tenbarge's stomach had been.

"Oh my God," Armstrong said, "that shell hit him right in the gut. Let's get Harlan outside. We can come back for Alvin later. He's dead."

Using the utmost care and with Armstrong holding the remains of Stefan's shattered arm, they carried the driver outside and laid him gently on the deck of the tank. The tourniquet had slowed the bleeding from his arm to a dribble, but to Armstrong, his husky friend looked as small and shrunken as "a frail little old man." Stefan's eyes were still open, and his lips were moving, but Armstrong couldn't make out what he was saying.

"Harlan's hardly got any blood left," Armstrong said to Okum. "If we don't get him to an aid station, he'll be dead in a few minutes."

Seconds later, two corpsmen and a group of stretcher bearers materialized. While the medics administered plasma to Stefan, Armstrong and the other crewmen went back inside the ruined tank and hauled out Tenbarge's body.

Corporal Floyd Cockerham arrived in his own Sherman at about this time, and he was stunned by the scene before him. "Harlan was a bloody mess," Cockerham recalled. "I didn't see Alvin when they were taking him out, but Jack told me he was terribly messed up."

According to Cockerham, the passage through the hills where the attack took place had been used many times, and Marine tankers were aware of a vulnerable spot along one of the slopes. What they didn't realize was that the night before, the Japanese had set up a concealed 47-millimeter gun armed with thermal antitank rounds to attack American tanks as they returned from action.

"I don't know why the Japs waited to strike until the return trip," Cockerham said. "Maybe they thought we'd be out of ammo and unable to retaliate, but they were wrong. We always had plenty of ammo for occasions like this. Several of our tanks did return fire, and when they ceased firing there was no response from the enemy gun."

Eventually, the corpsmen found their way to a blood-drenched Jack Armstrong. He was sitting on the ground, leaning against a rock, staring blankly at a razor-sharp piece of shrapnel he'd found caught in the leg of his dungaree pants after leaving the tank.

"Come on, son, we've got a stretcher for you," one of the medics said. "Let's get you over to the aid station and get you checked out."

"But there's nothing wrong with me, Doc," Armstrong protested.

"You've lost a lot of blood there, son, and you look like hell. You need medical attention."

"This isn't my blood," Armstrong said. "It belonged to some friends of mine."

"Look, we're trying to help you, Mac," said a burly Marine manning one end of a stretcher. "Now get on the stretcher and don't make problems." There was the vaguest hint of a threat in his voice.

Armstrong was too drained and grief-stricken to argue any further. He shrugged, took a last look at the hulk of the "Ticket to Tokyo," and allowed the stretcher bearers to carry him away.

⌒

ON MAY 8, the Sixth Marine Division arrived to assume responsibility for the westernmost sector of the Tenth Army front, which followed a jagged line across southern Okinawa and was manned by troops of four divisions. Other major changes in the composition of American front-line forces were about to occur over the next few days as well.

On May 10, the 96th Division returned from a ten-day rest to take over positions on the east end of the line from the Seventh Division's three infantry regiments—the 184th, 32nd, and 17th—which were finally relieved after thirty-nine consecutive days in the combat zone. The central portion of the front was held by units of the 77th Division's 306th and 307th Infantry regiments, and to their immediate right were the First Marine Division's First and Fifth Marines. The Sixth Marine Division's 22nd Marines was the first of its three infantry regiments to deploy on the line at the west end of the front.

These realignments, accomplished in driving downpours of rain and seas of mud, brought thousands of fresh troops into the contested ridges. But despite this influx, General Buckner was in no rush to throw his Tenth Army troops into new frontal assaults against fanatically defended enemy positions. Time after time, the experiences of the past month had shown dramatically that such assaults came at a high cost in infantry yet produced no greater territorial gains than more conservative tactics. Major General Andrew Bruce's 77th Division had achieved impressive success with a strategy of concentrating maximum firepower on one limited objective at a time. It made for slow going, but it worked, and, at that point, Buckner appeared more than willing to try Bruce's tactics.

Unfortunately for the infantry, however, Buckner's boss, Admiral Kelly Turner, still insisted on speed. Turner reminded Buckner daily of the need to conclude the Okinawa campaign with all possible haste. The Navy was suffering mightily under the onslaught of the kamikazes, he emphasized, and each additional day that ground fighting dragged on, the greater the toll on Task Force 58, the highly vulnerable radar picket ships, and American shipping in general.

Buckner responded to Turner's impatience by ordering the last thing that any of his infantry field commanders wanted: another general offensive—the largest yet—relying on the same brutal assault tactics as before. This time, it would be a coordinated attack across the full length of the line, from one coast of Okinawa to the other. Led by crack infantry regiments from all four divisions, the attack's objective was as simple as it was difficult: to smash the Shuri Defense Zone once and for all, overrun General Ushijima's own headquarters, and force the Japanese defenders to flee, surrender, or die.

All participating units would jump off simultaneously at 7:00 A.M. on May 11, with the two Marine divisions, the First and Sixth, responsible for the western half of the front, and the two Army divisions, the 77th and 96th, responsible for the eastern half.

The Deadeyes of the 96th Division, who had suffered the greatest losses in the repeated attacks on Kakazu Ridge, had now received replacements to fill the gaps in their ranks. Thus reinforced and fresh from a ten-day rest, this most experienced of the Army divisions on Okinawa drew the job of breaching the Japanese flank on the east and gaining control of Conical Hill, a cone-shaped formation jutting almost 500 feet above the coastal plain. Conical was the anchor of the east end of Ushijima's defensive line and had been a major thorn in the Tenth Army's side since late April. It had to be taken if the enemy line was to be broken.

In the left-center portion of the front, next to the sector occupied by the Deadeyes, the 77th "Statue of Liberty" Division was to attack south of the town of Maeda over terrain that was relatively flat but marked by stretches of rough, broken ground and a number of small, craggy peaks. Among them were the fancifully named Chocolate Drop and 250-foot-long Flattop Hill, part of which extended into the 96th's sector. If the 77th succeeded in penetrating the enemy defenses, its ultimate goal was to advance some 3,500 yards and capture Shuri Castle and Ushijima's headquarters. It would be a long, arduous two-mile trip through a tortuous maze of ridges, with every step of it directly under the guns of the Shuri heights.

The First Marine Division, meanwhile, was to attack parallel to the 77th in the west-central sector of the front and also fight its way directly toward Shuri through an equally forbidding series of hills and ravines. The first major obstacle facing the First was Dakeshi Ridge, which loomed just a few hundred yards ahead of it as the offensive jumped off. Next was Wana Ridge, and beyond it, Wana Draw—names that would add an unforgettable new chapter in the proud history of the Old Breed.

This topographical morass formed the cornerstone of Ushijima's Shuri Defense Zone, and the Japanese soldiers defending it were under orders to "hold without fail." The First's bitter—yet ultimately successful—struggle against similar cave-riddled ridges and fight-to-the-death defenders on Peleliu was expected to give the division an important edge in this mission.

Finally, the fresh troops of the Sixth Marine Division were handed the job of striking down the west coast of the island to sever the right side of the Japanese line, attack across the Asa Kawa River, and drive to the Asato estuary. Then the division was to turn east, bypassing the ravaged city of Naha and cutting behind Ushijima's stronghold in the Shuri heights. From there, the Sixth was to advance up the Kokuba River Valley toward the town of Yonabaru, thus encircling the core of Ushijima's defenses.

Only three small hills—none of them more than fifty feet high—stood in the way of the Sixth. None of the division's rank-and-file infantrymen knew what to call these nondescript little knobs when the offensive started. Indeed, they appeared so insignificant from a distance that there seemed no genuine need to name them at all.

But the identities bestowed on them by the Sixth Division Marines who repeatedly tried, failed, and tried again to take them would become synonyms for the most horrific struggle in the division's history—as well as symbols of the extraordinary courage and heroism it took to win that struggle.

Among those who survived the three hills, they are inevitably remembered as Horseshoe, Half Moon, and Sugar Loaf. First, though, the division had to cross the Asa Kawa River, and that turned out to be one hellaciously tough job in itself.

WHEN HE ENLISTED in the Marine Corps in January 1943, nineteen-year-old Ray Schlinder had one overriding goal: to be a number one machine gunner. At the time, he didn't know a .30-caliber Browning from a slingshot, but he achieved his goal by stepping boldly into line with a newly formed machine-gun section and making friends with Sergeant Bill Enright, a squad leader from Indiana, Schlinder's home state.

"Enright handed me a training manual about three inches thick and told me to memorize every word of it in the next three days, or else," Schlinder recalled. "'Otherwise,' he said, 'you're right back in a rifle platoon.'"

Schlinder spent every available minute, day and night, studying the manual, and when time came to test his skills on the firing range, he passed with flying colors. A little later, when he found a pair of rusty clippers and trimmed another friend's hair, he also inherited the job of company barber in K Company, Third Battalion, 22nd Marines.

"So here I was, a number-one machine gunner and the barber for 235 guys," he said, "and I didn't know what the hell I was doing in either case. One day a second lieutenant came in and asked for a flattop, and when I got through with him, he looked like I'd hit him with a hand grenade. The next day, I was fired as company barber and told to spend full time being a number-one machine gunner. That suited me fine."

When the Sixth Marine Division was formed on September 1, 1944, Corporal Schlinder became a charter member. He'd landed on Okinawa on Love Day and spent the next four weeks in what he called a "machine gunner's paradise" on the north end of the island. "That's where you shoot like you're on a target range, and nobody shoots back," he explained.

The "paradise" ended abruptly three hours before dawn on May 10, when Schlinder's machine-gun section was transported by truck to the north side of the Asa Kawa River

"It's sink or swim from here, guys," said Lieutenant Colonel M. O. Donohoo, the battalion CO. "We're going across."

"We waded across the river in chest-deep water, and there were no shots fired at us on the way," Schlinder recalled, "but once we got on the other side, all hell broke loose."

Japanese riflemen and machine gunners caught the battalion in a savage crossfire between a fortified promontory jutting into the sea on the Marines' right and a thirty-foot bank on the left where the enemy had built a series of gun emplacements.

"The situation's bad," Colonel Donohoo reported to Colonel Merlin F. Schneider, the regimental commander. "We're getting hit, but we're across the river, and we're going to stay."

Schlinder, along with PFC Ray Kieman of St. Paul, Minnesota, the number-two gunner in the squad, and some other Marines were fortunate enough to be next to a large concrete drain pipe with a couple feet of water in it, and they lost no time crawling inside it. "I had a big pack, and it was tough trying to keep my nose above water," said Schlinder, "but it sure beat the hell out of getting shot."

For two days, the battle on the riverbank raged. The stalemate was finally broken when General Shepherd, the division commander, ordered a Bailey pontoon bridge built across the river by Marine engineers, and two companies of the Sixth Tank Battalion were brought up to run interference for the infantry. The battalion's Company B had tried to move in earlier to provide armored fire support, but its medium Shermans had bogged down in the mud and silt of the riverbank.

The engineers worked under repeated Japanese artillery barrages fired at two-hour intervals from the Shuri heights during the night of May 10–11. Despite having several men injured by flying rock from the shelling, the engineers worked on, finishing the bridge about 10:00 A.M. on May 11, then watching, grimy and bleary-eyed, as the long line of tanks streamed across it.

A short, red-haired engineer leaned out a truck window to wave the tankers on as they passed. "We'll do it again whenever you need us," he hollered. "Blast all the bastards to hell!"

One flamethrower tank in particular took the little engineer at his word. When it turned its giant torch on a cave housing an enemy ammunition dump, the explosion sent rocks and boulders flying in all directions.

"A big rock hit my buddy Kieman and smashed his leg," said Schlinder, "but when I got to him, he was lying there with a big grin on his face and smoking a Camel."

"Eat your hearts out, you guys!" Kieman exulted. "By God, I'm going home!" Kieman would spend weeks in a cast, and his damaged leg would give him problems for years to come, but many a man in the 22nd would willingly have traded places with him—especially if they'd known what lay ahead.

By the end of the day on May 11, the Sixth Division had driven forward between 700 and 1,000 yards, mopping up pockets of enemy resistance behind its lines as it went. That afternoon, Schlinder's Third Battalion had taken a heavily fortified cliff area that ran all the way to the sea. It would require another day of savage fighting, plus help from units of the 29th Marines, but the enemy's Asa Kawa defense line was starting to crumble. By late on May 13, Marine units had advanced up to 2,000 yards, but they'd suffered more than 800 casualties in the process, and the men who were still able to function were exhausted.

Directly ahead of them, blocking a broad corridor leading into the heart of the Shuri heights, was an irregular rectangular bump of a hill that overlooked the upper Asato River and an intervening stretch of ragged, choppy ground.

The advancing 22nd had first come within sight of the bump when the rains temporarily slacked off and the mist lifted on May 12. Because of its shape, the infantrymen were quick to give the bump a name.

They called it Sugar Loaf, but there was nothing sweet about it.

CHAPTER NINE

Bitter Toll at Sugar Loaf

B Y MID-MAY, the Okinawa campaign had already lasted longer than the fight for either Iwo Jima or Saipan, and most Americans on the island, from the lowliest privates on up to General Buckner and his division commanders, could tell that the end of it was nowhere in sight. Neither was the end of the infernal rain.

For combat-weary men sunk to their knees in Okinawa's soupy red mud or treading water in overflowing foxholes with enemy ordnance rumbling overhead, the ceaseless fighting and recurrent downpours seemed destined to last forever. This feeling was amply illustrated in a series of May-datelined letters from PFC Al Henderson of the 96th Recon Troop to his wife in Arkansas:

- "It rained here all night last night and has rained all day today. Sure is sloppy. You can't hardly walk, the ground is so muddy and slick. . . ."
- "I don't think there's a hill over here that doesn't have two or three caves running clear through it and twenty or thirty different openings. Looks to me like the Japs have been digging over here for ten years or longer. It sure makes the going slow. . . ."
- "I sure hope this rain hurries and quits. It's so sloppy you can't walk without slipping and sliding in every direction. . . ."
- "I didn't get a letter today, baby doll, but I know they are just held up somewhere. Only four or five letters came in for the whole outfit. I guess it's so rainy and muddy that the planes can't take off. It has rained all day again. . . ."
- "I don't see how the Japs can hold out much longer. They know they are whipped, and it can't end any too soon for

me. I hope Russia hops on the Japs. I think they would quit if Russia got in the war. I look for the sun to come out tomorrow, but it will probably take a week for everything to dry out. . . ."

- "It's raining here again today. It doesn't look like it will ever stop. Sometimes I think the big guns cause it to rain—just jar the rain loose from the clouds. I hope it rains all the time when I get home to you, precious, because we will be snuggling every second, rain or shine. . . . I feel like I've been gone a million years, and there's never been a second of it that I haven't missed you. . . ."

THE MORNING OF MAY 13 found the thin ranks of the Sixth Marine Division's 22nd Marines, Second Battalion, dug in several hundred yards from the foot of Sugar Loaf Hill, licking their wounds from an abortive tank-infantry assault on the hill the afternoon before.

The Tenth Army's Okinawa casualty count now stood at more than 18,000, but based on the experiences of the last twenty-four hours, U.S. commanders feared the worst was still ahead, and they were right. As an ugly harbinger of things to come, the week just past (May 5 to May 12) had added 4,500 American dead and wounded to that overall total.

General Ushijima's 32nd Army had its back to the wall now, and his soldiers knew they were doomed. Since the only remaining goal for the Japanese was to kill as many Americans as possible, the coming week's toll was likely to run even higher.

Nobody in the 22nd Marines doubted that probability—least of all the men of G Company, Second Battalion, who'd had the misfortune of leading the attack of May 12.

For the first 900 yards of the advance, casualties were light for the company's three rifle platoons, but as they neared the high ground, enemy fire increased to a roar, and concealed 47-millimeter guns began knocking out the supporting Shermans of the Sixth Tank Battalion, leaving the infantry exposed.

With two of his platoons helplessly pinned down, Captain Owen T. Stebbins, the company CO, and his executive officer, Lieutenant Dale Bair, led the remaining forty-man platoon forward in a heroic, but ill-advised, charge.

After a 100-yard advance up the front side of the hill, only a dozen men were still standing. Stebbins was among the seriously wounded with machine-gun bullets in both legs, and no sooner had Bair taken charge of the survivors than he was hit by a piece of shrapnel that tore a large chunk of flesh from his leg. But the burly young officer kept on fighting, even after he was struck again in the left arm. With the injured arm hanging useless at his side, Bair wielded a light machine gun with his right arm, spraying bursts of fire at every visible Japanese.

With only twenty-five men and a few tanks left, and using smoke grenades and smoke shells as cover, Bair led the final push up Sugar Loaf until a third enemy hit knocked him down and out of the battle. Exactly four members of the attacking platoon, along with a handful of men from the other two platoons, reached the top. They had no chance of holding it. The best they could do was rescue numerous wounded Marines, Bair among them, as they retreated back down the slope.

Three times that afternoon, Marines of G Company had reached the summit of Sugar Loaf, and three times they'd been driven off with horrendous casualties by Japanese mortars and grenades. But this was only the beginning.

THE PROBLEM facing the Sixth Marine Division was strikingly similar to the one that had confronted the Army's 96th Division a month earlier at Kakazu Ridge—a local defensive juggernaut encompassing far more than a single hill and supported by massed enemy artillery. The Sugar Loaf complex consisted of three hills instead of one—a fact that was just now dawning on the Sixth's regimental and battalion commanders. What they still didn't fully grasp, however, was that, as unimposing as it looked, this three-hill complex was also the enemy's most important remaining system of defenses protecting the Shuri heights.

Sugar Loaf itself was a puny hill barely three city blocks long, but it was the centerpiece of an ingeniously designed triangle of mutually supporting, intensively fortified enemy strongpoints. It was bracketed by Half Moon Hill to the southeast and a curving plateau called the Horseshoe to the south. Within the Horseshoe's curve on its reverse side was a deep depression that gave the Japanese near-impregnable mortar positions, assailable only by short-range rifle and grenade attacks.

Each hill rose abruptly from otherwise flat and barren ground, offering no covered approaches into the defensive maze, and each was an integral part of an interconnected labyrinth of deep tunnels, concealed machine-gun, mortar, and antitank positions, augmented by pillboxes on both forward and reverse slopes. Any ground force trying to outflank one of the three hills exposed itself to fire from the other two as well as from Shuri. Hence, none of the three could be seized independently; they had to be taken together as one objective. After the losses suffered since crossing the Asa Kawa River, Colonel Harold C. Roberts's depleted 22nd Marines lacked the manpower to complete the job alone, but for the time being, that job remained squarely on the shoulders of the 22nd's understrength rifle platoons.

Action on May 13 was limited to probes by the Marines, aimed at gauging the strength of the enemy positions. Apparently, the probes were less than revealing, either of enemy numbers or determination. As a periodic report issued by division headquarters at the end of the day blithely observed: "The enemy has lost possession of the important tactical terrain between Naha and the Asa Kawa, and by the end of the period, no heavily organized enemy defenses had been noted to the division's front."

At this point, size estimates of the local enemy force were based mostly on guesswork, but it was generally believed that each of the three hills was held by only about a company of Japanese. In actuality, the Sugar Loaf–Half Moon–Horseshoe complex was defended by about 2,000 fresh troops, including some Okinawan conscripts but mostly from the 15th Independent Regiment of Japan's 44th Brigade. Ignorance of these facts was undoubtedly one reason for the decision to send the 22nd's already-disheveled Second Battalion—whose F and G Companies had been reduced to skeleton strength in the fighting of May 12—in another all-day attack on May 14.

This time, however, there was one important change in strategy: The attacking Marines would no longer concentrate on Sugar Loaf alone but would move simultaneously against all three fortified enemy hills.

The morning of the attack dawned to typical May weather on Okinawa—sullen skies, low-hanging clouds, and incessant rain. Lieutenant Colonel H. G. Woodhouse Jr., commanding the Second Battalion, spent most of the morning waiting for the go-ahead to move his men out.

In briefing his company commanders that morning, Woodhouse had originally designated the three targeted pieces of enemy high ground as Hills One, Two, and Three. Hills One and Three, each rising only about thirty feet above the plain, were what soon came to be known respectively as the Horseshoe and Half Moon.

During the briefing, some of the officers suggested that fifty-foot-tall Hill Two, the largest of the group and the attack's main objective, should be redesignated as Hill One. To avoid confusion, Woodhouse renamed it Sugar Loaf—probably the first official use of the nickname, which was quickly adopted throughout the division.

The plan called for a coordinated attack, with units of the First Marine Division advancing in tandem with troops of the Sixth to cover the latter's left flank, but logistical problems caused a delay. Finally, at 11:30 A.M., Brigadier General William T. Clement, assistant commander of the Sixth, arrived at Woodhouse's command post with written orders directing the battalion not to wait on the First Division but to attack as soon as possible.

"You are to attack immediately and continue the attack at all costs," Clement told Woodhouse. "Repeat—at all costs."

The order worried Woodhouse, and he expressed his concern to Lieutenant Ed Pesely, commanding the decimated remnants of Fox Company. "It sounds like something out of World War I," Pesely later recalled Woodhouse saying of the order. "It's not the school solution, but we've got to comply."

By the time the attack started, it was after 2:00 P.M., and the short-handed Marine units involved quickly found themselves in trouble. Woodhouse had assigned just one Fox Company rifle platoon each, supported by several tanks, to seize the Horseshoe and Half Moon. Once the crests of the hills were in Marine hands, the platoon on the Horseshoe was to be relieved by E Company while G Company relieved the other platoon on Half Moon. At that point, all three F Company rifle platoons would converge to capture Sugar Loaf. That, at any rate, was the wishfully optimistic plan.

By about 2:20 P.M., aided by covering fire from artillery and tanks, Lieutenant Rodney Gaumnitz's First Platoon of Fox Company made it to the top of the Horseshoe but was pinned down under heavy enemy fire from Sugar Loaf proper. Meanwhile, a few members of the Second Platoon, led by Lieutenant Robert Hutchings, reached the summit of Half Moon, but they took dozens of casualties along the way from fire on their unprotected left flank and left rear, and the survivors were soon forced to withdraw.

At 3:00 P.M., Colonel Woodhouse knew his battalion would have to have help if it hoped to hold any of the ground it had taken, much less gain more. After he contacted regimental headquarters to plead for more troops, K Company of the 22nd's Third Battalion was ordered into the fight—but this concession didn't come without a price.

"General Shepherd has ordered that the division objective (Sugar Loaf) must be taken before dark," said the curt message from regiment, "without fail and regardless of consequences."

Faced with this ultimatum, about 4:30 P.M., Woodhouse ordered his battalion forward one more time to make a final attempt while it was still daylight. Supporting artillery pounded all three hills for half an hour. Then, under a smoke screen, led by four tanks, and with E Company providing covering fire, F and G Companies jumped off a few minutes after five. It took more than two hours of hard fighting and heavy casualties before survivors of the two companies reached the slopes of Sugar Loaf. Of the 150-plus Marines who started the advance, only four officers and forty enlisted men—the equivalent of a single rifle platoon—were still able to stand. Three of the four supporting tanks lay disabled behind them.

Among the survivors, spirits were abysmally low. Daylight was rapidly fading. Soon it would be dark, and the drained, demoralized troops were a long way from friendly ground.

As the little group of Marines huddled at the foot of the hill, Major Henry A. Courtney Jr., executive officer of the Second Battalion, called them together to propose a drastic plan. Courtney's idea was straightforward, unorthodox, and dangerous, and it also violated some of the basic combat precepts instilled in every Marine from his earliest days at boot camp.

The major wasn't known as a particularly persuasive talker, a charismatic leader, or an officer who enjoyed great rapport with his enlisted men. On the contrary, he had a reputation as a somber, silent, rather standoffish type.

Yet within the next few moments, Courtney somehow managed to transform a few dozen tired, nervous young men into a fighting machine that refused to quit or accept defeat.

IN THE SIX MONTHS since he'd joined the Second Battalion, Courtney had picked up the nickname "Smiley" among some Marines because of the dour expression he often wore. But since the landing on Okinawa, the twenty-eight-year-old reserve officer from Duluth, Minnesota, a lawyer before the war, had also proved his courage under fire and displayed a high tolerance for pain—not once but many times.

Unlike some execs who were content to hang around the battalion CP doing detail work, Courtney preferred front-line action. Early in the campaign he'd led the 22nd Marines' advance to the north end of Okinawa, walking for most of the way in the "point" position well ahead of the battalion's main body. On May 10, he'd been hit in the right thigh by shell fragments during an enemy artillery barrage but refused to be evacuated. On May 12, he'd stayed all night in a G Company foxhole, offering quiet support to its battered troops after most of their officers were killed. And he'd spent the entire day of May 14 with the assault companies in the thick of the fighting.

Now, during a lull between artillery and mortar barrages, Courtney stared into the intent young faces around him and calmly outlined his plan: "Men, if we don't take the top of this hill tonight, the Japs will be down here to drive us away in the morning. I have a plan, and if it works, we'll take the top of the hill. I want volunteers for a banzai charge of our own!

"When we go up there, some of us are never going to come down again. You all know what hell it is on the top, but that hill's got to be taken, and we're going to do it. What do you say?"

The most outspoken dissent to Courtney's plan came from Lieutenant Robert Nealon, one of only two remaining G Company officers, who'd just arrived on the scene with twenty-six more men carrying sorely needed ammo and rations. Nealon said he and his men had been sent by Colonel Woodhouse to relieve F Company troops on Hill Three (Half Moon), "and that's what I intend to do."

Also voicing reservations was Lieutenant Ed Pesely, F Company's exec and a Silver Star recipient on Guam. Pesely had assumed command of the company after Captain Mike Ahearn, the CO, was wounded by machine-gun fire earlier in the day. Courtney told Pesely that men from F Company were already on top of Sugar Loaf—a statement that Pesely seriously doubted.

"We should join them there," Courtney said. "It'll be easier to do it tonight in the dark than to take the hill tomorrow in daylight when the enemy can see every move we make."

Normally, Marines didn't attack at night; in fact, any Marine who ventured from his foxhole in the dark was at risk of being shot by his comrades. Pesely was uneasy enough about the idea that he quietly contacted Woodhouse on the radio and told him about Courtney's plan. He was disappointed, however, when Woodhouse agreed that the plan might work.

Meanwhile, except for a few dubious veterans, the enlisted men were generally rallying to Courtney's call. Dour in demeanor though he may have been, the major's attack plan had inspired them. As the Sixth Marine Division's official history put it: "There was determined, even eager, willingness in their eyes."

Though he still disagreed with the decision, Lieutenant Pesely knew he was outvoted. "He [Courtney] slapped a few men on the back and cajoled others until all agreed that we would go with him," Pesely recalled much later.

"We're going to need lots of grenades for this trip," Courtney said. "Let's round up all we can find and take as many as we can carry with us. When we get near the crest of the hill, I want everybody to throw grenades over the top and onto the reverse slope as fast as you can."

~⊃

IT WAS A FEW MINUTES before 7:00 P.M., and dusk was settling over Half Moon Hill when acting Sergeant Walt Rutkowski, a nineteen-year-old G Company rifle-squad leader from the south side of Chicago, saw Lieutenant Nealon, his platoon leader, approaching. When Nealon first spoke, Rutkowski felt a weak surge of relief at what the lieutenant was saying—or, more correctly, at what he *thought* Nealon was saying.

"There's only fifty of us left in George Company," Nealon told him. "I want you to take twenty-five men, and Corporal [Steve] Stankovich can take the other twenty-five. . . ."

The company had made it across the Asa Kawa River with 215 combat-capable Marines. Now more than three-fourths of those men were gone, and the rest were obviously in no condition to keep fighting. Even so, elation rose in Rutkowski's chest. "For a second, I was sure Nealon was gonna tell us to withdraw back to our lines and get some rest," he recalled. "It was like a big weight was being lifted off my shoulders."

But then Nealon went on: ". . . and get over to that other hill [Sugar Loaf] on the double as soon as we get some smoke. When it gets full dark, we're going to the top of the damned thing."

Rutkowski caught his breath as the weight of Nealon's order slammed down with crushing force.

—⁓

To THIS DAY, considerable disagreement exists concerning the exact number of Marines in the little band that Major Courtney led up the forward slope of Sugar Loaf and to its crest that night. Some sources place the number as low as forty-four. The official Sixth Division history says that forty-six men stormed the hill. But assuming that most of the fifty Marines led to Sugar Loaf by Rutkowski and Corporal Stankovich on orders from Lieutenant Nealon actually got there and that about forty were already there with Major Courtney, it seems possible that up to ninety men went up the hill.

Walt Rutkowski knows only one thing for sure—that he was one of them.

The overcast sky was completely dark when the group started its ascent, the only light coming from flares fired by Navy ships offshore and reflected off the low clouds. "Courtney was in a hurry to go," Rutkowski recalled nearly sixty-one years later, "but some of my BAR guys hadn't shown up yet, and I wanted to wait for them."

"What're you waiting for?" Courtney demanded.

"We need some more BARs," Rutkowski said.

"There's no time," the major snapped. "We've got to move." He called for supporting mortar fire, then turned to the waiting Marines. "I'm going up to the top of Sugar Loaf Hill. Who's coming along?"

The men surged forward en masse, closing around Rutkowski and pushing him ahead of them until he and Courtney were shoulder to shoulder. As they mounted the steep, slippery forward slope, Courtney was a few feet away on Rutkowski's immediate left, and a Fox Company BAR man was on Rutkowski's right.

They stopped a few feet short of the crest and flattened themselves against the rocky hillside. Then Courtney hollered down the line: "Use your grenades!"

Almost simultaneously, at least 100 grenades sailed over Sugar Loaf's crest, and the little hill shook from the force of their explosions on the reverse slope. The Marines' ears were still ringing when Courtney jumped to his feet, waved his arms, and started clambering up the hill. Rutkowski was close beside him, his boondockers sliding on the wet rocks. To his right, Rutkowski saw the BAR man struggling forward, and, as another flare momentarily lit the sky, he also caught a glimpse of Corporal Stankovich off to his left.

Seconds later, they were on top of Sugar Loaf Hill and trying to dig in on the rocky summit. Machine-gun and rifle bullets buzzed around them like bees, but Rutkowski got the feeling that most of the fire was from adjacent hills and that the Japanese were shooting blindly. He was more concerned about the enemy grenades that now began sailing up from the reverse slope and exploding on the crest. There was also intermittent mortar and artillery fire.

"Maybe I ought to throw a smoke grenade," said the BAR man on Rutkowski's right.

"What good's that gonna do?" Rutkowski said. "It'll help the Japs more than it will us."

"We need a shovel to dig with," the guy said. "I think I know where I can find one." He handed his BAR to Rutkowski and disappeared.

Courtney abruptly nudged Rutkowski. "I see a bunch of Japs down there," he said, pointing almost straight ahead toward the edge of the reverse slope. "They just came out of a hole, and it looks like there's about twenty of them."

Rutkowski's eyes darted to where Courtney pointed. The enemy soldiers were no more than thirty yards away, and even as the major spoke, they started hurling grenades. Rutkowski swung the BAR in their direction and opened fire.

A SHORT DISTANCE away along the hilltop, Private Wendell Majors of G Company ejected one eight-shot clip from his M-1 and reached for another. As he did, he realized to his horror that the nest of Japanese he was firing at, lurking just below the crest of Sugar Loaf on the reverse slope, was using the bright flashes from Marine rifles as aiming beacons for their grenades—Majors's own red-hot M-1 included.

Majors had spent much of that afternoon watching his buddies being shot to pieces around him in the assault on Half Moon Hill. "The Japs cut us down like a mowing machine in a hayfield," recalled the erstwhile country boy, who'd grown up on an eighty-acre farm near Searcy, Arkansas.

Now the surviving Marines of G Company looked to be in an even worse position. In fact, Majors couldn't imagine how their situation could be more desperate. He shut his eyes for a moment, remembering what his older brother, also a Marine, had told him when Majors announced his intention to enlist in the Corps:

"Take my advice, little brother, and join some other branch of the service—any other branch but the Marines!"

As if in reply, he heard someone shouting his name: "Majors! Majors!"

Majors didn't answer. If he could've gotten his hands on the shouter, he would've strangled him with no trace of remorse. Every Marine knew the Japanese would seize any opportunity to kill an American officer, and if any spoken word signaled "officer" louder and clearer than "Majors," Private Majors had never heard it. Self-preservation had been his main reason for assuming the nickname "Deacon," but now, in the heat of battle, someone had forgotten, and there was going to be hell to pay.

It came in the form of a sputtering enemy grenade that sailed out of the darkness, hit the ground a couple feet from Majors's shallow foxhole, and hopped right in. Majors recognized it instantly for what it was, and he groped frantically around the bottom of the hole in search of it—only he couldn't find it. All he could do, at the last possible second, was jump out of the hole and throw himself away from it.

The blast blew dirt and fragments of rock all over him and hurt his ears, but he was okay otherwise. He rolled into a firing position, leveling the M-1 and was wondering what to do next when he remembered a trick that Gary Cooper had played on the Germans in the World War I movie *Sergeant York.* Maybe—just maybe—the same trick would work with the Japanese.

Majors cupped his right hand around his mouth and made a low gobbling sound in good imitation of a strutting turkey gobbler. Then he lay still and waited.

Ten seconds passed ... fifteen ... twenty ... Majors repeated his gobble, and a helmeted Japanese head appeared over the rim of the hill about forty feet away. A moment later, another appeared beside it. It was odd, Majors thought, but the Japanese, like the Germans in the movie, couldn't seem to resist their curiosity about the gobbling sound.

He emptied another eight-round clip, killing both enemy soldiers, but Majors's ordeal was far from over. His volley of shots caught the attention of a Japanese machine gunner, who opened fire immediately as

Majors scrambled into a slight cleft in the hilltop. By his calculations, the gunner expended an entire belt of ammo, missing with every round except one. It creased the calf of Majors's leg but caused no serious damage.

By now, Majors's rifle was too hot to touch, and its wooden stock was actually smoking from the ceaseless fusillade he was laying down. But as he tried to run and reload at the same time, singeing his fingers in the process, Majors stumbled and jammed the barrel of the M-1 into the muddy ground, rendering it useless. He couldn't find the foxhole he'd left, so he jumped blindly into another one—landing squarely on a rifle propped against the side of the hole with its bayonet pointing upward. The blade stabbed through the back of Majors's thigh and came out his groin.

"Ohhh God!" he muttered through clenched teeth as he struggled to pull the blade free. When he did, a stream of blood gushed out. To Majors, it seemed to spurt a foot into the air. He was sure for a while that he'd severed a main artery and was going to bleed to death, but he kept stuffing sulfa powder into the wound and applying pressure to it until the bleeding finally stopped.

A little later, a G Company comrade, PFC Jack Houston, jumped into the foxhole and put a field dressing on the wound. By this time, Majors was dozing periodically but waking at intervals to wonder what tricks of fate had conspired to place him in this sorry mess.

Actually, Majors had made a valiant effort to obey his brother's advice and enlist in the Navy. In fact, he *had* enlisted in the Navy, but one day later, when he arrived at the induction center, he'd found a Marine gunnery sergeant waiting to pounce.

"I'm short four men," the gunny said. "I need four guys to volunteer for the Marines."

After much swearing and many aspersions on the recruits' manhood, the gunny got his quota of volunteers, and Majors had breathed a sigh of relief. Then, as the sergeant started to leave, he grabbed up Majors's enlistment papers and unaccountably yelled: "Come on, Majors, you're a Marine, too!"

Now, as he lay in a sea of darkness and pain, Majors could only ask himself the same question over and over: *What could that gunnery sergeant possibly have had against me?*

PFC WALT RUTKOWSKI was still sandwiched between Major Courtney and the F Company BAR man, who had just returned with a
shovel, when he heard the telltale sound of an incoming round—either
a mortar or artillery shell—a split second before it exploded two or
three yards behind him.

The force of the blast blew all three of the men forward and knocked
them to the ground. As the sound of the shell burst died, Rutkowski dis-
tinctly heard Courtney and the other Marine let out almost identical
groans. He also felt a peculiar sensation in his left arm, just above the
elbow.

"Are you guys all right?" Rutkowski asked. He listened intently, but
there was no answer. He tried to crawl toward Courtney, but his arm refused to cooperate. "Corpsman!" he yelled weakly. "We got men hit over
here!"

In less than a minute—or so it seemed to Rutkowski—a medic
showed up and crouched down beside Courtney. "Who is this guy?" he
asked. "Do you know him?"

"Yeah," Rutkowski said. "It's Major Courtney."

The corpsman's voice was tired and unimpressed. "Well, he's dead,"
he said, crawling over to the BAR man. "This one's dead, too."

"But I was right between them when the shell hit," Rutkowski said,
"and both of 'em were groaning afterward."

"Then you must've been damned lucky," the medic said wearily.
"These other two weren't."

The corpsman put a dressing on Rutkowski's arm, told him it was
broken, and gave him a shot of morphine. "You'll be okay," he said. "We'll
get you evacuated as soon as we can, but I can't say when that'll be." Then
he vanished as quickly as he'd come.

Rutkowski drifted off for a while—he had no idea how long—until
another exploding shell jerked him back to consciousness. This one hit
about as close as the first one, only much nearer to Courtney. It blew the
major's body two or three feet into the air and hurled it completely over
Rutkowski.

When the body flopped back to earth, Rutkowski caught a glimpse
of Courtney's face, but it was no longer really a face, just an unrecogniz-
able mass of torn flesh, cartilage, and bone.

Rutkowski was too numb to know if he'd taken any additional shrapnel from the latest shell, but he did know he was lucky.

Thank God I'm still alive, he thought. *Now if I can just make it through the night . . .*

<hr />

IT WAS ABOUT 1:00 A.M. on May 15, and a cold rain had been blowing in off the East China Sea for the past several hours, when Lieutenant Reginald Fincke, the recently appointed CO of K Company, Third Battalion, 22nd Marines, reported to Colonel Woodhouse at the regimental commander's CP.

Fincke had assumed command of K Company just two days earlier, after his predecessor, Lieutenant Paul Dunfey, had been wounded at the Asa Kawa River, but the new CO was highly respected by his men as a compassionate and resourceful leader.

"The situation on Sugar Loaf is very critical," Woodhouse told him. "The lines are thin, and the Japs are counterattacking in strength. Replenish your supplies, and stand by to take your company up there."

When Fincke returned to the CP around 2:00 A.M., the situation on Sugar Loaf had grown even worse. "According to the reports I've gotten, only eight or ten men are still holding out on top of the hill," Woodhouse said. "If we lose Sugar Loaf, we'll lose everything we've gained and paid dearly for. I want you to take your company up there and hold it at all costs. I want to see you there in the morning."

Within minutes, K Company moved out in the darkness from the positions it had held on the Horseshoe, and its ninety-nine men and four officers reached the crest of Sugar Loaf by about 2:30 A.M. without a single casualty.

As he climbed the hill, carrying a tripod and ammo for his .30-caliber machine gun, Corporal Ray Schlinder thought back over the past few days and the beating the regiment had already taken. Just hours earlier, he'd been bullshitting with his buddies about where they might be this time next week. Now, with this "take the hill at all costs" order, he realized that none of them might be alive when the sun came up.

On the other hand, Schlinder had already made it through some tough times. A few nights before, while the 22nd was still advancing along the seawall on the west coast of the island, he'd set up his water-cooled Browning pointing seaward, then gathered enough rocks to build a substantial little fort around it in case of a forced landing by the Japanese.

As darkness fell, Schlinder had seen a group of men approaching. "Who's there?" he challenged.

"Second Platoon with chow," came the reply.

A little later, more figures appeared on the beach, moving toward him in a tight bunch. He'd tensed, feeling for the one grenade he was carrying but trying to calm himself at the same time.

Just take it easy. Probably just more Second Platoon guys.

The figures had been about twenty yards away when Schlinder noticed their round, bullet-shaped helmets. "Who's there?" he'd yelled again. This time, there was no reply, but Schlinder already knew the answer to his question.

He'd jerked the pin out of his lone grenade, but something snapped inside, and it malfunctioned. He'd thrown it into the water and opened fire with the .30, then kept firing until nothing moved on the shoreline in front of him.

"The next morning, we counted thirty-eight dead Nips out there," Schlinder recalled years later. "But once we started up Sugar Loaf, we never had any easy targets like that again."

In sickening contrast, the bodies he now saw as the company moved up Sugar Loaf's forward slope were all Marines. There were scores of them—too many to count—sprawled and scattered in every direction. "I crawled over dead Marines and pieces of dead Marines all the way up the hill," Schlinder said. "I wondered if some of them might still be alive, but I couldn't take time to check."

Schlinder's light .30-caliber machine gun was one of eight carried up the hill by the K Company Marines, and his first priority on reaching the top was to find a place to set it up.

"All right, men," he heard Lieutenant Fincke say, "find yourself a hole and get in it."

Schlinder noted that many of the holes he passed already had Marines in them, but it was hard to tell the living ones from the dead. As he searched for somewhere to put his weapon, the Japanese opened up with their own machine guns, knee mortars, and artillery.

"All at once the hill was alive with bursting shells," Schlinder said. "I don't know how I ever made it, but I finally jumped into an empty slit trench near the reverse slope."

With no radio communication available, Fox Company's Lieutenant Pesely had helped guide the troops from K Company up the hill by shouting instructions at intervals during their ascent. But in the confusion after the newcomers reached the top, he was unable to make contact with any of them, although he heard someone he judged to be an officer ordering a machine gun to be set up.

Almost as soon as the machine gun began firing, its position came under enemy mortar fire. Three or four mortar rounds struck within seconds of one another, one of them exploding virtually on top of the gun, destroying it, wiping out its crew, and mortally wounding Lieutenant Fincke, who was directing fire against the enemy mortar.

The blast mangled both of Fincke's legs, leaving only twisted tendons, shredded flesh, and shattered bones. Worse, when two Marines loaded the lieutenant on a stretcher and tried to take him down the hill, one slipped on the slick ground and dumped him over the edge, watching in helpless horror as his body tumbled all the way down the slope. He was probably already dead when he fell, but no one could say for sure.

Moments after Fincke's death, Pesely heard a voice beside his foxhole. "Where's Fox Company?" it asked.

"This is it," Pesely replied. "What's left of it anyway. I'm Ed Pesely."

"I'm Jim Roe, King Company exec," the voice said. "Lieutenant Fincke's dead, so I guess I'm in charge of the company now. How do you want us to deploy?"

"Just spread out on top of the hill and dig in as quietly as you can and wherever you can," Pesely said. "You guys're damned brave to climb into a mess like this, but we're happy as hell to see you."

"Thanks," said Lieutenant Roe. "I wish I could say I was happy to be here."

Ray Schlinder fared somewhat better than the ill-fated machine gunner killed with Fincke, but his position near the edge of the reverse slope also came under intense grenade attacks and mortar fire, and his ability to return fire was strictly limited by a steep drop-off just a few feet in front of his position.

"I was about as close as you could get to the backside of the hill," Schlinder said. "There were a bunch of Nips right below me—practically underneath my trench—so I got the idea that I might do better with grenades than with my gun."

Schlinder passed the word to Marines behind him to bring up as many grenades as they could, and he was soon rewarded with three full cases. During his high school days in Milwaukee, Ray had played catcher on the baseball team, and he'd gotten pretty adept at throwing out runners trying to steal second base. Now he put his throwing ability to the supreme test—as if the bases were loaded, and it was the ninth inning of the seventh game of the World Series.

"There was this one group of Japs that was maybe fifty yards away," he recalled. "I didn't think I could throw a grenade that far, but I decided to try. I came up a little short, but I sure scared the shit out of them."

For close to an hour, the Japanese kept coming, and Schlinder kept tossing grenades over the edge of the cliff as fast as he could pull the pins. As best he could calculate, he threw about 300 of them altogether. Make that 301.

"I was busy throwing when I felt something hit me in the right thigh," Schlinder recounted. "I looked down, and it was a Nip grenade. In reflex, I jerked it up and pitched it back over the edge. There were so many explosions around me that I never knew if it went off or if it was a dud, but I really got into it after that. I made up my mind to clean out the whole damned front of the hill."

UP AND DOWN the Marines' thin line, similar examples of courage and determination were commonplace.

Brawny, red-haired Corporal Donald "Rusty" Golar, a G Company machine gunner, former longshoreman in San Francisco, and self-described "glory hunter," blazed away with his .30-caliber Browning until he ran out of ammunition. Except for himself and two riflemen, no one else was still standing to hold the section of Sugar Loaf's crest where Golar's group had dug in.

"Gotta use what I got left," Golar yelled to Private Don Kelly, a rifleman crouching nearby. Drawing his .45, Golar emptied it at charging Japanese until it, too, ran dry. Then he hurled it at the nearest enemy soldier and scrambled around the hilltop, scooping up grenades from fallen comrades and throwing them across a small defile into Japanese caves with what the Sixth Marine Division's official history called "wonderful accuracy."

Eventually, the grenades also ran out, but as dawn broke on May 15, Golar found a BAR lying next to a dead Marine and fired a steady stream of rounds from it until it jammed.

"Nothing more to give 'em now," he told Kelly. "Let's get some of these wounded guys down from here."

He bent down, carefully lifted a Marine with a gaping chest wound, and carried him toward the slope of the hill. Kelly heard the crack of a rifle shot and saw Golar stagger, but the husky redhead managed to place the wounded man gently on the ground and stumble over to a ditch.

"I saw him sit down and push his helmet over his forehead like he was going to sleep," recalled Kelly. "Then he died."

WALT RUTKOWSKI wasn't sure how long he'd been lying in the same spot, clutching his M-1 in one hand and Major Courtney's .45 automatic in the other. He'd had enough strength to crawl over to Courtney's body and get the pistol, but since then, his wounded leg had stiffened up, and he found it hard to move.

By his estimate, it was getting close to first light when a baby-faced Marine who looked to be about sixteen years old came trotting out of the darkness and dropped down beside him.

"Hey, man, I'm a replacement," the young Marine said, as if that weren't obvious. "Are you okay?"

"I got hit in the leg," Rutkowski said, "but it could be worse."

"I came over to give you a boost, man. Look, I've got a machine gun. I don't know how it works, but you probably do."

Rutkowski glanced at the weapon the young Marine was holding, then shook his head. "It's not gonna do either one of us much good," he said. "The back plate's gone off of it, and it won't fire without it. What'd you do with the plate?"

The young Marine looked disappointed and shrugged. "Aw, I threw it away," he said. "I didn't want some Jap to find it and be able to shoot it. I guess I wasn't thinking straight."

"Well, the gun's worthless the way it is," Rutkowski told him.

The young Marine shrugged again, flung the machine gun to the ground, and scurried back into the darkness.

IT WAS ABOUT 5:00 A.M. on May 15 when a knee mortar round hit within three or four feet of Ray Schlinder and finally ended his grenade-throwing epic. It rammed a golf ball–sized fragment into his chest cavity, sliced completely through his right lung, and knifed into his liver. Another fragment also buried itself in his left wrist, but that was a minor concern compared to the other wound.

Minutes earlier, the first friendly voice Schlinder had heard in hours had interrupted his marathon game of pitch. The voice belonged to Schlinder's squad leader and close friend, Sergeant Bill Enright.

"Hey, Ray, Farnsworth's been hit. I don't know how bad."

Enright referred to Private Vinone "Vern" Farnsworth, the gunner manning another .30-caliber Browning some forty yards away.

"You think he's still alive?" Schlinder asked.

"I don't know," Enright said. "All I know is he was hit."

"Well, I'm gonna go see about him. He may need help."

"Okay, good luck," Enright said, and scrambled away down the trench.

Schlinder had made it only about halfway to Farnsworth's position when the shell struck. Dazed by the blast, he thought at first it had merely knocked the wind out of him, but as he gasped for air, he felt something warm and wet running down his side.

"I pulled off my shirt and sweatshirt," Schlinder recalled, "and I saw this hole in my chest. It was about the size of a silver dollar, and bleeding pretty bad, and I started thinking about what a helluva mess I was in."

I'm the farthest guy out on top of this rock, and if the Japs take the hill again, I'll lie here and bleed to death. I can't do anything for Farnsworth now. I gotta find some help for me!

Clutching the hole in his chest, Schlinder pulled himself to his feet and ran as well as he could toward the north slope of Sugar Loaf. Within a few seconds, he was totally winded, and his wound seemed to be bleeding faster than before. Wobbly and dizzy-headed, he slid over the slope and tumbled a few yards down it until he hit a pile of rock and rubble and lay there panting.

After a couple of minutes, Schlinder caught his breath sufficiently to let out a few weak yells, and, miraculously, his cries were heard by Pharmacist's Mate First Class Frank Mack, a Navy corpsman.

"Ray was in bad shape with a heckuva hole in him, and I could tell he was pretty torn up inside," Mack recalled many years later. "I really wasn't sure he was going to make it, and we'd had so many wounded that I didn't have much in the way of supplies left to work with."

"Damn, I'm glad to see you, Doc," Schlinder muttered.

"Just take it easy, and I'll do what I can, but I'm almost out of everything," Mack told him. The only thing the corpsman could find to plug the hole in Schlinder's chest was a small first-aid packet, now empty of its original contents but bulky enough to slow the bleeding. Mack also pulled Schlinder under an overhanging ledge, where he was somewhat protected, both from the Japanese and the elements.

"Hang on," Mack whispered. "We're trying to get some amtracks in here to pick up the wounded. We'll get you out as soon as we can."

"Do me one last favor before you go, okay?"

"What's that?" Mack asked.

"Hand me my .45," Schlinder said. "If the Nips come down this slope, I'd like to take as many of them with me as I can."

Mack took the pistol from its holster and pressed it into Schlinder's right hand. "Good luck," he said.

Schlinder lay motionless until the sun came up. Behind him at the foot of the north slope, he could hear amtracks being hit by mortar and artillery fire, but one finally managed to reach the base of the hill. Soon afterward, Schlinder saw Mack and two Marines approaching. They lifted him onto a stretcher and carried him downhill to the amtrack. It was crowded with about twenty-five other grievously wounded Marines.

"I was almost out of blood when they loaded me on the tank, but a lot of guys were worse off than me," Schlinder said. "I saw guys in all kinds of bad shape. Guys missing arms, guys missing legs, guys shot through the head. One of my buddies, PFC Fred Sanchez from New Mexico, was hit in the guts and dying. He didn't live to get to the aid station."

Schlinder later learned that only three of the sixty-five able-bodied men who had marched south a week earlier with K Company's weapons platoon emerged unscathed from the Sugar Loaf ordeal.

"I spent the next nine and a half months in military hospitals, and I'm still carrying a piece of shrapnel around in my liver," he said nearly sixty-one years later. "But I was damned lucky. I'll never know how any of us made it off that hill alive."

AT 7:30 A.M. on May 15—just thirty minutes before a planned new Marine assault on the Sugar Loaf complex—a powerful Japanese counterattack drove the last few remaining men from Major Courtney's group off the summit of Sugar Loaf. (Although the charge led by

Courtney had ultimately proved futile, he would be posthumously awarded the Medal of Honor.)

Within an hour and a half, the enemy counterattack stretched along a 900-yard front into the 29th Marines' zone, and it kept rolling until early afternoon. By the time the advance was halted, much of the hard-won ground in front of Sugar Loaf had also been lost.

In three days of savage combat, the Second Battalion of the 22nd Marines had lost more than 400 men—40 percent of its strength. Meanwhile, units of all three infantry battalions of the 29th Marines were now thrown into the thick of the fighting before Half Moon Hill—but with few positive results. The night of May 15–16 found both regiments bogged down well short of the crests of Sugar Loaf and Half Moon.

On the afternoon of May 16, the Marines of the 22nd reached the crest of Sugar Loaf four times—and four times they were driven back by massed mortar and artillery fire and Japanese infantry counterattacking from caves. At the same time, troops of the 29th were taking a brutal pounding on Half Moon. By 5:00 P.M., they were trying to dig in on the crest of the hill, but a maelstrom of shellfire made their situation untenable, even after extensive use of smoke. Before dark, they were forced to withdraw to a smaller ridge to the north.

"The frustrating thing about those hills was that they just looked like barren little humps covered with tree stumps left by Navy gunfire," said First Lieutenant Bob Sherer, who led the machine-gun section of Fox Company when the 29th joined the fight. "There was no outward indication of all the caves and tunnels inside."

Snipers with Nambu machine guns took a heavy toll on officers of the 29th, and within a few hours, Sherer found himself commanding Fox Company's First Rifle Platoon. "We got on Sugar and stayed long enough to fight off several Jap counterattacks, but we couldn't hold," he said.

"All told . . . May 16 was as bitter a day as the Sixth Division had seen or would see," concluded the division's historian several years later.

Yet, for all practical purposes, at the end of that bitter day, the division found itself locked in virtually the same disheartening stalemate that it had faced four days earlier.

The battle for Sugar Loaf was, in fact, only half over.

CHAPTER TEN

The Limits of Human Endurance

W HILE UNITS of the Sixth Marine Division were being bled white on the slopes of Sugar Loaf, Half Moon, and the Horseshoe, all three infantry regiments of the First Marine Division were pressing an advance parallel to the Sixth on the east. They were also absorbing a similar bludgeoning from enemy defenders around Dakeshi Ridge, Wana Ridge, and Wana Draw.

By afternoon on May 12 (L-plus-42), the Seventh Marines had managed to dislodge the enemy from the summit of Dakeshi, breaching the first of three Japanese defensive lines in the First Division's sector and virtually annihilating the remaining troops of Japan's 62nd Division. The next day, May 13, the subterranean headquarters of Major General Suichi Akikawa, a Japanese brigade commander, came under intensive attack, with the general and his staff personally trading grenades with Marine riflemen. Late that evening, acting under direct orders from General Ushijima, Akikawa and a handful of survivors slipped through Marine lines and fled.

On the morning of May 14, the Seventh Marines launched a major new attack at Wana Ridge, a nettlesome strip of high ground forming the northern wall of Wana Draw. In a coordinated assault, the First Marines drove toward the point where the ridge ended at the mouth of the draw. When both attacks failed to reach their objectives, General del Valle, the division commander, concluded that Wana Draw couldn't be taken by infantry unless tanks were brought up to provide support and covering fire.

General Ushijima, too, recognized U.S. tanks as a major key to the battle's outcome. "The enemy's power lies in its tanks," the Japanese commander told his officers in a memo. "It has become obvious that our battle against the Americans is a battle against their tanks."

For Corporal Jack Armstrong, commander of the "Ticket to Tokyo II," and his crew, this meant increased high-risk exposure to the deadly

Japanese 47-millimeter antitank guns that had already destroyed the original "Ticket to Tokyo," killed one crewman, and cost another his arm. Having felt the 47s' lethal bite once, Armstrong and his men had an acute case of the jitters going in.

"I was glad the new tank was a regular Sherman M4 without the flamethrower because of that big tank of napalm that was mounted inside," Armstrong recalled. "But when we started across Wana Draw, it felt like every gun on the island was zeroed in on us."

Even maintenance personnel of the First Marine Tank Battalion regularly ventured into harm's way to repair disabled Shermans. PFC Frank Nemec, a Peleliu and Cape Gloucester veteran of Czech descent whose experience with tractors and other heavy machines on a central Texas farm had made him a natural for the tank service, was severely injured as he tried to replace a 165-pound tank battery under fire.

"By this time, we were short of tanks, and we had to rebuild anything that could be rebuilt," Nemec said, "but after I hurt my back working on that battery, I couldn't do anything—even tie my shoes. I was in the hospital for almost a year."

Under the circumstances, Nemec felt he earned his Purple Heart as honestly as any rifleman who took a bullet or grenade wound.

For Jack Armstrong and his crew, meanwhile, their streak of bad luck continued. To give the enemy as little time as possible to reorganize or reinforce, the battalion operated in relays at Wana Draw and Wana Ridge, with one wave of tanks attacking while a second rushed back across the draw to reload. Armstrong's tank was returning from its attack when disaster struck, but this time, instead of one of the dreaded 47s, the villain was a "teakettle" land mine that blew "Ticket to Tokyo II" off the ground and hurled its commander out of the turret.

"When we hit that thing, it made the loudest explosion I ever heard," Armstrong said, "and the next thing I remember was lying outside the tank on the ground."

He was groggy from a blast concussion, bleeding from one ear, and stinging from several shrapnel wounds to his arms. Miraculously, no one else in the tank was hurt—all escaped through the bottom hatch to the safety of another Sherman that stopped to help—but the same wasn't true of the infantry fire team assigned to Armstrong's tank.

"The fire team was right beside the tank, and they never had a chance," Armstrong said. "They were all wounded, and I think at least two of them were killed."

Moments later, Armstrong watched in a daze as the tank that had rescued his crew stopped on a slight rise a few dozen yards away and turned its 75-millimeter cannon on the crippled "Ticket to Tokyo II." "It gave me a heartsick feeling to watch their gunner demolishing our own tank," he recalled much later, "but it had to be done to keep our equipment from falling into enemy hands."

The Fifth Marines, meanwhile, advanced on the village of Dakeshi, only to collide head-on with a strong system of enemy defenses in an area identified on maps as the Awacha Pocket. If the Japanese line could be broken here, the heart of the Shuri Defense Zone would be exposed to direct assault. But as had so often been the case since the first days of May, the weather was to prove as tenacious an enemy as the Japanese.

"When our battalion dug in in front of Awacha, our mortars were emplaced on the slope of a little rise about seventy-five yards behind the front line," noted PFC Gene Sledge, the K/3/5 mortarman. "The torrents of rain were causing us other problems besides chilly misery. Our tanks couldn't move up to support us. Amtracks had to bring up a lot of supplies because the jeeps and trailers bogged down in the soft soil."

Typically, though, the places where ammunition was most needed were inaccessible even to amtracks. Weather conditions being what they were, virtually every rifle bullet, grenade, and machine-gun round aimed at the enemy first had to be carried for some distance on the backs and shoulders of enlisted men slogging through thick mud, driving rain, and ceaseless enemy fire.

It was backbreaking—and morale killing—work that, in Sledge's words, "drove the infantryman, weary from the mental and physical stress of combat, almost to the brink of physical collapse." It reached the point that profanity and verbal abuse were heaped on the manufacturers of the wooden boxes in which .30-caliber rifle bullets were packed. Each box contained 1,000 rounds of ammo and weighed more than fifty pounds, yet offered only a shallow fingerhold at either end to the two men needed to handle a single box. On the other hand, the makers of boxes for grenades and belted machine-gun ammo drew applause for equipping their containers with rope or metal handles.

Books and movies on the war generally ignored such onerous aspects of a combat infantryman's life, Sledge complained, and left the impression that plentiful supplies of ammo were always within easy reach when needed. "But the work (of hauling ammo by hand) was something none of us would forget," he said. "It was exhausting, demoralizing, and seemingly unending."

What was happening, although it was never apparent to many who suffered through it until it reached crisis level, was a gradual erosion of mental discipline and psychological control. Compounded by deteriorating physical stamina, acute lack of sleep, grief over lost buddies, unmitigated anger, inescapable fears, and failing hopes for one's own survival, an insidious form of mental illness became a raging epidemic on Okinawa.

It caused usually reasonable men to curse the makers of the ammo boxes they carried and stressed-out officers to berate brave men for what should've been viewed as commendable acts of courage. It touched off hair-trigger temper tantrums among enlisted men—sometimes bordering on mutiny—against officers and NCOs. It blinded men to everything except a mindless need to hide or run, and it drove some of their buddies to condemn these men as cowards for cracking up under pressure, "losing their guts," and lapsing into the infamous "1,000-yard stare."

Arguably, the final month of the Okinawa campaign did more than any other battle in modern history to add such terms as "battlefield psychosis," "combat fatigue," "posttraumatic stress syndrome," and "shell shock" to America's vocabulary. All are terms for the same invisible virus of despair that wounds the mind and psyche as disastrously as bullets, bombs, and shellfire ravage human flesh and bone, and whose aftereffects often linger for a lifetime.

The virus manifests itself when men are swept beyond the limits of human endurance—and tens of thousands of cases of it were recorded at Okinawa.

⌐

PROBABLY NO RIFLE COMPANY in the First Marine Division had been led by a more admired set of commissioned officers during the savage battle for Peleliu than K Company, Third Battalion, Fifth Marines, and no group of enlisted men ever held its officers in higher esteem.

But Peleliu exacted an even heavier toll on K/3/5's leadership than on its rank-and-file troops. Less than 100 hours before the Marines were withdrawn from combat, First Lieutenant Ed "Hillbilly" Jones, commander of the Third Platoon, had been gunned down by a sniper. Captain Andy "Ack-Ack" Haldane, the company's beloved CO, had been shot through the head on the next-to-last day of the fighting. Both Jones and Haldane had been with the company since Guadalcanal, and both were Silver Star recipients.

When K/3/5 was pulled off the line at Peleliu after thirty straight days of battle, only two of its commissioned officers remained alive and unwounded—First Lieutenant Thomas "Stumpy" Stanley, the company exec, and Second Lieutenant Charles "Duke" Ellington, commander of the mortar section.

Eight months later, in mid-May 1945, the entire cast of Peleliu officers was gone from K/3/5, except for Stanley, who was nursing a severe case of malaria and only a few days from being evacuated to a hospital.

"We'd lost more lieutenants than I could count, much less remember, during the first six weeks at Okinawa," said mortar section leader Sergeant R. V. Burgin, "and without badmouthing any of our replacement officers, I'd have to say that their levels of experience and leadership were a cut or two below what we'd had at Peleliu."

Replacing Ellington in command of the mortar section was Robert "Scotty" McKenzie, a "boot" second lieutenant fresh from an Ivy League school and a total stranger to combat. On the rest-camp island of Pavuvu, as K/3/5 prepared for Okinawa, McKenzie's loud pronouncements about the havoc he planned to wreak on the Japanese when he met them in battle made Peleliu and Cape Gloucester veterans either cringe with embarrassment for the young shave-tail or laugh in his face.

"The first time one of our guys gets hit, I'm gonna take my Ka-Bar in my teeth and my .45 in my hand and charge those damned Japs!" McKenzie would rail while the veterans smirked and rolled their eyes.

"I was embarrassed for Mac," said Gene Sledge, "because it was so obvious that he conceived combat as a mixture of football and a Boy Scout campout."

In early May, McKenzie had learned the truth about combat in one painful lesson, and his reaction had borne no resemblance to his earlier illusions. When he saw his first man killed in action and came under massive artillery fire for the first time, he dug the deepest foxhole that anyone in the company could remember seeing. Long after all his men had finished their own digging, McKenzie was still at it, burrowing like a groundhog as enlisted men threw barb after barb at their lieutenant.

"Ain't it about time you took your Ka-Bar and .45 and charged them Nips, Mac?" jibed Corporal Snafu Shelton.

"Hey, if you dig that hole much deeper, Scotty, they may get you for desertion," said Sergeant R. V. Burgin.

"We kept our comments respectful because of his rank," Sledge recalled later, "but we gave it to him good for all the bravado and nonsense he'd been mouthing."

Many years after the war, Burgin was more charitable than many toward his former platoon leader. "Scotty was green as grass, but he grew up a lot on Okinawa," he said. "I'd get so mad at him sometimes I could've killed him, but I couldn't stay mad. He developed into a good Marine."

When Lieutenant Stanley's malaria reached the point where he had to be hospitalized, the men of K/3/5 found themselves confronting yet another officer problem—and this one was no joking matter. Assigned as the company's new CO was First Lieutenant George Loveday, who had served briefly as executive officer but remained a stranger to most of his men. Many of them, according to their own recollections, soon wished they never had to see him again.

Where McKenzie was merely brash and immature, Loveday had the personality of a walking booby trap. He was known, less than fondly, as "Shadow" for his ability to slip up behind a Marine who was doing something the new CO didn't like and explode without warning. At any slight provocation, Shadow would throw his green fatigue cap to the ground and stomp it into the mud while roundly cursing anyone who aroused his ire.

PFC John Redifer, one of Sergeant Burgin's veteran mortarmen, felt the sting of a particularly virulent Loveday outburst on a day when a work party of ammo carriers, including Gene Sledge, found themselves pinned down in a ravine by a Japanese machine gun. Redifer's "sin" was coming to their rescue by hurling smoke grenades and summoning a tank.

"The smoke hid us from the gunner, but he kept firing intermittent bursts down the draw to prevent our crossing," Sledge remembered. "Slugs popped and snapped, but we made it across . . . hugging the side of the tank like chicks beside a mother hen."

Shadow's reaction was to pitch a fit. "You stupid son of a bitch!" he howled at Redifer. "What the hell do you think you're doing, exposing yourself to enemy fire like that? Don't you have any goddamn brains?"

Redifer took the dressing-down quietly, but he was clearly dismayed. As Loveday stormed away, the Marines whose lives Redifer had just helped save could scarcely stifle their fury.

"It was just the first of many such performances I was to witness," said Sledge, "and they never ceased to amaze and disgust me. . . . [H]ere was this ranting, raving officer actually cursing and berating a man for doing something any other officer would have considered a meritorious act. It was so incredibly illogical that we couldn't believe it."

As he looked back across six decades on the totally different—yet equally bizarre—behavior patterns of Lieutenants McKenzie and Loveday, Sergeant Burgin sensed a common thread that might help explain both officers' actions.

"Battle fatigue can take a lot of different shapes and forms," he said, "and officers sure as hell weren't immune to it. If anything, they were probably under worse mental strain than the guys who served under them. On Okinawa, men tried to deal with stress in lots of ways. Yelling and cussing and trying to dig foxholes to China were just a few of them."

PSYCHIATRY IN GENERAL—and especially the quest for effective treatment for psychiatric disorders induced by the stresses of combat—was still in its infancy in 1945. Military doctors on Okinawa, inundated by men with severe physical wounds and armed with little or no experience in treating psychiatric patients, were forced into hit-or-miss responses to the influx of "head cases."

Near the town of Chatan in the First Marine Division's zone, a special hospital was set up for men whose minds had snapped under the rigors of battle. One patient was a young Marine who had lapsed into a comalike state after a Japanese mortar round burst near the foxhole he shared with a buddy.

Doctors found no evidence of concussion in the Marine—and his buddy was unhurt—but the patient had passed out cold when the shell exploded, and when he awoke, after prolonged unconsciousness, he was irrational, unaware of his surroundings, and shaking uncontrollably.

By this time, the chief physician had seen enough shell-shock cases to notice that many victims were unable to verbalize their feelings because of negative emotions. To overcome the problem, the patient was injected with a chemical solution that freed him of his resistance to talk, then questioned at length by the doctor in charge.

As a visiting observer described it later: "When the man had finally been brought to the point where he and his buddy were in the shell hole together, the doctor suddenly stamped on the deck, hit the wall with his fist, and shouted 'Mortar!'

"No actor could have portrayed fear like this man did. He kept gurgling, 'Mortar . . . mortar . . . mortar . . .'"

Asked what he was going to do now, the man replied, "Dig deeper! Dig deeper!"

When the doctor told him to go ahead, the man dropped to his knees and went through frantic digging motions until the doctor managed to quiet him and get him back to bed.

Such experimentation wasn't expected to produce a cure. At best, it merely provided a few leads that might help steer some of these patients back from the "psycho ward" toward normalcy.

ONE LIKELY CONTRIBUTOR to the epidemic of battle fatigue on Okinawa was a newly instituted practice of sending fresh, untested replacement troops directly into front-line units while the battle was being fought. A total of 180 officers and 4,065 enlisted men were "absorbed" during May into depleted infantry companies of the First Marine Division. Similar waves of replacements were simultaneously bolstering other divisions' raw numbers but doing little to sustain their combat capability.

While the new policy filled vacancies in the ranks more rapidly than in the past, many veteran field commanders condemned it as a failure.

Okinawa: Victory in the Pacific, a Marine Corps monograph published in 1955, was outspokenly critical of the policy: "Strength in numbers is one thing, and fighting efficiency is another. Feeding raw, usually inexperienced replacements into the front lines during action had proved anything but successful. The new replacements actually hampered the companies, since the new men had no conception of what they were getting into."

Green replacements were often characterized as being "out of phase." As the monograph explained: "[T]hey were standing when they should have been down; they were down when they should have been up and moving. They seldom had time to get acquainted with their fellow squad or platoon members before they were moving into action; there was a lack of confidence felt by the veterans and a definite lack of unity . . . because of these 'strangers.'"

Corporal Ray Schlinder and other survivors of the battle for Sugar Loaf Hill know by heart the toll of casualties recorded during that hellish weeklong fight. They know the Marines took the hill eleven times before they held it, and that 2,662 of their comrades were killed and wounded there. They don't relish talking about it, but they also recall that 1,552 Marines—replacements and veterans alike—suffered disabling mental disorders during the slaughter.

"When I think about guys who cracked up," said Schlinder, "I always remember 'Big John'—a sergeant from Montana. He was one of the best, bravest Marines I ever knew, but when he saw a close friend shot through the jugular vein and bleed to death before anyone could help him, it broke Big John up, and he went over the edge.

"I never thought any less of him for it, though."

⁓

Marine Lieutenant Quentin "Monk" Meyer and the men of his Fourth Joint Assault Signal Company had often found time hanging heavy on their hands during the month of April. In fact, being forgotten on Love Day and left to languish all night in a Higgins boat may have been the most exciting things that happened to them during the first thirty days of the Okinawa campaign.

When May arrived, though, everything changed. Once the First Marine Division went into combat, the JASCO unit—whose job was to call in naval gunfire whenever it was needed to support a ground assault—had stayed busy day and night. In hopes of better coordination between Navy firepower and Marine infantry units ashore, every rifle company had been assigned a specific warship as its fire-support partner. In Meyer's view, this arrangement was vastly superior to the old "catch-as-catch-can" system employed in previous campaigns, but it also meant longer hours and a more demanding job for Meyer and his men.

The lieutenant made mention of this fact on the morning of May 11 as he stole a few minutes to dash off a brief predawn letter to his fiancée, Francie Walton, back in New York.

It seems that I can't find time to write a decent letter. I have so much to say but must resort to this until our battalion settles down. . . .

As Meyer wrote, the Second Battalion, Fifth Marines, was mopping up the last organized Japanese resistance in the Awacha Pocket while 1/5 and 1/7 followed along in its wake, cleaning out bypassed enemy strong-points. But Meyer's thoughts were drifting 10,000 miles away and twelve months into the past.

My darling, it was just a bit more than a year ago that we were to-gether. It was a wonderful corner of the spring—a spring I shall always re-member. I think leaving you was one of the most difficult things I have ever done, but we still have all the seasons of our lives ahead, and they will be happy years. . . .

By 6:00 A.M., the five-man team under Meyer's command was at its operations post, and Meyer was directing fire from a Navy cruiser at enemy targets. The team included Private Gil Quintanilla, a spotter/scout/sniper whose Thompson submachine gun provided the bulk of the group's firepower; PFCs Raven L. Rummell and John Hein; two Marine radiomen; and a Navy radio operator.

"We knew there were still some Jap snipers holed up in caves in our area," Quintanilla recalled, "and when Monk spotted a sniper, he went after 'em, even though that wasn't our main job."

Around 6:30, the cruiser was ordered to cease firing, and word came down that the JASCO team was to return to the battalion command post to begin an eighteen-hour break. "I called Monk on the radio and told him to come on back to the CP," recalled PFC Hein later, "but he said he wanted to wait around for a while to make sure everything was going all right."

A little more than two hours later, a shaken Quintanilla called from the observation post to tell Hein that Meyer and PFC Rummell had been hit. "They'd both gone out with a squad that was cleaning up a last pocket of resistance in that immediate area," Hein said. "About nine o'clock we got word that Rummell was wounded and Monk was dead."

The last thing Quintanilla heard Meyer say as he and Rummell headed out was: "Hey, Quint, let me borrow your tommy." After sixty-plus years, memories of that request still burn in Quintanilla's mind.

"Usually, in a situation like that," he recalled, "Monk would say, 'Grab your tommy, Quint, and let's go,' but this time he just asked for the tommy and didn't invite me along, so I handed him the gun, sat down in my foxhole, and watched him and Rummell disappear around the corner of a little hill. They were heading for a good-sized cave about sixty yards away."

About fifteen minutes later, two pairs of stretcher bearers appeared from the direction of the cave. One was carrying Rummell, who was groaning and bleeding from a neck wound. Quintanilla went over to the other stretcher and stared down at Meyer's body.

"I felt like I'd been hit myself," he said. "My heart was in my throat, and my stomach was churning. I was shaking like hell."

He removed Meyer's watch, compass, maps, and various personal gear from the body and called Hein at the battalion CP to report what had happened. Then Quintanilla used Meyer's compass to lead the JASCO team back to safety. At the CP, someone handed him a cup of grapefruit juice laced with grain alcohol to calm him down.

Some discrepancies remain, even today, in the accounts of Meyer's death. Both Rummell, who saw it happen, and the doctor who examined the body maintained that he was killed instantly by a sniper's bullet. Another Marine who was nearby at the time contended that Meyer stepped on a land mine.

"Personally, I've always thought it was a grenade that got him because I saw shrapnel wounds on his body," Quintanilla said, "but those could've been made after he died. I don't guess it would've made much difference to Monk how it happened, anyway. I know he didn't want to die because he had unfinished business at home, but he was one helluva gung-ho Marine."

"His courage was legend," wrote Hein in a letter to Meyer's parents in early September 1945. "He always picked the most dangerous jobs, and he did them fearlessly and well. His energy knew no bounds."

On Peleliu, Hein pointed out, the Navy fired 61,000 rounds at the Japs, and, of these, Meyer was directly responsible for 11,000. "I think this will let you know how well Monk did his job," he said.

Meyer closed his final letter to Francie Walton with these words:

I love you much, my little darling, and always will. This is just to let you know that all is well with me and that you are always in my thoughts.

LIKE THE FIRST and Sixth Marine Divisions, the Army's 77th and 96th Divisions were contending with their own lists of demonic hills with fanciful names as the middle of May arrived. Among the maze of ridges that enjoyed brief, bloody fame on the agonizing march toward Shuri were Chocolate Drop, Flattop, Love, Oboe, and Sugar.

But the tallest and most formidable of the lot was Conical Hill in the 96th's sector. General Hodge, the 24th Corps commander, handed the responsibility for seizing Conical to Colonel Eddy May's 383rd Infantry, the same regiment that had been instrumental in wearing down enemy resistance on Kakazu Ridge. Because of the tenacious series of attacks directed by May at Kakazu, Hodge was convinced that he was the best man to tackle Conical.

Called Utanamori by the Japanese, Conical was almost 500 feet high and topped by a tall round cone. To put themselves in position to attack it, May's troops would first have to advance some 800 yards down a hogback to another high point called Sugar Hill (not to be confused with Sugar Loaf). But if Conical, Sugar, and the hogback could be taken, their loss would spell disaster for General Ushijima's Shuri Line and its defenders. It would open Yonabaru, the third largest town on Okinawa, to attack and allow the 96th's Deadeyes to advance up the Yonabaru-Naha highway, drive behind Ushijima's entrenchments, join forces with Marines advancing from the west, and block any enemy attempt to escape to the south.

Foreseeing this threat, Ushijima had assigned about 1,000 well-armed, well-trained troops to defend Conical, the majority positioned in the hills to the west, which the Japanese believed would be May's route of attack. Instead May sent two companies of his Third Battalion up the north slope of Conical. By afternoon on May 13, with General Buckner observing from May's command post, the GIs were dug in about fifty feet below Conical's cone-shaped crest—a sheer topographical oddity that offered no defensible positions—without incurring a single casualty on the way up.

Over the next three days (May 14–16), the Deadeyes repelled a half-dozen Japanese counterattacks without giving ground. Meanwhile, General Hodge sent the rested, reinforced Seventh Division in a fast-moving strike around the Japanese lines. The division's target was the Yonabaru-Naha highway. If the Seventh could seize the road and move west along it, it would make a further retreat to the south by Ushijima's forces impossible. It was a big "if," but the potential prizes it offered were the collapse of the Shuri Line, the seizure of Shuri itself, and the end of Japan's 32nd Army.

But before this could happen, the four American divisions bearing down on Shuri faced another devastating ordeal. The ten days between

May 11 and May 21 would be described by historians as "the most terrible of the extraordinarily bitter Okinawa campaign."

Ruinous losses were incurred during this period by all the American divisions now inching their way toward Shuri, but nowhere were these losses more brutally felt than among the Marines of K/3/5.

⌒

FOR THE FIRST TIME in his life, Corporal Sterling Mace had lost his infectious sense of humor. The Shuri Line had stolen it from him and replaced it with a pervasive feeling of doom, punctuated by bursts of anger, spells of dizziness and disorientation, fits of shaking, and interludes of abject sorrow.

The symptoms deepened as each passing day brought new episodes of horror and irreplaceable loss. But it was two incidents in particular, occurring just a couple of days apart, that proved to be the final straws that propelled Mace into a full-blown crisis.

On the morning of May 7, when Mace noticed his foxhole mate, PFC Bob Whitby, reading what appeared to be a letter from his wife in Florida, he paid no attention at first. But a half hour later, when Whitby was still slumped over the letter with tears streaming down his face, Mace became concerned.

"What's the matter, man?" Mace asked. "You get some bad news?"

Whitby was eight years older than Mace—an "old guy" with twin two-year-old daughters at home—but he stood just five feet four, and his short stature made him seem almost boyish. His shoulders shook with sobs like a brokenhearted child as he tried to speak.

"It's . . . it's my kids," he muttered, wiping his face on his sleeve. "My wife says they can't sleep at night because they miss their daddy so much, and they keep asking her when I'm coming home."

"Just take it easy, Bob," Mace said, trying to sound reassuring. "You're gonna make it fine. Everything will be okay."

Whitby didn't seem to hear. He raised his head to stare at Mace with vacant, bloodshot eyes. His voice trembled, and a new wave of tears flooded his cheeks. "When *am* I coming home, Sterling? What's going to happen to my girls if I don't make it? That's all I can think about, and it just keeps eating at me. Damn, I can't take it anymore."

Mace leaned down, awkwardly patting Whitby's shoulder. In his mind's eye was the image of old "Pops" Whitby, trying in vain a few days earlier to jump across a ditch under enemy fire with legs far too short for the job. Whitby had narrowly missed being hit that day, Mace thought. Next time, who could say if he'd be so lucky?

"You need to go to the battalion aid station and see a doc," Mace said quietly. "There's a corpsman down there named George Chulis. He's a good guy. He can give you something for your nerves."

Mace wasn't sure if his buddy had heard anything he'd said until Whitby finally struggled to his feet, picked up his gear, and began walking listlessly toward the rear. They didn't see each other again for more than fifty years.

Two days later, a cluster of exploding knee mortar rounds killed PFC Garner W. Mott, another young father from rural Miami County, Ohio, and another close friend of Mace's. In Mott's case, however, he never saw his son, Nicky Joe, who was only ten months old at the time of his father's death.

"Mott was a great guy, the kind of guy everybody in the outfit liked and respected," Mace said. "The only thing he ever talked about was that boy of his, and I'm sure his last thoughts were of Nicky Joe. His death was proof to me that the good really do die young. It took me a long time to get over it."

Each day, it seemed, the list of lost buddies grew longer and harder to bear. Two days after Mott's death, Mace himself almost bought the farm when a shell fired from an eight-inch Japanese gun more than a mile away blew him completely out of his foxhole. His platoon mates rushed to him through the swirling smoke, almost certain that Mace was dead, but the explosion had only knocked him cold and punctured his eardrum.

The incident that finally pushed Mace over the edge came on May 9, when he volunteered as a stretcher bearer to carry out wounded Marines from Wana Ridge. After the close call with the artillery shell, Mace would take any opportunity to be out in the open, rather than being "trapped" in a foxhole.

Among this group of casualties were two aides assigned to future Illinois Senator Paul Douglas, who'd entered the Corps as a fifty-year-old private and quickly advanced to the rank of major (with the help, it was said, of political friends in Washington, including President Roosevelt). Also wounded in Mace's immediate area was Sergeant Alex Henson, a squad leader in K/3/5's machine-gun section, and his gunner, PFC Emmitt Bishop.

"While we were struggling to get these guys out under heavy enemy fire, I found an abandoned jeep," Mace recalled. "I said to myself, 'I can find a better use for this thing than just sitting here,' and with the help of some other stretcher bearers, I started loading up the wounded on the jeep. When we got to the aid station, this ninety-day-wonder second lieutenant, who'd only been there a day or two, came over and demanded to know where I got the jeep."

Mace explained that the vehicle had been abandoned and that he was using it to transport severely wounded men, but the lieutenant was less than understanding.

"You're not authorized to have that jeep, and you may have left some officer stranded out there," the lieutenant flared. "You take it back where you found it, and get back to your post, or, by God, I'll write you up on theft charges."

As Mace drove back toward the front, Japanese artillery shells began bursting around the jeep, and with every explosion, he felt his grip on reality being blasted loose. His hands began to shake so violently that he could hardly hold the steering wheel. Waves of dizziness and nausea swept over him.

He jerked the jeep to a halt without really knowing where he was and noticed a familiar corpsman frowning at him. "What's the matter, buddy?" the medic asked. "You look like hell. Are you okay?"

"Don't you hear that damned shelling?" Mace yelled. "Jesus Christ, don't you hear it? Get down! Get down!"

The corpsman grabbed Mace by the shoulders and stared into his eyes. "You gotta get yourself the hell out of here, Mace," he said. "Get back to the aid station, and tell 'em you need a sedative. You're in no shape to be up here."

The shaking and dizziness grew worse as Mace stumbled back the way he'd come. The next thing he remembered was lying on a cot, cursing the replacement lieutenant, and screaming about the shelling. Two doctors were leaning over him, arguing.

"He's gone totally psycho," he heard one doctor say. "We'd better get some restraints on him before he hurts himself or somebody else."

"It's another case of battle fatigue," said the other doctor. "I'll give him a shot to calm him down."

Mace saw the second doctor pick up a hypodermic syringe, and he felt the sting as the needle broke the skin of his upper arm. After that, he remembered nothing else until he woke up several hours later aboard a hospital ship.

AT ABOUT THIS SAME TIME, Corporal Robert C. Doran, a fire team leader in K/3/5's Second Platoon, was dying of multiple wounds on Dakeshi Ridge as PFC Harry Bender held him in his arms.

"I guess he was delirious, or maybe he really thought I was Lieutenant (Bucky) Pearson, commander of the First Platoon," Bender recalled. "He kept staring into my face and whispering, 'Bucky, hold this hill. My blood's up here.'"

Soon after Doran died, the Marines were forced to withdraw.

THERE WERE TIMES as May wore on when Sergeant R. V. Burgin seemed, in every sense, to be the real commander of K/3/5's mortar section, not merely its senior NCO. Burgin's experience and combat savvy gained in three major Pacific campaigns had honed his battlefield instincts and skills to an edge that young Lieutenant Scotty McKenzie, Burgin's boss, couldn't approach, much less match.

On May 15, less than a week after subjecting himself to savage enemy fire to pinpoint the location of a Japanese machine gun, then directing a mortar barrage that "blew the gun one way and the gunner the other," Burgin locked horns with McKenzie in classic fashion. On a psychologically healthier battlefield under less wrenching mental stress, the confrontation between the veteran platoon leader and the greenhorn lieutenant might have earned Burgin a court-martial. But as it was, it was scarcely noticed and quickly forgotten.

By now, most men were so stressed that their attitudes and behavior patterns ranged from stoic resignation to bitter defiance. "The cursing and outbursts of rage didn't seem to help," recalled PFC Gene Sledge, a witness to the head-butting contest between McKenzie and Burgin, "although no one was above it when goaded to the point of desperation and fatigue."

It was in this atmosphere, and during an exhaustive series of orders and counterorders, moves and countermoves carried out in mud up to knee-deep, that Burgin ignored a direct command from McKenzie—and wiped out a force of at least fifty Japanese as a result.

As one of the Marines' most seasoned directors of mortar fire, Burgin had spent a lot of time observing a long, narrow ridge where entrenched Japanese had repulsed attack after attack by Marine infantry over a three-day period, even when the attackers were backed by heavy artillery. From his observations, Burgin deduced that the enemy defenders were in a narrow gully that sheltered them from artillery fire, yet they might be vulnerable to mortars, which could blanket a small area with fire on a steeper trajectory.

"I want us to register in three mortars so that one fires from right to left, one fires from left to right, and another one fires along the crest of the ridge above the gully," Burgin told PFCs Sledge, Vincent Santos, and John Redifer, Corporals Snafu Shelton and George Sarrett, and other mortar veterans. "Then, if we fire them all at once in a coordinated pattern, the Japs can't possibly get away."

When McKenzie heard about Burgin's plan, he emphatically ordered the tough-talking Texan to call it off.

"You can't do that," he said. "We can't spare the ammo."

Unfazed, Burgin grabbed the phone, called the company CP, and explained what he wanted to do. "Can you get us the ammo?" he asked.

"No problem," the CP responded.

A short time later, Burgin's voice crackled over the sound-powered phone: "Mortar section, on my command, fire!"

"No! Stop!" yelled McKenzie over the phone. "I order you not to fire."

"Go to hell, Scotty!" Burgin snapped. "Mortar section, fire on my command! Commence firing!"

"We fired as Mac ranted and raved," recalled Sledge. "When we finished firing, the company moved against the ridge. Not a shot was fired at our men."

More than fifty Japanese dead were found in the target area, all killed by K/3/5's 60-millimeter mortar fire. After a stone-faced McKenzie walked away, one of the mortarmen grinned at Burgin.

"I guess you showed old Mac a thing or two," he said.

"Just forget it," Burgin told him. "I don't want to hear any more about it. No need to rub the lieutenant's nose in it. That's not gonna help anybody."

On the morning of May 20, the streak of good luck that had carried Burgin unscathed through two major battles and most of another finally started to run out.

"I had an inkling something bad was gonna happen that day," Burgin recalled. "Corporal Jim Burke and I were on a patrol, and a 150-millimeter

Jap gun was giving us hell. We jumped into some shell craters just as a round from the 150 hit within a few feet of us. It completely buried me in dirt—they had to dig me out—but I didn't realize I was hurt until later."

About two o'clock that afternoon, the patrol got caught between dueling U.S. and Japanese artillery, with several Corsair fighters zooming in to help.

"The shell that got me hit the top of the ridge we were on and sent shrapnel flying all over hell," Burgin said. "One jagged piece about three inches long hit me in the back of the neck."

Burgin made it to an aid station under his own power through continuing artillery fire. By dark, he was lying inside a huge tent at a field hospital, surrounded by other wounded men and doctors who kept wanting to give him shots.

"I don't need another one of those things," he grumbled to one medic approaching him with a needle. "I've already had three shots. What I need is something for this pain in my stomach."

"Have you been near an exploding shell?" a nurse asked.

"About as close as I could be and still be alive," Burgin told her.

"You've got a concussion," she said. "I'll get you something for it."

As she hurried away, Burgin realized the concussion must have been caused by the shell that had briefly buried him alive that morning. K/3/5 would be without his expertise for eighteen days, but he'd get back to the company in time to take part in the final phase of the battle.

At the time, Burgin had no idea that he'd soon be awarded a Bronze Star, not for directing the mortar attack that killed fifty Japanese but for his earlier role in finding and silencing the enemy machine gun.

PFC BILL LEYDEN's turn came five days later on May 25—the day before his nineteenth birthday. After suffering a serious wound to his left eye at Peleliu, Leyden had lost the illusion of invulnerability that he'd carried into his first battle. Along with dozens of good friends, he'd also lost most of his fear of physical harm.

When he awoke that morning and pulled himself up into a sitting position on the edge of his foxhole, Leyden was first puzzled, then concerned, about the unresponsiveness of his foxhole mate, PFC Marion Vermeer. The instant Leyden tried to talk to Vermeer, he could tell something was seriously wrong.

Both of them were bone-tired, red-eyed from lack of sleep, tense, and dispirited from the endless shelling. Right now, they were in a bit of a lull, but the enemy guns could open up again with the heavy stuff at any second. Leyden's guts were like coiled springs, but Vermeer appeared strangely relaxed as he sprawled on his back at the bottom of the foxhole.

As members of the same rifle platoon, the two of them had shared a foxhole dozens of times in the course of two major battles. They'd also shared much else.

They'd been wounded within minutes of each other during a firefight in late September 1944, but both had recovered in time to rejoin K/3/5 before the company sailed for Okinawa. They'd shared in the loss of two company commanders—Captain Andy Haldane, killed by a sniper on the next-to-last day of combat on Peleliu, and Lieutenant Stumpy Stanley, evacuated from Okinawa a few days earlier with a raging case of malaria.

On Peleliu, they'd survived some of the nastiest, most savage fighting imaginable, but Okinawa had already lasted nearly twice as long, and there was still no end in sight. On Okinawa there was less hand-to-hand combat than on Peleliu, and except for the rain, the weather was less unbearable than Peleliu's 115-degree heat. The smell of decaying corpses was somewhat less overpowering, and even the terrain wasn't quite as impossible. But the tension born of the near-constant long-range enemy artillery fire on Okinawa was even harder on the nerves.

"You awake, man?" Leyden mumbled. "Do you hear what I'm saying?"

It wasn't a fair question, Leyden thought. He could hardly remember what he'd just said himself.

Vermeer didn't move or acknowledge the questions. He lay motionless in the foxhole, his right leg across Leyden's boondockers, his eyes wide and vacant, his face devoid of expression.

Leyden frowned. "What the hell's wrong with you?" he demanded. In recent days, he'd seen several cases of what they called "battle fatigue," and Vermeer had all the symptoms. He still neither moved nor spoke in response. The night before, the brawny former lumberjack from Washington State had seemed okay, but now he was acting like a zombie.

"Hey, man, I think you'd better—"

The rest of Leyden's words were lost in the rumble of an incoming shell, a flash of dark fire, and the earsplitting blast of a Japanese 75. Leyden was aware of someone screaming as the force of the explosion spewed him skyward. He, too, cried out as he sailed through the air—or thought he did—but maybe the sound was only in his brain: *Our Father and hail Mary!*

For a second, he was sure he saw Saint Peter sitting on a cloud, grinning at him with apparent approval. His devout Irish-Catholic mother would be proud. "He died with a prayer on his lips and Saint Peter smiling down on him," she would tell her friends.

I'm dead, he thought. *I must be dead.*

He wasn't, though—even if the first of his comrades to reach him thought he might be better off if he were. When he hit the ground twenty feet from his foxhole, one of his eardrums was blown out, and the little finger on his right hand was gone. His body was peppered with shrapnel wounds from his chest to his knees. Blood oozed from a dozen punctures in his abdomen.

Nothing much was left of Vermeer or PFC Roy Bauman, the other occupant of the foxhole. In the next foxhole over, PFC Archie Steele had been killed instantly, and PFC Louis Verga was mortally wounded but still moaning in pain.

"Oh, God, somebody shoot me," Verga pleaded. "Please, somebody shoot me!"

In his foxhole about thirty feet from the blast area, PFC Harry Bender had been knocked down by the force of the explosion but was otherwise unhurt. He rushed to the aid of his platoon and squad mates, but found there was little he could do. One of Bauman's legs was blown off above the knee, and Vermeer's body was mangled almost beyond recognition.

"Verga was splattered really bad, too," Bender recalled. "You could hardly see him for the blood, and everybody knew he was done for, but none of us had the guts to put him out of his misery."

Bender tried his best to get Leyden to talk to him, but Leyden's only coherent response was to ask about Bauman and Vermeer.

"The stretcher bearers are taking them out now," Bender told him. He couldn't bring himself to say more.

⌒

ON MAY 26, slightly more than twenty-four hours after Bauman, Steele, Vermeer, and Verga were killed, K/3/5 lost Private Frederick "Junior" Hudson, an athletic seventeen-year-old from St. Louis, who had joined the Marines to avenge the death of his brother at Tarawa. Hudson was blown apart by Japanese artillery fire. Also killed by an enemy shell that day was PFC George Pick, a K/3/5 newcomer. Corporal Roy R. "Railroad" Kelly, a veteran of Peleliu and Cape Gloucester, was wounded.

These casualties brought the total number of the company's killed and wounded since Love Day to seventy-six—almost one-third of a rifle company's authorized strength—but it was fairly typical of the in-action losses in other Marine and Army units.

The vaunted Shuri Line was beginning to crumble, but it was exacting an excruciating price. By the last days of May, more than 28,000 Americans would be dead, wounded, or missing in action at Okinawa. When the battle was officially declared over on June 21, total casualties among Tenth Army ground forces stood at 39,420. Losses to Navy personnel aboard ships at sea were unprecedented—more than 10,000 killed and wounded in Japanese suicide attacks.

Ground troops afflicted with combat fatigue, battlefield psychosis, and mental breakdowns weren't included in any of these figures. But best postwar estimates placed that number at close to 30,000—just slightly below the number of WIAs who sustained physical wounds serious enough to require hospitalization of a week or longer.

IT WAS A TIME when exhausted, stressed-out men would grasp at any positive straw, no matter how small or trivial, to fend off unbearable depression, uncontrollable panic, or maniacal rage. As he squatted in a flooded foxhole on May 20 to write a letter home, PFC Al Henderson of the 96th Recon Troop managed to find solace by extolling the many utilitarian virtues of his well-worn steel helmet.

"You can do a lot of different things with your helmet," he observed. "You can wash in it, shave in it, cook coffee in it, or use it to urp in when you get sick. You can put gas in it to clean your gun, dig a hole with if you don't have a shovel, sit on it, and use it to dip water out of your foxhole if it gets too deep. It's quite an invention."

Significantly, however, Henderson omitted any mention of the helmet's main intended function—to help prevent GIs like himself from getting their skulls torn apart by ricocheting bullets or flying shrapnel.

CHAPTER ELEVEN

Divine Wind—Part II

THE RELENTLESS CAMPAIGN of Divine Wind attacks that began at Okinawa on April 6–7 went on with a vengeance for nearly two and a half months. Even after an American victory seemed assured on land, remnants of Japan's Kamikaze Special Attack Corps still aimed coordinated waves of death and destruction at the U.S. Navy.

Kikusui, or "Floating Chrysanthemum" Number One, in which 355 suicide planes and pilots had been thrown at U.S. ships supporting the invasion, was followed in quick succession by Kikusui Two (April 12–13) with 185 kamikazes, and Kikusui Three (April 15–16) with 165 suiciders.

After an eleven-day lull, while Japanese commanders searched their empire for planes of any description to transform into high-explosive manned missiles, the Divine Wind attacks resumed with scaled-down numbers. Available aircraft for Kikusuis Four (April 27–28) and Five (May 3–4) totaled only 115 and 125 respectively.

Several additional Floating Chrysanthemum strikes were tentatively planned, but Japan's ability to launch them depended on locating enough flyable—and expendable—planes. The Japanese had stashed several thousand attack aircraft in secret revetments scattered across their empire in preparation for their last stand at home, but except for these "untouchables," they were literally running out of planes. Their determination, however—and their ability to make grandiose, if unrealistic, plans—remained undiminished.

Kikusui Six, scheduled to begin May 11, was a key component of a complex scheme that turned out to be Tokyo's last major offensive effort of the war, as well as the high-water mark of the Divine Wind's second phase.

On May 8, Admiral Matome Ugaki, commander of Japanese naval forces on the southernmost home island of Kyushu, had been informed by the high command that two divisions of troops would be sent aboard destroyers to reinforce General Ushijima's beleaguered 32nd Army. For this force to reach its destination, Tokyo said, kamikazes would have to knock out some of the radar pickets northwest of Okinawa while simultaneously hobbling Task Force 58 with mass attacks against its carriers. To further impede U.S. interference, the Japanese planned to crash-land airborne troops at Okinawa's two main airfields, Yontan and Kadena, in a suicide mission to destroy American planes on the ground.

To find enough planes by May 11 to carry out this expansive scheme, Ugaki spent the next two days combing not only Kyushu but Japan's northern islands for every aircraft capable of taking off. By the night of May 10, Ugaki had achieved the seemingly impossible: He'd rounded up about 150 kamikazes, ranging from sleek new Kawanishi "Arrow" fighters to decrepit World War I–vintage biplanes, plus eighteen Judy dive-bombers and a force of fighter escorts to attack the American carriers.

Thereafter, even if the May blitz was an unprecedented success, the Divine Wind could be expected to diminish to a faint gasp. The kamikaze corps no longer was made up wholly of volunteers; willingly or not, entire flying units were being assigned to one-way missions. The most critical problem was that this latest Kikusui would leave the mechanical resources of Japan's army and naval air forces at the point of exhaustion. Yet Tokyo believed the sacrifice was worthwhile if it meant holding off the American juggernaut from the home islands for a few more weeks.

The final outcome of the Floating Chrysanthemums campaign was, by now, fairly predictable. In the meantime, the greatest trial by fire in the history of the U.S. Navy would continue to exact a calamitous toll on its men and ships.

⁓

ON THE MORNING of May 11, Lieutenant (j.g.) Douglas Aitken, the slender, sandy-haired radar officer on the destroyer *Hugh W. Hadley*, had just come off the graveyard shift and was finishing a breakfast of scrambled eggs and toast when the ship's loudspeakers gonged, then squawked an alert:

"General quarters! General quarters! All hands to battle stations! Enemy aircraft approaching!"

It was 7:40 A.M. when the first reports of bogies to the northeast reached the *Hadley* at Radar Picket Station Fifteen, some forty-five miles northwest of Bolo Point on Okinawa. The 2,200-ton Sumner-class vessel, commanded by Captain Barron J. "Joe" Mullaney and carrying a crew of 22 officers and 340 men, was one of the Navy's newer destroyers—launched just the previous July. She was named in honor of Commander Hugh W. Hadley, USN, killed in action in the Solomon Islands while commanding a Navy transport division.

The *Hadley* was Aitken's first duty station after completing the Navy's officer training school at Columbia University. As a charter member of her crew, the twenty-two-year-old Cincinnati-born lieutenant, who now called Palo Alto, California, his home, felt both proprietary pride and deep concern for his ship.

Still, as he stood up from his breakfast table, wiped his mouth, and hurried toward the Combat Information Center (CIC), where he'd just spent the night, he wasn't particularly alarmed. In fact, after dozens of general quarters alerts over the past few weeks—the most recent one before dawn that same morning—his prevailing attitude was more aggravation than fear.

Oh, God, he later remembered thinking, *not another one!*

This call to quarters, however, would be different from all the others. Aiken had scarcely stepped from the wardroom into the passageway outside when the voice on the loudspeakers blared again:

"Commence firing! Commence firing!"

A second later, the order was followed by the thunderous boom of the *Hadley*'s five-inch guns—the first of more than 800 rounds they would fire that morning. For Aitken and every other man aboard the *Hadley,* the next 100 minutes would feel like 100 years.

⸺

THE *Hadley* had been taking its turn on picket duty for the past week, alternating between several remote stations north of Okinawa, part of a radar net circling the island like a loose string of beads. The picket stations were merely designated points in the sea, usually between forty and fifty miles from Okinawa, where destroyers with the strongest available radar units, each manned by specially trained five-man crews, were assigned to watch for enemy ships and planes.

Assignment to one of these stations was perhaps the most unenviable duty that a Task Force 58 destroyer and its crew could draw. No less than sixty destroyers and destroyer escorts had been seriously damaged or sunk since April 6—most while on radar picket duty.

Like all modern U.S. destroyers, the *Hadley* was fast—top speed thirty-five knots—and well endowed with firepower. She mounted six five-inch/.38-caliber dual-purpose guns in three batteries of two guns each, two quad-mount 40-millimeter guns, two twin-barrel 40s, and sixteen 20-millimeter AA weapons.

Accompanying the *Hadley* at Station Fifteen was the *Evans*, a destroyer of similar size, speed, and armament, captained by Commander Robert Archer, a Naval Academy classmate of Mullaney, the *Hadley's* skipper. Also along were four "small boys"—three LCIs (landing craft, infantry) converted to gunboats and equipped with rockets, 40s, and 20s, and the *LSM(R) 193*, a medium landing ship converted to a rocket launcher and mounting a single five-inch gun. All shared the advantage of being well armed for their size and difficult to hit from the air.

A squadron of twelve Corsair fighters was also assigned to the station, and they'd been circling the two destroyers since about 6:00 A.M. "Those Marine pilots did a marvelous job that morning," Aitken would recall many years later. "Without them, I doubt that any of us would have lived through it."

Destroyer crewmen learned to measure the proximity of approaching enemy planes by which type of guns they heard firing: If only the five-inchers were in action, it meant the attackers were still some distance away. If the 40s were firing, the planes were getting close, and when the 20s started chattering, the bogies were right there.

As Aitken darted down the ladder to the lower deck—located below and one room aft of the bridge (usually a primary target in an air attack)—both the 40s and 20s opened up with everything they had. The ship lurched violently as the captain ordered the helmsman to zigzag at thirty knots.

The CIC was a hotbed of chaotic activity when Aitken got there, and more officers and men were rushing in. All of them, Aitken included, were bracing themselves for an impending explosion and shouting the same questions: "What's going on? How many planes are there? Where the hell did they come from?"

"Only one so far," a young radar man told them. "He slipped in under the air search radar, and nobody noticed him on the surface search. Lookouts spotted him when he was only a few miles out."

"Yeah, we splashed the bastard when he was still 1,500 yards away," said an operator from the *Hadley's* central radio room next door. "But I hear there's more on the way—a lot more!"

Among those streaming into the center was Lieutenant Commander Robert M. Brownlee, the ship's executive officer. "The kamikaze was an old Jap float plane loaded with gasoline," he said. "He made quite a bonfire when he hit the water. We were lucky."

"Hey, look at this big blip on my screen," one of the radar men yelled. "It's starting to separate out now. There must be fifteen, twenty bogies in there!"

"How far away?" Brownlee asked.

"About fifty-five miles," said the radar guy.

"What about our CAP?" someone asked, referring to the U.S. carrier task group's Combat Air Patrol.

"They're vectored and on their way to intercept," said the exec, picking up the phone to the bridge. "They won't be able to stop all these damned things, though. We're going to have a lot of firing to do. Alert the *Evans* and the other ships."

Within seconds, another, even larger group of bogies showed up on air search radar, spaced about fifteen to twenty minutes behind the first group. Because of the distance, it was impossible to get an accurate count, but the new blip looked big enough to contain scores of additional planes.

By now, Aitken's breakfast wasn't setting well with him, but the churning in his stomach had nothing to do with the quality of the toast and eggs he'd just eaten. Filling his gut like a lead weight was the ominous feeling that each of the little blips now materializing on the radar screen was a kamikaze bound straight for the *Hadley*'s bridge and the communications nerve center just beneath it.

⌒

UNKNOWN TO AITKEN or anyone else at Radar Picket Station Fifteen, the ordeal they were about to endure could have been much worse if not for two isolated earlier developments. One was a disastrous accident caused by Japanese carelessness at Kokobu airfield on Kyushu. The other was early and effective interception of the enemy force by American planes.

As a group of non-kamikaze Judy dive-bombers bound for the strike against U.S. carriers took off before dawn from Kokobu, they flew directly into the path of a flight of Val suiciders taking off simultaneously from another part of the field. The resulting melee of midair collisions and explosions—probably the worst such incident of the war—cost the raiders fifteen planes that they could ill afford to lose, including seven Vals assigned to attack the Station Fifteen pickets.

Carrier-based Corsairs and Hellcats, along with Marine fighters from Yontan and Kadena airfields on Okinawa, also thinned the attackers' ranks well before all of them reached their intended targets. Pilots from Task Force 58's carrier group combined for sixty kills, both kamikazes and nonsuicide attackers, and land-based American flyers shot down another nineteen enemy planes.

Even so, the approximately fifty kamikazes that began orbiting like vultures above the *Evans* and the *Hadley* around 8 A.M. brought with them problems enough.

The suiciders, mostly young, inexperienced pilots flying unfamiliar, inferior aircraft, had nonetheless perfected a more sophisticated—and deadlier—strategy as the Kikusui campaign unfolded. Early on, the kamikazes had usually attacked one or two at a time, making it relatively easy for experienced gunners on ships with good firepower to blast them into the sea before they could do any harm. But now they routinely attacked in multiples of three, four, even a half-dozen planes at once, sharply increasing the odds that at least one would get through to the target.

The solitary enemy float plane that had heralded the approach of the kamikazes minutes before the main body of attackers appeared was a notable exception to this rule. As such, it had given the *Evans* and the *Hadley* another significant advantage: time to take evasive action and make sure their gun crews were fully prepared for what was coming.

From their respective bridges, separated by a couple of miles of seawater, Commanders Mullany and Archer watched the first of the hellbirds peel off from the main formation and zoom toward their ships.

"All gun crews, commence firing," they said in near unison.

⸺⸺

STANDING NEXT TO Captain Mullaney on the *Hadley*'s bridge was Seaman First Class Jay Holmes, manning the fire control director for the port side quad-40 mount on the poop deck below. Although Holmes, from Ogden, Utah, was only eighteen years old and less than a year out of high school, he was well experienced at his battle station, having weathered a dozen or more small-scale kamikaze attacks since the Okinawa campaign began. But neither he nor Mullaney had ever witnessed anything like what they were staring at now.

The skies to the north were black with Japanese planes—more than Holmes had ever seen at one time—and they were closing fast. Darting in from the west to contest their approach were several Corsairs. In the distance, puffs of black smoke filled the air above the *Evans* as her five-inch batteries poured out a steady stream of fire.

"My God, look at all those damn bogies," Mullaney shouted above the thunderous roar of the *Hadley*'s own five-inchers just below as he reached out and grabbed Holmes by the shoulder. The captain, a flamboyant, tough-talking Irishman, was a seasoned destroyer man who was highly respected by his crew, but he was clearly alarmed at the sight.

"I see them, sir!" Holmes shouted back. Truthfully, he could see hardly anything else. "They're all over us, but they're still out of range for the 40s."

As the man in charge of fire control for the quad-40s, Holmes was responsible for turning on the power to the battery, which couldn't be fired manually, and for alerting the gun captain by phone of approaching targets that might not be visible to the gun crew in the tub mount. At the twist of a lever at Holmes's fingertips, the four guns in the mount could be fired automatically as long as the loaders provided a steady supply of ammo, although they had to be aimed by the gunners in the tub.

From all indications, Holmes thought as he tugged the lever, the 40s were about to get a workout like they'd never had before.

The attackers included every conceivable kind of aircraft—lightweight trainers, ancient biplanes with open cockpits, early-model Zekes, combat-worn Vals, and rumbling old Bettys. "Some were sneaking in just off the water, and others were diving at us from all directions," Holmes recalled. "You couldn't blame the captain if he was tense and scared. We all were."

The *Hadley*'s fighter director officer, studying the radar in the CIC with Doug Aitken, now estimated the total number of incoming enemy planes at 156, all apparently suiciders. They appeared to be flying at varying altitudes in five distinct raiding groups, ranging in size from twenty to fifty planes.

"From this time on," said the official report of the action compiled afterward by Commander Mullaney, "the *Hadley* and the *Evans* were attacked continuously by numerous enemy aircraft coming at us in groups of four to six planes on each ship. . . . The tempo of the engagement and the maneuver of the two destroyers at high speed was such as to cause [them] to be separated by distances as much as two or three miles. This resulted in individual action by both ships. Three times the *Hadley* suggested to the *Evans* to close for mutual support . . . but each time the attacks prevented [it]."

One suicide plane, attacking with three others, zoomed straight for the bridge, narrowly missing Mullaney and Holmes. "That was my worst scare," said Holmes. "He looked like he was going to fly right through us. His wing scraped the side of the ship close to the waterline as he crashed into the ocean."

DURING THE NEXT forty-five minutes or so, gun crews on the *Evans* knocked fourteen suicide planes out of the sky in rapid succession and at a rate of almost one every three and a half minutes. Holmes and his comrades on the *Hadley* ran a close second, scoring twelve kills during the same period. More than two dozen additional enemy planes had been splashed so far by Corsair fighters. Miraculously, despite the fury of the attacks, neither destroyer had suffered more than superficial damage.

"The paint was blistering on our gun barrels," recalled Seaman First Class Leo Helling from Kansas City, who'd been switched just two days earlier from his job as first loader on the *Hadley*'s portside quad-40s to a new job as fuse setter on the number-one five-inch battery. "All of the 40s were so hot that the guys were worried about them setting something on fire," Helling said. "They got off over 8,900 rounds within about ninety minutes."

Helling wasn't too happy about his recent change of battle stations. During the *Hadley*'s many calls to quarters, he'd become well acquainted with several members of the 40- and 20-millimeter gun crews. He'd developed strong friendships with guys like Seaman First Class John M. Epelley Jr., who manned one of the 20s nearby; Gunner's Mate D. C. Bass, a talented carpenter who spent his spare time designing kitchen cabinets; Seaman First Class Vaughn Lewis, who'd suggested taking a liberty together when they got back to friendly shores; and Seaman First Class Charles Green, an "old man" of thirty-eight with a wife waiting at home and enough points to get him there, if he ever got to use them.

There was no way for Helling to know that, when that fateful morning was over, he would owe his life to being transferred from the highly exposed quad-40 tub mount to the solid-steel sanctuary beneath the five-inch battery.

⌒

IN ALL LIKELIHOOD, Helling was also unaware that one of his shipmates, Seaman First Class Fred Hammers, had recently been transferred, at his own request, in exactly the opposite direction—or that Hammers's decision would come within a hairsbreadth of costing him his life that morning.

"I was trained to help operate our five-inchers, but I didn't like it much down there in the hole," Hammers recalled many years later. "So one day I saw Captain Mullaney on deck, and I asked him if I could move to one of the 20-millimeter guns instead."

"I've got just the gun for you," Mullaney told him. "From here on, you'll be the gunner on that port-side 20 just below the bridge—and when the fireworks start, by God, you better be sure and protect *me*!"

Hammers, a southern California native who'd finagled his way into the Navy in the summer of '42 at age sixteen, had been extremely pleased with his new battle station, at least until that morning of May 11, when he had every reason to think he should've stayed in the hole.

"I had two kids as loaders who were less than a year out of boot camp," he said, "but they stuck right with me, and the three of us did well."

Hammers kept the manually operated gun firing constantly, except for one brief interval when he ran out of ammo and his loaders had to rush below and haul up more.

The Japanese planes zoomed in from all directions, so many of them that Hammers had a hard time concentrating on a single target, but his lieutenant helped.

"To the right, Hammers!" the lieutenant yelled. "A little more to the right! A little more!"

A Zeke that was close enough for Hammers to count the rivets in its fuselage spouted flame and careened into the ocean, bringing an exultant yell from the lieutenant: "Nice shooting, Hammers! See there, you got the bastard! Now go to your left! Your left, damn it, your left!"

I may die out here this morning, Hammers thought, *but whether I live or die, I'll never have this much fun again!*

Around nine o'clock, the two destroyers' good fortune rapidly turned sour. Mullaney received word from Combat Air Patrol that the covering squadron of Corsairs was out of ammo and low on gas, and most of its planes were returning to base to reload and refuel. Four planes lingered behind briefly to offer what help they could for as long as possible, but except for the "small boys," the *Hadley* and the *Evans* were essentially on their own.

The kamikazes moved quickly to seize the advantage. At 9:07 A.M., a Japanese Judy dive-bomber crashed the bow of the *Evans,* causing severe damage but failing to slow either the destroyer's speed or rate of fire. Moments later, the ship's gunners splashed a second kamikaze streaking in from port, but a third suicider, gliding just off the waves from another direction, refused to go down.

"We could see our 20-millimeter batteries hitting the plane," Captain Archer said, "but it kept on coming."

A bomb aboard the plane detonated near the *Evans*'s after fire room, causing flooding that spread rapidly to the after engine room. Then, while Mullaney and others watched helplessly from the *Hadley*'s bridge, two more kamikazes crashed the *Evans* amidships within seconds of each other. They blew up both forward boilers, set off raging gasoline fires aft, knocked out power to the batteries, and strewed the decks with the bodies of dead and wounded sailors. Among the seriously injured was the ship's executive officer, Lieutenant L. W. Gillen.

As the destroyer lay powerless and dead in the water, Seaman First Class Robert Stonelake switched his twin-mount 40 to manual control in time to single-handedly down yet another suicider, who fell just short of the ship. It was the nineteenth—and last—kill of the morning credited to the *Evans,* and Stonelake's action may have been all that saved the ravaged ship from sinking.

As it was, her hulk remained afloat with thirty dead crewmen and twenty-nine wounded aboard. Three miles away, meanwhile, the rest of the hovering hell-birds turned their full attention to the *Hadley.*

"This was the granddaddy of them all," recalled Jay Holmes, who watched the onslaught from the bridge. "We didn't have time to count, but the records show the kamikazes came at us ten at a time. As good as our gunners were, there was no way we were going to stop them all."

The mass attack began at 9:20 A.M., when an Oka rocket bomb narrowly missed the ship. Seconds later, another suicider aimed for the bridge but overshot it and hurtled between the *Hadley*'s twin stacks. A wing sheered off, ripping out a section of the destroyer's rigging and its main radio antenna but causing little other damage.

From his post underneath the five-inch batteries, Leo Helling heard or felt a hard bump and glanced up toward the bright patch of daylight a deck above him in time to see his gun captain duck sharply and almost lose his footing.

"God almighty, that was close!" the gun captain howled.

It wasn't as close as the next one, however. The second hit came squarely on top of the port-side quad-40 that had been Helling's battle station until two days ago, fatally wounding every member of its crew. As the plane exploded, the pilot released a bomb into the same area, wiping out several other 40- and 20-millimeter mounts. The plane's blazing wreckage then careened into the deckhouse atop the main afterdeck, engulfing in flames the lockers and living quarters for most of the *Hadley*'s junior officers.

Seaman First Class Franklin Gebhart, gun captain on one of the starboard 40s, thought for sure that the first suicide plane "had my name on it," but its glancing blow merely bounced him against some torpedo tubes and knocked the wind out of him.

"I ordered my men to abandon ship, and they all jumped but two, who kept firing," Gebhart recalled. "Then another kamikaze hit the gun and killed them both, and I jumped overboard, too. I was bobbing around out there when I saw one of our Corsairs, whose ammo was totally gone, come down on top of a Jap plane and ride him down into the water."

On the bridge, Jay Holmes still hoped his besieged ship's luck might hold if it could somehow get through the next minute or so. But the hope faded as a second kamikaze crashed the ship just aft of amidships.

A moment later, the third successful suicide plane applied the kiss of death to the *Hadley* when it crashed the reeling destroyer amidships at the water line on the starboard side. As the plane hit, the pilot released a 500-pound bomb that exploded underneath the ship.

Almost immediately, with seawater pouring through the gash in her side, the *Hadley* began listing sharply to starboard. Fire rooms, boilers, engine rooms, and turbines rapidly flooded. All power went off throughout the ship. Columns of billowing black smoke rose from out-of-control fires.

When the *Hadley*'s big guns fell silent for the first time in an hour and a half, Jay Holmes didn't notice. He turned and saw Captain Mullaney yelling orders at somebody, but Holmes couldn't detect the slightest sound. Constant exposure to the roar of the five-inchers, particularly when they swung around toward port, had left him stone-deaf in both ears.

Inside the CIC, Lieutenant Doug Aitken was shaken by the sharp jolts of the explosions. He knew the ship had been badly hurt, but he'd been unable to see any part of the action from his post in the radar room, so he had no idea where or how severe the damage was.

Fighting his way to the outer door of the pitch-dark CIC, Aitken got his first clear look at the mortally wounded vessel. He was stunned by what he saw.

"The fantail was awash, which was bad news," he said, "and our list to starboard was several degrees and worsening, and that was more bad news. What we didn't know at the time was that the bomb that exploded under the ship had left a fifty-six-inch hump in her keel. By any statistical measurement, she should've sunk—but she didn't."

Aitken felt a curious sense of detachment as he realized that his living quarters and all his personal possessions had been obliterated by the blasts and the raging fires they touched off.

"My room was right in the middle of all that," he recalled many years later. "If I'd been in my bunk when the plane hit, there wouldn't have been enough of me left to pick up with a sponge. As it was, I came out of it with nothing except what I was wearing, but that was the least of my worries at the time."

Seaman Second Class Don Hile struggled up a ladder from the sudden, impenetrable darkness a deck below the *Hadley*'s now-silent five-inch batteries with stars flashing inside his head and a hot, hard pain stabbing through his neck and lower. Hile's regular job was in the CIC tracking planes on radar, but his battle station was in the magazine area, where he'd been removing caps from five-inch rounds when the third kamikaze smashed into the ship.

Knocked from his feet by the impact, Hile had hit face-first against the heavy hoist used to lift the fifty-pound shells into the magazine. A wave of dizziness passed over him, and for a moment, he was afraid he was going to fall.

"Keep moving, man," said a voice behind him. "We gotta get out of here. It feels like we're sinking."

Hile tried to answer, but his whole face felt paralyzed, and he couldn't open his mouth. As he stumbled out onto the deck, staggered toward the ship's rail, and prepared to jump, he knew for a certainty that his jaw was broken.

ON THE BRIDGE, Captain Mullaney was trying to contact fire- and flood-control teams and rescue parties searching for wounded when Lieutenant Commander Brownlee, the exec, ran up from the CIC.

"Captain, we've been hit!" Brownlee panted, his face the color of ashes.

"Holy Christ, man, I *know* we've been hit!" Mullaney erupted. "Now get the hell down below and see what you can do to help get the wounded off. We may have to abandon ship, but I don't want to give the order if there's any way to avoid it."

He turned to his navigator, thirty-five-year-old Lieutenant Ned E. Wheldon of Hollywood, California. "Are any of our engines working? Can we move at all?"

"Negative, sir," Wheldon said, shaking his head. The navigator had achieved a degree of fame among the other officers aboard because of his mother's habit of enclosing a four-leaf clover in every letter she wrote him. Wheldon had accumulated hundreds of the good luck symbols, but they hadn't been much help that day.

"I want every flag on the ship raised," Mullaney told a young ensign, standing in semishock nearby. "By God, if the *Hadley*'s going to the bottom, she's going down with all flags flying!"

By about 9:30 a.m., the ship's chief engineer and the damage control officer delivered their first reports to Mullaney, and neither could offer any encouragement. Their conclusion: With the ship in danger of capsizing and unable to defend herself, the situation appeared hopeless. Engineers were securing the forward boilers to keep them from blowing up, but ammunition exploding in the roaring fires created a perilous situation.

"All right, I'm giving the order to prepare to abandon ship," Mullaney said grimly a moment after hearing the reports. "Spread the word."

Life rafts and floats were put over the side. A party of about fifty men and officers was organized to remain aboard and make a final effort to save the *Hadley*. All wounded personnel were lowered over the side into the rafts to await pickup by the "small boys."

Many crew members didn't wait for a Jacob's ladder to take them over the side of the ship. They simply took a running leap and dived into the sea.

"Because of the way she was listing, I was really worried about getting away from the ship," remembered Leo Helling, "so I just pulled off my shoes and jumped in with no life jacket or anything. I'd heard a lot about how hard it was to swim away from a ship that was going down, but I didn't have much trouble. I swam to a life raft where a bunch of other guys were holding on, and in a few minutes, the LSM picked us up."

"I ran for all I was worth right off the side of the ship," added Jay Holmes. "My legs were still running full speed when I hit the water."

With his ship apparently sinking beneath him, and his ammunition again exhausted, Fred Hammers raced to the *Hadley*'s starboard side, where another 20-millimeter gun was standing abandoned. He fired the gun's last few rounds at a Japanese float plane, then scrambled to the rail and looked down at the roiling sea. He was preparing to jump when he turned to see his two best buddies, Seamen First Class Bruce Hill from Philadelphia and Johnny Huff from Texas.

"We gotta go!" Hammers yelled. "Captain says abandon ship."

"You shoot down any Japs?" Huff wanted to know.

"Yeah, my lieutenant gave me credit for three kills," Hammers said, "and those ain't probables, man! Those are definites!"

The three sailors had scarcely hit the water before another Zeke came streaking in and bullets from his wing guns splashed the water around them.

"It was the first time all morning I'd really been scared," Hammers recalled. "There was no place to hide, and I figured that Jap was gonna kill all three of us."

Suddenly a Marine Corsair, possibly the last one remaining in the area, swooped down toward the low-flying Zeke. The Corsair's pilot was obviously out of ammunition, but he set his own plane virtually on top of the Japanese plane, and to Hammers's disbelieving amazement, he forced it down toward the water.

Hammers's voice still shook with emotion more than sixty years later as he recalled what happened next: "The guy in the Corsair chewed that Jap's tail completely off with his prop and rode him right into the sea. There's no question at all that he saved our lives. He was one courageous son of a bitch."

SATISFIED THAT BOTH the *Evans* and the *Hadley* were finished, the surviving Japanese attackers wasted no further time on the two floundering destroyers but turned their attention to bigger game.

Shortly after 10:00 A.M. on May 11, at least fifty suicide planes swooped down on Task Force 58's carrier group with disastrous results for American ships and sailors. Admiral Marc Mitscher, commanding the carriers, watched from the bridge of his flagship, the *Bunker Hill*, and found himself much too close to the action for comfort.

Effectively using rain clouds and low-altitude approaches to play hide-and-seek with U.S. radar, two kamikazes—a Zeke and a Judy divebomber—were right on top of the *Bunker Hill* when they popped suddenly out of an overcast sky and attacked from two directions at once.

The Zeke streaked in from the flagship's starboard quarter, crashing into lines of parked planes and igniting numerous gasoline fires. Before it skidded overboard and exploded, the plane released a bomb that blasted through the side of the ship and gouged out a section of the flight deck. On the heels of the Zeke, the Judy roared down from astern in an almost-vertical dive, its bomb load exploding another section of flight deck at the base of the island and triggering more massive fires.

Listing badly to starboard and blazing furiously, the *Bunker Hill* appeared doomed by the hundreds of gallons of aviation fuel spilling over its flight deck and the dozens of heavily armed aircraft in the path of the wind-whipped flames. The big ship almost certainly would've sunk if not for the skill and steady nerves of Captain George A. Seitz, her skipper, and Commander Charles J. Odenhal, her navigator, who managed to reverse her course, changing the list to port and allowing the flammables and explosives on deck to slide into the sea.

It took firefighters five and a half hours to bring the inferno under control, and the damage it left behind knocked the *Bunker Hill* out of the war. She and the carrier *Franklin*, ravaged by kamikazes several weeks earlier, rank as the two worst-damaged carriers of World War II to survive. Her casualties totaled 396 killed or missing and 264 wounded.

Many sailors were killed instantly on the flight deck, but many others were trapped below in smoke-choked passageways. Machinist's Mate Harold Fraught tried desperately, but without success, to reach the only small porthole in a narrow corridor, but the opening was inches too high. "I was just about to give up," he said, "when someone pushed me through." The helpful rescuer, whose identity was never determined, pushed a total of seven men to safety. The other eighteen sailors in the corridor died, the rescuer among them.

The engine of the Japanese Judy, blown from the exploding plane, had hurtled into the *Bunker Hill*'s flagship office, killing three of Admiral Mitscher's staff officers and eleven enlisted men. Mitscher himself, slightly shaken but unhurt, quickly moved his headquarters to the carrier *Enterprise*. That same afternoon, he ordered two of his remaining carrier task groups to steam north for a new round of raids aimed at grounding the hell-birds once and for all.

The target: twenty-three airbases on the Japanese home islands of Kyushu and Shikoku from which kamikazes were known to operate.

BACK AT RADAR PICKET STATION FIFTEEN, where two other destroyers had been dispatched to assume patrol and picket duty, the disabled *Evans* was taken under tow about noon for the dismal voyage to the growing graveyard of ships at the Kerama Retto. Meanwhile, aboard the even more seriously damaged *Hadley*, still miraculously afloat with the help of "small boys" who lashed themselves to her to keep her from capsizing, some sixty seamen and officers continued fighting to save the ship and dispose of classified materials in the event she had to be abandoned.

The last contact between the two battered ships and their skippers came in a message scribbled by Captain Mullaney on a scrap of paper and transmitted to Captain Archer on the *Evans* by flashing light signals:

CAPTAIN BOB—
BELIEVE I CAN SAVE MY SHIP. I AM PROUD TO
HAVE FOUGHT THIS BATTLE WITH YOU.
SINCERELY, JOE

In the action report prepared later, Mullaney went into much greater detail concerning the rescue efforts taking place at the time: "A truly amazing, courageous, and efficient group of men and officers, with utter disregard for their own personal safety, approached the explosions and fires with hoses, and for fifteen minutes kept up this work. The torpedoes were jettisoned, weights removed from the starboard side, and finally, the fire was extinguished, and the list and flooding controlled . . . although the ship was still in an extremely dangerous condition."

Except for personnel required for these efforts, all other members of the crew—including 30 dead and 121 wounded—had either been removed from the *Hadley* or left the ship under their own power. Pending the arrival of a hospital ship, most of the severely injured were first transported to the *LSM(R) 193*, the largest of the "small boys," for treatment.

As Seaman Leo Helling was helped from the raft where he'd clung with a dozen other men for what seemed a long time, he spotted a familiar—but horribly burned—figure lying on a stretcher on the deck of the landing ship.

Moving closer, Helling recognized Seaman John Epelley, his friend from one of the port-side 20s that had been engulfed in flames by a crashing suicider. Most of Epelley's uniform had been burned away, and his exposed skin was terribly blackened and blistered. He'd always been a small guy and fairly short—about five feet six at most—but now he seemed smaller than ever, as if the fire had shrunk him somehow.

Helling stopped, wanting to say or do something but not knowing what. He watched silently as another acquaintance knelt on one knee beside the stretcher and spoke softly to Epelley: "Hey, John, I'm glad to see you made it, buddy. Everything'll be okay now. You'll be going home."

"Yeah . . . glad . . ." Epelley whispered through seared lips. "Be nice . . . go home."

Helling was amazed that Epelley was conscious and able to talk. When he was fresh out of boot camp in the spring of 1944, Helling himself had come down with a case of scarlet fever that morphed into rheumatic fever and almost killed him. He'd been hospitalized for five months, and sometimes he thought he'd never get well—but he finally had.

For a moment, a spark of hope for Epelley flickered in Helling's chest, and he wanted to go over and tell his friend not to give up. Then his rational mind took over, and he knew there was no use. Epelley had burns over more than half his body, and he was already slipping into shock. He died a short time later, long before receiving any meaningful medical treatment—not that it would've changed anything.

Afterward, Helling was left to stare out to sea, thinking about what a good-natured, pleasant guy John Epelley had been and pondering the incomprehensible workings of fate.

That could be you lying there instead of him, you know. It could just as easily be you.

Helling had never found out who took his place as first loader on the port-side quad-40 mount where the kamikaze had hit. Now he was glad he hadn't.

AMONG THOSE who remained aboard the *Hadley* and hard at work was Lieutenant Doug Aitken, whose responsibilities as radar officer included proper disposal of all classified materials and military data. Aitken remained in the CIC until afternoon.

Navy regulations required that top-secret documents—in this case including detailed invasion plans for Japan—be placed in heavy, perforated canvas bags with lead weights sewn into the bottoms, then dropped overboard. Coding machines and other sensitive equipment also had to be deep-sixed in similar fashion.

"I was a good swimmer, and I'd been a water polo player in high school," Aitken recalled, "so I had absolutely no doubt that I could swim away from the ship safely if I had to. In the meantime, I had a bunch of things to do, and I tried to stay focused on the job at hand."

One of Aitken's closest friends, Ensign Wallace Kendall, a Marylander who served as the ship's unofficial photographer, was working close by in the CIC. But Aitken's mind drifted periodically to other friends whose whereabouts and condition were still unknown. Among them were Lieutenant Patrick McGann, who, as the *Hadley*'s gunnery officer, had probably been the busiest man aboard that morning, and Ensign Tom Dwyer, the ship's torpedo officer, who'd been a classmate of Aitken's at the officers school at Columbia.

Now and then, images from his boyhood also flashed across Aitken's mind's eye. He remembered the court of honor where he'd received his Eagle Scout award and how proud his parents had been. Doug had been a very good Scout, too, if he did say so himself. Scouting had helped make him a better Navy officer, and its famous motto, "Be prepared," had always served him well—at least until now.

But how the hell, he mused, *could anyone possibly be prepared for something like this?*

THE *Hugh Hadley* never sailed another inch under her own power. She was towed first to Ie Shima, then to the Keramas, where she was berthed beside another gutted destroyer, the *Aaron Ward,* which had been built just ahead of her at the same shipyard in San Pedro, California. After she was placed in a floating dry dock, divers determined that the bomb damage to her keel was beyond repair. Eventually, she was towed all the way back to the States, where she was stripped and sold for scrap.

But the proud record left behind by the *Hadley* survives to this day. Of all the U.S. ships that fought the kamikazes, she is credited with the most official kills—twenty-three. Both Captain Mullaney and Lieutenant McGann, her gunnery officer, were awarded Navy Crosses for their stellar performances on May 11, 1945. Other individual decorations received by members of her crew included four Silver Stars, one Legion of Merit, six Bronze Stars, and approximately 100 Purple Hearts. In addition, her crew was awarded a Presidential Unit Citation by President Harry S. Truman.

For its outstanding gunnery, rescue, and towing efforts, and other assistance to the *Hadley, LSM(R) 193* also received a Presidential Unit Citation—the only one among the more than 1,000 LSMs in action during World War II to receive this honor.

As a final footnote, perhaps the most fortunate member of the

Hadley's crew on May 11 was Lieutenant (j.g.) Bill Winter, assistant gunnery officer in charge of 20- and 40-millimeter guns, who'd been ordered ashore two days earlier for training in five-inch weapons.

"I was on the beach when the suicide attacks came," said Winter more than sixty years later. "I lost some good friends on the *Hadley,* and I should've been right there on the bridge, directing fire by phone. Some people might say I was the luckiest guy in the Navy that day, but I'm still mad as hell about it."

KIKUSUI SIX continued on May 12–14 with a hodge-podge of about 180 kamikazes and nonsuicide planes attacking radar picket stations south of Okinawa and again going after Admiral Mitscher's carriers.

On May 13, which happened to be Mother's Day, the hell-birds descended on the well-traveled destroyer *Bache,* on picket duty at radar station 9 southwest of Okinawa, and gave her the worst battering of her tough, colorful life.

Commissioned in 1942 and a veteran of Pacific battles stretching from Attu to Leyte to Iwo Jima, the *Bache* had already fought off one series of suicide attacks in Okinawan waters. She'd also experienced moments of glory that were rare for a destroyer, having torpedoed and sunk three enemy vessels, including a battleship and a cruiser, at the battle of Surigao Strait in the Philippines. But this would be her last and most futile fight.

At 7:07 A.M., an old Val lumbered in from the port side and laid waste to the *Bache* amidships, knocking out all steam and electrical power, starting numerous fires, killing forty-one American sailors, and wounding thirty-two more. When the fires were brought under control, the forlorn ship was towed, like so many others, to the Kerama Retto.

"It was much like a funeral march," recalled Lieutenant Clement R. McCormack, the *Bache*'s fighter control officer, "especially as the number of casualties became known. There was an air of disbelief that it could happen to us because our gunnery had been so good."

After makeshift repairs, however, the *Bache* made it all the way back to New York, limping along with only one operational engine. It wasn't possible to find an empty berth for her in any of the West Coast repair yards; they were all filled to capacity with other damaged destroyers from Okinawa.

THE JAPANESE saved one of the most spectacular strikes of Kikusui Six for last.

On the morning of May 14, a Zero piloted by Japanese Lieutenant (j.g.) Tomai Kai burst from a cloudbank at full throttle 1,500 feet above the carrier *Enterprise*—the storied "Big E" and Admiral Mitscher's latest flagship. With Mitscher looking on helplessly from the flag bridge, Tomai (whose calling cards were found in the wreckage of his plane) avoided a firestorm of AA fire, crashed his plane at a fifty-degree angle through the wooden flight deck, and released a bomb a split second before he died.

Having been targeted by kamikazes numerous times before, the *Enterprise* and her crew were well prepared. Stored planes had been drained of gasoline and disarmed. Watertight hatches were closed and sealed. Fuel lines had been emptied and refilled with carbon dioxide. Crewmen on the flight deck were protected by flash-proof gear. As a result, a disaster that might otherwise have sunk a carrier of the *Enterprise* class and slaughtered half its crew was mostly avoided.

Thirteen sailors were killed and sixty-nine wounded, but without the advance precautions, the toll might easily have been a dozen times as high. The fires that broke out were contained and extinguished within a half hour. The "Big E" was soon able to continue on her way, and Mitscher was able to remove his long-billed baseball cap, pat his bald head, and jokingly remark: "By God, if the Japs keep this up, they're going to grow hair on my head yet!"

Tempering all this good news, however, was one unhappy fact: The kamikazes had removed the *Enterprise* and her air group from the Okinawa campaign—and all further combat operations for the duration of the war—as effectively as if they'd been destroyed in one huge fireball. The carrier's next stop would be the repair facilities at Bremerton, Washington, where it would take many months of work and refitting to make the "Big E" whole again.

The Divine Wind had scored one last major triumph, and Mitscher was forced to find yet another flagship, this time the carrier *Randolph*. But Tokyo's central underlying objective in launching Kikusui Six—to reinforce General Ushijima's ground forces in southern Okinawa with two divisions of fresh troops and possibly prolong the land battle for weeks—proved beyond her grasp.

Despite the heavy losses to the kamikazes, the American naval presence in the East China Sea was simply too powerful to risk the loss of two entire Japanese divisions. This fact, coupled with a shortage of destroyers to ferry troops and an increasingly desperate lack of fuel oil, caused the reinforcement plan to be canceled by the Japanese high command. The fresh troops never arrived.

CHAPTER TWELVE

The Crowded, Angry Skies

MAJOR GENERAL CURTIS E. LeMAY never set foot on Okinawa during the battle for the island, but as leader of the U.S. Army Air Force's 21st Bomber Command, he probably deserves as much credit for America's eventual victory as any of the on-site U.S. commanders who managed the ground campaign.

That isn't to say that the stern, square-jawed LeMay was a dedicated—or even willing—participant in the fight for Okinawa. He complained bitterly when Admiral Chester Nimitz, commander in chief of U.S. forces in the Pacific, pulled LeMay's heavy bombers away from their strategic raids against Japan's industrial centers to target air bases on Kyushu, where virtually all Okinawa-bound kamikaze missions originated. But LeMay did as he was ordered, and his pilots and bombardiers most likely spared the lives of thousands of American soldiers, sailors, and Marines as a result.

On March 27, 1945, five days before Army and Marine assault troops went ashore on Okinawa, LeMay dispatched 151 of his B-29 "Superfortresses"—the most awesome long-range bombers the world had yet seen—to strike the airfields on Kyushu.

Again on March 31, the eve of Love Day, 137 B-29s from LeMay's command blasted the same Kyushu facilities again. The damage done in these two raids probably explains why no large-scale kamikaze attacks were launched during the Okinawa invasion itself, when U.S. troop ships and their human cargoes would have been at their most vulnerable.

All during April and early May, as the struggle for Okinawa continued, the B-29s returned to Kyushu at regular intervals to plaster major kamikaze bases as demanded by Admiral Nimitz. The giant bombers were unable to stop the suicide squadrons completely, but they cut deeply into the available supply of kamikaze planes and kept the Japanese scrambling to find replacements for those the B-29s destroyed. All told, the 21st Bomber Command flew ninety-seven tactical missions against Kyushu airfields during this period and claimed to have destroyed nearly 500 Japanese planes. It's difficult to imagine how much greater the damage and loss of life on U.S. Navy ships might have been if not for the preemptive strikes ordered by the tough-talking thirty-eight-year-old LeMay.

The raids on Kyushu airstrips continued until May 11, when Nimitz released the B-29s to resume their systematic destruction of every major Japanese city. LeMay would have preferred a much earlier release date. By the time U.S. troops landed on Okinawa, he believed his B-29s had completed their kamikaze-killing assignment.

Perhaps more strongly than any other high-ranking American officer, LeMay believed that his B-29s, using conventional weapons, could bomb Japan into submission without an invasion of her home islands, and he continued to focus on this goal even while diverting planes to Kyushu.

On April 13, for example, in the midst of the anti-kamikaze campaign, 327 B-29s dumped more than 2,000 tons of incendiary bombs on a section of Tokyo known to house huge stores of armaments, virtually obliterating eleven square miles of the city. Two days later, 300 Superfortresses struck a second massive blow at Tokyo, Yokohama, and Kawasaki, leaving ten square miles of desolation in their wake.

At about this same time, the 21st Bomber Command was bolstered with the arrival of two new wings of B-29s. This gave LeMay the capability, for the first time in the war, of launching 500-plane raids against Japan on a routine basis. He jumped at the opportunity to demonstrate "the power of the strategic air arm" and to reassert his conviction that his command could force Japan to surrender within six months, "providing its maximum capacity is exerted unstintingly."

This campaign of mass destruction continued without letup all during May, but Monday, May 14, was the day when, as LeMay phrased it, "My dream began to come true." On that date, 472 Superforts dropped 2,500 tons of bombs on a Mitsubishi industrial complex in Nagoya. "This was a daylight attack," LeMay exulted, "and we lost exactly one airplane each to fighters and to flak."

By mid-June, the six most important industrial centers in Japan's home islands had vanished into a wasteland of bomb craters and charred debris. In the city of Kobe alone, more than 51,000 buildings were destroyed. Of the six urban areas of Tokyo, Yokohama, Osaka, Nagoya,

Kobe, and Kawasaki, comprising a combined total of 257 square miles, more than 105 square miles had been blasted to rubble, and thousands of Japanese civilians had been killed. Millions more were left homeless.

~⌐

MOST OF THE B-29 missions flown during the Okinawa campaign were launched from bases on Guam, Saipan, and Tinian, and all involved long flights over water. As LeMay's no-quarter bombing campaign intensified, a sharply rising number of B-29s damaged by flak or encounters with Japanese fighters were forced to ditch at sea on the way home or make emergency landings on Iwo Jima.

This caused many in the bomber command to look longingly at Okinawa, with its proximity to Japan, as a potential B-29 base. But any attempt to utilize the island for this purpose would have to wait until the ground fighting ended. As home bases for the Second Marine Air Wing, both the Yontan and Kadena airstrips had been turned into first-class fields capable of handling almost any type of aircraft—except for bomb-laden B-29s, which required longer runways for takeoff. Once the Okinawa issue was settled, either field could be converted with relative ease into a base for B-29s.

By early May, two squadrons of smaller four-engine B-24 Liberator bombers were already being rotated between Yontan and Tinian to target Japanese shipping in the East China Sea. But as long as Japanese resistance continued on Okinawa, both fields had other priorities. The B-24s had to share limited space with long-haul transports and Marine and Army fighter squadrons, lined up wing tip to wing tip along their parking aprons. The crowded conditions left little room for anything else.

Although a few bombing and strafing missions were flown from the two airfields against targets on the islands just south of Kyushu, operations at Yontan and Kadena were mainly focused on two objectives much closer at hand: providing close air support for U.S. ground forces and defending against air attacks by kamikazes and other Japanese planes. After the island of Ie Shima, just off the west coast of Okinawa, was secured by U.S. troops on April 22, its three airstrips were quickly repaired and utilized by the B-24s for ongoing raids against Kyushu.

Both Yontan and Kadena had been securely in American hands since early afternoon on Love Day, with scarcely a shot fired in either's defense. In the days that followed, however, Yontan had been subjected to almost nightly aerial attacks that made life a torment for the men quartered there. Incoming bombs, shells, and machine-gun bullets became such a routine part of life that a welcoming sign erected by Yontan's Marines incorporated a none-too-subtle warning to visitors:

WELCOME TO YONTAN—EVERY NIGHT A 4TH OF JULY

For the first month of the campaign, the Japanese had done everything in their power to keep the Americans from making meaningful use of the airfields. Kadena, located three miles nearer than Yontan to the Japanese heavy artillery at Shuri, had been shelled with particular regularity. As American ground forces pressed south, however, a long lull in the fireworks had ensued. For several weeks, no enemy planes had threatened, and no artillery rounds had struck from the Shuri heights.

Then came the evening of May 24, the night the war returned to Yontan.

IN HIS TENT near the edge of the field, Tech Sergeant Walt McNeel, a mechanical crew chief for Marine Night Fighter Squadron VMF(N)-542, awoke with a start to the sound of air raid sirens. It was shortly after 10:00 P.M., and McNeel was dog-tired from a long day in the squadron's prop repair shop. The only thing he wanted was a good night's sleep, but he was about to be rousted from his bed by one of the most bizarre incidents of the Pacific war.

Everything had been so quiet around the field recently that McNeel first thought he must be dreaming, but when the wail of sirens continued, he jumped up and grabbed for his pants. Even if it was a false alarm, he thought, there was no sense taking chances.

McNeel vividly remembered the mid-April afternoon when he'd driven to Kadena to meet with the manager of the prop shop there, arriving just in time to get a good scare from a lone enemy attacker.

"We were standing at the end of the runway when we heard a roar and looked up to see a Jap fighter-bomber heading straight for us," McNeel recalled. "He dropped a bomb just as we jumped into a revetment, and something—maybe a bomb fragment, maybe a rock—hit this guy's pipe and knocked it right out of his mouth."

A day or two later, on April 17, attacks on Yontan and Kadena had occurred off and on all day, including several by kamikazes. Marine Corsairs based at the two fields had blasted no less than thirty-eight enemy planes out of the sky that day. There'd been little enemy activity in the area since. In fact, the most recent Japanese attack on Yontan had come on the night of April 26, when a few planes had bombed the same tent area where McNeel was now bivouacked. All hands had been safe in their foxholes, however, and no one was hurt.

Now it was almost a month later, and McNeel and the other ground crewmen living in tents on the fringes of the airfield while permanent barracks were being built had almost quit worrying about being strafed or bombed—almost but not quite. When McNeel heard dozens of anti-aircraft batteries open up in unison, he knew for sure this was the real thing.

As he jumped into his shoes and ran for the large communal foxhole designated for ground crewmen, he heard loudspeakers blaring across the field:

"Pilots, man your planes! Bogies closing!"

⌒

EIGHT TWIN-ENGINE Japanese bombers were roaring toward Yontan through the dark northeastern sky. They were intent on far worse mischief than an ordinary bombing run or even a "standard" kamikaze attack. Their mission had originally been scheduled as part of the massed suicide raids of May 11. Logistical problems had interfered, but after a delay of almost two weeks, the Japanese high command had decreed that the mission take place as planned.

An even dozen of the attacking planes, all Mitsubishi Sallys, had taken off from an airfield on Kyushu, but four had developed mechanical problems and turned back. Several others were intercepted by U.S. night fighters and never reached the vicinity of Yontan. Three more were riddled by Yontan's 40- and 90-millimeter antiaircraft batteries and crashed nearby.

Only one plane accomplished its mission, executing a wheels-up belly landing on Yontan's main northeast-southwest runway with a "cargo" of about a dozen Japanese "Giretsu" commandos armed with grenades, rifles, and satchel charges of TNT. Joined by the plane's crew and possibly some survivors from the three other downed Sallys, the raiders proceeded to demonstrate how much destruction can be caused in a matter of minutes by a few determined, well-trained men. Their fiery sweep across Yontan field has been called the first and only airborne assault of the war in the Central Pacific.

Airfield personnel were ill prepared to face enemy troops attacking on the ground, and the raiders fanned out on foot with amazing speed, blowing up every parked American plane they could reach. McNeel and his comrades in the foxholes could only watch in helpless shock as flames from exploding U.S. aircraft lit the night sky. No one in the group had thought to buckle on a handgun, much less grab a rifle, as they fled their tents for cover.

"At worst, we expected the plane to be loaded with bombs, not crack demolition teams," McNeel recalled many years later. "If even half of those twelve bombers had managed to land, it's hard to imagine what they could've done. As it was, that one planeload of raiders did damage enough."

In all, nine U.S. planes were destroyed—three Corsair fighters, two Navy Privateers, and four transports. Twenty-nine others, including two B-24 heavy bombers, were damaged, and 70,000 gallons of aviation gasoline stored in two fuel dumps went up in bright orange flames.

Confusion and wild shooting by U.S. personnel caused most of the American casualties. Lieutenant Maynard C. Kelley of VMF(N)-533, the duty officer in the control tower, was mortally wounded after he turned on floodlights to illuminate the attackers, and they opened fire. Eighteen other Americans sustained nonfatal wounds.

PFC JACK KELLY, a ground crewman in the same squadron as McNeel, had spent the early part of the evening listening to "Tokyo Rose" on the radio. Later, he'd been working on the flight line getting one of the F6F Hellcats ready for its nightly mission when the air raid sirens sounded. He quickly finished what he was doing and darted for the bomb shelter. "The evening began quite sanely but developed into the wildest experience of my life," Kelly recalled.

The belly-landing Sally skidded along one of Yontan's two fighter strips, sparks flying as her steel fuselage scraped the pavement. She lurched to a halt no more than 100 yards from the shelter where Kelly and seventeen other Marines huddled as the heavily armed Japanese commandos begin jumping out of the plane.

"We were defenseless in the bomb shelter and at their mercy if they'd seen us," said Kelly. "One Jap grenade thrown into the shelter would've KO'd our whole group."

To the rescue came two other members of VMF(N)-542, First Lieutenant Clark "Bucket" Campbell and Tech Sergeant Chan Beasley, along with several Marine guards with Thompson submachine guns. Before chasing after the raiders, Campbell ordered the ground crewmen—including Kelly, armed only with a screwdriver—to form a defensive perimeter around the shelter.

Moments later, as he stood guard alone in the darkness, Kelly heard someone shout: "Whoever goes there better answer up!" A shot followed almost immediately, striking Kelly in the foot.

"Hold your fire, you dumb son of a bitch," Kelly hollered, and the firing ceased as several of Kelly's buddies ran to his aid. They cut off his boondocker shoe with a Ka-Bar knife, put sulfa powder on his wound, and applied a dressing as best they could.

Along with Kelly, two other men from VMF(N)-542—Staff Sergeant Benjamin Masciale and PFC Vincent Polidaro—were also wounded, probably by friendly fire, and all were evacuated. Tech Sergeant G. M. Stanley was injured by debris from one of the blown-up planes but elected to stay with the squadron.

The threat to Yontan ended shortly before 1:00 A.M. on May 25 when the last Japanese raider was killed as he tried to hide in some underbrush near the field. By daylight, the bodies of sixty-nine Japanese, all presumably Giretsus or crew members from the planes, had been collected and counted. Some appeared to have committed suicide. No prisoners were taken.

⸺⚬

THE CONCEPT of separate night-fighter squadrons, made up of planes specially designed and equipped for fighting in total darkness, was still relatively new when the battle for Okinawa began. But by the end of the campaign, three Marine night-fighter squadrons—VMF(N)-533, 542, and 543, each made up of fifteen F6F Hellcats, thirty pilots, plus several dozen support personnel—were flying missions every night from Yontan and Kadena. The Army's 548th Night Fighter Squadron also operated out of Okinawa with five P-61 Black Widows.

The Navy had seen the need for night fighters in the early days of the war but encountered many practical problems in integrating them into carrier operations. By mid-1945, although the Navy maintained three carrier-based night-fighter squadrons in the Pacific, ground-based Marine squadrons had clearly established themselves as the U.S. military's leaders in developing night-fighting technology, tactics, and skills. Among them, the three Marine night-fighter squadrons operating from Okinawa accounted for sixty-eight enemy kills and spared American servicemen on land and sea untold trauma.

Intercepting enemy aircraft at night was impossible without radar. But although the Navy had led the way in developing radar beginning in the 1920s—and had even given it its name (a word derived from "radio detection and ranging")—it was the British who first applied it in aerial combat during the London blitz in 1940.

At the time of the Japanese attack on Pearl Harbor in December 1941, both the Army and Navy had a handful of crude radar devices in operation, including one in Hawaii that showed the approaching enemy planes but whose operators couldn't find anyone in authority to tell on a sleepy Sunday morning. But there were no radar-equipped planes in America's arsenal in late 1941 and no airborne controllers to operate them in coordination with ground-based radar units.

By early 1943, as America's daytime air superiority grew increasingly apparent in the Pacific, the Japanese began resorting more and more to nighttime bombing raids, and the need for radar-equipped night fighters became more pressing.

First, though, numerous technical problems had to be overcome by trial-and-error refittings of radar scopes, antenna, oxygen equipment, guns, and gun sights. The first U.S. Navy and Marine night-fighter squadrons of F4U Corsairs didn't arrive in the Pacific combat zone until September 1943, and the AI (air interception) radar they used was primitive and hard to operate. The first confirmed kill by one of these planes didn't come until late October.

By the spring of 1945, however, Grumman Aircraft had built 1,500 specially modified Hellcats—designated as F6F-5Ns—for night-fighter and reconnaissance work. They employed the newly developed APS-6 radar system, which was simple to operate, had a range of 5.5 miles, and weighed only 250 pounds. Installed in a bulblike pod on the plane's starboard wing, the radar unit provided a blip showing the target's altitude as well as a view to the rear of the American plane when another aircraft approached within 180 yards.

EVERY NIGHT-FIGHTER pilot had to pass a twenty-nine-week training course, in which he learned to fly solely on instruments, operate the six knobs that controlled his radar, and locate and destroy enemy aircraft in total darkness. For Marine night fliers, the course included three months of intensive flight training at Cherry Point, North Carolina. These were some of the reasons why only four Marine night-fighter squadrons were in operation as of mid-1945. Three of them were based on Okinawa.

"I had hoped to become a fighter pilot, but this was a newly created field," recalled First Lieutenant Lloyd J. Parsons, a native Californian who flew out of Yontan with VMF(N)-542. "How could fighter aircraft engage the enemy at night? The answers weren't too long in coming. . . .

"At the Marine Corps Air Station at Cherry Point, North Carolina, we learned to fly the plane and watch the radar at the same time. I'm still astounded that the equipment worked, with its maze of wiring, miniature tubes, and bulkiness. How the antennae stayed on was a mystery, since it turned at 18,000 RPMs out there on the right wing tip."

It worked well enough, however, on the night of May 13 (Mother's Day), as Parsons was flying a Hellcat nicknamed "Melancholy Baby" through the seemingly endless starlit skies northwest of Okinawa.

Suddenly, Parsons's radio crackled to life, and he heard the curt voice of his ground-based radar controller: "There's a bogie in your area. Find him."

This wasn't the way it was supposed to happen, Parsons thought. Part of the controller's job was to vector the pilot into a trailing position behind the enemy aircraft, then provide the altitude, air speed, and direction of the quarry. But on this night, the ground-control radar wasn't working properly, so all the controller could do was warn Parsons that the bogie was "in the vicinity."

With his adrenaline pumping at full throttle and his hands flying around the cockpit, adjusting knobs, flipping switches, and trying to keep his "Baby" upright, Parsons searched the inky skies, but neither his naked eye nor his radar screen offered any encouragement at first.

With no further word from ground control, Parsons flew one direction, then another. He dived, then climbed, turned, and turned again. He was about to give up when a telltale flicker of light popped up on his radar screen. His prey was six miles dead ahead and flying away from Parsons at the same altitude.

Careful now! Don't lose him! he admonished himself, jamming the throttle forward. *Oh, damn, now I'm closing too fast. Slow down! Slow down!*

On his first pass, Parsons overshot his target, and he felt his heart sink as he threw the "Melancholy Baby" into a tortuous, hard-over turn.

It's too late, his mind screamed at him. *You've lost him! He's gone!* But he kept one eye glued to the radarscope, and seconds later, the blip on the screen reappeared. Parsons was behind the enemy plane now, still at the same altitude, and in much better position for the kill.

There she is, silhouetted against the stars. A twin-engine Jap Frances, not a friendly. Oh, please don't have a belly gunner. The blue-flame exhaust from my idling engine is a dead giveaway.

In the near-total darkness of the cockpit—essential to remain invisible to the prey, prevent night blindness, and enable night-fighter pilots to obtain required visual contact before firing—Parsons fumbled for the gun-sight switch. He closed to within fifty feet of the target, then backed off a little and opened fire with his six .50-caliber machine guns.

Both engines of the enemy bomber burst into flame at once, and the ruptured motors showered the Hellcat's windshield with a solid coating of oil. For a moment as he veered away, Parsons saw the big red meatball on the bomber's fuselage glow vividly against the dark sky. Then the plane exploded, and the burning pieces of it floated gently down toward the East China Sea.

Parsons took a deep breath and grinned as he radioed his controller. "Ground control from Topaz 29," he said. "I've got Jap oil all over my windshield, and I can't see out. Give me a vector home."

—⁓—

It wasn't the sort of job that many pilots relished. Three out of every four evenings, the Okinawa night fighters took off at dusk on missions that normally lasted between two and a half and four hours—sometimes two of them per night. During these missions, each pilot operated in pitch-dark isolation, assigned to a specific sector and strictly forbidden to leave it, even in hot pursuit of enemy aircraft.

Their designation as night fighters, however, didn't mean they could take life easy once the "day shift" took over. Frequently, even after completing their night's work, they were also pressed into service for daylight bombing and strafing runs against enemy ground targets. Yet because of their small numbers, specialized skills, and perilous line of work, members of each squadron took great pride in their jobs. They also became like close-knit families.

⌒

AS OF EARLY 1942, Frank O'Hara had been an eighteen-year-old student at a Catholic seminary near his native Kansas City, Missouri, with every intention of entering the priesthood. Now, just over three years later, O'Hara was a Marine first lieutenant flying an F6F Hellcat on nightly missions with VMF(N)-542.

"Suddenly, everybody I knew was going into the service," O'Hara recalled decades later, "and something told me I needed to change my plans."

Sometimes the twenty-one-year-old pilot still marveled at his own personal transformation from prospective "man of the cloth" to flying Leatherneck. More recently, though, his thoughts had been focused on his bad luck in letting an enemy plane slip away from him—an incident that had indirectly contributed to the loss of his close friend and squadron mate, Lieutenant Fred Hilliard.

"I was on that plane for forty minutes before he slipped over into the next sector," O'Hara recalled many years later. "I was close enough to see Hilliard shoot the first Jap down. Then he took off after another one, and I lost radio contact with him. We never found Fred or his plane, and he was officially listed as missing in action."

Death was never very far away for the men of VMF(N)-542. In addition to Hilliard, Second Lieutenant William W. Campbell also failed to return after splashing a Japanese plane, and Second Lieutenant Clyde H. Hill was killed when his F6F crashed on the airstrip. Even before leaving the States, the squadron had suffered fatalities. Major Robert O. Hawkins, executive officer of 542, and Lieutenant E. L. Leimbach had been killed in separate crashes during training at Cherry Point in 1944.

The first confirmed kill by an Okinawa-based night fighter came on April 16, shortly after VMF(N)-542 had begun regular missions from Yontan, when First Lieutenant Arthur J. Arceneaux, a slender, dark-haired twenty-year-old from south Louisiana, blasted an attacking enemy plane out of the sky. By the time he arrived at Yontan, Arceneaux had spent hundreds of hours providing air cover for the Pacific Fleet and had seen combat at Peleliu and Yap, but as he recalled decades later, "Okinawa was where the *real* action began."

Even before reaching the island, the squadron's ship, the escort carrier *Sitko Bay,* was attacked by kamikazes, and Arceneaux and his fellow pilots had to launch prematurely by catapult 600 miles at sea as the ship's guns downed an enemy suicide bomber a short distance away. "Before I realized what was going on," said Arceneaux, "I was airborne in the middle of a full-blown war."

Every plane in the squadron suffered damage in escaping the melee, and necessary repairs delayed their first action until April 16. Around dusk that evening, Arceneaux and Lieutenant Bill Campbell took off on the squadron's initial combat mission—and quickly found themselves in a dogfight with two Japanese Zeroes.

"At about 10,000 feet, we saw a destroyer below us being attacked by the Zeroes," Arceneaux recalled. "We could see the ship zigzagging and the bomb drops narrowly missing it on either side."

Arceneaux immediately peeled off with his .50-caliber wing guns blazing, and he could see his tracers hitting one of the Zeroes as Campbell zoomed after the other enemy plane. Arceneaux's target coughed smoke as the F6F-5N Hellcat streaked past so near that Arceneaux could see the pilot's face in the cockpit of the Zero. Wheeling back for another pass, Arceneaux fired another short burst from his .50s, and the Zero blew up in a tremendous fireball, dangerously close to the pursuing Hellcat.

"I didn't learn until I got back to Yontan that the other Zero had latched onto my tail," Arceneaux said. "Luckily for me, Bill Campbell joined the chase and shot the Japanese fighter down. After that, he was more than just a good friend; he was the guy who'd saved me from meeting my Maker."

A few days later, Major Robert Porter, a Guadalcanal veteran who had succeeded Major William C. Kellum as CO, scored two kills on one of his first missions with 542. Captain Wallace E. Sigler, the squadron exec, would become an ace with five and a half kills to his credit—all of them "flamers."

ON THE INKY NIGHT of May 1, 1945, First Lieutenant Herbert Groff, a country boy who'd grown up on a Missouri farm 100 miles from St.

Louis, was cruising under 20,000 feet in his patrol sector when a voice broke through the static on his radio: "This is ground control. I've got a contact for you. Range about five miles and closing. Altitude 25,000 feet. Do you read?"

Groff blinked his eyes and stared at the six-inch radar screen in front of him. It appeared to be totally devoid of blips. "Roger," he said, "but I'm not picking up anything on my screen."

Groff was only moments away from the invisible line defining his assigned sector, and he knew there'd be hell to pay if he ventured beyond it, but this was his first chance at a kill, and he wanted it so much that he could almost taste it. This was no time for his radar, which was generally dependable but far from foolproof, to go on the blink.

"Night fighting was not only relatively new," Groff recalled later. "It was also hard and hazardous because a pilot was almost totally dependent on his instruments."

He put his Hellcat into a steep climb, adjusted one of the control knobs on the radar unit, and felt his pulse accelerate when a bright pinpoint of light appeared on the screen. "I've got him!" he said. "He's coming straight at me!"

"Good hunting," said ground control.

A minute later, Groff spotted the plane visually. It was a twin-engine Betty medium bomber, flying alone and heading for God knew where. Whatever its destination, he told himself, it wasn't going to make it.

As he streaked toward the target, Groff's finger found the firing button on the Hellcat's .50-caliber wing guns. At just over 100 yards, he opened fire.

"I'd fired a little less than 1,000 rounds when I saw the Betty burst into flame," Groff said. "As it turned out, it was the only opportunity I ever had to down a Japanese plane, and I was determined to make the most of it."

He followed the burning wreckage down until it splashed into the sea and the flames went out.

⁓

LIKE GROFF, many Marine airmen—whether on day or night patrol—were every bit as eager to get at the enemy as their counterparts on the ground. But none was more tenacious in his quest for a kill than twenty-eight-year-old Lieutenant Robert R. Klingman of VMF-312, a former enlisted man in both the Navy and the Marine Corps.

On May 10, Klingman was assigned as wingman for Captain Kenneth Reusser during combat air patrol over Ie Shima when they spotted a twin-engine Nick fighter on a photo reconnaissance mission 15,000 feet above them. All four planes in the patrol group climbed to investigate, and the enemy plane headed for higher—and much colder—altitudes to try to elude them.

One of the pursuing planes was forced to drop out of the chase at 32,000 feet, another at 36,000, but Reusser and Klingman fired enough ammunition to lighten their planes sufficiently to reach 38,000 feet, where Reusser used up his remaining .50-caliber rounds to riddle the Nick's left wing and engine. Left to continue the chase alone, Klingman closed to within fifty feet of the Nick, only to discover that his wing guns were frozen and wouldn't fire.

Frustrated but determined, Klingman attacked the enemy plane with the propeller of his Corsair. On his first pass, he damaged the Nick's rudder and slashed into its rear cockpit, where the Japanese gunner was pounding frantically on his own frozen guns. When a second pass inflicted more prop damage to the Nick but left Klingman dangerously low on fuel, he elected to stay and finish the job anyway. His third pass severed the Nick's stabilizer and sent the plane into an out-of-control spin that sheared off both its wings as it plunged seaward.

Klingman managed to nurse his Corsair back to Kadena and make a dead-stick landing with part of his prop missing, his plane peppered with bullet holes, and fragments of the Nick stuck in his cowling.

Two days later, Klingman was back on patrol when his hydraulic system failed and he bailed out instead of trying to crash-land on a beach with only one wheel. He was plucked from the sea by a destroyer-escort, and that evening he was a dinner guest of Admiral Richmond Kelly Turner, overall commander of the amphibious forces at Okinawa, aboard Turner's flagship.

"I'm hoping some of your luck will rub off on me," Turner reportedly told Klingman.

ON THE NIGHT of May 16, exactly a month after the first kills by Art Arceneaux and Bill Campbell, the same two fliers spotted three Japanese

"Kate" float planes practicing landings and takeoffs in a well-lighted area near an island halfway between Okinawa and Japan. This time Campbell led the attack, and before Arceneaux could catch up with him, he saw one of the float planes burst into flame.

Instantly, all the lights below went dark, and Japanese antiaircraft batteries and machine guns filled the air with fire.

"What's going on?" Arceneaux yelled into his radio mike. "Do you read me, Bill?"

"I shot down one of those Kates," came Campbell's faint reply through crackling static, "but the yellow so-and-so almost got me, too."

"What do you mean?" Arceneaux replied. "Are you okay?"

The sky around Arceneaux was suddenly ablaze with searchlight beams, streaking tracer bullets, and bursts of flak, some of them close enough to shake his plane. The only sound from the radio was unbroken static.

"Come in, Bill," he shouted. "We've got to cut out of here. Can you hear me?"

Arceneaux waited, holding his breath, but there was no response. A second later, he fired both his five-inch rockets at what he thought was a Japanese AA battery, then streaked south as fast as his Hellcat would fly.

"Only God knows why I wasn't hit," said Arceneaux, "but it was a long, lonesome trip home—and a mighty sad one, too."

Three nights later, Arceneaux avenged the loss of the friend who'd saved his life by sending another Kate float plane flaming into the sea. He never knew if this Kate was one of the three that he and Campbell had been after when Campbell disappeared.

⸺

AMONG THEM, the fliers of VMF(N)-542 shot down nineteen enemy aircraft during the Okinawa campaign. "We were pretty proud of what our pilots accomplished, although the squadron next door, VMF(N)-533, got thirty-two kills," said Tech Sergeant Walt McNeel.

To demonstrate their pride, McNeel and Sergeant C. J. Haines, another ground crewman, spent several days constructing a scoreboard showing one Japanese "meatball" for each enemy plane downed by their squadron, then put it on prominent display for the benefit of visitors to Yontan.

ALTHOUGH THE JAPANESE kamikaze campaign grew more feeble with each passing day, it remained a factor to be reckoned with and a cause of near-constant alerts aboard Navy ships as June began. When Japanese Admiral Matome Ugaki launched Kikusui Nine on June 3, he did so with only about 100 planes, including 64 Zeroes, 6 ancient Val dive-bombers, and a hodgepodge of 31 Army planes. Their first strike was a total washout because not one of the enemy planes reached its intended naval target, thanks to aggressive interception by carrier-and land-based Marine Corsairs, whose pilots claimed thirty-five kills and sent the surviving Japanese planes limping back to Kyushu.

Part of the interceptors' success could be credited to a high-level change, a few days earlier, in the Navy's Pacific command structure. On May 27, command of the U.S. Fifth Fleet and Task Force 38 was transferred to Admiral William F. "Bull" Halsey, whose aggressive leadership was already a Navy legend and which stood in sharp contrast to the more cautious philosophy of his predecessor, Admiral Raymond Spruance.

Spruance had viewed the primary mission of his fast carrier group as providing close air support for the Okinawa ground campaign and had used the bulk of his attack aircraft for that purpose. Halsey, to the contrary, was determined to strike the kamikazes on their home turf. One of his first orders on assuming command was to intensify attacks on Kyushu, while using the planes and pilots of Rear Admiral "Jocko" Clark's Task Group 38.1 to maintain air coverage on Okinawa. Halsey also ordered Marine Air Group 14 to move its squadrons of land-based Corsairs from the Philippines to Okinawa after determining that space could be found for them at Kadena and Yontan.

Although impeded by a small but vicious typhoon that seriously damaged the cruisers *Pittsburgh, Miami,* and *Baltimore* and destroyed the forward sections of the flight decks on the carriers *Bennington* and *Hornet,* Halsey managed to keep the pressure on Kyushu. He assigned Rear Admiral A. W. Radford's Task Group 38.4 to continue attacking the kamikaze bases even while the storm raged.

Meanwhile, the Army Air Force's 318th Fighter Group had begun operating from Ie Shima off Okinawa's northwest coast, using powerful, high-speed P-47 Thunderbolts—for which even Japan's newest Zeroes were no match—against Kyushu's fifty-plus airfields with devastating success.

Kikusui Nine scored its last major hit against an American ship on June 6, when one of a handful of Japanese army planes and naval floatplanes crashed into the U.S. minelayer *J. William Ditter*, ripping a gaping hole in its side, killing ten crew members, and injuring twenty-seven others.

The swan song for Kikusui Nine came on June 7, when a late-afternoon attack by two suicide planes on the destroyer *Anthony* at Radar Picket Station One failed to hit the target. One enemy pilot bailed out after his plane was hit by the destroyer's gunners. The other kamikaze fell thirty feet short of the ship, causing no significant damage and killing no one other than its pilot.

By this time, according to reports by Japan's own Fifth Air Fleet, only 570 serviceable aircraft remained on Kyushu out of the thousands that had been based there. Almost all of these surviving planes were designated for aerial defense against the mounting U.S. attacks on the Japanese home islands. Only forty-six flyable attack aircraft were left on Kyushu, and fewer than a dozen of these were available for kamikaze flights.

For the "Floating Chrysanthemums," blooming season was over.

CHAPTER THIRTEEN

Collapse of the Shuri Line

A S THE AIR WAR RAGED and May wound down, the going was painfully slow for American troops on the ground. Historian Robert Sherrod calculated that the U.S. Tenth Army gained an average of 133 yards per day during the period from April 7 through May 31—impressive numbers for a college running back, perhaps, but not much to brag about for an assault force of 183,000 men.

Troops of the five attacking U.S. divisions lost track of the times ground was gained, lost, regained, and lost again. Yet every bloodstained foot of their advance pressed Japan's 32nd Army deeper into a corner and eventually left its commander, General Ushijima, with only two options—another major retreat or swift annihilation.

By May 20 (L-plus-49), the stubborn ring of outer defensive works guarding Shuri was sustaining serious cracks. For the Americans, the pieces to a diabolical puzzle were finally starting to fit together, albeit at a frightful cost. Ushijima's Shuri Defense Zone was about to disintegrate.

⁓

FOR MORE THAN A WEEK, Wana Ridge and Wana Draw had been a bloody nemesis for troops of the First Marine Division. Lying virtually in the shadow of Shuri castle and the commanding heights where the heaviest concentration of Japanese artillery was positioned, Wana Draw was described by one historian as "a giant moat that might have been created for the slaughter of anyone mad enough to enter it." PFCs Manuel and Salvador Rivas of A Company, First Battalion, First Marines—reputedly the only pair of identical twins serving in the same company in the entire Corps—had their own name for the draw. The brothers from El Paso, who had served together in the Pacific since Guadalcanal, called it Death Valley, and for good reason.

"We ate and slept with the bloated bodies of Japs and our own men," recalled Manny Rivas, "and the only safe place to get any relief from the artillery fire was in the Okinawan tombs. There were six guys from El Paso in A Company, and Sal and I were the only ones who made it out alive. It was Death Valley, all right."

Bordering Wana Draw on the south was the barrier ridge of the same name, which not only blocked the advance of the First Marine Division but also contributed artillery support to enemy defenders in the Sugar Loaf–Horseshoe–Half Moon complex of hills in the Sixth Marine Division sector to the southwest.

The thin ranks of the Seventh Marine Regiment, who had carried the brunt of the Wana attack for eight days, were barely hanging on when their sister regiment, the First Marines, fresh from a week of rest, moved in on May 17 to relieve them.

"We were shot to pieces and beaten bloody," said Corporal Melvin Grant, a flamethrower operator in E/2/7. "Easy Company had gone into the line with 240 men. Now we were down to 26, and there was no way we could hold our positions any longer."

The Seventh's attacks against the intricate network of Japanese fortifications on Wana Ridge often ended with wounded Marines helplessly pinned down and unable to retreat, Grant recalled. "On one occasion, we had snipers firing at us from all directions," he said. "My flamethrower assistant was lying beside me, shot through the thumb. My first sergeant was lying behind me, shot through both eyes. A Mexican buddy of mine was in front of me, shot through the shoulder. One of the snipers fired at me seven times, but every shot missed. I counted the bullets as they hit the dirt. I played dead, and he finally stopped shooting."

⌐

FOR TWO WEEKS, Corporal Jimmy Butterfield, squad leader in the First Platoon of G Company, Second Battalion, First Marines (G/2/1), had been caught up in a sticky web of grief and depression that he couldn't seem to shake.

Normally, the nineteen-year-old Peleliu veteran—known as "Butts" to his buddies—was a talkative, easygoing type. But since his closest friend, PFC Harold W. "Chappy" Chapman, had been killed on May 5, Butterfield had been a different person. Not even the letters from Mary, his fiancée back in his hometown of Glens Falls, New York, could dispel his gloom.

Every night, he slept alone in his foxhole, shunning all attempts by his squad mates at companionship or conversation. And each day, he awoke with the same cold heaviness in his chest, as if he were carrying around a fifty-pound lead weight where his heart was supposed to be.

"Chappy and I had both grown up around Glens Falls, and we'd been best friends ever since we ended up in the same outfit at boot camp at Camp Lejeune," Butterfield recalled. "I usually checked with him first thing every morning, but the day he was killed I had a badly wounded guy in my squad who was losing a lot of blood, so I didn't see Chappy. I didn't know he was dead till my lieutenant told me. It really took the wind out of my sails."

Aggravating Butterfield's grief was an irrational thought that kept drumming inside his head like an accusation of guilt:

If only I'd been able to talk to him that morning, maybe it wouldn't have happened. Maybe he'd still be alive right now if it wasn't for that.

Now it was midmorning on May 19, and another in what seemed to be an endless series of attacks by the First Marine Division against the Japanese-held ridges around Wana Draw was in full sway. It was a beautiful, clear day—one of the last the Marines would see for the rest of the month—and the attack got off to a promising start with the platoon making steady gains.

"I had the middle squad, and these guys were damn good," Butterfield said. "We took a couple of small ridges without much trouble, but as we started up a larger, steeper ridge—so steep we had to crawl on our bellies to climb it—we came under heavy enemy fire that stopped us in our tracks."

Moments later, Butterfield glanced to his right in time to see blood fly as a rifle bullet struck Corporal Whitey Hargus squarely in the face. The wounded man pitched forward, sliding down the face of the ridge toward Butterfield, who struggled to his feet and ran to Hargus's aid.

Butterfield grabbed the corporal and pulled him over the crest of the ridge and out of the line of fire just as two other Marines rushed over. One of them was Sergeant Steve Godfrey, a hard-bitten platoon leader from Chicago. The other was Private Edward Brugger, a recent replacement from Buffalo.

"Jesus, we gotta get a corpsman up here," said a shaken Godfrey, staring at the mass of torn flesh where Hargus's nose and cheekbones had been. "This guy's really bad off."

As Godfrey scrambled down the hill, yelling for a corpsman, Butterfield glanced toward him and started to say something. But before he could get a word out, another rifle bullet—probably from the same sniper that had felled Hargus—smashed into his own face, squarely between the eyes.

Instantly, everything went black. Butterfield threshed in pain, feeling for his eyes but finding only blood.

"Where the hell are you guys?" he moaned.

If anyone answered, he didn't hear. Brugger, with tears of shock and horror gushing down his cheeks, was already running back down the slope as hard as he could go, searching for a medic and stretcher bearers.

"Somebody help me," Butterfield gasped. "I can't see a thing."

Then an enemy mortar round hit a few feet away, showering his mangled face and head with fragments. Butterfield scarcely felt the rash of new wounds from the shrapnel as he lapsed into unconsciousness.

⁓

AFTER THE EXHAUSTED Seventh Regiment had limped to the rear, Butterfield's surviving comrades of the First Marines slugged their way into the high ground on Wana Ridge. In savage fighting, they not only managed to take the hilltop but also to silence some of the Japanese 75-millimeter guns that were holding back the Sixth Division on Sugar Loaf Hill.

This breakthrough at Wana was one of the keys to solving the thorny riddle of Sugar Loaf. Another turned out to be what the Sixth Marine Division history called "an insignificant depression, hardly large enough to be dignified by the name of 'valley.'" This depression, running north and south to the east of Sugar Loaf, came to the attention of General Shepherd, the division commander, during a conference with Colonel William J. Whaling, commander of the 29th Marines, when it was noted that troops had passed through the defile several times without drawing enemy fire.

Based on this information, Shepherd took a major gamble in hopes of breaking the stalemate that was bleeding away his division's strength and morale. The general decided to move all three battalions of the 29th Marines through the depression in column. Then, once past the depression, each battalion was to attack one strong point in the Japanese defensive system, bringing all principal components of the system under simultaneous assault.

On the morning of May 17, elements of each assigned battalion launched coordinated attacks. In three attempts to take Sugar Loaf's summit, Captain Alan Meissner's Company E, Second Battalion, was beaten back in fierce hand-to-hand fighting that cost 160 casualties—two-thirds of the company's strength. The First Battalion also failed to achieve its objective and was forced to withdraw after nightfall by heavy artillery fire from Shuri. But the Third Battalion fared somewhat better, gaining and holding the reverse slope of Half Moon Hill, strengthening the regiment's left flank, and placing it in a good position to resume the attack the next day.

By now, the Japanese had driven troops of the Sixth Marine Division off Sugar Loaf nearly a dozen times with staggering losses, but General Ushijima realized that this latest coordinated assault had left his defenses seriously weakened. Without reinforcements, he knew that his defenders would soon be forced to yield this crucial complex of high ground.

During the night of May 17–18, Ushijima tried to send several hundred fresh troops into the Sugar Loaf–Horseshoe–Half Moon ridge system, but American observers spotted their movement and called in a devastating artillery barrage that inflicted heavy casualties and forced Ushijima to cancel his plan.

Soon after first light on May 18, Lieutenant Colonel William G. Robb's Second Battalion, 29th Marines, tried again to take Sugar Loaf, this time supported by tanks. The previous evening, a determined Robb had phoned Colonel Whaling, his regimental commander, and confidently predicted better results on the next try.

"We can take it," Robb had assured Whaling. "We'll give it another go in the morning."

Early on, however, it looked as if this assault would be repulsed like all the others. The supporting tanks had severe problems negotiating minefields on both sides of the hill, and six of the Shermans were disabled within the first hour and a half. Even so, the battalion worked its way far enough along the flanks of the hill to attempt another tank-infantry assault with the remaining Shermans, using a plan devised by Captain Howard Mabie of D Company.

"We can send half the command around the right side of the hill with tank support," Mabie said, "and when they get the Japs' attention, we'll send the rest of the troops and tanks around the opposite flank."

The plan worked to perfection. The tanks circled the hill from both sides while the infantry sealed caves on the reverse slope. Then the two groups of attackers joined forces, and this time there would be no retreat. After a furious, hourlong firefight with grenades, mortars, rifles, and bayonets at close quarters, Second Battalion Marines were in firm control of Sugar Loaf's crest. Despite continued heavy fire from Horseshoe Hill to the south and a nighttime counterattack by the Japanese, the Marines would never relinquish Sugar Loaf again.

Early on May 19, as the Fourth Marines moved in to relieve the 29th, there was still heavy fighting on the south slopes of Sugar Loaf, and the Horseshoe was still held by the enemy. The Third Battalion, Fourth Marines, commanded by Lieutenant Colonel Bruno Hochmuth, was subjected to particularly heavy artillery fire from the Shuri heights. The men of 3/4 suffered forty casualties during the morning, but they held their ground.

By late afternoon on May 20, Hochmuth's Third Battalion, again supported by tanks and aided by flamethrowers and cave-sealing demolition teams, had gained control of the Horseshoe. With fire support from the 22nd Marines, the Third Battalion also seized and held the western end of Half Moon Hill, despite taking heavy losses. At nightfall, Companies K and L of 3/4 held high ground that dominated Japanese mortar positions in the depression behind (south of) the Horseshoe, and troops of Company I, Third Battalion, had moved in on the left to bolster the front line.

Japanese resistance around Sugar Loaf would continue for several more days, and early on May 23, elements of the First Marine Division, including K/3/5, were sent into the Sixth Division zone to help secure Half Moon. The men of the Fifth Marines had seen carnage enough in their own sector—the westernmost reaches of Wana Draw were only a few hundred yards from Half Moon—but the scenes they faced after crossing into the slaughterhouse occupied by the Sixth defied description.

～⊃

PFC GENE SLEDGE and his buddies had spent close to a week almost within shouting distance of Half Moon Hill, but only when they entered the Sixth Division's sector early on May 23 were they struck by the full horror into which they marched.

On its way to Half Moon, Sledge's mortar squad had to pick its way through scores of Japanese dead, many of whom still lay where they'd fallen up to two weeks earlier. Most combat veterans took the sight of enemy corpses in stride, but when they began to pass untended Marine dead, it came as a sickening shock.

A few feet to the mortarmen's left, the bodies of six Marines lay side by side and facedown, so close together that they'd almost surely been killed by the same artillery shell. Sledge suspected that the six were new replacements so terrorized by the shelling that they failed to heed the warnings of officers and senior NCOs not to "bunch up." They were only the first of many. Decomposing corpses—both Japanese and American—littered the landscape in all directions.

"From the foxhole where I was pinned down on Half Moon, I could see the bodies of about thirty-five dead Americans and dead Japs," said PFC Harry Bender of K/3/5's First Platoon. "The smell of death was everywhere."

"It was the most ghastly corner of hell I had ever witnessed," Sledge recalled. "As far as I could see, an area that had previously been a low, grassy valley with a picturesque stream meandering through it was a muddy, repulsive open sore on the land . . . choked with the putrefaction of death, decay, and destruction."

In a slight depression near the mortar section's gun pits lay about twenty dead Marines, their bodies on stretchers and covered with ponchos, waiting to be taken to the rear for burial. From all indications, they'd been waiting for quite a while. Other Marines lay where they'd died—in many cases days earlier—in shell craters and foxholes half filled with muddy water. They still clutched rusting weapons as swarms of flies buzzed around them.

Japanese 75-millimeter shells from Shuri still whined in the sky and crashed to earth, making it obvious why so few of the dead Marines had been removed. Sugar Loaf had been taken, but continuous enemy artillery fire made any move from cover to help exposed wounded men—much less collect the dead—enormously risky for any Good Samaritan who tried.

"Around each corpse, maggots crawled about in the muck and then were washed away by the runoff of the rain," said Sledge. "There wasn't a tree or bush left. . . . Shells had torn up the turf so completely that ground cover was nonexistent. . . . The scene was nothing but mud; shell fire; flooded craters with their silent, pathetic, rotting occupants; knocked-out tanks and amtracks; and discarded equipment—utter desolation."

By NIGHTFALL on May 20, it had become apparent to both sides that the Japanese defensive juggernaut anchored by Sugar Loaf had been weakened beyond repair. Without this nondescript fifty-foot hill and those flanking it, the entire Shuri Defense Zone—encompassing the port of Naha, the town of Yonabaru, the heavy artillery that had mauled U.S. forces for weeks, and General Ushijima's own headquarters—would soon be indefensible for the Japanese.

The news that Sugar Loaf had been secured brought an elated message from General Geiger's Third Amphibious Corps headquarters to General Shepherd: "Resistance and determination with which elements of your division attacked and finally captured Sugar Loaf is indicative of the fighting spirit of your men. My hearty congratulations to the officers and men concerned."

When Colonel Robb, whose battalion had finally secured Sugar Loaf's crest, was interviewed by a reporter a day or two later, he paid tribute to the 2,662 Sixth Division Marines killed and wounded during the merciless ten-day fight for the hill.

"It was a helluva price to pay," Robb said, "but we took the damned thing."

ON MAY 13, while the Marines were trying to claw their way up Sugar Loaf, Half Moon, and the Horseshoe, the Army's 96th Division finally reached the top of Conical Hill on the east side of the island. Then, for the next three days, the Deadeyes held it against a series of determined Japanese counterattacks and relentless mortar and artillery fire.

The 96th continued to be harassed by Japanese dug in on smaller hills in the area until May 21, when Lieutenant Colonel Daniel Nolan's Third Battalion of the 381st Infantry took Sugar Hill and the unnamed hogback between Sugar and Conical, alleviating that problem. Now, with the northern and eastern faces of Conical held securely by troops of Colonel Eddy May's 382nd Infantry, Japanese mortars and machine guns could no longer threaten U.S. troop movements along the eastern coastal flats from positions on Conical.

General Buckner, the Tenth Army commander, congratulated May, calling his regiment's seizure of Conical one of the "most brilliant" examples of small-unit tactics that Buckner had ever seen.

Near the center of the island, meanwhile, the Army's depleted 77th Division continued its own stubborn chipping away at the Shuri defenses—a process that had cost its 305th Infantry fully 75 percent of its manpower in a ten-day period. Nevertheless, with the well-rested Seventh Division back in action nearby, the 77th was ready to join the all-out drive against Shuri that everyone sensed was just ahead. Shuri Castle was in the 77th's sector, and Major General Andrew D. Bruce, the division commander, believed his battered legions had earned the right to claim it before anyone else did.

⁓

At this point, General Hodge, commander of the 24th Corps, knew that the battle for Okinawa could be shortened dramatically if the Tenth Army could avoid another reenactment of the nightmares before Shuri and Kakazu. The only way to achieve that goal was to bottle up the enemy at Shuri instead of letting him slip away to the south, as he'd done at Kakazu, and Hodge devised a strategy for doing exactly that. His plan shaped up like this:

The combat-toughened Seventh Division (Attu, Kwajalein, Leyte), recently reinforced, fresh from a ten-day rest, and assigned to a relatively quiet sector of the front west of the 96th's zone, would sweep east around the Shuri defenses to Yonabaru, Okinawa's third largest town. The division would then wheel west along the Yonabaru-Naha road to hook up with the Sixth Marine Division near the west coast, sealing off Ushijima's escape route from Shuri and preventing him from forming a new defensive line farther south. If this maneuver succeeded, the Japanese would be surrounded, and Hodge believed the battle for Okinawa would be all but over.

It was a sound plan—one that might have worked—if a new round of torrential rainstorms hadn't descended on the front a few hours after Conical Hill fell to the 96th on May 21. In the opinion of many who witnessed it, this deluge was the worst yet on Okinawa. It went on for days and caused untold trouble and misery.

As PFC Gene Sledge of K/3/5 put it: "The almost continuous downpour . . . turned Wana Draw into a sea of mud and water that resembled a lake. Tanks bogged down, and even amtracks could not negotiate the morass. Living conditions on the front lines were pitiful. Supply and evacuation problems were severe. Food, water, and ammunition were scarce. Foxholes had to be bailed out constantly. . . . Sleep was nearly impossible."

Despite the rain, which continued almost nonstop for more than a week, the Seventh Division's surprise southward thrust, led by the 184th Infantry, came off without a hitch. By dusk on May 23, troops of the 184th had gouged a 2,000-yard hole in enemy lines south of Yonabaru and were driving disorganized Japanese defenders ahead of them. Meanwhile, Colonel Mickey Finn's 32nd Infantry, assigned to spearhead the westward push, moved into position to start its dash across the island.

Then the lashing rains left the whole operation stranded in an incredible quagmire. The dash slowed to a crawl and the crawl to a standstill. Tanks sank hull-deep into the mud and stalled there while men waded up to their thighs in the ooze, cursing helplessly as they struggled to free the massive Shermans. In each divisional sector from east to west, the situation skidded from bad to worse. Unpaved Highway 13, the only road connecting Yonabaru and Naha, became one long tangle of motionless vehicles marooned in a sea of mud.

By the afternoon of May 25, there were mile-long columns of vehicles clogging the road, and the mud grew deeper by the hour. Moving the approximately 175 tons of supplies per day needed by the Seventh—not including ammunition—from Yonabaru westward became an impossibility. There was no way to drain the roadway because its surface was almost level with surrounding rice fields, and no rock or crushed coral was available to fill yawning mud holes. During the last week of May, the Army's 13th Engineering Battalion dumped more than 1,000 truckloads of rubble, scraped up from the ruins of Yonabaru and other towns, into holes on Route 13 to try to keep supply lines open.

"Without the rain, we could have moved considerably faster and caused the Japs a lot of trouble," said General Archibald Arnold, commander of the Seventh. "Even so, we kept moving, which is remarkable enough in that mud."

Among the bogged-down equipment was "Galloping Gertie," the 37-millimeter antitank gun named for Tech Sergeant Porter McLaughlin's aunt, and the jeep that was trying to pull it.

"The jeep really wasn't much help in all that mud, and we had to wade in there and manhandle the gun most of the way," McLaughlin recalled. "In fact, some of the jeeps got stuck so badly that our tanks rolled right over them in order to keep moving. The mud was so deep that it would suck your shoes right off your feet. When it did, it was almost impossible to dig them out of the stuff, and when we tried to dig foxholes, they immediately filled up with water."

Scattered Japanese forces also directed a series of harassing attacks against Colonel Finn's advancing 32nd Infantry from various hills and ridges along the route. Fierce fighting broke out between Companies K and I and Japanese occupying a group of hills including Mabel, Minnie, Hetty, and Duck, leaving ten men dead, including Lieutenant Amos De-Lazier, a K Company platoon leader, and sixteen others wounded.

As the rain continued, four of the five U.S. divisions found themselves stopped cold, except for minor patrol activity. Only the Sixth Marine Division managed to keep grinding ahead, although at a glacial pace, first into the skeletal ruins of Naha, empty of civilians but defended by a Japanese naval engineering battalion, then south toward the overflowing Asato River. Some Marines tried to use Okinawan ponies as pack animals to move supplies, but in several instances they were forced to shoot the ponies after they bogged to their necks in the sucking mire.

But the worst thing of all about the incessant rain was that it gave General Ushijima desperately needed time to formulate a plan of his own for slipping out of the Tenth Army's grasp and escaping to fight another day.

⌒

IT WAS CLOSE TO MIDNIGHT on May 22, and torrents of rain were cascading off the ancient, shell-scarred battlements of Shuri Castle, when General Ushijima called together his staff and senior commanders in a cave far below to talk strategy. Almost all agreed that attempting to hold the Shuri heights beyond the next few days was out of the question. The Americans were on the verge of breaking into the heart of the shrinking Japanese defensive bastion, which was now too small even to shelter the estimated 50,000 men remaining in the 32nd Army. After debating other possible courses of action, most of the officers agreed that the best decision was to withdraw to the Kiyamu Peninsula eleven miles to the south at the tip of the island and establish a new defensive line along the Yaeju Dake–Yuza Dake Escarpment.

In contrast to the U.S. Seventh Division's route over the unpaved five-mile-long loblolly between Yonabaru and Naha, the 32nd Army could accomplish its withdrawal via all-weather Highways 3 and 7, which ran parallel to each other and almost due south.

The new line of defenses already had enough natural and man-made caves to accommodate the whole Japanese garrison, and sizable stores of weapons and ammunition had been left there when the Japanese 24th Division moved north to Shuri in early April.

Ushijima ordered the removal of ammunition and wounded to begin immediately, utilizing some of the 100 light trucks that had been kept safely hidden at Shuri. Service and communication units would go next, and the artillery, with 50 percent of its heavy guns still operable, would follow. Most of the combat units would wait until May 29–30 to move out, and some would stay behind on the Shuri perimeter long enough to screen the others' withdrawal.

Unlike General Hodge's plan for containing the Japanese, Ushijima's elaborate scheme was born of desperation. In all likelihood, it would have failed miserably in anything resembling normal weather conditions. But as it was, ceiling-zero visibility kept U.S. observation planes grounded for the better part of a week, and Ushijima took maximum advantage.

THE WEATHER CLEARED slightly on May 26, enough to allow a few aerial reconnaissance missions, and American pilots saw long columns of Japanese troops marching south. Scattered among the troops were throngs of what appeared to be civilians clothed in white. (Leaflets had been dropped over Shuri earlier, advising civilians to leave the area and to identify themselves as noncombatants by wearing white.)

Unhampered by the rain and mud, the cruiser *New Orleans,* the battleship *New York,* and other Navy ships began targeting the southbound roads on which enemy troop movements had been reported. More than fifty Marine aircraft also flew bombing and strafing sorties over the roads, selectively striking at enemy troops but undoubtedly hitting civilians as well. (The leaflets had warned civilians to stay away from Japanese military units, but many either didn't understand or failed to heed the warning.)

Late on the afternoon of May 26, pilots also spotted a column of soldiers moving north from the island's southern tip. After assessing this visual evidence, U.S. intelligence mistakenly concluded that Ushijima's forces were still mounting a strong defense of Shuri while evacuating civilians and wounded and bringing up reinforcements from the south.

In fact, except for a rear guard of about 5,000 men, the survivors of Japan's 32nd Army were moving south as rapidly as possible, and a report prepared by Ushijima's staff noted that the withdrawal was "proceeding in good order without any signs of confusion due to slackened enemy pressure."

Actually, however, the situation wasn't nearly as rosy as the report implied. Despite a ceiling of total zero on May 29–30, which grounded all U.S. flights for most of the period, American planes used the few brief openings they had to strike telling blows on the retreating Japanese. Ushijima had estimated before the withdrawal that 50,000 troops remained in his command, but a recount following the retreat showed only 30,000. This indicated that, not counting the 5,000-man rear guard, many of whom perished, some 15,000 Japanese soldiers were lost en route from Shuri to the new defensive perimeter.

Estimates indicate that a like number of civilians also died on the roads leading south.

IN THE FINAL ANALYSIS, the fact that U.S. intelligence had again misread the intentions of the Japanese had little bearing on the outcome of General Hodge's attempt to cut off Ushijima's retreat. The rain and mud were unquestionably the principal culprits that allowed up to two-thirds of the Japanese troops to escape and negated the entrapment planned by the Seventh Division and the Sixth Marine Division.

The Japanese rear guard also contributed to the success of the withdrawal by making it seem as if far more than 5,000 enemy troops were still defending the Shuri bastion. When strong U.S. patrols were sent out on probing missions all along the front, they immediately met stiff resistance. Typical reports from returning patrols read, "No indication of Japanese withdrawal" and "Does not appear that resistance has lessened."

Early on May 27, however, irrefutable evidence emerged that some sort of general Japanese withdrawal was in progress when units of the Sixth Marine Division entered Naha to find that the Japanese had virtually abandoned the ravaged port city. This discovery led General Buckner to dispatch urgent instructions to his army:

"Indications point to possible enemy retirement to new defensive position with possible counteroffensive against our forces threatening his flank. Initiate without delay strong and unrelenting pressure to ascertain probable intentions and keep him off balance. Enemy must not—repeat not—be permitted to establish himself securely on new position with only minimal interference."

By this time, General Ushijima had apparently learned—or guessed—that a concerted American effort was under way to pinch off his escape routes. Operating in the rain, patrol spearheads from the Seventh Division's 184th Infantry reached the town of Inasomi two miles southwest of Yonabaru with no sign of organized resistance. But when the Seventh's main body of combat troops tried to follow the same path, they were met in force by elements of the Japanese 62nd Division, hastily dispatched by Ushijima to shore up his right flank.

⁓

THE INTERMINABLE DOWNPOURS finally gave way to a bright sun on May 28, although intermittent showers hung on for a couple more days, delaying a prolonged drying-out. The ground was so saturated and unstable that it would take a week or more for it to solidify sufficiently to support the weight of tanks.

By the morning of May 29, most Japanese soldiers left in the vicinity of Shuri were guarding the withdrawal routes to the south, and Shuri itself was only lightly defended. As the Seventh Division's history notes: "It was, of course, too late to encircle the Japanese, but Tenth Army was anxious to straighten out and consolidate its lines in preparation for a drive south in pursuit of the enemy."

All that was really left to be decided for the five U.S. divisions converging on the all-but-abandoned Japanese citadel of Shuri was the question of who would be first to reach the ruins of Shuri Castle and claim the victory—tainted though it was.

Much to the chagrin of the 77th Division, whose sector included the castle, that honor would go to members of Captain Julian D. Dusenbury's A Company, First Battalion, Fifth Marines. They slipped through an opening in the enemy lines near Wana Draw early on May 29, routed a small group of Japanese in the castle courtyard, and climbed to the top of its high parapet. There Dusenbury, a devoted South Carolinian, raised a flag—not the Stars and Stripes, as it happened, but the Confederate Stars and Bars.

"When we learned that the flag of the Confederacy had been hoisted over the very heart and soul of Japanese resistance, all of us southerners cheered," said K/3/5's PFC Gene Sledge, a native of Alabama. "The Yankees among us grumbled, and the Westerners didn't know what to do."

The banner was later replaced by an American flag that had flown over Guadalcanal and the battle colors of the First Marine Division.

The town of 17,500 inhabitants that had once nestled at the base of the castle had virtually vanished into a tortured moonscape of shell craters, piles of rubble, and shattered stone. The only recognizable structures were the bell tower and outer concrete walls of a small Methodist church. Everything else, including the twenty-foot-thick walls of the castle, had been pounded to powder by more than 200,000 rounds of U.S. artillery and countless bombs.

When Tech Sergeant Porter McLaughlin and the rest of the Seventh Division's 32nd Infantry arrived in the Shuri area after completing their delayed trek from Yonabaru, they found that little military equipment had been left behind by the departing Japanese. There was no evidence that their withdrawal had been anything but orderly.

"What we did find, though, was an incredible number of bodies," McLaughlin said. "Up in the ridges where the Marines had fought, bodies and pieces of bodies of dead Marines were scattered everywhere, and there were lots of dead Japs, too. Many of them had been lying there for a week or more, and the smell was so terrible you hated to breathe."

Meanwhile, there was still Japanese resistance to be dealt with, and the mud remained as unforgiving as ever for those who had to traverse it by foot. As one 96th Division officer described his men's progress—or lack thereof: "Those on the forward slopes slid down. Those on the reverse slopes slid back. Otherwise, no change."

IN THE 96TH DIVISION'S SECTOR, scattered resistance continued on May 30 from a few isolated pockets of Japanese defenders, but for the most part it was quiet, even in places where the infantry had encountered savage resistance a day or two before. Two small hills code-named Hen and Hector were exceptions. Both were fiercely defended by significant forces of Japanese, and two companies from the 96th's 382nd Infantry were sent in to clean them out in coordinated assaults. Among a six-man patrol assigned to move out ahead of Company G to probe enemy positions on Hen Hill was PFC Clarence B. Craft, a husky ex-truck driver from San Bernardino, California, who was seeing his first combat since joining the division as a replacement a few days earlier.

The group hadn't gone far when the Japanese opened up with machine guns, rifles, and a hailstorm of grenades from a deep trench just beyond the crest of the hill. Almost instantly, three members of the patrol fell wounded, and two others hit the dirt and took cover, but Craft kept charging ahead without breaking stride, hurling grenades as he went and firing his M-1 at any hint of movement he saw.

From the crest of adjacent Hector Hill, PFC Donald "Si" Siebert, another young replacement also involved in his first action, watched Craft's one-man war with awed admiration.

"Once at the top of Hector, I glanced to my right at the George Company attack," Siebert recalled later. "A single soldier was standing astride the trenches, firing into them. . . . We were able to bring the fire of our BARs to the rear of the ridge and Hen Hill, preventing [the Japanese] from firing up at this man. But he apparently needed little help from us."

Craft received the only assistance he did need from several of his G Company comrades, whom he waved forward to form a chain behind him to hand up grenades and TNT satchel charges. He cut down the crew of an enemy machine gun, paused to reload his M-1, then hurled a TNT charge into a cave where several stunned Japanese had taken refuge. When the charge failed to ignite on the first try, Craft retrieved it, relighted the fuse, and threw it again, sealing the cave shut.

In single-handedly routing the enemy from Hen Hill, Craft killed at least twenty-five Japanese—a feat described by General Hodge as the "most remarkable I've heard of in a lifetime of soldiering"—without suffering so much as a scratch. He paused only once in his rampage, long enough to grab a sword from a dead enemy officer. "I figured the rest of the guys in the company would've stripped that field clean of souvenirs by the time I got back," Craft explained.

On November 1, 1945, at the White House, Craft was awarded the Medal of Honor by President Harry S. Truman in recognition of his "utterly fearless and heroic attack" against Japanese positions that had repulsed earlier U.S. assaults in battalion strength.

For several days, the troops that General Ushijima had left behind to shield the retreat of his main force continued to harry the American mop-up of the areas around Naha and south of Shuri, thus delaying a general advance southward by the Tenth Army.

Many of the most bitterly contested former Japanese strong points had been abandoned completely. On May 30–31, men of the First Marine Division moved unchallenged through the Wana area, where they'd been held at bay for nearly two weeks and suffered hundreds of casualties, then hooked up without incident with GIs of the 96th Division.

The heaviest enemy resistance was still being faced by the banged-up Sixth Marine Division as it slugged its way through the hills east of Naha against Japanese navy troops and scattered rear guards. But by June 1 the Sixth had broken through the thin Japanese lines to reach the Kokuba River and its estuary, which separated Naha from the Oroku Peninsula.

The Shuri line was history, but the U.S. command was as confused over the whereabouts of the remaining Japanese forces as it had been on April 1, sixty long days before. Tenth Army commander General Buckner and his staff still didn't fully realize Ushijima's intentions, and they seriously underestimated the effectiveness of his plan. Buckner himself clung to the belief that the Japanese withdrawal had come too late and that the Americans could catch the Japanese before they were able to form a workable new defensive perimeter.

"It's all over now except for cleaning up pockets of resistance," Buckner confidently predicted at a press conference on May 31. "This doesn't mean there won't be stiff fighting, but [Ushijima] won't be able to organize another line."

That same day, most of the 77th Division was assigned to the inactive sector formerly held by the 96th for rest, rehabilitation, and reinforcement. Only the artillery battalions of the 77th and its 305th Infantry Regiment remained in the combat zone to provide fire support and aid in mopping up isolated enemy holdouts.

The following morning, June 1, with the Army's Seventh and 96th Divisions again positioned on the left (east) side of the front and the First and Sixth Marine Divisions on the right (west) side, the drive began to find and finish off the Japanese defenders—wherever they might be.

SURVIVING MEMBERS of General Ushijima's rear guard remained at predesignated defensive lines until June 4, when the last of them evaporated into the countryside and made their way south.

By this time, Ushijima was settled into his new headquarters in a cave deep in the bowels of Hill 89 outside the town of Mabuni. His remaining forces were quickly organizing the defense of the Kiyamu Peninsula along the Yaeju Dake–Yuza Dake Escarpment, which ran, with only the briefest of breaks, all the way across Okinawa's two-mile-wide southern tip.

With the U.S. Tenth Army moving cautiously toward him along the same routes that his own army had used to escape Shuri, Ushijima had time to reflect on what intelligence officers of the First Marine Division would soon be calling his "properly deft withdrawal."

Clearly, he had thwarted and frustrated the Americans again—not getting away as cleanly as in the retreat from Kakazu Ridge but conserving his strength very effectively nevertheless. Still, the courtly general must have asked himself what he'd really accomplished. More than 62,500 members of his army were now dead, and the rest were still in a trap, even though it was one of their own design.

Ushijima had fulfilled his only goal: He'd bought additional time for his surviving troops—and for his besieged homeland. No one yet knew how much time was left for the 32nd Army, but a realistic estimate was about three weeks. That appeared to have been the assessment of Ushijima's staff, considering that only a twenty-day supply of rations had been brought to the 32nd Army's new command post.

Knowingly or not, Ushijima had also won the bitter admiration of his enemies. As Colonel Cecil Nist, intelligence officer for General Hodge, commander of the U.S. 24th Corps, wrote in summarizing the week of May 26 through June 2:

"Although the forces of General Ushijima are destined to defeat, his conduct of the defense of Okinawa had been such that his spirit can join those of his ancestors and rest in peace."

CHAPTER FOURTEEN

The End of an Army

O N JUNE 5, the rains finally stopped, and the ocean of mud that had covered southern Okinawa for a month slowly began drying out. Marines and GIs pulled off their sodden combat boots, peeled away their rotted socks, and got their first look in weeks at their tortured toes.

PFC Gene Sledge, whose Fifth Marines had gone into reserve on June 4 after being relieved on the line by the First Marine Regiment, was shocked by the condition of his feet when he removed his boondockers. Back in April, Sledge had traded a candy bar to a soldier for a pair of Army-issue wool socks, which he valued highly because they were much more comfortable when wet than the Marines' standard cotton ones. But when Sledge saw how "slimy and putrid" his socks were, he had no choice but to trash them.

"With regret, I threw my prize socks aside," he said, "and spaded dirt over them as though covering up a foul corpse." Along with them, he also buried most of the skin from the soles of his feet, which clung to the socks and sloughed off in large strips, leaving his feet red, raw, and cracked.

"Damn, Sledgehammer, your feet stink like hell," said Sledge's buddy, PFC Myron Tesreau, who soon discovered that his own were equally odorous.

Sledge's mortar section and the rest of K/3/5 were drastically under-strength at this point and overdue for a break. On June 1, the company had suffered thirty-six casualties as it mopped up in the Shuri area. With these losses, K/3/5 was down to about 100 enlisted men and 3 or 4 offi-cers, well below half its normal complement.

The whole regiment was in much the same weakened condition, and rumors circulated that the Fifth Marines might not be committed to combat again on Okinawa—but the rumors, as usual, proved false. The break would be brief and replacements too few to fill the gaps in K

Company's ranks before it returned to action at a place called Kunishi Ridge.

⌒

EVEN AFTER THE SUN came out and the skies cleared, rank-and-file combat troops of the Tenth Army found few bright spots in their situation. Their nerves were as raw as their feet, their tempers as foul as their socks. Sun or no sun, the haggard conquerors of Shuri now faced the prospect of repeating the bloody ordeal of May. It was almost too much to bear.

"By this time, we all knew the Japs had outsmarted us again," recalled acting Sergeant Jack Armstrong of the First Marine Tank Battalion. "We were mad as hell that they'd been allowed to slip away, but, even worse, we were at the point where we really thought this thing was never going to end. We weren't even sure where the Japs had gone after they pulled back from Shuri, but we knew exactly where *we* were—stuck in the mud and right back at square one."

Despite General Buckner's confident assertion that the enemy wouldn't be able to form a substantial new defensive line before the Tenth Army found him and overran his shrunken forces, the southward advance began cautiously. As in the drive on Shuri, the Seventh and 96th Infantry Divisions were positioned on the left (east) side of the island and the First and Sixth Marine Divisions were on the right (west). The situation was eerily reminiscent of the one two months earlier before Kakazu. No one could be certain where the Japanese would set up their first defensive perimeter, so simply locating the enemy was the Tenth Army's initial priority.

The assignment for General Arnold's Seventh Division—to seal off the Chinen Peninsula and keep the Japanese from escaping into its rugged hills—was largely a wasted effort since General Ushijima had never planned to move his troops in that direction. Nevertheless, the Seventh carried out its mission quickly and in good order, rounding up 13,000 civilians in the process and moving them to safety. Meanwhile, the Deadeyes of the 96th drove down the center of the island toward the town of Iwa and a strip of high ground beyond it.

On the west side of the advance, the First Marine Division moved to block enemy access to the Oroku Peninsula just as the Seventh Division was doing with the Chinen Peninsula on the opposite coast. The Sixth

Marine Division was to seize Oroku itself, a mission that included the last amphibious landing of the war and the first serious fighting of the post-Shuri campaign.

Defending Oroku, which juts into the sea just south of Naha, were about 2,000 well-armed Japanese navy troops under Rear Admiral Minoru Ota, who had deployed his force along an east-west ridgeline fortified with more than 200 machine guns and small-bore cannon salvaged from wrecked aircraft. Until the peninsula was secured, Naha harbor would be unusable by American ships.

General Geiger, commanding the Third Marine Amphibious Corps, expected the main Japanese defenses on Oroku to be across its base and facing inland, so he planned to flank them with a landing by the Sixth Division on the northern tip of Oroku. The assault assignment went to the Fourth and 29th Marines, with support from two companies of the Sixth Marine Tank Battalion, commanded by Lieutenant Colonel Robert L. Denig. Only about seventy serviceable amtracks were available, barely enough to transport the two regiments. All the others had either been destroyed or worn out hauling supplies through the mud.

After landing on Oroku on June 4, it took the Marines only two days to overrun Naha airfield, once the busiest on Okinawa. But on June 7, they stumbled upon an awesome network of underground enemy tunnels, some up to 300 yards long, equipped with electric lights and built in three levels. Within this labyrinth were battalion-sized caves equipped as sleeping quarters for enlisted men, officers' quarters outfitted with plush furniture, well-equipped hospitals, galleys, and storage areas—most of them now unoccupied.

Brigadier General William T. Clement, assistant commander of the Sixth and a veteran of Bataan, described the system of caves on Oroku as "stronger than [those on] Corregidor." Necessarily, the advance slowed to a crawl while these were checked out.

Also slowing the advance—and exacting a heavy price in U.S. tanks—were the heaviest concentrations of land mines the Marines had yet seen in the campaign. Buried in thick mud, the mines had to be located and removed by disposal teams, who ventured out ahead of the Shermans to do their high-tension work. Even so, the mines, along with satchel charges and cannon fire, claimed a total of thirty tanks. The Japanese on Oroku had no 47-millimeter antitank guns; if they had, none of the Marine tanks might have survived.

Also fortunate for the Marines, about four-fifths of the 10,000 seasoned combat troops originally under Admiral Ota's command had been withdrawn from Oroku and sent to deal with crises elsewhere. If Ota's force had remained at full strength and its underground citadels fully manned, the fight for Oroku could have lasted for weeks. As it was, the Marine rifle companies owed their success in large part to the stout nerves of Colonel Denig's tankers.

"Orchids to C Company's tanks," said a message to Denig from Fourth Marines headquarters. "Company I had been unable to move until the tanks came in to support them. Many weapons were captured, many Japs killed. It was a successful afternoon. The gains were due to the tank support."

WHEN G COMPANY, 29th Marines, had come ashore on Love Day, it had counted 235 men in its ranks, including 7 guys who shared the last name White. None of the 7 were directly related as far as they knew, but friendships developed among them that welded them into a tight, if informal, fraternity. By the morning of June 9, however, only 20 of the company's original Love Day members were still in action and of the White contingent, only Privates James S. and Robert S. White remained fit for duty.

Actually, Jim White, a husky, dark-haired youngster from Kansas City, Missouri, had already been wounded twice—first in mid-May, when a 47-millimeter shell hit a few feet from him, buried him in dirt, and left him with a concussion, then on June 6, when mortar fragments tore up his left thumb. Both times, he'd refused to be evacuated.

"I had to carry my M-1 with both hands because of my thumb," he recalled much later, "but I could still use it okay—and a BAR, too—and I figured the company needed me. We had less than 100 men left in the whole Third Battalion [out of 1,000], and I was a damned good rifle shot if I do say so."

Other Whites in G Company had fared far worse than Jim. In mid-April, PFC John White had been shot through the chin during an assault on Mount Yaetake. On May 14, Jim's close friend Private W. W. "Red" White had been hit in the buttocks by a huge chunk of shrapnel from the same mortar round that ripped another Marine's head off on Half Moon Hill.

When Jim had pulled his buddy out of the shell hole where the mortar shell had struck, Red was barely conscious, but he was yelling at the top of his lungs to his unwounded comrade, Private R. R. "Railroad" White:

"Hey, Railroad, I got my ticket home right in the ass!"

On that same day, Private Henry White had had his leg torn off by another mortar blast, and Private W. F. White had been hit in the thigh by grenade fragments. A few days later, "Railroad" White had been evacuated after losing a toe in a truck accident.

Now the faces of his five departed comrades flashed through Jim White's mind as he made his way cautiously up a hill on the Oroku Peninsula under heavy fire. When White saw a Marine fall nearby and heard him scream in pain, he immediately started crawling to the man's aid.

"By this time, we didn't have any corpsmen left; they were all dead or wounded," he recalled. "So I tried to help the guy, but then a Jap sniper opened up on me with a 7.7-millimeter rifle."

As White felt twin streaks of pain knife through his legs, he saw three other Marines hit nearby at almost the same exact second. Leaving a trail of blood behind him, he managed to turn around and drag himself to the relative safety of a gully.

"I crawled back about fifty yards, through two or three inches of mud and water at the bottom of the gully," White recalled. "There were bloated Jap bodies all over the place, and I had to crawl over them because I was too weak to go around them. Finally, I got back to a rear area where a couple of guys put me on a truck with a bunch of other wounded. One guy died on the way to the field hospital. He was awash in his own blood, and I was bleeding just about as bad."

Jim White would later learn that Private Robert White, the last unscathed member of the "clan" in G Company, had himself been evacuated with bullet wounds to the chest and left arm shortly after Jim had fallen.

As Jim observed more than sixty years later: "I guess seven just wasn't our lucky number."

IT TOOK THE FOURTH and 29th Marines five days of "blowtorch and corkscrew" fighting, plus help from the 22nd Marines, to wear down the embedded Japanese. But by June 10, the enemy defenders were squeezed into a narrow pocket in the northeast corner of the peninsula between the towns of Oroku and Tomigusuki and completely surrounded.

At the height of the battle, a one-man blitz against enemy positions around Tomigusuki Castle, an ancient pile of coral near the eastern edge of the peninsula, helped seal the victory. Private William H. Lowe, a rifleman in the 22nd Marines, braved fierce enemy fire to blast no less than seventy-five Japanese caves, a feat that Lowe modestly described in these terms: "When the Japs fired on us from caves along a ridge, we worked our way up the opposite slope. A couple of buddies brought up the TNT, tied the blocks, and put fuses in the charges. I lighted and threw the going-away satchels into the caves."

When the blasting was done, 114 Japanese bodies were counted, according to Lieutenant Rex Dillow, Lowe's platoon leader.

On June 11, eight battalions of Marine infantry, supported by tanks, launched a coordinated attack to smash the last major pocket of enemy resistance on Oroku. They had to negotiate several more concealed minefields under a crossfire from enemy machine guns, but by afternoon the pocket was cleared.

Sensing that the end was near for his forces, Admiral Ota sent a final radio message to General Ushijima's headquarters, now relocated in a deep cave near the town of Mabuni on the southern coast:

"Enemy tank groups are now attacking our cave headquarters. The naval base force is dying gloriously at this moment. . . . We are grateful for your past kindnesses and pray for the success of the Army."

The next morning, Marines attacking from the west and south routed the remaining Japanese defenders and broke into the heart of their subterranean bastion. So extensive and elaborate was the network of tunnels, corridors, and caves that it took Marine patrols two days to locate the bodies of Admiral Ota and five of his staff officers, all of whom had committed suicide. The corpses were found lying in state in a headquarters of solid concrete at the center of the complex.

For the first time in the campaign, enemy troops began surrendering in significant numbers during the fight on Oroku. One group of thirteen Japanese soldiers surrendered to a 29th Marines platoon led by Sergeant James E. Higdon Jr. Another group of twenty-plus was talked into surrendering by PFC Harry M. Tuttle, an interpreter, with the help of a captured Japanese warrant officer. The top prisoner taker was Lieutenant Spencer V. Silverthorne, a veteran language officer and former Williams College football star, who accepted the surrender of fifty-six Japanese in a single day, including one who was pointing a BAR at him.

"The muzzle kept looking bigger and bigger as I approached," Silverthorne said later. "By the time I got within three feet, I would've sworn I was walking up on a 155 howitzer." Assuring the Japanese soldier that he had nothing to worry about, Silverthorne firmly pushed the weapon to one side. For his bravery and coolheadedness, he was awarded a Silver Star.

Many other Japanese chose to die fighting or take their own lives, and the Sixth Marine Division paid dearly for its victory. By the time the mop-up was completed on June 13, a total of 1,608 Marines had been killed and wounded in the ten-day fight for Oroku. According to General Shepherd, the division commander, 4,000 Japanese were killed (this claim seems inflated because records show Ota having only about half that many men), and 200 were taken prisoner.

For its tenacity and sacrifice, the division received commendations from Generals Buckner and Geiger, and Shepherd lauded the "indomitable spirit and professional skill" of his men.

⁓

WHILE SHEPHERD'S MARINES had their hands full on Oroku, troops of the Seventh and 96th Divisions advanced south at a slow-but-steady pace, deprived of close support by their armored and artillery units because of mud and miserable road conditions. On June 7–8, the Seventh ran into stiffening resistance on the outskirts of the town of Gushichan, while the 96th, having captured Iwa town, held forward positions near the villages of Tomui and Shindawaku.

Ahead lay the looming heights of the Yaeju Dake–Yuza Dake Escarpment, shielded by an unseen but lethal barrier of Japanese artillery. From here on, the going would be as tough as anything the Tenth Army had yet experienced on Okinawa. The escarpment stretched across the width of the island's southwestern tip, anchored by four major defensive strong points: Kunishi Ridge, a mile-long coral precipice in the First Marine Division zone on the west; the Yaeju Dake and Yuza Dake peaks, towering 400 and 340 feet respectively above the 96th and Seventh Divisions' sectors; and Hill 95, a massive 300-foot limestone outcropping paralleling the east coast and providing unobstructed fields of fire all along the bluff line's eastern face.

Topographically, there was no vulnerable spot in the new Japanese line. All northern approaches to the base of the escarpment were via long stretches of low, level ground, ending abruptly at a wall of sheer 160-foot bluffs and exposed to interlacing fire from the front, right, and left. The plateau atop the cliffs was studded with craggy limestone and coral outcroppings and, like every other system of enemy-held high ground on Okinawa, honeycombed with fortified caves. The only natural avenue into the enemy stronghold was a narrow valley dominated by high ridges on both flanks.

The escarpment was an even more formidable natural barrier than either Kakazu Ridge–Kakazu West or the Sugar Loaf Hill–Wana Draw–Wana Ridge complexes—lynchpins of the Shuri Line. In this case, however, there were two critical differences between this Japanese defensive complex and the others—manpower and firepower.

In the high ground protecting Shuri, the Americans had faced the bulk of General Ushijima's well-entrenched, well-prepared, combat-tested 110,000-man 32nd Army. Now that army had shrunk to fewer than 30,000 men, many of them lightly trained replacements from rear-echelon units and the Okinawan *Boetai* home guard Even if all of them had been seasoned battle veterans, their number wasn't nearly enough to man the escarpment effectively. In addition, fully three-quarters of their machine guns had been lost, and stocks of ammunition for their artillery and heavy mortars were running low.

The third, and most important, difference between the enemy's current situation and his earlier ones was that this time there could be no further withdrawal or retreat. There was nowhere left to go. The 32nd Army had run out of maneuvering room. With that inescapable fact in mind, Ushijima issued a final summary order to his dwindling ranks: "The present position will be defended to the death, even to the last man. Needless to say, retreat is forbidden."

ON JUNE 6, the small port of Minatoga on Okinawa's southeastern coast—and only about a mile north of Hill 95—had been opened by U.S. forces without appreciable enemy opposition. This enabled a steady flow of ammunition and other vital supplies to bypass the mud and bad roads and cover most of the distance to shortage-plagued combat units by water.

During the next three or four days, clear skies, a continuing dry-out, and feverish work by military engineers at last allowed tanks, amtracks, trucks, and artillery that had been bogged down far behind the Tenth Army's advance to move into positions to support the supply-starved infantry.

By June 8, a second water supply route, this one on the west coast north of the town of Itoman, was opened by the First Marine Division as it swung south after helping bottle up the Japanese on Oroku and punched its way to the sea. After being on short rations for more than a week, the division was finally able to evacuate its casualties and enjoy a full meal, courtesy of the first LVTs to arrive.

As patrols from the Second Battalion, Seventh Marines, probed south of the Mukue Gawa River on June 9, they ran into heavy small-arms and machine-gun fire and were forced to retreat back to the opposite bank. From there on, resistance mounted, and repeated attempts to cross the river and take the towns of Itoman and Tera were soundly repulsed.

Lieutenant Colonel Spencer Berger, thirty-two-year-old commander of 2/7, utilized a landing craft some 200 yards offshore as an observation post to try to pinpoint enemy positions and determine if his men could make a landing on the beach to relieve a platoon that had been cut off on a reconnaissance mission.

Berger, a native Californian who had dropped out of law school to join the Marines in 1935 and become one of the Corps' youngest battalion COs at Peleliu, ordered the rest of E Company to reinforce the besieged platoon. But heavy enemy fire repulsed an attempt to cross the river on foot, and an effort to move the Marines to the opposite bank by LVT was also beaten back.

"The Japs really opened up on us," Berger recalled much later, "and I lost one of my best company commanders that day when Captain Hank Grasse was killed crossing the river."

The next morning, June 10, Berger sent Companies G and F over a ten-foot seawall, and they waded 400 yards to gain the south bank of the Mukue Gawa and attack the town of Itoman.

That same day, elements of the First Marine Tank Battalion, along with other Army and Marine armored units, began reaching the front lines. By late that afternoon, with the beat-up Fifth Marines still getting a rest, 2/7 and units of the First Marines were drawn up facing Kunishi Ridge across 1,500 yards of mercilessly open ground. What Army historian Roy Appleman has described as "the most frantic, bewildering, and costly close-in battle on the southern tip of Okinawa" was about to begin.

Before the main assault, some of the newly arrived tanks were to be sent out in small groups to probe the enemy's strength. It was the most dangerous kind of assignment a tank crew could draw, especially with no accompanying infantry fire teams to guard against enemy demolition teams armed with TNT.

But since the Japanese were believed to have lost most of the 47-millimeter guns that had wreaked such havoc on U.S. tanks earlier, and to be short of ammo for the few that remained, division headquarters decided to take the risk.

AT FIRST LIGHT on Sunday, June 10, acting Sergeant Jack Armstrong, commander of the M4 Sherman tank nicknamed "Ticket to Tokyo," awoke with feelings of foreboding. For a second, he couldn't understand why he should feel that way; then he remembered the orders he'd been handed a few hours earlier, and he shuddered.

Armstrong and his crew had drawn the unenviable assignment the night before, along with two other tanks from their company: In a half hour or so, the three Shermans would head south along a narrow draw that meandered across the flat, treeless plain toward Kunishi Ridge. Their orders were to get as close to the ridge as possible and try to locate major Japanese strongpoints.

"Wake up, Ben," Armstrong said, jostling PFC Ben Okum, the onetime bar owner from Detroit who'd be manning the bow gun on the "Ticket to Tokyo." "Time for a little Sunday morning sightseeing tour."

Okum sat up, frowned, and mouthed a silent expletive.

The rest of the crew gathered for a quick, tasteless breakfast of K-rations, and a friendly corpsman stopped by with a bottle of medicinal brandy. "Have yourself a shot of this, Jack," he said, holding the bottle out to Armstrong. "You guys can use a little liquid reinforcement."

Armstrong wasn't much of a drinker, but he took a swig from the bottle in hopes of melting the cold, ominous ball in the pit of his stomach. Then he extended the bottle to the young replacement lieutenant who was going along on the mission as an observer.

"Want one for the road, sir?"

"Might as well," the lieutenant said. "Here's luck!"

"I think we're gonna need it," said Stephen Smith, the driver.

"We'd better saddle up," Armstrong said. "We've got no infantry with us today, and we have the honor of being the lead tank."

"Hot damn!" Smith said.

The distance from their starting point to the base of Kunishi Ridge was only about eight-tenths of a mile, as the crow flies, but it was much farther on the route the tanks were taking, and progress would be painfully slow. Two roads, of sorts, led across the flats, but Armstrong's orders were to follow the narrow draw, which meandered toward a break in the ridge. As the three tanks moved out, their route was almost parallel to the ridge, looming in the distance on their right. A series of rice paddies and cane fields bordered the draw on their left.

Having an extra person aboard made for cramped quarters inside the tank and a heightened level of discomfort since everybody was already feeling edgy. As tank commander, Armstrong stayed in the turret with the hatch open for the first little while, studying the lay of the land through his field glasses and giving the lieutenant full use of the space they'd otherwise have to share.

About twenty minutes into the mission, though, they came under enemy fire for the first time, and Armstrong was obliged to duck down, button up, and make do with his periscope from that point on. The fire was mostly small-arms rounds that bounced off the "Ticket to Tokyo" as harmlessly as pea gravel. Now and then, a Japanese machine gun would also open up, and although it posed no threat to the tank's crew, the sharp clatter of slugs against the Sherman's armor was harder on the nerves than the sporadic *ping-ping* of rifle bullets.

"Hey, boss, I just want you to know something," Smith yelled back at Armstrong from the driver's seat. "If we have to get out of here in a hurry, we're gonna be in a helluva lot of trouble. This damn draw's too narrow to turn around in."

"I know that, Steve," Armstrong yelled back, "so the best thing to do is just keep moving forward, okay?"

"Can anybody spot any of the Japs that are firing at us?" the lieutenant asked. "Is there any way to return fire?"

"Negative," said Okum from his gunner's seat up front. "They're all holed up on that ridge and out of sight."

As the "Ticket to Tokyo" rumbled slowly along, the constant pounding of bullets against the tank grew almost unbearable. It gave Armstrong the most trapped, harried feeling he could ever remember.

"By now, all of us were feeling really strange," he recalled many years later. "We were just holding our breath and waiting for the Japs to open up with artillery or mortars. So far all we'd gotten was small stuff, but we knew the big stuff had to be coming."

"If those bastards had any 47s, they'd have blown us open like a can of beans by now," Okum shouted above the din. "They can't hurt us with that small-arms crap."

"They can blow our treads off with a satchel charge if they get close enough," yelled Private David Spoerke from his rear seat at the 75-millimeter cannon.

The lieutenant turned to face Armstrong, leaning slightly forward until their faces were only a couple of feet apart. "We're in a very tedious spot here, Jack," Armstrong heard him say. "Everybody needs to keep a sharp—"

At that instant, an armor-piercing artillery shell roared through the center of the tank, its shrieking blast obliterating the last few words of the lieutenant's warning. It missed Armstrong by inches, but its force slammed him hard against the steel hull of the Sherman.

When he was able to sit up and focus his eyes, the first thing Armstrong saw made him cringe. The lieutenant's abdomen was split open from his rib cage to his crotch, and his exposed intestines squirmed in a glistening red pile in his lap. The young officer's lower left arm dangled by a thread, and blood streamed from his shattered elbow.

Armstrong was too deafened to hear what the lieutenant was saying, but he managed to read his lips.

"Oh, God, Mama, help me . . ."

⌒

Before infantry units of the First Marine Division would be able to attack Kunishi Ridge directly, they were forced to deal with Japanese defenders embedded on two secondary points of high ground immediately north of Kunishi—Yuza Hill and Hill 69.

By nightfall on June 10, troops of 1/1 had gained control of Yuza Hill, with the help of excellent artillery support from the 11th Marines, but they were still fighting like hell to hold it. The artillery had kept the Japanese pinned down until infantry units gained a foothold on the hill, but losses were heavy. The two assault companies in the attack suffered 120 casualties during the day, including every officer in C Company, which by evening was commanded by a mess sergeant. Hard fighting continued through the night, and a major Japanese counterattack was repulsed at 4:00 A.M. on June 11.

GIs of the 96th Division, who were supposed to be advancing in tandem with the First Marines, were stopped cold at Yuza Dake peak, a short distance to the east, resulting in a serious alignment problem. The Marines' advance had carried them well ahead of the Army troops, leaving a dangerous salient in the U.S. lines and exposing the Marines' eastern flank to concentrated mortar and artillery fire from Yuza Dake.

On Hill 69, west of the village of Osato, two companies of the First Marines also had a tough fight on their hands during the night of June 10–11. In the darkness, a large group of civilians began moving through the area occupied by Lieutenant Richard B. Watkins's E Company, which had been sent up a short time earlier to reinforce F Company.

Heeding repeated admonitions from their commanders to spare civilian lives whenever possible, the Marines initially held their fire. Then someone noticed that about every fifth "civilian" was actually an armed Japanese infiltrator. When the Marines opened fire, more enemy troops charged out of the darkness from both sides, brandishing swords and bayonets, and pandemonium ensued.

Lieutenant Watkins killed two attackers with his .45 while talking on the phone to Lieutenant Colonel James Magee, commander of the First Battalion. Two women who burst from a cave and ran into Company E's bivouac area were warned to halt, then shot dead when they refused. Both were found to be carrying TNT satchel charges and grenades. When the shooting stopped, forty dead Japanese soldiers were counted, along with several dead civilians who had been forced to serve as decoys.

⌐

WITH YUZA HILL and Hill 69 taken—although still under heavy enemy fire—two battalions of the Seventh Marines jumped off at dawn on June 11 on a mission to clear the village of Tera and the coastal town of Itoman of enemy resistance and remove the last remaining defensive obstacles to Kunishi Ridge itself.

The advance went well at first. The First Battalion seized Tera with relative ease and also took the high ground immediately south of the village. But when the Second Battalion drove into Itoman, it was a completely different story. Itoman was a hornet's nest of entrenched Japanese.

As First Marine Division historian George McMillan explained in *The Old Breed:* "Itoman was not easy. The battalion lost five officers in seven minutes. There were caves in the outskirts of the town, and the streets were mined."

By June 12, Itoman had been declared secure, although stubborn little pockets of enemy resistance remained, and Japanese artillery fire from Kunishi and Yuza Dake still fell on the town at intervals as mop-up operations continued.

Poised on the southern edges of Tera and Itoman, the Marine combat units stood a mere 800 yards from the foot of Kunishi Ridge. Now General Pedro del Valle, commander of the First Marine Division, confronted one of the thorniest questions of the Okinawa campaign: How to get enough of his men alive across that 800-yard meat grinder to assault the ridge itself?

Del Valle's answer was to steal a page from the Japanese book of tactics and send the first wave of his assault force against Kunishi in total darkness. It was almost unheard of for Marines to attack at night, but these were rare circumstances.

Colonel Edward W. Snedeker, commanding the Seventh Marines, committed one company each from his First and Second Battalions to the predawn operation, with H hour set for 3:30 A.M. on June 12. Chosen for this dubious distinction were C/1/7 under Captain Richard Rohrer and F/2/7, led by First Lieutenant John W. Huff. B and G Companies were assigned to a second assault wave to follow at 5:00 A.M., immediately after daybreak.

The initial attack took the Japanese completely off guard. C Company surprised and wiped out several small groups of enemy soldiers as they prepared breakfast, and F Company also reached its assigned objective atop the ridge with no major problems. The Japanese quickly regrouped, however, and when the two support companies moved up at dawn to reinforce those on the ridge, they were pinned down by enemy machine guns and had to withdraw. A second attempt by B and G Companies, with tank support, was repulsed by Japanese artillery, and a third assault, launched at 8:15 A.M. under cover of smoke, was also beaten back, this time by murderous machine-gun fire.

Early in the afternoon, C/1/7 and F/2/7 found themselves isolated

atop Kunishi and facing a situation hauntingly similar to the debacles at
Kakazu and Sugar Loaf. The Marines held the crest of the ridge, but
deeply entrenched Japanese, backed by artillery, controlled the reverse
slope and commanded every forward approach. Thus, the Marines
couldn't be reinforced—and they also couldn't retreat.

As General del Valle ruefully recalled later: "The situation was one of
those tactical oddities of this peculiar warfare. We were *on* the ridge; the
Japs were *in* it, both on the forward and reverse slopes."

The only possible answer was to use tanks to reinforce and resupply
the two cut-off companies and evacuate their wounded. By now, the
Japanese had several deadly 47-millimeter antitank guns positioned to
contest such a move, but when the first wave of tanks moved out at 3:55
P.M. on June 12 carrying critically needed supplies, the 47s were strangely
silent, and all tanks returned safely. On the second trip, fifty-four men
from A Company were loaded aboard nine Shermans, then unloaded
through their bottom hatches to reinforce C Company. The same tanks
brought out twenty-two wounded Marines, the first of many that would
flood aid stations at Tera and Itoman that evening.

⁓

MARINE PRIVATE William V. "Bill" Niader had been on Okinawa for
less than a month, but he'd already established himself as a go-getter
who would gladly tackle any job. Niader was well experienced by now
as a stretcher bearer, and when the tanks began bringing wounded men
from Kunishi into Itoman, he quickly volunteered, even as enemy artillery rounds still fell in the area.

Since reaching Okinawa on May 16 with the 46th Replacement Battalion, Niader had been assigned to Headquarters and Service Company,
Second Battalion, Seventh Marines, where his good nature and willing
hands had won the admiration of his CO, Captain Maurice Cavanaugh.

On his nineteenth birthday two weeks earlier, Niader had written a
letter to his parents back home on Orono Street in Clifton, New Jersey,
assuring them "not to worry because I'm OK."

Around 5:00 P.M. on June 12, Niader and a buddy, Private Harry
Switzer, were carrying a critically wounded Marine toward a temporary aid
station in Itoman when an enemy shell exploded about fifty yards away.

"Let's hurry it up," Niader yelled. "That one was a little too close for
comfort!"

He and Switzer broke into a trot, being careful not to spill their suffering cargo, and they made it to the aid station without further problems. As a corpsman attended the wounded man and Switzer squatted nearby to catch his breath, Niader turned back toward where other wounded still waited. He'd gone only a few dozen steps when another artillery round struck within ten feet of him, blasting him to the ground.

Niader was unconscious but still breathing when Sergeant Don Fach and a corpsman reached him. A chunk of shrapnel had ripped a gaping hole in his stomach, and he was bleeding profusely.

"Not much chance he'll make it," the corpsman said, "but let's get him to the rear."

Niader died soon after, and fifty-five years later, Fach still mourned his death. "He was always among the first to volunteer for special details, assignments, or missions," the sergeant recalled in June 2000. "He was a terrific person, the kind of guy you liked to be around and have in your squad."

In a letter to Niader's mother, Captain Cavanaugh expressed similar sentiments: "It is typical of William that he met his death in the manner that he did . . . helping others in the most dangerous and necessary humane tasks that a man can undertake in combat."

WHILE THE FIRST MARINE DIVISION grappled with Kunishi Ridge on the west, Army troops of the Seventh Division's 32nd and 17th Regiments were mounting similar assaults on the eastern end of the front against Hill 95 and Yaeju Dake.

General Arnold, the division commander, ordered a general attack against the two enemy strongholds for 1:00 P.M. on June 8, with Colonel Mickey Finn's 32nd Infantry assigned to hit Hill 95. During two days of bitter fighting, a small group of GIs led by Captain Tony Niemeyer helped secure the pointed hilltop by dragging a 200-foot fire-resistant hose up the slope, attaching it to a flame-throwing tank on the flats below, then using it to spray Japanese positions with searing streams of napalm. Although enemy troops still held parts of the slopes below, the first small break in General Ushijima's last line of defense had been achieved.

At the same time, Colonel Francis Pachler's 17th Infantry assaulted the broad face of 1,200-yard-long Yaeju Dake, an escarpment averaging

170 feet in height and topped by a 100-yard-wide coral shelf. About 500 Japanese were embedded in elaborate cave defenses along the ridge with small groups of snipers clustered at the base.

The attack was preceded by a thunderous artillery barrage joined by every available weapon from 105 howitzers down to 37-millimeter anti-tank guns. Companies I and K of the 17th's Third Battalion led the infantry assault, supported by a platoon of tanks, on the morning of June 9. Rather than the main northern mass of Yaeju Dake itself, their first objectives were two small secondary ridges at the south end of the escarpment, but both companies quickly ran into trouble, and the drive ground to a standstill.

Progress was slow but fairly steady for the next three days, during which flamethrowing tanks supporting the 17th Infantry expended 38,000 gallons of napalm against Japanese caves and bunkers. By June 13, the Third Battalion had gained control of several key points of high ground. Lieutenant Colonel William E. Siegel's Second Battalion seized the town of Azato, killing 122 Japanese and taking another strategic coral outcropping designated as Hill 8. At the end of the day, three companies of the 17th formed a solid 1,600-yard front anchored by dominating positions across the Seventh Division's sector of the escarpment.

CONCLUDING THAT Kunishi Ridge couldn't be secured by the Seventh Marines alone, General del Valle ordered the First Marines to attack a point on the ridge east of where men of the Seventh were clinging to the crest. He also told the Fifth Marines to cut short their rest break and prepare for combat within twenty-four hours.

In the interim, Marine tanks continued to bring in supplies and reinforcements and to carry out wounded while Japanese positions were continuously pounded by Marine artillery and Navy guns. Rocket ships moved in close to shore to rake enemy defenses on the reverse slopes of Kunishi, Yuza Dake, and Yaeju Dake. Many of the friendly rounds fell within 250 feet of Marine positions on Kunishi's crest.

Before dawn on June 14, two platoons of riflemen from E/2/1 and one platoon from G/2/1 clawed their way to the summit of Kunishi, but support units were turned back by heavy machine-gun fire, leaving the men at the crest isolated in an area just seventy-five yards wide. When dawn broke, enemy fire increased sharply and continued without letup all day. Marine casualties soared with one company losing six of its seven officers. Tanks were sent in, but they were too busy evacuating wounded and bringing in ammo, water, and blood plasma to contribute much tactical support.

On June 15, five days after Marine Sergeant Jack Armstrong had escaped death when his third tank was crippled with him inside, a fellow tank commander approached him with a sympathetic offer.

"I'm heading over to Kunishi Ridge to take some supplies and bring back some wounded," the other guy said. "Want to ride along?"

Armstrong managed a weak laugh. "Are you kidding?"

"No, I'm serious. I figured you'd be getting all antsy sitting around here without a tank."

Armstrong shook his head, thinking of the young replacement lieutenant with a severed arm and a lapful of intestines; of his driver, Corporal Harlan Stephan, wallowing in his own gushing blood as he drove their tank to safety; of his close friend, Corporal Alvin Tenbarge, blown almost in half by a land mine.

"Thanks, buddy, but I'll pass," he said. "I've had my three strikes, and I'm glad I'm out."

⸺◠⸺

No one in the Fifth Marines was overjoyed when the regiment returned to combat on June 15, relieving battered units of the First Marines on Kunishi Ridge and Yuza Dake. When veterans of Cape Gloucester and Peleliu were ordered to start their move to Kunishi before dawn on June 17, there was considerable bitching in the ranks.

"We were stubborn in our belief that nobody but the Japanese, or damned fools, moved around at night," said PFC Gene Sledge of K/3/5. "But moving up under cover of darkness was the only sane way to . . . get across the open ground without being slaughtered."

As for those persistent false reports that the Fifth Marines wouldn't be sent back to the front lines on Okinawa because of its weakened condition, most of the men took their disappointment in stride.

"Hell, we all knew they couldn't finish the job here without K/3/5," cracked Sergeant R. V. Burgin, who'd returned to his mortar section during the Fifth's rest break after being hospitalized with wounds for seventeen days. "Now let's get after it."

Burgin's words were small consolation to Sledge as he stared through the darkness at the shadowy silhouette of Kunishi Ridge. "Its crest looked so much like Bloody Nose that my knees nearly buckled," he said. "I felt as though I were on Peleliu and had it all to go through again."

When daylight came, one group of K/3/5 riflemen moved east along the ridge and another worked its way up the slope under heavy sniper fire. Burgin's mortar section didn't bother to set up its guns because the fighting was too close in, but the mortarmen stood by to serve as stretcher bearers, fill gaps in the line left by fallen riflemen, and intercept any enemy infiltrators from below.

"Snipers were all over the ridge and almost impossible to locate," Sledge said. "Men began getting shot one right after another, and the stretcher teams kept on the run."

The teams tied the wounded onto stretchers for the steep trip down to a protected area at the base of the ridge, where the stretchers were tied onto the rear deck of tanks and walking wounded were helped inside. Then the tanks roared away in clouds of dust toward an aid station while riflemen peppered the ridge with M-1s and BARs to keep the snipers from killing the exposed wounded aboard the Shermans.

AT SUNRISE ON JUNE 17, Corporal Melvin Grant was almost too tired to stand up. He and his flamethrower had spent the previous day "processing" some of the last enemy caves on Kunishi Ridge, and then he'd stood watch all night to keep the jittery young replacement who shared his foxhole from firing indiscriminately into the darkness. But when he heard that his younger brother, nineteen-year-old PFC Scott Grant, was in the immediate vicinity, Melvin came wide awake.

Both brothers from Oklahoma had been on Okinawa since Love Day, sometimes within a few hundred yards of each other, yet they'd met only once in all that time—and then barely long enough to share a hug and a can of C-rations. Because Melvin was attached to E/2/7 of the First Marine Division and Scott was a demolitions man in A/1/22 of the Sixth Marine Division, their paths almost never crossed. Now, however, Scott's outfit was moving in to relieve some of the hardest-hit First Division units on nearby Mezado Ridge, a westward extension of Kunishi. The news energized his older brother almost as much as a good night's sleep.

"I couldn't stand to think about him being so close without trying to see him," Melvin recalled more than sixty years later. "When I heard that

Scott's unit was on our right flank, I made my way over to the foot of Mezado Ridge and started looking for A Company."

Melvin finally located Second Lieutenant Robert Johnson, the A Company CO, and explained the situation. "Sorry, man," Johnson said, "but A Company's already committed and under fire. There's no way I can let you go up there. It's too dangerous."

"Listen, Lieutenant," Melvin said. "I'm one of 26 men left in my company out of the 235 we started with. I'm not afraid of getting shot at. It's worth it for a chance to see my brother."

"I sympathize, Corporal, but the answer's no. Permission denied."

Melvin turned away, sick with disappointment.

Later that day, the 22nd took the crest of Mezado as Melvin watched helplessly from a distance. Then Melvin's battalion pulled back two miles and bivouacked for the night. He'd never felt more exhausted in his life, but he couldn't sleep for worrying about Scott while their last conversation replayed itself over and over in his mind, like a stuck record.

"*Eat, drink, and be merry,*" Melvin heard himself saying as they polished off the can of C-rations, "*for tomorrow we may die.*"

"*If one of us has to go,*" Scott replied, "*I hope it's me because you've got a wife and kid at home.*"

———

CORPORAL CLAUDE BOHN felt as if he'd been running and stumbling for hours through the coral crags of Mezado Ridge. His legs were lead weights, and his lungs were ready to burst, but he couldn't stop now. It was the morning of June 18, and Bohn had promised his wounded platoon leader, Lieutenant Robert Jordan, that he'd get Jordan's urgent message to the company CO. The fate of the platoon depended on it:

We're in big trouble. We can't hold here without reinforcements; we don't have enough men. We've got to have artillery support in here, and smoke—lots of smoke!

As Bohn ran, a Japanese machine gun opened fire from his left, and he dove for the first hole he saw. When he jumped into the hole, he landed squarely on top of three Marines huddled there.

"Where you goin' in such a hurry?" one of them asked. "You can get shot that way, you know."

Bohn, who'd quit high school in Green Bay, Wisconsin, to join the

Marines at seventeen and reached the Pacific in time to fight at Guadal-canal, lay for a moment at the bottom of the hole, struggling for breath and unable to answer.

"Gotta get a message to A Company," he managed to croak. "My platoon's cut off up on the hill. Can't hold without help."

"You're all done in, man," said the youngest of the three Marines. "We're a demolition team with A Company, and I know where the CP is. I'll take the message the rest of the way."

"I can't let you do that," Bohn rasped. "It's too risky."

But before Bohn could move or say another word, the young Marine sprang to his feet. Instantaneously, the enemy machine gun chattered again, and Bohn saw the young Marine's body stiffen in midair, then tumble limply back into the hole.

"Scott! Scott!" one of the others yelled. He crawled to the fallen Marine and turned his body over. "Oh, God, he's really shot up bad."

Five bullets had slashed through the young Marine's rib cage and upper abdomen. He was plainly beyond help, but his eyes were open, and he was trying to say something.

"Tell my mother I died like a Marine," he whispered. Seconds later, his eyes dimmed, and his breathing stopped.

"He's gone," said the Marine leaning over him.

"I'm sorry," said Bohn. "Christ, why did he have to jump up like that?" He shook his head. "What's the guy's name?"

"Scott Grant," one of the others replied. "Damn good demo man."

"I gotta go," Bohn said. "I got twenty men depending on me. You guys cover me, okay?"

Both Marines in the hole raised their M-1s and fired in the direction of the machine gun as Bohn scrambled over the edge and ran for all he was worth.

⁓

EARLY ON JUNE 18, PFC Gene Sledge was rescuing a wounded comrade, PFC Leonard Vargo, with bullet wounds in both feet, from under the gun sights of a Japanese sniper. After dragging Vargo to safety, Sledge turned for a moment and looked south from his vantage point near the top of Kunishi Ridge. What he saw made him realize for the first time that the battle for Okinawa was almost over.

"I felt a sensation of wild exhilaration," he recalled later. "Beyond the smoke of our artillery to the south lay the end of the island—and the end of the agony."

Over the past forty-eight hours, the Tenth Army had pulled out all the stops, throwing everything it had at the enemy with a determination bordering on mania. On June 16, Marine and Army troops had witnessed what may have been the most devastating example of concentrated artillery fire of the Pacific war when twenty-two U.S. artillery battalions—264 guns—all fired at once, obliterating a large concentration of Japanese troops in the town of Makabe.

Sensing final victory, Marines fought like madmen on Kunishi Ridge, wresting it inch by inch from enemy snipers and machine gunners despite horrific casualties. In three days of fighting, K/3/5 lost forty-nine men and one officer, including virtually all of its most recent replacements and leaving it at barely 20 percent of its authorized strength.

Many of the companies in all three infantry regiments of the First Marine Division were equally depleted. But to add punch to the division's continuing attacks, the Eighth Marine Regiment of the Second Marine Division, which had returned to the area in early June to seize two small offshore islands, was sent to Okinawa and attached to General del Valle's command. He committed the Eighth to action on June 18, hoping its fresh troops would speed the collapse of organized enemy resistance.

On the east side of the island, meanwhile, GIs of the Seventh and 96th Divisions were attacking with equal vengeance and at a comparable cost in casualties. After seizing Yaeju Dake on June 14, Deadeyes of the 381st and 382nd Infantry regiments took Yuza Dake two days later, and troops of the Seventh overran the headquarters of the Japanese 44th Brigade on June 17.

That same day, the Marines secured Kunishi and hooked up with Army troops to the east. Marine tanks circled behind enemy lines to fire directly into Japanese positions on Kunishi's reverse slopes, paving the way for the climactic breakthrough. Soon after, infantry units of the Fifth and Seventh Marines cleared the last of the caves on Kunishi and Mezado Ridges, and by afternoon the nearby village of Kunishi was in American hands as well.

At another press conference that evening, General Buckner summed up the situation to media representatives: "We have passed the speculative phase of the campaign and are down to the final kill."

This time, Buckner's optimism was fully justified. As he spoke, the

Tenth Army was in firm control of an unbroken line of dominating high ground, stretching all the way across the southern tip of Okinawa, from Kunishi and Mezado Ridges on the west to the cliffs overlooking the east coast. General Ushijima's headquarters, deep beneath Hill 89 south of the town of Mabuni, was only a few hundred yards from the American lines.

In a practical sense, Japan's 32nd Army no longer existed as a cohesive defensive force. One of its two remaining infantry regiments would soon be annihilated to the last man; another was virtually surrounded. But even in disarray, scattered enemy units, especially those few possessing artillery, still had the ability to strike hard and painfully.

It would take four more days of fierce fighting to bring the battle for Okinawa to its official close, and General Buckner himself would be among its final victims.

CHAPTER FIFTEEN

A Civilian Catastrophe

O F ALL THE CALAMITIES to come out of World War II, few are more
tragic or heartrending than the plight of tens of thousands of Okinawan civilians caught in the lethal netherworld between two vast
armies. The exact number who fell victim to bullets, explosives, napalm,
untreated illness or injuries, asphyxiation, starvation—and their own
suicidal panic—will never be known.

They died like flies without regard to age, gender, or degree of inno-
cence: frail old men, pregnant women, mothers clutching newborns,
round-faced toddlers, barefooted cripples, sailor-suited schoolgirls—an
estimated 140,000 in all, maybe more. Almost every surviving Okinawa
combat veteran saw civilians who had been killed, civilians being killed,
or civilians killing themselves.

Many American soldiers were aggrieved by the slaughter and did
what they could to prevent it. Others either didn't give a damn or became
so hardened to the largely self-inflicted massacre as time went on that
they scarcely noticed. One Marine platoon leader, who watched scores of
civilians throw themselves off cliffs as the battle was ending, described
the spectacle and his feelings in these terms:

> It was like ants when their nest has been dug up.
> Mass confusion. Civilians running here, running there,
> looking for a place where their fall wouldn't be broken
> on the way down, for a rock below where they could hit
> full. . . . We didn't shoot them, but we didn't try to stop
> them either. Seeing civilians do all that didn't bother
> me one bit, not one iota. Maybe I was half crazy myself
> by that time, I don't know. . . . I'd seen a lot of horrors
> by then, including one of my men killed only a few
> hours before. What I was worried about was whether

> one of those milling ants would turn around and try to
> blow us up.

The carnage mounted to a catastrophic climax as final defeat closed in around the Japanese 32nd Army, but it had begun nearly three months earlier, almost as soon as the first U.S. troops set foot on the small islands off Okinawa's west coast.

⁓

ON THE NIGHT of March 28–29 (L-minus-3), PFC William Kottas had been among other GIs of the 77th Division's 306th Infantry who heard a series of loud explosions and screams while bivouacked on the island of Tokashiki in the Kerama Retto. None of the troops left their defensive perimeter in the dark, but when they investigated the next morning, they came upon a gruesome tableau. The bodies of 150 civilians, many of them women who had clutched grenades to their bodies and blown themselves to pieces, lay in twisted heaps. Numerous fathers had strangled their children, then killed themselves. Army medics tried in vain to save a few victims who were still alive.

In all, 325 civilians died as suicides on Tokashiki, and about a dozen others were beheaded by the Japanese as traitors or spies.

Captain Frank Barron, commander of A Company of the 305th Infantry, told of encountering similar horrific scenes on the neighboring island of Zamami. "Within thirty minutes or less [after landing]," Barron said, "two of my men brought in an Okinawan civilian. As they came upon him in a cave, he cut his own throat; he had just killed his wife and two children to spare them the treatment they had been told would be their fate at the hands of the Americans."

During its second day on Zamami, Barron's advancing company came upon a group of civilians huddled at the edge of a steep precipice. One woman held a baby in her arms and another had a two- or three-year-old child clinging to her side.

"They were about thirty or forty feet away from me," Barron recalled, "all staring at us like little frightened animals."

Seconds later, the entire group disappeared over the cliff. Barron and his men rushed forward in time to see their bodies bouncing off the walls of the precipice as they plunged to their deaths.

What Barron and his comrades couldn't know at the time was that all the natives on Zamami had been ordered by the Japanese to kill themselves when U.S. forces landed on the island. Records obtained later indicated that more than 170 men, women, and children obeyed the order. Those who resisted were stabbed, strangled, suffocated, or clubbed to death, usually by members of their own families.

These scenes were tragic harbingers of things to come on Okinawa itself.

———

By most accounts, rank-and-file Japanese soldiers had little sympathy or regard for their smaller-statured Okinawan cousins, whom they considered cloddish, culturally backward inferiors. At best, they treated the Okinawans like children; at worst, like cattle. Tens of thousands of the island's young males were conscripted into the 32nd Army, and the natives' property, including their sacred family tombs, was routinely commandeered for military use.

Just before the invasion, when the Japanese regulars retreated to their elaborate fortifications in the southern ridges, the only troops they left behind to mount a token defense of the beachhead and Yontan and Kadena airfields were about 3,500 members of an all-Okinawan *Boetai* or home guard. These ill-equipped, ill-trained young men—some of them no more than fourteen or fifteen years old—were, in almost every instance, the "Japs" encountered, and frequently killed, by American forces during the first few days of the campaign.

Beginning in the fall of 1944, virtually every Okinawan male of anywhere near military age, and regardless of physical condition, had been conscripted by the Japanese. In addition to those who actually bore arms with General Ushijima's combat units, many others served as laborers to dig caves, haul supplies on their backs, and manhandle military equipment. In all, about 25,000 were inducted, leaving only women, children, and old men to tend Okinawa's small farms.

Nevertheless, the Okinawans generally looked up to the Japanese and believed what they were told by Japanese officers and enlisted men—a situation that led to one of the most dramatic examples of mass brainwashing in human history. Despite friendly overtures from countless GIs and Marines, especially early in the campaign, many civilians had been so thoroughly indoctrinated with dehumanizing anti-American propaganda that nothing the invaders said or did could assuage the natives' deeply instilled fears.

For Americans of the twenty-first century to understand how this was possible, it's necessary to realize how primitive and unexposed to modern outside influences the life of a typical Okinawan was in the spring of 1945. Except for Japanese military machines, for example, there were only about 250 motor vehicles in all of Okinawa, many of them charcoal-burning buses, for an average of about one vehicle for every 2,000 people. Small wonder that the island had, in the words of one Western observer, "an excellent network of horrible roads."

Journalist John Lardner, writing in the May 19, 1945, issue of *The New Yorker,* offered stateside readers one of the first graphic descriptions of Okinawa's native population:

> [E]very Marine regarded Okinawans as Japs and
> would split no Oriental hairs whatever except to concede
> that these "Japs" looked very harmless and beaten down.
> The Okinawans we saw at first, cowering in the thatched
> houses of the little village of China—an apt name, since
> Okinawans are more like Chinese peasants than anything
> else—or hiding in nearby caves, were all women, old
> men, and children, every male civilian between 16 and 40
> having been herded south by the Jap army for labor duty.

Early on, the overriding concern of Okinawan families was finding a safe refuge from the fighting. Most of them left their farm crops, livestock, homes, and barns to the mercy of the American troops and hid in the most secure places they could think of—their hallowed ancestral tombs. But the Japanese, too, wanted to make use of the tombs because they made highly effective bomb shelters and bunkers.

The least risky, most efficient way to deal with a tomb suspected of harboring a deadly enemy, of course, was to toss a grenade into it and see what blew out. This happened with some frequency until American forces began to realize that many tombs were occupied only by harmless, helpless civilians.

On the other hand, the Japanese had callously designated a sizable percentage of the tombs, especially those in strategic areas, to be converted into heavily armed gun emplacements and snipers' nests, in some cases with civilians also occupying their depths. As knowledge of this situation spread, U.S. troops began using smoke grenades to flush out occupants of the tombs, rather than deadly phosphorous grenades that caused hideous burns. Such humanitarian adjustments undoubtedly slowed the Tenth Army's advance, but they provided evidence to the natives that not all Americans were monsters, even as Japanese abuse of the Okinawan tombs kindled anger in some civilians.

Once the situation became apparent to GIs and Marines, they made an honest effort to avoid spilling innocent blood in the tombs while still taking care to protect themselves. Marines, in particular, had never dealt with a large, potentially unfriendly civilian population during the war (civilians had been few to nonexistent in their previous Pacific combat zones), and they also had a deep-rooted protective instinct against taking prisoners.

Knowing this, the U.S. War Department began taking steps, several months before the invasion, to hold civilian casualties and suffering to a minimum. As part of this effort, a carefully structured military government organization was set up, composed of physicians, medical corpsmen, quartermasters, civil administrators, interpreters, military officers trained in bivouac operations, and engineers to oversee construction of detention camps for refugees. The job of the "milgovt," as it was known, was to move unarmed civilians out of combat zones to safe rear areas as quickly as possible.

Small teams of milgovt personnel were assigned to follow closely in the wake of advancing combat units to provide food, water, and medical care for sick or wounded civilians. Among the supplies brought ashore by each of the four U.S. divisions landing on Love Day were 70,000 pounds of rice and soybeans to be distributed to needy civilians by the milgovt teams.

Aboard their Okinawa-bound troopships, American fighting men had received briefings and brochures emphasizing the "simple, polite, law-abiding," and unwarlike character of the island's natives. Many Army assault troops were also taught a few helpful phrases in Japanese to facilitate communication, but this instruction was apparently more hit-or-miss among Marine units.

As Lardner reported, most Leathernecks viewed Okinawans merely as more "Japs," who might look and act somewhat differently from those the Marines had previously encountered but who were still subject to suspicion and definitely not to be trusted. Many Army veterans felt the same way, and even the War Department brochures cautioned that most civilians were still loyal to Japan.

"All they know about Americans is what they get from Tokyo propaganda," the handouts warned, "so you can expect them to look at you as though you were a combination of Dracula and the Sad Sack—at first, anyway."

What Tokyo was telling the Okinawans, and what was being reinforced by a large majority of the Japanese soldiers Tokyo had sent to their island, was that the Americans were devils, in the most literal and loathsome sense of the term. They were devils whose sole desire was to kill Okinawans in the most brutal, merciless ways possible. They would shoot Okinawan men on sight, but instead of a quick kill, they preferred to leave their victims writhing in agony for as long as possible. They would rape and torture Okinawan women and butcher their children before their eyes. At times, they would pretend to be friendly, but the gifts of candy or other food they offered were always laced with poison.

To emphasize these points, some Japanese soldiers supplied the Okinawans with grenades so that they could blow up themselves and their children before the American devils could subject them to their unquenchable bloodlust. But when U.S. troops began finding grenades hidden on civilians, their first assumption was that the explosive charges were intended to hurt or kill Americans, rather than as instruments of self-destruction.

Hence, every confrontation between traumatized natives and wary invaders held the potential for violent tragedy. It may have been somewhat worse in the early going, but what no American could anticipate was the depth, intensity—and obsessive power—of many Okinawans' fear. It seemed to have a life of its own.

By their very nature, the Okinawans were a peaceful, nonaggressive people, who hadn't seen armed conflict on their soil in more than 300 years. Then the Americans had come, first to rain fire bombs and high-explosive shells on their cities and towns and later to storm ashore by the tens of thousands, sweeping across the countryside, brandishing their awesome weapons and, it seemed, searching for Okinawans to brutalize and murder.

"The most pitiful things about the Okinawan civilians," said PFC Gene Sledge of K/3/5, "were that they were totally bewildered by the shock of our invasion, and they were scared to death of us. Countless times they passed us on the way to the rear with fear, dismay, and confusion on their faces."

As a microcosmic example of the unrelenting dread experienced by civilians fleeing before the American invaders, author George Feifer cites the case of eleven-year-old Shigeko Sonan, eldest daughter of a family in Gushikawa, a village seven miles east of the landing beaches, near the east (Pacific) coast.

Although ordered by the Japanese to evacuate before the landing, the family had elected to stay, and Shigeko, her three younger sisters, and their pregnant mother were terrorized by the preinvasion bombs and shells, some of which landed in their village.

In school, Shigeko had been taught all about "subhuman Americans who drowned deformed infants and killed healthy but unwanted babies by bashing their heads against a wall," wrote Feifer in his book, *Tennozan: The Battle of Okinawa and the Atomic Bomb*. "She knew about their racist yearning to destroy and depopulate Divine Japan, except for the few attractive women they planned to keep for their insatiable animal lust."

Not surprisingly, Shigeko was petrified with fear when the invaders began marching toward Gushikawa. When an American plane flew overhead, she believed it was shooting directly at her as she took cover.

After the girl's father made his way home from working as an enforced laborer for the Japanese, the family decided to flee with as much food as they could carry and try to reach the northern village where they'd been assigned. But a bombed-out bridge forced them to leave their provisions behind, and they struggled on by foot, traveling only at night.

The family came close to starvation, but when Shigeko and the other children accepted chocolate and K-rations from the Americans, their parents threw the food away, fearing it was poisoned. Eventually, the children's hunger won out, and they ate some of the food, anyway. Otherwise, they subsisted on boiled grass, tree bark, edible palms, and discarded half-rotten sweet potatoes.

As the family fled from one end of the island to the other, some of the huts where they hid were burned by advancing U.S. troops, and Shigeko witnessed the rape of a young woman by two American soldiers. At the scene of a fierce battle, they came upon dozens of blown-apart Japanese corpses. Too weak from hunger to dig deep enough to bury the bodies completely, they collapsed from exhaustion among the corpses, stuffing leaves in their noses in an effort to block out the smell.

The family's plight continued for more than three months and might have lasted longer if Shigeko's mother hadn't given birth while seriously ill with malaria. The children were walking skeletons, and, because of her illness, Shigeko's mother had no milk for the baby. Faced with all this, the girl's father finally brought his family down from the mountains and surrendered to the Americans.

Within a few hours, they were in a detention camp, where they were fed and sprayed with DDT, but the ordeal had been too much for Shigeko's four-year-old sister, who died a few days later of illness and malnutrition. Surviving family members weren't allowed to return to their village for ten months after the fighting ended, and when they got there, all their possessions were gone.

Despite this, the Sonans were luckier than most Okinawan families. Only one family member had succumbed to their ordeal; none had met violent death at the hands of the American devils, and none had committed suicide. Shigeko had learned that some Americans could be kind, but she still couldn't bring herself to trust them completely.

❧

ON L-PLUS-1, Corporal Don Dencker of the 96th Infantry Division's 382nd Regiment, Second Battalion, had paused in the drive east across the island when he confronted his first civilians. As Dencker and his buddy, PFC Ernie Zimmer, were setting up their mortar and dining on K-rations, they noticed an Okinawan woman come out of a cave on a nearby hill. She glanced down at the two GIs for a moment, then quickly ducked back inside.

Dencker hadn't seen even one Japanese soldier, either dead or alive, since coming ashore, but he decided the cave warranted investigation. With Zimmer covering him, he drew his .45 and approached to within about fifty feet of the entrance.

"De-tay-ko-ee!" Dencker yelled. The strange-sounding phrase meant "come out" in Japanese and was among three or four potentially useful expressions included in the GIs' preinvasion orientation.

Dencker waited. When nothing happened, he eased closer to the cave and yelled again:

"De-tay-ko-ee!"

This time, seven figures slowly emerged—three women, two children, and two old men—and stood staring at Dencker in obvious terror. When he motioned them forward, they took a few halting steps toward him, then stopped. The women sobbed and whispered nervously to each other.

"Move! Move!" Dencker shouted, advancing to within a few feet of the group and pointing to the path that led down the hillside. The Okinawans still stood there immobilized by fright until one old man stepped forward. He pointed to the pistol in Dencker's hand, then to his own head, repeating the gesture several times until its meaning became distressingly clear: He was asking—actually pleading—for Dencker to shoot him in the head.

Dencker refused, of course, and after several more minutes, he managed to coax the group down from the hill and into the company's defensive perimeter. When two MPs showed up a short time later and led the civilians away to one of the detention centers hurriedly being set up in rear areas, Dencker felt a surge of relief. For the time being, he thought, the war was over for these Okinawans, and they'd been spared—in part, at least, from themselves and their own anguished fears.

But as Dencker and his comrades would later see with their own eyes, thousands of other innocent noncombatants would be denied this little group's good fortune. Within the next few days, they would come across the bodies of dozens of civilians who had died of self-inflicted wounds.

CORPORAL DAN LAWLER of K/3/5's machine-gun section had never seen kids refuse to eat candy—not until now. But the little Okinawan boy, who looked about seven years old and had ventured out of a cave with his younger sister, was adamant about it. When Lawler held out a K-ration chocolate bar to the boy, he shook his head so hard that Lawler was afraid it would fall off his skinny shoulders.

"They were the cutest damn kids you ever saw," Lawler recalled more than sixty years later. "Neither one of them appeared to be injured, but they were both so scared they were shaking, and their clothes were streaked with dried blood."

Lawler continued to hold the chocolate bar out toward them, smiling and awkwardly repeating a phrase that he thought meant, "Don't be afraid. Come on out, and we'll give you some food."

The boy shook his head again, his eyes wide with fright.

"The kid thinks the candy's poisoned," said Lawler's assistant gunner.

"The Japs've told these people if they ask us for anything we'll kill 'em. Maybe if you took a bite of the candy yourself, the kid might change his mind."

Lawler shrugged and bit off a corner of the bar. He chewed it up and swallowed it, then licked his lips. "See, it's good," he coaxed. "Come on, try it."

The boy took a couple of steps forward with his sister peeking out from behind him, then he hesitated and shrank back.

Lawler broke the other corner off the bar and ate it, too, with elaborate expressions of enjoyment. "Umm, that's really delicious! You'd better come on and get it before I eat it all."

The kids couldn't stand it any longer. The boy sidled up to Lawler, took what was left of the bar, broke off a piece for his sister, then gobbled down the rest. He managed a small smile as he turned and shouted something toward the cave.

Then a whole group of Okinawans crept out into the daylight, smiling, bowing, and moving in slow motion with their eyes glued to Lawler and the other Marines. There were eight of them in all—two other children, two women, and two ancient, virtually toothless men.

"We gave them all some candy," Lawler recalled, "but they still refused to touch it unless one of us ate some of it first. You could tell they didn't trust us as far as they could throw us."

DURING THE CALM interlude after the landing, scenes like those above were repeated countless times, and many ended, at least temporarily, on a hopeful note. At first, the Marines and GIs saw nothing even remotely threatening about the civilians they encountered. In fact, in the early days of the campaign, when many U.S. units were encamped for days in the same area, some native farmers conducted a lively trade with the troops in fresh vegetables, eggs, and other edibles.

But as the fighting intensified and moved farther south into the most heavily populated areas of Okinawa, casualties and suffering among civilians grew steadily more horrific. As of late May, when General Ushijima made his decision to abandon his Shuri Defense Zone, an estimated 100,000 civilians remained south of the Shuri Line—and directly in the path of the advancing Tenth Army. Within another month, most of them would be dead.

The governor of Okinawa, Ei Shimada, one of the few high-ranking Japanese officials who truly sympathized with the plight of the Okinawan people, pleaded with Ushijima to keep his forces where they were and make his final stand at Shuri. Withdrawing to the south would result in a devastating number of civilian deaths, Shimada argued, but Ushijima's mind was made up. Prolonging the battle remained the foremost priority of Tokyo's military planners, who had always considered the Okinawan population expendable, anyway, and Ushijima was determined to follow his superiors' directives.

Amid the massive withdrawal that followed, hordes of civilians compounded the coming disaster, first by disregarding Japanese orders to evacuate to the safety of the Chinen Peninsula, then by failing to heed the flood of leaflets dropped by American planes. The leaflets urged them to wear white, stay clear of Ushijima's retiring army, and turn themselves in to U.S. troops as soon as possible, but the civilians' fear and distrust prevailed. Many wore white, but they clogged the same roads used by withdrawing Japanese troops, where they were highly vulnerable to U.S. bombing raids and artillery strikes.

Up to the very last days of the fighting, many civilians clung to the belief that the 32nd Army would somehow turn the tables on the American invaders and drive them into the sea. Sticking close to Japanese troops may have given them an unfounded sense of security, when, in fact, it put them in jeopardy from the Japanese as well as the Americans.

As Ushijima's army deteriorated into small groups, desperate soldiers sought any means to elude advancing U.S. forces. Many attempted to slip past American lines by posing as civilians and mingling with women and children.

"Near Itoman, we set up trip wires across the road that would set off flares if anybody hit one of them," recalled Lieutenant Colonel Spencer Berger, commanding the Second Battalion, Seventh Marines. "That night, a mass of people—about 150 of them—came along and set off our flares. Many of them appeared to be women in kimonos, but then our guys noticed that some of them were also wearing boots."

Berger hesitated only a few seconds before ordering his troops to open fire. Almost every member of the group was killed—including more than forty kimono-clad Japanese soldiers. "I might've been executed as a war criminal for that order if the Japs had won the war," Berger noted ruefully many years later. "But under the circumstances, I didn't feel I had any other choice."

Clearly, the more civilians who surrendered to the Americans, the fewer "human shields" would be available to fleeing Japanese soldiers. It remains uncertain how many civilians were killed by the Japanese to prevent them from giving themselves up, but the number was likely considerable.

"In the desperation of the enemy's position," noted a Sixth Marine Division field intelligence report issued on June 17, "civilians have become vagrants who represent an additional difficulty for the defenders . . . disrupt[ing] the enemy's communications, organization, and morale. Reports have been received to the effect that Japanese soldiers have been shooting civilians who made efforts to surrender. It is probably true that civilians would welcome an opportunity to surrender themselves to our forces. . . . The Japanese thus far have shown no inclination to give them that opportunity."

Between June 1 and June 23, when the battle for Okinawa would officially end, American land and naval artillery eclipsed their earlier bombardments by pouring nearly 7 million rounds into the compressed southern area where the refugees crowded among the remnants of Ushijima's army. Dead and dying civilians littered the roads and roadsides as dazed orphans and maimed adults dragged past, some crawling on hands and knees, with no concept of where they were going.

To Tokuyu Higashionna, an Okinawan schoolteacher who crossed the area while trying to reach the town of Kyan on the southern coast, the scenes of mothers carrying dead children and living children lying on the corpses of dead mothers defied description. It was, he said, "Utter horror . . . dead everywhere . . . *everywhere!* . . . literally hell."

Every tragedy seems to have its elements of irony. The irony of this one was that, if the Okinawans had only done as they were instructed by either the Japanese or the Americans, the vast majority of civilian deaths could have been avoided. The Chinen Peninsula, which juts into the Pacific Ocean about four miles southeast of the town of Yonabaru, and where the civilians had been ordered to go by the 32nd Army, was almost totally untouched by the fighting. Likewise, if the noncombatants had assembled on the west coast highway and avoided Japanese troops, as the American leaflets urged, they also would have found safe haven, along with sufficient food and water, in the detention camps.

As it was, however, close to 15,000 civilians are believed to have died during the retreat from Shuri alone—about the same toll suffered by

Japanese troops—and those who survived then found themselves in a grinding trap between the armies from which there was no escape.

⸻

DURING THE ARDUOUS weeks since the landing, K/3/5 machine gunner Dan Lawler had acquired an intriguing—if somewhat macabre—new hobby. Whenever he came across the body of a dead Japanese, provided there was enough time and the body wasn't too far gone, Lawler would dig through the soldier's pack and pockets in search of photographs. He'd discovered that a surprising number of enemy soldiers carried pictures of themselves, as well as those of wives, children, and other family members, and Lawler gradually built an extensive collection of these photos of nameless dead Japanese.

Pictures made good souvenirs because they didn't weigh much or take up much space in Lawler's pack, and after a couple of months, he had dozens of photos in his collection. Many of the subjects in the pictures had fallen victim to Lawler's own .30-caliber air-cooled Browning; others had been killed by parties unknown, but to Lawler, each of the faces and forms in the pictures had its own arresting characteristics. In his brief interludes of free time, the handsome nineteen-year-old from upstate New York found that poring over the photos and studying the images offered an oddly satisfying diversion from the hell around him.

In the first days of June, as the First Marine Division moved south from Shuri, K/3/5's route of march took it through a shell- and bomb-blasted village—the name of which no one in the company knew or really cared to know.

"We'll take a five-minute break here," the platoon sergeant shouted, "but be ready to move out when I give the word."

As Lawler set down the tripod for his machine gun, his attention was drawn to the nearby remains of a two-story wood-frame building. It was badly damaged with its roof blown off and two of its outer walls mostly demolished, but Lawler was immediately fascinated by the possibilities for photo-collecting that it might contain.

I bet there's pictures in there, he thought. *Maybe lots of pictures, and if I hurry, I've got just enough time to take a look.*

Lawler nudged his assistant gunner, who was carrying their 1918-model Browning. "Watch the tripod for a minute," he said. "I'm going to check out that building over there."

"What for?" the assistant gunner asked. "It's a total wreck, just like everything else around this godforsaken place."

"Never mind," Lawler said. "I just want to have a quick look."

When he reached the building, he found the front door standing open and partially off its hinges, and when he moved cautiously through the doorway, he could tell that it had, until very recently, been a school. The foyer was strewn with broken glass, pieces of roofing, splintered boards, books, papers, and other debris.

Several bodies, all of which appeared to be young females, were scattered across the floor, and the remaining interior walls were splashed with their blood. They hadn't been dead long—probably only a few hours, Lawler figured—because there was no detectable smell. He shuddered as he stepped around the bodies. Hanging crookedly on one wall was what he'd come searching for—a framed photograph.

The glass in the frame was so spattered with blood that he could barely make out the picture behind it. But when he removed the frame and the glass, Lawler found himself staring at a formally posed group picture containing more than fifty solemn Oriental faces. Only five of the figures in the photo were mature and male, almost certainly faculty members. The rest were girls who appeared to be in their early or midteens. Lawler couldn't be sure whether they represented the entire student body of an all-girls school or perhaps only one class. They were dressed in everything from kimonos to middy blouses and frilly dresses. Some were extremely pretty, others downright homely, but to Lawler, the most striking thing about the photo was that almost none of the students was smiling.

Was it because they had orders not to smile? he wondered. *Or could they somehow sense what was coming?*

He felt an urgent desire to leave, to walk away from this place of crushed young hopes and battered young bodies, to pick up his tripod and march on, to throw down the picture and try to forget what he was seeing. But something compelled him to venture farther into the gutted structure.

The upper story of the building was almost entirely gone, but portions of the first floor had a grotesque air of normalcy about them. In the wreckage of a classroom, neatly written Japanese word symbols were on the blackboard. Some students were still at their desks. Others were sprawled on the floor, their arms and legs akimbo, their books and papers scattered around them. Blood was everywhere. All of them were dead.

Lawler stared again at the photo, wondering how many of the same young girls staring back at him from the picture were among the fresh corpses in the ruins of the school. He folded the picture roughly and shoved it into his knapsack as he stumbled back outside.

⁓

THE GIRLS at the devastated school in the bombed-out town were a tiny fraction of the 100,000 Okinawan civilians who perished, according to reliable estimates, during June 1945. The majority of these died during the last ten days of the battle—many by their own hands—as it became increasingly clear that the 32nd Japanese Army was defeated and that the American "devils" would soon control the whole island.

"The civilians were in just terrible shape—wounded, starving, terrified," said PFC Edward "Buzzy" Fox, a machine gunner in Company G, Second Battalion, 22nd Marines. "You never saw such fear on faces, but we still couldn't trust them because of the gung-ho ones mixed in."

Evidence collected over the six-plus decades since the Okinawa campaign ended strongly suggests that extremely few Okinawan civilians were actually "gung-ho" enough to stage deliberate attacks against Marines or GIs. But the thousands who leaped to their deaths from high cliffs, slashed their children's throats, or blew themselves to bits with Japanese-provided hand grenades to avoid American brutality are ample proof that the Americans' distrust was returned a hundredfold.

Some sources contend, however, that the majority of Okinawans didn't commit suicide but became victims of disease, starvation, Japanese atrocities, and indiscriminate American bombing and shelling. "[T]he greater number of civilians slaughtered on Okinawa . . . more often died in days or weeks rather than minutes," wrote historian George Feifer, "with that much more time to witness the agony of their families."

Meanwhile, some of the same Japanese soldiers in whom the Okinawans had placed infinite trust became the natives' worst enemies. As the soldiers grew more desperate for food, water, and temporarily safe shelter, they systematically slaughtered men, women, and children who got in their way. Numerous eyewitness accounts tell of Japanese soldiers murdering crying children in cold blood for fear their cries would attract Americans to the soldiers' hiding places.

Military deaths on both sides of the battle totaled just under 120,000—at least 20,000 fewer than the number of noncombatants who died during the same period, according to official estimates. Virtually every Okinawan lost family members to the battle. About one of every three civilians living on the island in the spring of 1945 was killed. Hundreds of years of accumulated Okinawan culture were obliterated, along with the island's entire economy and physical infrastructure.

As author Feifer notes, "[I]t would have taken 150 atomic bombs to wreak on Japan the equivalent cultural and material devastation and to kill a comparable number of Japanese."

As terrible as the slaughter was, however, it could have been worse. As the Japanese 32nd Army was collapsing and during the final mop-up by American forces, approximately 80,000 Okinawan civilians surrendered to GIs and Marines. Up to half of these were wounded, and many might well have died without the food, medical care, and other assistance they received at U.S. refugee centers.

CHAPTER SIXTEEN

A Somber Victory

A ROUND NOON on June 18 (L-plus-79), General Buckner paid one of his frequent visits to front-line positions to see for himself how his units were faring. Buckner's supreme confidence in his own troops had never wavered over the past eleven weeks, despite the Tenth Army's many bloody setbacks. He knew that the successful end of the Okinawa campaign was close at hand—perhaps only hours away—and he was determined to witness the final act of the drama at close range.

By this stage of the battle, "Buck" Buckner had accumulated more than his share of critics and detractors. Some were enlisted men and field officers in his own army, who faulted Buckner's refusal to approve a second amphibious landing on Okinawa's southern coast and his reliance on brutal "corkscrew and blowtorch" frontal assaults. Others were media "armchair generals," who deplored the campaign's high human cost and its slow progress from the safety of their desks in Washington and New York.

Homer Bigert, a correspondent for the *New York Herald-Tribune,* accused Buckner in football parlance of adding to the casualty toll by repeatedly pounding the Japanese in "the middle of the line" instead of making an "end run." David Lawrence, author of the nationally syndicated column "Today in Washington," repeated this charge and went a step further, implying that Buckner and other Army generals failed to "understand the dynamics of island warfare" and should have let the Marines take charge of the campaign. Lawrence also called the Okinawa campaign "a worse example of military incompetence than Pearl Harbor" and accused U.S. officials of covering up the resulting "fiasco."

Most high-ranking Army and Navy commanders, however, solidly supported Buckner's conduct of the battle and defended his decisions. These included Navy Secretary James Forrestal; Admiral Chester Nimitz, commander in chief of U.S forces in the Pacific; General John Hodge, commander of the Army's 24th Corps; and Admirals Richmond Turner and Marc Mitscher, the highest-ranking naval commanders at Okinawa. Nimitz, for one, held a news conference on Guam on June 17 to give Buckner a firm vote of confidence. The Marine commanders, if they disagreed, at least maintained a discreet silence.

Even those who took issue with Buckner's Okinawa strategy respected his courage, tenacity, and willingness to put himself in harm's way in close proximity to the actual fighting. But it was these very character traits that spelled tragedy for the Tenth Army commander on the early afternoon of June 18, only three days before the island was declared secure.

Despite urgings from his staff to delay his visit to the front, Buckner came to the freshly taken Kunishi ridgeline around noon to observe an assault by infantrymen of Colonel Clarence Wallace's Eighth Marines of the Second Marine Division against one of the few remaining enemy strong points. Wallace's regiment, which had taken part in the Love Day feint at Okinawa's southeast coast, was attached to General del Valle's First Marine Division, and Del Valle lost no time in ordering its fresh troops into combat.

Buckner was accompanied by Colonel Wallace and several other officers as he watched and photographed the Marines' advance for close to an hour from a hastily prepared forward observation post. About 1:15 P.M., with the attack going smoothly, he decided to visit another part of the front, and he was telling the others good-bye when five Japanese artillery shells—some of the last to be fired by the enemy—burst in rapid succession nearby. The blasts struck one of two huge protective boulders on either side of the observation post, showering the post with chunks of rock, shards of coral, and metal shell fragments. At least two pieces of this debris struck Buckner squarely in the chest and abdomen.

Corporal Claude Bohn, thoroughly exhausted from his ordeal of the night before, had been dozing fitfully on Mezado Ridge at a point adjacent to Buckner's party when he was jerked awake by the roar of incoming rounds in time to see the shells hit.

"The general was off to my left and maybe 400 yards away," Bohn recalled, "and I had a clear view of the shell bursts that got him. As far as I know, they were the only ones the Japs fired that afternoon."

The shots, as it later developed, were by no means random. Around 1:00 P.M., Buckner's group of officers had been spotted by a member of a Japanese artillery battery on a nearby ridge. None of the enemy soldiers knew the officers' identity, only that they appeared to be high-ranking, but the gunners rushed to get their lone remaining weapon ready to fire and to take advantage of a "miraculous" opportunity.

One member of the gun crew was quoted by author-historian George Feifer as saying that, as soon as the shells were fired, the Japanese retreated deep into their cave, fully expecting "a return gift of a thousand shots from [the Americans] for every shot from us."

When medical personnel reached Buckner, he was bleeding too heavily from his gaping wounds to be evacuated, although he was smiling and semiconscious. A corpsman struggled frantically to slow the loss of blood, but within ten minutes, Buckner was dead, still wearing a smile on his handsome face. Ironically, none of the officers accompanying Buckner suffered so much as a scratch, but just over an hour later, Colonel H. C. Roberts, commander of the 22nd Marines of the Sixth Marine Division, was killed by a sniper near another observation post.

When word of Buckner's death reached the headquarters of Commander in Chief, Pacific Ocean Area, in Hawaii, Major General Roy Geiger, commander of the Third Marine Amphibious Corps, was named to succeed Buckner in command of the Tenth Army. It was the first—and it remains the only—time in U.S. military history that a Marine Corps general has commanded an entire American army. (Within a few days, Geiger would turn over the command to the Army's Lieutenant General Joseph W. Stilwell.)

Buckner was the highest-ranking U.S. officer killed in action in World War II. When the headquarters staff of Japan's 32nd Army heard the news by radio in its subterranean fastness beneath Hill 89, many of the officers are said to have cheered, including General Cho, the army's fiery second in command. But General Ushijima reportedly remained silent, except to offer a prayer for his fallen counterpart.

Buckner's death came as a shock back in the States, and accounts of his simple burial service in an Army cemetery on Okinawa, filed by almost 1,000 news correspondents now covering the war's only remaining active battlefield, ran on newspaper front pages across the nation. The numerous high-ranking officers in attendance watched a detachment of riflemen fire a volley of shots, followed by a brief artillery barrage as Buckner's personal three-star flag waved beside the Stars and Stripes.

Ushijima and Cho had received a message from Buckner on June 17, in which the U.S. commander warned that "destruction of all Japanese resistance . . . is merely a matter of days" and urged them to spare their remaining troops by surrendering. They both had laughed at the message, but, by this time, Ushijima undoubtedly recognized the truth of Buckner's words and the inevitability of his own situation.

On the very day of Buckner's death, Ushijima had sent his apologies to Imperial General Headquarters and the people of Japan for his failure to achieve victory at Okinawa. "It has come to the point," he informed Tokyo, "where we are about to deploy all surviving soldiers for a final battle—in which I will apologize to the emperor with my own death."

Dismissing all Western logic and reason, Samurai tradition dictated that more fighting must be done, more blood spilled.

⁓

In a tactical sense, the battle for Okinawa may have been all but over on June 18, the day General Buckner fell, but for the Marines of K/3/5, that date would rank as the costliest twenty-four hours of the entire campaign. No fewer than thirty-three men were evacuated with wounds that day, and four—Corporals Stanley W. Arthur and John Wishnewski and Privates Alexander Doyle and Richard L. Williams—were killed in action.

Most of PFC Harry Bender's closest buddies in K/3/5's First Platoon were gone now, except for PFC William Tyler, an "old married guy" of twenty-four, with whom Bender regularly shared a foxhole. In many respects, the two Marines were as opposite as day and night. Tyler was a slender six feet two, and Bender stood barely five feet four, a difference that inspired their platoon mates to call them "Mutt and Jeff," and Bender was a tough street kid from Chicago, while Tyler was a quiet country gentleman from the rural hamlet of Cement, Oklahoma. Yet they'd been friends ever since making PFC together as new replacements on Pavuvu, and their friendship had steadily grown during the agony of Okinawa.

The last of K/3/5's June 18 casualties occurred around 11:00 P.M., some ten hours after Buckner's death, as Bender and Tyler huddled on the ground among a half-dozen Marines in what they believed to be a protected area.

"I heard the shell coming, and I've always believed it was friendly fire because the Jap artillery wasn't doing much by then," Bender recalled many years later, "but there was nothing any of us could do. It blew the hell out of an empty Jap pillbox behind us and splattered us all with shrapnel."

Bender was struck in the back, left arm, and both legs and blown several feet by the force of the blast. As he lay dazed and bleeding, he heard Tyler moaning off to his left. Crawling toward the sound, he paused to check on a blood-covered sergeant who had recently joined the company after being transferred from the peace and quiet of Panama.

"The sergeant was real bad off," Bender said, "and Tyler had a nasty-looking head wound and another wound in the back. I tried to talk to him, but he was pretty well out of it. Several other guys had been hit, too."

Despite his own multiple injuries, Bender managed to run about 100 yards to the company CP, where he enlisted the help of two corpsmen and some stretcher bearers and led them to Tyler and the others.

Out of breath and weak from loss of blood, Bender allowed himself to be placed on a stretcher. He was dimly aware of being carried through a cane field and of another pair of stretcher bearers carrying Tyler nearby. The next thing Bender remembered was being loaded into an ambulance. Beside him, Tyler was babbling incoherently and fighting his restraints, and Bender feared what his friend might do if he should get his hands free. Then everything faded.

When Bender woke up again, he was in a field hospital with a buxom young nurse leaning over him. She was dressing the wounds on one of his legs, and he was acutely aware that, except for some bandages, he was naked.

When she noticed that Bender was conscious, the nurse smiled at him. "How are you doing, little boy?" she inquired.

Bender felt himself blushing, but he tried to cover up his embarrassment with bravado. "Not too damned good," he said, "and I ain't no fuckin' little boy."

The nurse showed no reaction to Bender's profanity. She'd probably heard worse plenty of times because her smile never wavered. "Well, you're going to be okay, Marine," she said. "Just try to get some rest."

"Hey, where's my buddy, Tyler?" he asked.

She shrugged and shook her head. "I don't know who you mean. You were alone when they brought you in. What did you say your friend's name was?"

"Tyler. PFC William Tyler. He was right beside me in the ambulance."

"Sorry," she said. "They must've taken him somewhere else."

Although Bender would later learn from his platoon leader, Lieutenant Bucky Pearson, that Tyler survived his wounds, he would never see nor hear from his closest Marine Corps buddy again.

⟳

UNTIL THE FINAL Japanese defensive line was breached, U.S. commanders had been amazed at the levels of discipline and organization maintained by Japan's 32nd Army under increasingly adverse conditions. The breakdown occurred only when all hope of a Japanese victory was gone, but once it started, "it spread like an epidemic," in the words of Army historian Roy Appleman, quickly triggering both skyrocketing casualties and hordes of surrendering soldiers.

During the first seventy days of the Okinawa campaign, the number of Japanese prisoners taken by American forces averaged fewer than four per day. But as rank-and-file enemy troops sensed the futility of their struggle and U.S. propaganda leaflets exerted a positive effect, the daily numbers soared. The average jumped to more than 50 per day between June 12 and 18; hit 343 on June 19; and then 977, the highest daily number for the entire Pacific war, on June 20.

At the same time, Japanese casualty figures—in this case almost 100 percent deaths, many of them self-inflicted—hit stunning heights. After averaging about 1,000 per day during the first half of June, the toll climbed to 2,000 on June 19, to 3,000 on June 20, and to more than 4,000 on June 21.

"This tremendous rise in enemy deaths resulted from the sudden and complete imbalance between the opposing forces and from the resignation of many Japanese to death," Appleman observed. "During the last days of the battle, many bodies were found with the abdomen and right hand blown away—the telltale evidence of self-destruction."

⟳

BY THE MORNING of June 19, only two sizable concentrations of organized Japanese resistance remained. The first was located near the town of Medeera, about midway between the east and west coasts, where Japan's 24th Division and various smaller units were headquartered. The second, and most important, was centered around General Ushijima's headquarters beneath Hill 89 on the east coast and the nearby village of Mabuni, where the remains of the Japanese 62nd Division and other troops were holed up. Otherwise, only isolated local pockets of defenders still held out. The largest group—about 400 men commanded by Colonel Kikuji Hongo—was hiding in deep caves under Kunishi Ridge.

The mission to overrun Mabuni, Hill 89, and Ushijima's headquarters was handed to Colonel Mickey Finn's tired but tenacious 32nd Infantry of the Seventh Division.

"We'd parked our antitank guns and were mostly curing caves with flamethrowers at this point," recalled Tech Sergeant Porter McLaughlin, leader of a weapons platoon attached to the 32nd's Second Battalion. "Our division had killed more Japs during the week of June 10 to 17 than at any time since early May. We'd actually counted 4,288 Japanese bodies around Hill 95 and Yaeju Dake."

Because of these losses and the enemy's increasingly desperate situation, General Arnold, the Seventh Division commander, felt that many of the remaining Japanese troops were near the breaking point and might accept an opportunity to give themselves up. Leaflets were dropped behind enemy lines declaring a one-hour cease-fire along the entire eastern side of the U.S. front, during which safe passage would be guaranteed to Japanese who discarded their weapons and surrendered.

"We didn't think much of the idea," McLaughlin said, "because, frankly, it was easier to kill them, but we respected the general's wishes."

At 3:30 P.M. on June 17, the Seventh's infantry units signaled the start of the cease-fire by shooting off a series of flares that spread red smoke across the division's entire portion of the front. Then interpreters, using loudspeakers mounted on tanks, invited the Japanese to come forward unarmed and enter American lines.

The results were disappointing in that not a single Japanese soldier accepted the invitation, although a few ventured close enough to make faces at the GIs before retreating to their own lines. In truth, almost nothing happened except that one GI was wounded by enemy fire and one loudspeaker was riddled by bullet holes. "The infantrymen were disgusted," noted the official Seventh Division history, "since they had been killing Japanese at a lively rate until the firing ceased."

The cease-fire may, however, have created some residual benefits that weren't immediately apparent. As the division history added, "[I]t is probable that Japanese officers were especially watchful during the hour-long lull in fighting to prevent desertion. It also appears probable that this demonstration served to convince the Japanese of the truth contained in American surrender leaflets and was thus a contributing factor that later made possible the capture of large numbers of enemy soldiers."

When the interpreters directed their loudspeaker messages toward Okinawan civilians, the results were much more favorable. Nearly 600 civilians were taken into custody by Seventh Division troops, and interpreters later identified sixty members of this group as Okinawan conscripts and another fifteen as Japanese deserters.

Over the next two or three days, scores of Japanese soldiers surrendered to units of the Seventh. An undetermined number of others attempted to do so, but they weren't always successful.

"We were moving up a hill, using smoke grenades to mop up a bunch of caves, when three Japs jumped out of some tall grass and ran toward us in their underwear," recalled Porter McLaughlin. "I drew my .45 and emptied it at them, but I missed them all. They ran in the opposite direction for a short way, then blew themselves up. I didn't realize until later that they were trying to surrender. Our leaflets had instructed them to pull off their uniforms when they were surrendering, but nobody bothered to tell me."

LOSSES BY THE ARMY'S 96th Division during the closing days of the campaign closely approximated those of K/3/5 and the Fifth Marines. The Deadeyes' line companies were so thin and worn that the 305th Infantry of the 77th Division was attached to the 96th, much the same as the Eighth Marines had been attached to the First Marine Division, to keep its attack from losing momentum.

One of the last members of the 96th to be killed in action was Brigadier General Claudius Easley, its fiery assistant commander and architect of some of the Deadeyes' most brutal assaults on Kakazu Ridge. On June 19, a day after General Buckner's death, Easley also went to the front to check on the progress of his troops.

When a Japanese machine gun opened fire and wounded one of Easley's aides, Lieutenant John G. Turbeville, the general crawled to the top of a knoll to try to pinpoint the location of the hidden gun. As he peered over the edge of the knoll, the machine gun fired another burst, and two rounds struck Easley in the forehead, killing him instantly.

Although his impetuous style had contributed to the loss of many lives in the 96th Division—including his own—Easley was widely mourned by the men who served under him. Corporal Don Dencker of L Company, 382nd Infantry, described the tough little Texan as "our spark plug," pointing out that Easley had been responsible for giving the 96th its designation as the "Deadeye" Division. The nickname was a tribute to Easley's heavy emphasis on marksmanship training for new recruits.

"A great soldier, marksman, and leader was dead," Dencker said. "June 19 was a sad day for the 96th Infantry Division."

Another Deadeye stalwart, Colonel Edwin T. "Eddy" May, commander of the 383rd Infantry Regiment, had also fallen victim to a Japanese machine gunner on June 5 as he stood outside his command post. May's death prompted division commander General Jim Bradley to describe him as "the finest soldier I have ever known." He was posthumously awarded the Distinguished Service Cross.

For men in the ranks, however, their deepest, most painful mourning was reserved for lost comrades who had fought beside them, shared their agony and their laughter, and become integral parts of their daily lives. One of the first acts of many GIs and Marines as soon as they came off the front lines was to seek out the graves of fallen friends.

"I'll never forget standing by a small wooden cross and saying my last good-bye to my friend Henry Rucker," recalled Sergeant George Peto more than sixty years after the last shots were fired. "From where I stood, I could see the road to Naha and the place where Rucker was killed, and I kept wondering why I'd been spared and he hadn't. I still wonder about it, and when I do, I still get all choked up."

ON JUNE 20, K/3/5 was among the first American units to reach the extreme southern tip of Okinawa. As they stood on a high cliff, looking down at the point where the waters of the Pacific Ocean and the East China Sea mingled together, the Marines were struck by the beauty of the sight, but they had no time to savor it. Below them, a firefight was raging as an Army infantry unit advanced from the left, exchanging fire with Japanese soldiers as they came. Rounds from Army heavy mortars exploded out in front of the advancing infantry.

That evening, K Company set up a defensive perimeter on the high ground overlooking the sea, and, as had happened so often before, the night was punctuated by the thunder of heavy weapons, the chatter of small-arms fire, and sudden confrontations with enemy infiltrators.

"We could hear the enemy soldiers' hobnailed shoes pounding on the road until a fatal burst of fire from some other Company K Marines sent them sprawling . . ." recalled PFC Gene Sledge. "Other Japanese swam or walked along in the sea just offshore. We saw them in the flare light. A line of Marines behind a stone wall on the beach fired at them."

Just before daylight on June 21, the sound of exploding grenades and wild shouts in Japanese echoed in an area where one of K Company's 37-millimeter guns was located. Sledge and his mortar-squad mates heard rifle shots, loud curses, and cries of "Corpsman! Corpsman!"

Two Japanese officers in full-dress uniforms and white gloves had hurled grenades at the crew of the 37, then charged, swinging samurai sabers. One Marine lost a finger trying to parry a saber blow, but both attackers were killed. When Sledge and a corpsman arrived on the scene, a dazed, grimy Marine stood over one of the bodies, methodically pounding the shattered skull of the dead enemy officer with his rifle butt.

"Brains and blood were splattered all over the Marine's rifle, boondockers, and canvas leggings, as well as the wheel of the 37-millimeter gun," said Sledge. "The Marine was obviously in a complete state of shock. . . . The poor guy responded like a sleepwalker as he was led off with the wounded."

Sledge and a couple of other Marines dragged the battered officer's body to the slope of the hill and unceremoniously rolled it over the edge.

Late that same afternoon, K/3/5 received word that organized enemy resistance on Okinawa had ended, and the island was now secured. Rumors ran rampant in the bivouac area that the beat-up Fifth Regiment would soon be boarding ships for Hawaii.

"We're headed for Waikiki," chortled a grinning Marine. "That's the straight dope."

It was a pleasant pipe dream but nothing more.

⌒

BY SUNSET on June 21, after three days of heavy fighting, Colonel Mickey Finn's 32nd Infantry had captured the town of Mabuni and gained control of the slopes and crest of sheer, 200-foot Hill 89, chopping up the pocket of resistance surrounding Ushijima's headquarters into smaller and smaller chunks. Finn's exhausted GIs then eliminated the smaller pockets one by one with flamethrowers, demolitions, and tanks until only the main headquarters complex inside the hill remained intact.

Meanwhile, the Seventh Division's 184th Infantry circled around the second enemy pocket to attack from the south as the Fifth Marines advanced from the west, and troops of the 96th Division closed in from the north through the town of Medeera, effectively sealing off the other Japanese strongpoint. On June 20, a courageous Japanese runner had managed to hand-carry a last message to Ushijima from the pocket where what was left of the 24th Division was holding out about a mile away. The message had served only to tell Ushijima what he already knew: The situation was hopeless.

It was these breakthroughs that convinced General Geiger, now the Tenth Army's acting commander, that it was time to declare a U.S. victory. On the evening of June 21, Geiger's headquarters reported that all organized resistance was at an end on Okinawa and scheduled an official U.S. flag-raising ceremony for 10:00 A.M. the following day.

As any infantryman in any line company could have told the brass, the celebration was premature. The Japanese were still fighting. American units were still suffering casualties. Although several of Ushijima's staff officers had been killed by U.S. explosive charges dropped down an air shaft into a room where they were meeting, the Japanese commander and most of his staff were still functioning and safe from immediate harm in the depths of their underground lair.

In fact, even as U.S. tanks were blasting shut cave entrances on Hill 89 above them, and men of the 32nd Infantry probed cautiously into the cavernous labyrinth of caves and tunnels carved into the hill, Ushijima and General Cho, his chief of staff, were issuing final orders to their troops and preparing for one last meeting with their subordinates.

SURRENDER HAD NEVER been an option for Ushijima and Cho. The law of the Samurai dictated that death in battle or ceremonial suicide were the only courses open to them. Their final orders to their scattered troops, members of the 32nd Army staff, and various commanders of units that were now mostly nonexistent were simply to fight to the death. Ushijima urged his soldiers still in the field to slip through American lines to the north and carry on guerrilla warfare as long as possible. Those within the headquarters complex were to stage a final suicide attack against the encroaching U.S. forces.

The only notable exception to the code of "death with honor" was Ushijima's chief operations officer, Colonel Hiromichi Yahara, the ingenious architect of Okinawa's defense. Yahara was ordered to try to reach Japan and present a detailed report to Imperial Headquarters on the strategy employed at Okinawa, in the hope that similar tactics could be used to defend Japan's home islands. (Yahara's mission failed when he was captured by U.S. troops while posing as a civilian. He was abnormally tall for a Japanese, and his extreme height made him stand out like a beacon among the squatty Okinawans.)

On the evening of June 21, with Colonel Finn's 32nd Infantry exploring and sealing a maze of caves directly over their heads, Ushijima and Cho hosted their staff at a sumptuous farewell dinner prepared by Ushijima's personal cook, Tetsuo Nakamuta. At 10:00 P.M., the group sat down to a multicourse meal of bean curd soup, canned meats, potatoes, fried fish cakes, fresh cabbage, rice, pineapple, tea, and sake. After dinner, General Cho broke out his last cherished bottle of Black & White scotch, and he and Ushijima solemnly toasted each other. Sake flowed freely among the other dinner guests until the early morning hours of June 22.

Shortly before 3:00 A.M., with a white moon rising above the western Pacific, most of the staff gathered their weapons and formed ranks to carry out Ushijima's last order—a final banzai charge up Hill 89 against the Americans who held its crest. As the assigned attackers departed, the small group of officers who stayed behind to ensure that nothing interfered with the suicides of Ushijima and Cho sang Japan's National Anthem, "Umi Yukaba." The chef, Nakamuta, was still working in the kitchen when Ushijima's orderly came to inform him in hushed tones that the two generals were preparing to commit hara-kiri.

Around 4:00 A.M., Ushijima and Cho, wearing full uniforms complete with medals and swords, stepped through a small natural opening in the rocky hillside and onto a narrow ledge above the ocean, where a white quilted coverlet and a white sheet were neatly laid out.

Lieutenant Kiyoshi Haginouchi, a Ushijima aide and one of a small group of officers who witnessed or assisted with the ceremony that followed, recalled Cho turning deferentially to his commander and saying: "Well, Commanding General Ushijima, as the way may be dark, I, Cho, will lead the way."

"Please do so," Ushijima replied, "and I'll take along my fan since it is getting warm."

After kneeling on the sheet and bowing to the eastern sky, each man unfastened his tunic to bare his abdomen, as a staff officer stood by with two daggers, their blades partially shrouded in white cloth. Another officer waited tensely with his saber poised.

Ushijima, being the senior commander, went first. Silently, he accepted one of the knives from the aide, grasped it with both hands, and with one hoarse shout, drove its blade into his belly. Almost instantly, the other officer's saber slashed down on Ushijima's neck, and his body flopped forward onto the blood-spattered sheet. Then the ritual was repeated with Cho, who left behind a brief handwritten note:

"I depart without regret, shame, or obligations."

At the moment of the two generals' deaths, the nearest American troops—members of Colonel Finn's 32nd Infantry—were only about 100 feet away, although separated from the suicide scene by many tons of rock.

Seventh Division troops discovered the bodies, still clad in their dress uniforms, several days later. The generals had been buried by orderlies in shallow graves below the ledge on which they died.

THE U.S. INFANTRYMEN might have been even closer to the suicides if the Japanese themselves hadn't blasted shut one main entrance to the headquarters cave complex and if the GIs hadn't encountered a confusing maze of caves and tunnels once they got inside Hill 89.

"One big cave we went into was divided into dozens of separate stalls," recalled Tech Sergeant Porter McLaughlin. "Some of them were dug back 150 feet or more into the cliff, and one room was filled with new socks in bundles the size of cotton bales."

As they felt their way forward through the maze, McLaughlin and his comrades routinely tossed smoke grenades into any openings they found. In some cases, the smoke poured out from a dozen or more other openings, but most of the subterranean compartments were unoccupied. "In this whole area, we found only one Jap, and he was propped against a wall dead," said McLaughlin. "The rest of it was totally empty of men, but I know now that we were very close when Ushijima and Cho killed themselves."

One of McLaughlin's buddies was at regimental headquarters later when Ushijima's cook was brought in. "The cook had seen the whole thing, and he was 'grief-stricken and crying,'" McLaughlin quoted his friend as saying. "To us, Ushijima was just another Jap, but apparently he was much loved by his men."

⁓

EVEN AS THE 32ND JAPANESE ARMY faded into history, Admiral Matome Ugaki launched a last-gasp kamikaze offensive from Kyushu on June 21–22. It was styled Kikusui Ten, although it bore little resemblance to the earlier "Floating Chrysanthemum" attacks. Only fifty-eight suicide planes actually reached the Okinawa area after numerous pilots aborted—even many kamikazes had now written off Okinawa as a lost cause and concluded that dying in its defense was pointless—and they managed a direct hit on only one U.S. ship.

At about 6:30 P.M. on June 21, a suicide pilot crashed into the seaplane tender *Curtiss*, touching off a fire that killed forty-one crewmen, injured twenty-eight, and sent the ship to the bottom. The only other loss was a deserted, previously hit decoy ship, the *Barry*, which was also sunk. Several other ships suffered minor damage from near misses.

The centerpiece of Kikusui Ten was supposed to have been six manned rocket bombs, known as Okas, launched from Betty bombers, but none caused any damage. Two failed to release from their mother planes and were hauled back to Kyushu; two were lost when their mother planes were shot down; and the two others missed their targets.

A handful of Japanese planes managed to elude the increasingly numerous and adept U.S. night-fighter squadrons—eighteen of which were now concentrated on and around Okinawa—and drop some bombs over the island. One struck a tree, knocking the U.S. command's central radio station off the air for a half hour and slightly injuring five Americans. The others fell harmlessly in uninhabited areas.

There were a few other isolated suicide raids after the night of June 21–22, but no more kikusuis. Authoritative U.S. estimates of Japanese aircraft losses during the campaign range up to 7,830 planes—both conventional and suicide types—while Japanese estimates are so unrealistically low that no correlation can be made between the two sets of numbers. Based on all existing evidence, however, it seems safe to say that about 1,900 kamikazes were destroyed at or around Okinawa. After sustaining such losses, Admiral Ugaki finally abandoned the attacks to conserve planes and pilots for the coming invasion of Japan.

IF THE BONE-WEARY MARINES and GIs of the Tenth Army thought they could relax once the Stars and Stripes were raised over southern Okinawa, they were sorely disappointed. As an admission that the island was, in fact, not nearly as "secure" as General Geiger's June 21 declaration indicated, the first order issued by General Joseph W. "Vinegar Joe" Stilwell when he succeeded Geiger as commander on June 23 was, in essence, to continue the fight.

Stilwell quickly organized and set in motion a ten-day mop-up sweep of the island by most active U.S. combat units. Their mission was to move north in one massive skirmish line, searching every square yard of ground, eliminating all remaining enemy resistance, and sealing the entrances to all caves where Japanese troops could be hiding. In addition, they were to retrieve any American dead, bury Japanese dead, and salvage usable equipment left on the battlefield by both sides.

One immediate concern was the enemy pocket around the ruined town of Medeera, where an undetermined number of enemy defenders from Japan's 24th Division were still holding out. The job of mopping up this area fell to the 96th Division's 381st Infantry, which captured or killed the last defenders on June 23. Units of the First and Sixth Marine Divisions, meanwhile, conducted a similar operation against scattered remaining enemy positions along the Kunishi ridgeline, while Seventh Division troops continued probing the bowels of Hill 89 and combing through the village of Mabuni.

Farther north, a line of blocking positions was set up in the hills above the Naha-Yonabaru Valley by units of the First Marine Regiment and the 307th Infantry. The goal was to prevent small groups of Japanese soldiers from infiltrating north to conduct covert operations, as they had been ordered to do by General Ushijima. All other units of the four active divisions joined the northward sweep.

The mop-up drive was punctuated by several bloody skirmishes with well-armed groups of enemy soldiers trying to infiltrate U.S. lines and scores of shootouts between American units and Japanese snipers hiding singly or in twos and threes. The caves that harbored these holdouts were systematically sealed with flamethrowers and demolitions charges, presumably entombing hundreds of Japanese, although no exact figures are available.

As the drive moved farther north, contacts with the enemy became steadily fewer, indicating that the blocking positions along the Naha-Yonabaru Valley had succeeded in keeping the disorganized remnants of the 32nd Army from crossing into the remote northern section of the island.

When the mop-up was successfully completed on June 30—three days ahead of schedule—an estimated 8,975 enemy troops had been killed, and 2,902 military prisoners had been taken. U.S. battle casualties totaled 783 for that period.

These statistics were added to a grim list of casualties on both sides. A precise body count showed 107,539 enemy soldiers killed in action. An estimated 23,764 more dead, including an undetermined number of Okinawan civilians, had been sealed in caves or buried by the Japanese, and 10,755 military prisoners had been taken. American losses (Army, Navy, and Marines) totaled 12,520 dead or missing and 36,631 wounded in action. Five of the six U.S. divisions involved suffered more than 1,000 KIAs each, with the highest toll recorded by the Sixth Marine Division with 1,622 dead. The 27th Infantry Division, which spent fewer days in combat than the other divisions, had the lowest number of KIAs with 711.

On July 2, the Ryukyus campaign was officially declared at an end. This time, the fighting really *was* over, but almost none of the victorious Americans felt like celebrating.

"We were told we'd be spending the month of July building a new camp and training area for ourselves," said Sergeant Jack Armstrong of the First Marine Tank Battalion. "Then we'd have a month or two to get ready to land in Japan—somewhere near Tokyo, we heard—for some really nasty street fighting. Boy, that was sure something to look forward to!"

At least, though, the combat troops finally had time to rest, eat real food, shave, shower, put on clean clothes, sleep in tents, open mail from home, and write letters back. "According to our regimental news sheet, the battle is over except for the mopping up," Tech Sergeant Porter McLaughlin wrote to his aunt Gertrude on June 24. "Thanks for the licorice and stationery you mailed in December. I finally got it."

While the rest of K/3/5 was still in the field, PFC Gene Sledge and several comrades were detached temporarily from the company and transported north by truck to where a new tent camp was being estab-lished for the First Marine Division. As the truck rolled smoothly through the same countryside where Sledge and his buddies had fought, he found the scenery strikingly transformed.

"Roads that had been muddy tracks or coral-covered paths were high-ways with vehicles going to and fro and MPs in neat khaki directing traf-fic," he observed. "Tent camps, quonset huts, and huge parks of vehicles lay along our route. We had come back to civilization. . . . It was exhilarating."

Rumors about R&R in Hawaii faded away as it became obvious that Okinawa would continue to be the division's home for the foreseeable fu-ture, but as Sledge put it, "We were like boys on a campout. The fear and terror were behind us. . . . [O]ur relief that the long Okinawa ordeal was over at last was indescribable."

The relief was short-lived as sinister scuttlebutt circulated about the imminent invasion of Japan proper, implying that American casualties would exceed 1 million men. Every member of K/3/5, which had sur-vived Okinawa with only twenty-six of its Peleliu veterans still on its ac-tive roster, knew that the company and the rest of the First Marine Division would be in the thick of the slaughter. "Nobody wanted to talk about that," said Sledge.

But inevitably everyone did.

⟶

ACCORDING TO STANDARD military procedure, men who had spent more than twenty-four months in the Pacific combat zone and fought in multiple campaigns during that time could expect to be rotated home for Stateside duty after a battle the likes of Okinawa. But the early summer of 1945 was an extraordinary time—a time when stan-dard procedure fell by the wayside as preparations for the assault on Japan moved forward.

A complex and confusing point system determined who would be re-deployed and who would remain to fight again, and the system was subject to considerable manipulation by military brass when necessity dictated.

As the official history of the Seventh Infantry Division noted:

> The decision to send everyone home who had more
> than eighty-five points was greeted with combined opti-

mism and skepticism in the division. Optimism was gen-
erated by the fact that the originals still left in the unit
were now veterans of almost two and a half years of overseas service. It was estimated that more than 7,500 men
were eligible to go home. Skepticism was brought on by
past experience with Army theory. Eighty-five points was
a nice, workable figure, but it soon became apparent that
to get immediate delivery Stateside, one had to have
about 120 points.

Meanwhile, many of the American combat troops who finished the
fight on Okinawa—those of the First Marine Division and the Seventh
Infantry Division—remained there. The 96th Division shipped out for
Mindoro Island in the Philippines in late July, a few days after the Sixth
Marine Division had departed for a rest camp on Guam, and the 77th
Division was also sent to the Philippines. Their escape, however, was only
temporary. These heavily experienced units were already penciled in as
key parts of an invasion force encompassing some forty divisions in three
armies.

Veterans grew more and more nervous as the weeks slipped past.
Now and then, a familiar face would vanish, but the redeployment
process was glacially slow. As the required point level gradually descended to 108—and the sweat level of the veterans steadily increased—
the same tormenting question repeated itself in their minds: Which
would come first, the invasion or a ticket home?

For recent replacements and others who clearly lacked the necessary
points, the bleakest imaginable future loomed. Everything they saw happening around them confirmed that much.

Even before the last shots were fired on the island, more than 95,000
military engineers, Seabees, members of construction battalions, and as-
sorted service personnel were hard at work transforming the island from
a battlefield into a massive staging area for the invasion that everyone
knew was coming. By mid-July, five airfields were in operation, each
crammed wingtip to wingtip with attack aircraft. Living quarters were
being built for a half-million military personnel, along with millions of
square feet of supply depots, ammunition dumps, mess halls, offices, and
service facilities. A modern port was under construction at White Beach,
and the battered port of Naha was being converted into a deep-water anchorage.

Some military planners had begun referring to Okinawa as the "England of the Pacific," comparing its emerging role to that of the British Isles during the buildup for the invasion of Normandy. But to tens of thousands of GIs and Marines who had just emerged from the most gruesome, grueling fight of their lives, the island they had conquered was now the jumping-off place into an even bigger, more horrendous version of hell.

In that prospect, as July melted into August, there was neither joy nor solace.

CHAPTER SEVENTEEN

The Atomic Bomb—and Reprieve

D URING LATE JULY and early August 1945, as both sides prepared physically for a struggle that stood to rank among the most brutal and destructive in human history, a profusion of high-stakes mind games, diplomatic posturing, and political skullduggery was unfolding behind the scenes.

After the fall of Okinawa, many in positions of authority in Japan, including Emperor Hirohito, realized that the war was lost and urgently desired to make peace before their already-devastated nation was reduced to one vast pile of bones and ashes. But the same intractable military clique that had seized control of the Japanese government in the 1930s and plotted the attack on Pearl Harbor—men who shared the mentality of the 32nd Army's late General Cho—still held sway in Tokyo.

The actual rulers of Japan in the spring and summer of 1945 were the "big six" members of the powerful Supreme Council for the Direction of the War, or SCDW. They included seventy-eight-year-old Baron Kantaro Suzuki, a retired admiral and a hero of the Russo-Japanese War who had taken office as Japan's new premier on April 7. Suzuki privately favored peace, but, as premier, he was little more than a puppet of the warlords, and he developed an unfortunate habit of issuing bellicose, badly timed statements at their behest. Foreign Minister Shigenori Togo was also a peace advocate, but he was kept silent by fear of reprisals from the militants.

Suzuki and Togo were often outvoted by the other four members of the SCDW—the war and navy ministers and the army and navy chiefs of staff—but there was confusion and indecision on both sides. As a case in point, on June 8, as the 32nd Army on Okinawa was entering its death throes, the SCDW approved a policy committing Japan and her citizens to a scorched-earth, to-the-bitter-end fight for their homeland. Ten days later, the council seemed to reverse course entirely by voting to ask the Soviet Union to relay a peace proposal to America and her Allies.

The Soviets, for their part, had no interest in playing peacemaker. Even when Hirohito proposed sending Foreign Minister Togo to Moscow with a personal message from the emperor to Premier Joseph Stalin, the Soviet government's response was evasive, discouraging, and slow to be delivered. Truth was, Stalin had already made up his mind to declare war on Japan, but he was waiting until such time as he could claim a share of the disintegrating Japanese Empire without having to commit his own troops to battle.

The Japanese people, meanwhile, were kept totally in the dark about the true state of affairs. When Okinawa fell, Premier Suzuki issued a statement—likely under pressure—that the defeat actually "improved Japan's strategic position" while dealing a "severe spiritual blow" to the United States.

On June 28, Tokyo radio admitted that American forces were "sure to attack" the Japanese homeland, then added provocatively: "The sooner the enemy comes, the better for us, for our battle array is complete." Official broadcasts also warned "peace agitators" of harsh punishment, and despite Japan's ruined cities and ravaged infrastructure, new government initiatives were announced to increase war production, build sturdier houses and more air-raid shelters for civilians, and stockpile food. Foreign Ministry official Toshikazu Kase later denounced this whole campaign of subterfuge as "extremely harmful nonsense," but like most others in the government, he dared not speak out at the time.

"The Japanese people were never told that their country was losing the war; even our capture of such key points as Saipan, Manila, and Okinawa was explained as a strategic withdrawal," wrote naval historian Samuel Eliot Morison. "Hence, anyone high in the government or armed forces who recognized the symptoms of defeat found himself in a cruel dilemma. Love of country impelled him to seek a way out of the war, but admission of defeat exposed him to disgrace or assassination."

Even Hirohito had no immunity from the antipeace faction. After Japan's surrender, when General Douglas MacArthur asked the emperor point-blank why he hadn't taken a stand against the war earlier, Hirohito drew his forefinger across his neck in the universal symbolic gesture meaning "I would've been cutting my own throat."

THERE WAS ALSO DISAGREEMENT and confusion in Washington about the Japanese situation during that spring of 1945. Under Secretary of State Joseph C. Grew, a personal friend of President Roosevelt who had served as U.S. ambassador to Japan in the pre–Pearl Harbor years, probably understood Japanese politics as well as any living American. As Grew listened from afar to the double talk coming from Tokyo, he sensed a legitimate interest by the Suzuki government in ending the war. He also believed that a single gesture by Washington—a promise to let the emperor keep his throne and title—might give Japan's peace advocates the momentum they needed to prevail.

Unfortunately, Roosevelt had been dead for six weeks, and Grew didn't know Truman very well, but heavy U.S. bombing raids on Tokyo on May 23 and 25 prompted Grew to visit the new president at the White House and propose just such a concession.

Truman expressed interest in the idea, but because of his short time in office, he hesitated to make a policy decision of this magnitude without input from his military advisers. He asked Grew to discuss the idea with Army Chief of Staff General George C. Marshall, Navy Secretary James V. Forrestal, and Secretary of War Henry L. Stimson. They, too, thought the idea had merit but felt the timing was wrong because (1) bad weather had brought the Okinawa campaign to a near standstill, and (2) under the circumstances, Tokyo might interpret the overture as an exploitable sign of war weariness in America.

Grew wasn't the type to give up easily. On June 18, with the Okinawa campaign nearly over, he again urged Truman to proclaim that the emperor could stay. When military leaders once more stalled for time, the president decided to defer his decision until his upcoming conference with Soviet Premier Stalin, British Prime Minister Winston Churchill, and Chinese Premier Chiang Kai-shek, scheduled to open at Potsdam in occupied Germany on July 16.

Although they didn't mention it to Grew, Truman's military chiefs had a third strong reason to decline or delay any concessions to the Japanese. A committee of high-ranking government officials and the nation's top atomic scientists had reported on June 1 that an atomic bomb with "devastating strength" was ready for testing. Assuming the test was successful, they recommended that the bomb be employed against a suitably large Japanese target as soon as feasible and that no advance warning be given.

On July 17, the second day of the Potsdam Conference, Churchill was informed that the first experimental atomic bomb had been success-fully detonated in the New Mexico desert.

"This is the Second Coming," Churchill exulted, "in wrath."

⁓

BACK IN THE PACIFIC, no one at Okinawa or dozens of other U.S. bases had yet heard the term "atomic bomb," much less received any indication that this "miracle of deliverance," as Churchill called it, was waiting in the wings.

With each passing day, the prospect of the impending invasion grew more oppressive, generating such feelings of futility and helplessness that many enlisted men even lost interest in their once-cherished beer ra-tions. Word filtered through the ranks that the invasion of Japan's home islands had been code-named Operation Downfall. It seemed ominously appropriate. No one expected to come through it in one piece.

"Everybody knew if he hadn't been hit so far, he soon would be," said PFC Dick Whitaker, a runner in Company F, 29th Marines, who'd re-ceived a wound and a Bronze Star in the massacre on Sugar Loaf Hill, "because we were going from the Oki slaughter to a much worse one."

One problem affecting the troops who remained on Okinawa—even those veterans who fully expected to be rotated home and not to have to fight again—was a lingering, bone-deep fatigue, both mental and physi-cal, that no amount of rest and relaxation seemed capable of assuaging. Another was simple boredom born of inactivity and a limbolike existence.

"It didn't make a rat's ass to me that we stayed on Okinawa," recalled Sergeant R. V. Burgin of K/3/5, a once-wounded veteran of three cam-paigns who'd been in the Pacific for two and a half years and had every right to expect to be sent home. "Our camp on the west coast near the Yontan airfield was as good or better than our old one at Pavuvu, but we were all just kind of numb and played-out. Some guys pulled guard duty, and there were a few work details, but otherwise, we really didn't have much of anything to do. I had two cousins with the Army on Okinawa, and I looked both of them up and had a visit. Other times, I'd just sit for hours watching planes land and take off. I was running in neutral so much of the time that a lot of that period is just a blank to me; I have no recollection of it at all."

⁓

ALONG WITH ALL the top-priority military construction taking place on Okinawa during that summer of '45, a few nonessential projects were also under way, designed to provide stressed-out, exhausted men a small measure of comfort and recreation. One such amenity was to be a swimming area along the western coastline for members of the First Marine Tank Battalion.

Although the ground in the area was sandy right down to the waterline, the submerged portion was composed mostly of razor-sharp coral, which had to be blasted loose and pulverized before men could walk on it barefoot without cutting their feet to ribbons. The water was also only about four feet deep at high tide, and the idea was to remove enough coral to create a "swimming hole" up to ten or twelve feet in depth. It was going to take a lot of dynamite to do the job.

When word got around about the project, everyone in the battalion was eager to see it completed, but as fate would have it, the man placed in charge of its dynamiting phase was none other than Private Howard Towry, the self-confessed "worst screwup" in the outfit.

The chief warrant officer overseeing the project probably had no idea that he was creating a scenario for disaster when he assigned Towry to handle the blasting, but many of the battalion's officers would soon see, hear—and, in some cases, feel—the results.

"I'd been to demolition school, and I knew how to handle dynamite, TNT, and stuff like that," Towry recalled many years later. "We hauled fifty-pound cases of dynamite about thirty or forty yards out into the water and positioned them in circles, then touched them off."

Everything went well until the last day of the blasting. The swimming area was almost complete, lacking only an anchored platform from which men could dive. Twenty cases of dynamite were left over, however, and the chief warrant officer instructed Towry to place them in a deep underwater hole, wait for the tide to come in, then detonate all twenty at once.

"He drove a stick into the ground and told me when the water got to that stick, I should blow the dynamite," Towry said. "He didn't say anything about checking the wind; he just told me to blow it. Then he left."

Towry followed the chief's instructions to the letter. When the incoming tide reached the stick, he "popped" the dynamite. The results were impressive, to say the least. Towry watched a geyser of seawater half the width of a football field erupt more than 100 feet into the air. When the sea winds caught the waterspout, it rolled like a tidal wave across a high bluff where the battalion's officers had their living quarters, along with their well-appointed mess hall, well-stocked cocktail bar, private latrine, and other facilities that were off-limits to enlisted men.

As it had dozens of times before during his military career, a horrified two-word exclamation flew from Towry's lips: *"Oh, no!"*

"The minute I saw it, I knew it was a horrible mistake," he said. "It looked like a hurricane hitting those officers' tents. It blew every single one of them down—I mean, it leveled their whole camp—and the next thing I knew, about fifteen officers were running toward me with blood in their eyes. Man, they were after my ass, I tell you."

At that moment, the chief warrant officer—a huge man who weighed close to 300 pounds—roared up in his jeep and jerked it to a halt squarely in the path of the charging officers.

"I told that boy to do what he did," the chief yelled, "so if you've got anything to say, you'll have to say it to me."

The chief's intervention may have saved Towry from at least a court-martial and possibly great bodily harm. But to his surprise, his misadventure with the dynamite established him as something of a hero among other enlisted men in the battalion.

"A lot of guys didn't like officers much," said Towry. "They considered them egotistical snobs, and they thought the whole thing was really funny. The swimming place turned out beautiful, and I was just glad to be alive."

THE INVASION OF JAPAN was too huge an undertaking to happen all at once. It would be divided into phases, the first of which, code-named Operation Olympic, was approved by Truman on June 18, the same day General Buckner was killed. It would target Kyushu, the nearest of the home islands to Okinawa, with three Marine and three Army divisions of the U.S. Sixth Army hitting the southern portion of the island on November 1. Three more Army divisions would land on the flat plain of Kyushu's northeast coast, and two additional divisions would stand by as a floating reserve.

The second phase, Operation Coronet, wasn't scheduled to happen until early spring 1946, when the Eighth and Tenth Armies were to assault the Tokyo Plain, while the First Army, transported around the world from Europe, provided a ten-division reserve force. The First,

Fourth, and Sixth Marine Divisions were designated to spearhead the amphibious assault aimed at seizing the Japanese capital.

Truman was disturbed by the heavy U.S. losses at Okinawa and Iwo Jima and the implications they had for Olympic and Coronet, and he demanded specific answers from the Joint Chiefs of Staff about the expected toll on Kyushu. General Marshall and Admiral Ernest J. King, chief of naval operations, expressed confidence that total casualties in Olympic should be no more than 31,000 killed and wounded, about the same losses as in the Luzon campaign. It was a number that Truman found acceptable, but it was also ridiculously low in the view of many historians.

Later evidence showed that this estimate had almost no basis in reality. It was largely based on MacArthur's early projection that Kyushu would be defended by only seven Japanese divisions and a couple of independent mixed brigades, a total of just over 200,000 men. Actually, the Japanese had eleven divisions, three mixed brigades, and three tank brigades—about 320,000 troops—available for ground defense. In addition, they could have committed more than 2,500 conventional aircraft and kamikazes to Kyushu's aerial defense.

MacArthur later delivered a far more realistic assessment of the cost of invading and capturing Kyushu, Japan's southernmost island, in a three-month campaign. In mid-June 1945, in response to pressure from Washington, MacArthur gave Marshall a drastically revised Kyushu casualty estimate of 106,000, including non-battle illnesses and injuries. Some planners believed that, if the Kyushu invasion succeeded in ending the war, the cost in U.S. losses would run even higher—to 132,500. If the rest of the home islands had to be invaded in two subsequent U.S. landings, the same planners projected, the bloodiest phase of Operation Downfall could drag on for another sixteen months with total American casualties exceeding 250,000 and even reaching 500,000.

Former President Herbert Hoover was convinced that even these estimates were far too low. Hoover sent a lengthy memo to Truman, urging him to consider a negotiated peace, rather than unconditional surrender, in order to spare "the lives of 500,000 to 1,000,000 American boys."

Author William Manchester, in his book *The Glory and the Dream*, put the looming ordeal in grim perspective when he wrote:

> The capture of Iwo Jima, less than eight square miles
> of volcanic ash, had cost 25,849 Marines. . . . Okinawa's

price had been 49,151. . . . If the Japanese could draw that much blood in the outer islands of their defense perimeter, how formidable would they be on the 142,151 square miles of their five home islands, where they would be joined . . . by every member of the civilian population old enough to carry a hand grenade?

TRUMAN WAS UNQUESTIONABLY swayed by the sharply rising casualty estimates. On July 26, he, Churchill, and Chiang Kai-shek issued a statement from their conference in Germany that became known as the Potsdam Declaration, outlining conditions under which Japan's "unconditional" surrender would be accepted.

Among other things, it called for (1) "elimination for all time" of the influence and authority of the Japanese militarists; (2) stripping Japan of all conquered territory and limiting her sovereignty to her four-island homeland and adjacent small islands; (3) occupation of Japan by Allied forces until a new order of "peace, security, and justice" could be established; (4) disarmament of Japanese military forces, whose members would be allowed to return home with a chance to lead "peaceful and productive lives"; (5) stern justice for all war criminals but guarantees of human rights and freedom of speech, religion, and thought to Japanese citizens; (6) retention of peaceful industries to sustain the Japanese economy while prohibiting any rearmament.

The declaration also pledged that occupation forces would be withdrawn from Japan as soon as the above objectives were fulfilled and "a peacefully inclined and responsible government" was established. It did *not* explicitly state, however, that the emperor could keep his throne. Truman and other leaders reportedly felt that the reference to "responsible government" was sufficient assurance that the Japanese would be allowed to choose their own future leadership, but this may not have been fully understood in Tokyo.

On the other hand, the warning included in the declaration should have been crystal-clear to the Japanese. It pulled no punches and came straight to the point. If the terms of the declaration were rejected, it stated, "the utter devastation of the Japanese homeland" would swiftly follow.

When the declaration was broadcast in Japan, it touched off heated debate over how to respond. Predictably, it was met with contempt by Japanese military leaders, but civilian "doves" embraced it as an opportunity to end the war without sacrificing national honor.

Foreign Minister Togo wanted to delay any official reply, fearing the cabinet's militants would approve nothing short of a total rejection, but Premier Suzuki again "jumped the gun." At a press conference on July 28, he denounced the declaration as an unworthy, unacceptable rehash of earlier Allied proposals, then boasted that increased Japanese aircraft production gave Japan new prospects of victory.

As Suzuki probably realized, there was no hope whatever that Tokyo's military zealots would soften their stand, regardless of how many civilian lives hung in the balance. "Even if the Japanese people are weary of the war," said Admiral Soemu Toyoda, commander of the Imperial Combined Fleet, "we must fight to the last man."

One of the most widely circulated patriotic slogans of that summer in Japan symbolized the warlords' determination that this "last man" reference apply as much to civilian men, women, and children as to the 4 million soldiers, sailors, and airmen remaining in the armed forces.

"One hundred million [will] die proudly," it proclaimed.

FROM POTSDAM, U.S. Secretary of State James Byrnes called Suzuki's statement "disheartening," but he expressed hope that Tokyo would change its mind before the conference adjourned. If not, Truman had already issued orders to the 20th Air Force to deliver the first two atomic bombs to the giant U.S. base on Tinian Island in the northern Marianas and to prepare to drop one of them on a Japanese city as soon after August 3 as weather permitted.

By the time Truman left Europe aboard the cruiser *Augusta*, no further word had been received from Tokyo. The die was cast. On August 2, still aboard the *Augusta* in the Atlantic, Truman issued the final order to General Curtis LeMay, whose B-29s had already obliterated much of urban Japan.

Inclement weather on August 3 and 4 delayed the mission, but when skies cleared on August 5, LeMay ordered the first bomb loaded aboard the *Enola Gay*, a B-29 commanded by Colonel Paul W. Tibbets. At 2:45 A.M. on August 6, Tibbets and his crew, accompanied by Captain William S. Parsons, a Navy ordnance specialist who was along to make final adjustments to the bomb, took off from Tinian's North Field for the 700-mile flight to Japan. Following in their wake were two observation planes whose job was to record the mission's results.

The target was Hiroshima, an industrial center of 350,000 people in southwestern Honshu, the largest of the home islands. It was one of only two important Japanese cities—the other being Kyoto—that hadn't yet been struck in force by the B-29s. Yet during the preceding weeks, thousands of U.S. bombers had flown over Hiroshima because it was near a key rendezvous point for the planes. Air-raid warnings had sounded day and night in the city, keeping citizens jittery. More than 100,000 residents evacuated during July and early August, leaving only about 240,000 present when the A-bomb struck. One rumor among many that circulated claimed that the Americans were saving something "special" for Hiroshima—and that one was true.

When the bomb exploded at 8:15 A.M. on August 6, up to half of the people in the city would either be killed outright or suffer hideous injuries that eventually proved fatal.

President Truman was still aboard the *Augusta* in the western Atlantic when he received confirmation that the mission had been successfully completed. His excitement was obvious as he spread the word, first to the presidential entourage, then to the ship's officers and men.

"This is the greatest thing in history," Truman told them.

⁓

WHEN WORD of the nuclear attack reached the men on Okinawa on August 10, they agreed almost unanimously with Truman's assessment.

As Marine Corporal Melvin Grant, whose brother Scott had been killed at Kunishi Ridge, recalled nearly sixty-one years after the first bomb fell: "We were thrilled, utterly thrilled when we heard the news. Using the bomb was the thing to do, and we did it, and I had absolutely no regrets. We did it to save lives, not only American but Japanese as well. My feeling was then, and still is now, that if there hadn't been a Pearl Harbor, there never would've been a Hiroshima or a Nagasaki."

"I was happy and relieved," added Sergeant Jack Armstrong of the First Marine Tank Battalion. "Hearing about the bomb gave all of us a big lift, and for the first time in a long time, we felt like there was a ray of hope. Maybe we wouldn't have to invade Japan after all. Maybe I'd actually make it home alive."

Marine PFC Wendell Majors was in a Navy hospital at Guam, recovering from his wounds on Sugar Loaf Hill and looking ahead with dread to being well enough to participate in the invasion of Japan, when he heard the news. "At the time, if I could've had a nuclear warhead that would fit on the end of my rifle, and I could've reached the Japanese homeland with it, I would've pulled the trigger," he recalled, in a voice still charged with emotion decades later. "I would've sunk the whole Japanese nation if I had to because that's what I thought it'd take to make them give up."

The horror of Hiroshima convinced Japan's highest ranking civilian leaders, including Hirohito, that Japan had no choice but to accept the terms of the Potsdam Declaration, yet it failed to dent the resolve of Japan's hard-core militants. Foreign Minister Togo took the lead in pushing for peace, but he and other "doves" in the government had to move cautiously. The warlords and their henchmen had shown no hesitation in murdering dissenters in the past and would almost surely do so again in the name of honor—even at the risk of destroying the entire nation.

Truman gave the Japanese three days to respond. When no official acceptance of the peace terms was received from Tokyo within that period, he ordered a second, even more powerful bomb detonated. The target initially selected was the city of Kokura, but a thick cloud cover forced the B-29 assigned to carry the bomb, piloted by Major Charles W. Sweeney, to divert to a secondary target—the city of Nagasaki, a major seaport and the largest industrial/military complex on Kyushu. This second bomb, code-named "Fat Man," exploded just after 11:00 A.M. on August 9, about six hours after the Soviet Union had declared war on Japan and sent its tanks rumbling into Manchuria.

An estimated 35,000 Japanese were killed instantly, and about 10,000 more would die of radiation poisoning in days to come. Thousands more were injured but survived.

The hard-liners were shaken, almost as much by the Soviets' actions as by the bombs, but they refused to acquiesce. An Imperial Conference of the Japanese War Cabinet's "big six," held in an air-raid shelter under the Imperial Palace with the emperor in attendance, dragged through the afternoon of August 9 and most of that night. Navy chief of staff Admiral Soemu Toyoda and army chief General Korechika Anami adamantly opposed Foreign Minister Togo's proposal to accept the Potsdam Declaration, arguing that their forces could defeat the Americans on Kyushu and win better terms.

Shortly before midnight, with the cabinet in a hopeless three-to-three deadlock, Premier Suzuki turned to Hirohito, reporting with regret that the cabinet was unable to reach a consensus and asking the emperor to take an unprecedented step.

"Your Imperial Majesty's decision is requested," Suzuki said.

As militants and peace advocates alike bowed in respect, Hirohito stood up and spoke in a voice trembling with emotion: "I cannot bear to see my innocent people suffer any longer. . . . How can we repel the invaders? . . . I swallow my own tears and give my sanction to the proposal to accept the Allied proclamation. . . ."

After the emperor left, Suzuki rose to address the other members of the SCDW. "His Majesty's decision should be made the decision of this conference as well," he said.

Under Japanese law, however, the conference had no authority to formally enact or enforce a national decision of this nature—only the cabinet could do that—so the SCDW adjourned the conference at 2:30 A.M. on August 10. A half hour later, the same six men convened a meeting of the cabinet and unanimously approved the emperor's decision.

At 7:00 A.M. that same morning, the governments of the United States and her Allies were notified that Japan would accept the terms of the Potsdam Declaration, with the understanding that the emperor would be allowed to remain as the country's sovereign ruler.

⁓

PEACE WAS ENTICINGLY close but not yet a fait accompli. Not quite.

A period of white-knuckle tension would continue in Tokyo for five more days, during which word of the emperor's decree would be withheld from the Japanese public. Over the next two weeks, various anti-peace plots would be hatched and a serious military coup attempt narrowly averted.

Washington sought to make it clear that, for the emperor to be retained as Japan's titular national leader, certain conditions would have to be met, as outlined in a note from Secretary of State Byrnes dated August 11. After the surrender, the extent of the emperor's role in government would be determined by the supreme commander of Allied occupation forces, and Japan's ultimate form of government would be decided by the "free will" of the Japanese people.

Receipt of the Byrnes note touched off a new crisis in Tokyo, where several top military leaders now demanded self-disarmament for their forces and either limited occupation of Japan by foreign troops or none at all. A fanatical group of young army officers tried to stage a coup to overthrow the cabinet and continue the war. In an effort to defuse the situation, Hirohito called on key senior army and navy officers to make sure that their troops obeyed his cease-fire order. War Minister General Korechika Anami summoned all officers of the rank of lieutenant colonel or higher, appealing to them to maintain control and warning against any overt attempt to thwart the peace decision. A similar warning was issued to naval personnel by Admiral Yonai, the navy minister.

On August 11, after the Byrnes note was sent, President Truman ordered a halt in all strategic operations against Japan by the 20th Air Force. Three days later, for reasons that remain unclear, the order was rescinded long enough to allow more than 1,000 B-29s to take off on bombing missions—a move that might have proved catastrophic to the peace process if the planes hadn't been recalled before they reached their intended targets.

As it turned out, only seven more B-29s would appear over Tokyo and other Japanese cities before World War II officially came to an end. They carried no bombs, only leaflets—5 million of them—each containing the text of the Japanese acceptance of the Potsdam Declaration and a translation of Secretary Byrnes's reply.

When the leaflets were distributed during the night of August 13–14, the Japanese people got their first indication of what was happening to their country. The emperor was shown one of the leaflets the next morning and warned by Premier Suzuki to make his peace declaration public as soon as possible. Otherwise, he risked losing control of the armed forces.

The following night (August 14–15), a group of diehard young officers confronted General Takeshi Mori, commander of the Imperial Guards, demanding that he and his men disobey the emperor's surrender order. When Takeshi refused, they assassinated him. The plotters also stormed into the studios of Radio Tokyo and tried to seize and destroy the master recording of Hirohito's peace announcement, scheduled to be broadcast to the nation a few hours later. When they failed, and an attempt to assassinate Premier Suzuki went awry, most of the conspirators committed hara-kiri, as did War Minister Anami; Admiral Takijiro Onishi, father of the Kamikaze Corps; and other high-ranking military officers.

BEGINNING EARLY on the morning of August 15, radios all over Japan repeated the same message: an announcement of utmost importance would be broadcast at noon. Few, if any, of the millions who gathered around loudspeakers in ruined cities at the appointed hour expected that announcement to be made by the emperor himself—much less that it would be an admission of Japan's defeat.

For the first time in history, the Japanese people heard the voice of their emperor. That, in itself, was incredible, but even more stunning was the ominous meaning of his words. The term "surrender" was never mentioned in Hirohito's statement, but its meaning was crushingly clear.

> We have ordered our government to communicate to the governments of the United States, Great Britain, and the Soviet Union that our Empire accepts the provisions of their joint declaration. . . . We charge you, our loyal subjects, to carry out faithfully our will. . . . Beware most strictly of any outbursts of emotion which may endanger needless complications, or cause ye to lose the confidence of the world. . . . Cultivate the ways of rectitude; foster nobility of spirit; and work with resolution so that ye may enhance the glory of the Imperial State. . . .

The gigantic conflict ignited by the warlords on December 7, 1941, was finally over. Japan had lost.

THE REACTION on Okinawa to the war's end ranged from silent shock and prayerful reflection to jubilant celebrations that more than matched those at home during the two-day national holiday declared by President Truman.

"We received the news with quiet disbelief, coupled with an indescribable sense of relief," said K/3/5's PFC Gene Sledge. "We thought the Japanese would never surrender. Many refused to believe it. Sitting in stunned silence, we remembered our dead. So many dead. So many maimed. So many bright futures consigned to the ashes of the past."

When Sergeant R. V. Burgin heard the news, he had left his buddies in K/3/5 and moved into temporary quarters near the port of Naha to await transportation home. "Everybody was damn glad it was over," he recalled, "and even though I'd been pretty sure I wouldn't have to go to Japan, it was a big relief to know there wouldn't be an invasion. I'd known from the beginning that we'd be on the winning side. It was just a question of if the Japs were going to quit, or we were going to kill them all, but when I envisioned every person in Japan as our bitter enemy—even the women and kids—it disturbed me. It would've bothered me a lot to go in there that way."

Uproarious celebrations did break out in parts of the First Marine Division's new camp on the Motobu Peninsula, but even these were tempered by bitter memories and tinged with continuing grief. "A lot of us got drunk and ran around like chickens with our heads cut off," recalled one Marine quoted in *The Old Breed*, "but I felt, and I think others felt, it was like doing what we were expected to do. Besides, that wasn't a very good place to celebrate. It seemed irreverent. It was only days before that your buddies had been dying. There were still lots of wounded men around in hospitals. You hear a lot about how they pitched a big one after World War I in the streets of Paris. Well, Motobu wasn't Paris."

As darkness descended on the evening of August 15, the skies above the island were lit by one of the largest pyrotechnic displays ever seen on Earth, as thousands of AA batteries on shore and aboard hundreds of Navy ships spewed endless streams of tracers and high-explosive rounds into the air.

On Mindoro Island in the Philippines, where the 96th Infantry Division had arrived on August 11 after weathering a particularly vicious typhoon at sea, there was similar revelry, in which shouts of joy were coupled with quiet introspection.

"Everyone in Love Company was energized by the news," said Corporal Don Dencker. "We congratulated each other as we drank our beer issue of three bottles apiece, but the celebration was surprisingly tame. There was no wild firing of weapons. My thoughts and the thoughts of others turned to our buddies who had been killed or seriously wounded."

On Guam, where the Sixth Marine Division had been sent after Okinawa, the first radio reports of Japan's surrender were received at about 10:00 P.M., after many of the men had gone to bed. As the reports hit home, Marines leaped from their cots and ran outside cheering and shouting, many in their underwear. Members of the 22nd Marines' regimental band broke out their instruments and led a spur-of-the-moment parade through company streets.

While others clustered around the radios, eager for further details about the surrender, First Sergeant Stanley A. Goff fulfilled a promise made months earlier to dress in his only good uniform of starched khaki and wallow in a mud hole.

Undoubtedly one of the quietest observances of the war's end was aboard the rocket ship *LSM(R) 198*, which had been on radar picket duty about 100 miles off Kyushu until receiving sudden orders to make a 180-degree turn and head for Hawaii.

"We didn't even know about the surrender until the next day," said Gunner's Mate Hank Kalinofsky, "although we suspected something big had happened when we changed course. Just a short time before, we'd still had kamikazes coming over. There was absolutely no celebration of any kind on the ship, and since there were only eighty-six of us on board, it would've been hard to keep it a secret. All I remember is a great feeling of relief. We weren't going to be supporting another invasion, after all."

The Fourth Marines had a totally opposite experience—and far less time to celebrate than the Sixth Marine Division's other regiments. On the same day that Japan surrendered, the Fourth—a reembodiment of the original Fourth Marines, whose survivors had been taken prisoner at Corregidor in May 1942—left Guam as one of the first U.S. units assigned to land on the former enemy's home soil. They would go ashore at Yokosuka four days before the signing of the peace treaty in Tokyo Bay.

The regiment's departure served as a sobering reminder that, although the war was now history, much remained to be done to secure the peace.

⁓

SURRENDER OR NO SURRENDER, there was still occasional hostile action on Okinawa and in the surrounding waters eight weeks after the island was declared secure, and it didn't end with Hirohito's acceptance of the Potsdam surrender terms.

On August 12, American forces in the area had been told to be on the lookout for a twin-engine Betty bomber, painted white and bearing green crosses on its wings and fuselage. The plane supposedly carried surrendering Japanese officers and was expected to land at the airfield on the island of Ie Shima off Okinawa's northwest coast en route to Manila.

"We were instructed not to shoot down this plane," recalled Radioman Joe Di Stanislao, a crewman aboard the U.S. cruiser *Columbia*. "However, instead of a white plane with green crosses, we got a torpedo plane that flew right over us and dropped a torpedo that hit the battleship *Pennsylvania*, anchored 1,000 yards away. The direct hit caused many casualties."

The venerable *Pennsylvania*, which had served as flagship of the U.S. Fleet before the war, had just returned from a full-scale refitting at Bremerton, Washington. It was lying at anchor in Buckner Bay (originally Nakagusuku Wan, which was renamed for General Buckner after his death) when it was struck. Twenty sailors were killed, and the wounded included Vice Admiral Jesse Oldendorf, commander of a newly created strike force of the U.S. Third Fleet, who was in the process of transferring his flag to the *Pennsylvania* from the battleship *Tennessee*.

Meanwhile, on Okinawa proper, American troops were still trading shots now and then with scattered Japanese holdouts—more than 700 of whom had managed to elude the Tenth Army's final mop-up of the island. The majority of these fugitives, almost 400 enlisted men and officers, many of them sick or wounded, were hiding in deep caves beneath Kunishi Ridge, led by Colonel Kikuji Hongo, a regimental commander in Japan's 24th Division. Another group of about 300 men under Captain Tsuneo Shimura was slowly making its way north in hopes of carrying on guerrilla action in mountainous, sparsely settled areas above the Ishikawa Isthmus.

When word of the surrender reached the holdouts, coaxing by American interpreters and testimony from Japanese POWs eventually convinced them that the war was truly over. By August 30, both groups on Okinawa, along with several small garrisons in the Kerama Retto, had turned themselves in to U.S. forces.

ON AUGUST 19, not one but two Betty bombers, each painted white and marked with green crosses, as stipulated, finally arrived at the airfield on Ie Shima. They were loaded with high-ranking Japanese officers who were to board an Army Air Force transport for a flight to Manila and a meeting with General MacArthur to arrange the formal surrender. The officers were greeted—none too cordially—by several

Marine machine-gun sections lining the tarmac on full alert with manned and loaded weapons.

"We were set up under the wing of a C-47 transport," recalled Corporal Dan Lawler, the K/3/5 machine gunner who was stationed at his .30-caliber Browning, "and, our captain told us, 'If these Jap officers make any funny moves, you guys mow 'em down. I mean wipe 'em out.'"

The Marines had no idea what to expect, since this was the first face-to-face meeting between Japanese and American officers, and among the group was Lieutenant General Torashiro Kawabe, deputy chief of staff of the Japanese army.

"Our officers thought it was too risky to let the Japs land on the main island," said Lawler. "They were afraid they might blow themselves up and take a bunch of Americans with them. I'll tell you this: If they'd pulled anything—I mean anything at all—I could've opened up on them without blinking an eye."

While the precautions taken at Ie Shima may seem extreme when viewed from more than six decades later, they were amply justified by events taking place in Japan at the time. The arrival of the specially marked Bettys had been delayed for two days after hotheaded Japanese army airmen threatened to shoot down any surrender mission that tried to take off.

In light of this and other incidents, including a thwarted plot by diehard kamikaze pilots to crash the battleship *Missouri* at the time of the surrender ceremony, a newly installed Japanese cabinet asked that the first landings by U.S. forces be delayed for several days. The request was granted, and the first U.S. troops didn't go ashore until August 28.

Evacuating the thousands of American and Allied POWs who were leaving abandoned Japanese internment camps and following broadcast and air-dropped instructions to gather at specified coastal rescue points was a top priority. Reports of threats by Japanese extremists to execute all these prisoners if Japan were invaded raised concerns about their safety, even after the peace agreement. Many were also half starved and desperately in need of medical care, including a number of survivors of the infamous Bataan Death March following Japan's conquest of the Philippines in early 1942. Every effort was made to get help to these men as quickly as possible via Navy ships that had recently played key roles in the Okinawa campaign.

ONE OF THE FIRST large vessels to reach the Japanese mainland was the heavy cruiser *Wichita,* which had also been the first major U.S. warship to arrive at Okinawa—and among the busiest once she got there, having survived attacks by kamikazes, torpedoes, and suicide swimmers.

Crew members of the "Old Witch" had already been jittery and on edge at the idea of steaming into the heart of the Japanese Empire before the official signing of the peace treaty, but when they learned their precise destination, their anxiety level increased still further.

"Our assignment was to go into Nagasaki harbor and liberate approximately 10,000 POWs who'd been held in a camp about twenty miles from the city," said Seaman Les Caffey. "This was less than two and a half weeks after the atomic bomb was dropped there, and we didn't have any idea what we might be heading into."

The *Wichita* was accompanied by a small convoy that included a destroyer, two destroyer escorts, two minesweepers, and a hospital ship, the U.S.S. *Haven.* Their orders were to lay to and stand by offshore until cleared to proceed into the inner harbor.

"All kinds of terrible rumors floated about the ship," recalled Ensign Ben McDonald, a young gunnery officer. "We heard that the Japanese government had sent observers to Nagasaki who never returned or reported. We heard that the radiation and other aftereffects could absorb or dissolve people—make them disappear—and that the area would be contaminated for centuries. We imagined a gaseous curtain extending from ground to sky that was lethal to anyone who entered it. Men who had fought the enemy fearlessly were now terrified of this unthinkable unknown."

The suspense mounted when two Navy flying boats intercepted the convoy and a contingent of scientists from the Manhattan Project that had created the atomic bomb came aboard the *Wichita.* Their assurances that the charred ground in Nagasaki was "probably habitable" did little to boost the crew's confidence.

"We were really scared—scared like never before," recalled McDonald.

After two days of testing ashore, the scientists reported that the radioactive waste from the bomb had dissipated, and it was safe for naval personnel to land. Members of the shore party were required to wear lead-lined protective clothing, however.

"The destruction was unbelievable," said McDonald. "The whole city was leveled, with only the hulls of a few stronger buildings outside ground zero still standing."

At first, there was no sign of human life, but frightened survivors, many of them covered by flash burns, gradually emerged, and several of the less seriously injured volunteered to serve as guides. "They showed us one small area near the main railroad station where 4,000 people were killed and another where 12,000 died," said McDonald.

The POWs were in terrible condition—walking skeletons caked with dirt and swarming with lice and other parasites. Those in the worst shape were treated aboard the *Haven,* while the others were placed aboard troop ships that would take them to the Philippines. In all, 9,700 were evacuated, including 1,512 American survivors of the Bataan Death March; others were British, Australian, Dutch, and Javanese.

AT 5:50 A.M. on August 30, men of the Second Battalion, Fourth Marines, commanded by Major Frank Carney, became the first American combat troops to set foot on Japanese soil—and, in fact, the first foreign invaders ever to do so.

As their landing craft neared the shores of Tokyo Bay, the Marines could see the high seawalls and fortresses of reinforced concrete that formed a solid line along the bay. They bristled with massive cannon, antiaircraft batteries, and weaponry of every description, all of which the Marines would have faced in an invasion. Now the fortifications were draped with white flags, as ordered by General William T. Clement, assistant commander of the Sixth Marine Division, who commanded the landing force, and all Japanese personnel had been removed except for small maintenance crews.

"I hope they mean it," said one Marine uneasily as he eyed the white flags over the ramp of his landing craft.

The forts were occupied without incident, however, and the few Japanese encountered by the Marines wore white armbands identifying them as essential maintenance personnel, as instructed, and they offered no resistance. Meanwhile, the regiment's First and Third Battalions seized the Yokosuka naval base and airfield, and, by midmorning, General Clement and his staff came ashore to set up a command post and accept the formal surrender of the area from a group of Japanese officers.

Some of the most riveting scenes to emerge from this emotional period took place at Yokosuka when members of the "new Fourth Marines" met 120 emaciated survivors from the "old Fourth" face-to-face for the first time.

As the regimental band played, the liberated heroes of Bataan and Corregidor sat down with heroes of Motobu Peninsula and Sugar Loaf Hill to enjoy a steak dinner, toast one another with Japanese beer, and exchange stories. Among them were two tearful half brothers, one from the old regiment and one from the new, who had never expected to see each other again.

The reunited brothers formed a microcosm of the best and worst times of the war, combining the agony of defeat and imprisonment with the euphoria of victory and peace.

AT 9:00 A.M. on Sunday, September 2, 1945, General MacArthur accepted Japan's formal surrender aboard the battleship *Missouri*, one of 258 American warships anchored in Tokyo Bay.

Admirals Nimitz and Halsey stood by, along with General Jonathan M. Wainwright, who had surrendered the Philippines to the Japanese in 1942, and British General Sir Arthur Percival, who had surrendered Singapore that same year—both fresh from Manchurian prison camps—as MacArthur made a brief statement:

"It is my earnest hope—indeed the hope of all mankind—that from this solemn occasion a better world shall emerge out of the blood and carnage of the past, a world founded upon faith and understanding, a world dedicated to the dignity of man and the fulfillment of his most cherished wish for freedom, tolerance, and justice."

Then, in a silent, frigid atmosphere, members of the Japanese delegation were motioned forward to sign the instrument of surrender. Foreign Minister Shigemitsu slowly stepped to the green-clothed table on his artificial leg and had to be shown where to sign by General R. K. Sutherland, MacArthur's chief of staff. Shigemitsu wrote his name on the document at 9:04 A.M., officially ending a war that had stretched over 1,364 days, 5 hours, and 44 minutes. MacArthur, Nimitz, Halsey, and Rear Admiral Forrest Sherman then signed for the United States, followed by signatories for each of the Allied nations.

At 9:25 A.M., with hundreds of Navy and Army Air Force planes roaring overhead in a massive aerial display, MacArthur closed the ceremony with these words: "Let us pray that peace be now restored to the world and that God will preserve it always."

Five days later, on September 7, a simple ten-minute surrender ceremony was conducted at Tenth Army headquarters on Okinawa with many of the Army and Marine combat troops who had fought there looking on. Control of the main island and its satellites in the Ryukyus was thereby ceded by Japan to the United States, to serve for more than half a century as the western cornerstone of America's worldwide defensive network.

Soon the troops who witnessed this event would be scattered in all directions—some home to the States, others to North China and Korea, still others to Japan itself. But regardless of where they went or how far, the front-line GIs and Marines who survived Okinawa would never really leave it behind.

Their last great battle had been won, but the bloodshed and misery endured by the winners would stain their memories and disturb their dreams for as long as they lived.

Epilogue

Love Day Plus Sixty-two Years

IN A VERY REAL SENSE, the American invaders never left Okinawa. U.S. occupation of Japan's home islands officially ended in 1952, but it wasn't until May 1972, after twenty-seven years as an occupied U.S. territory, that the island sometimes known as "the Great Loo Choo" was returned to Japan.

Today, the Prefecture of Okinawa is an integral part of Japan proper, rather than a disrespected stepchild, as it was before and during World War II. Yet it also remains the keystone of America's strategic defenses in the Far East and has served as the launching pad for U.S. military operations in Korea, Vietnam, and even the Gulf War of the early 1990s.

As this is written, some 30,000 Army, Navy, Air Force, and Marine personnel and their families are still based on Okinawa. Kadena Airfield, home to the largest base post exchange in the Pacific region, is among fifteen major U.S. military installations there, and the port facilities in the bustling capital city of Naha remain under U.S. Navy jurisdiction. All told, the United States controls about 10 percent of Okinawa's total land area, and even that isn't enough to fully satisfy the training needs of U.S. infantry units stationed there.

Except for this ongoing foreign presence, however, the visible aftereffects of the invasion of 1945 have long since been smoothed away by time, vast infusions of Yankee dollars, and the dedicated efforts of the Okinawan people. White Beach, where many of the American assault troops landed on Love Day, is now rated among the most beautiful and popular tourist beaches in the Pacific. The city of Naha, left in utter ruin by U.S. incendiary bombs and high-explosive shells, has risen from its own ashes to become a gleaming financial, educational, and political center with a population of about 325,000. Its mile-long Kokusai Dori entertainment district—teeming with restaurants, nightclubs, bars, and gift shops—stretches through the heart of the city, drawing visitors from across Japan and the Pacific Rim.

Naha Airport, the hub of the Ryukus, offers daily commercial flights to and from Tokyo and other major Japanese cities. The airport is connected by the Okinawa Monorail and the Airport Expressway to a downtown filled with thriving banks, corporate and government offices, a nine-story shopping mall, a huge public market, and other amenities. The city is dotted with such familiar names as AT&T, Baskin-Robbins, Burger King, and Toys "R" Us—and towering above it all are the gleaming walls of a painstakingly reconstructed Shuri Castle, now a registered UNESCO world heritage site and Naha's most popular tourist attraction. The old town of Shuri is now part of metropolitan Naha, which stretches north to the invasion beaches.

Kakazu Ridge remains where it always was, but few American veterans would recognize it today for the rows of apartment buildings surrounding it. Many of the smaller hills that formed lynchpins of the Shuri Defense Zone are virtually unidentifiable.

Some of the ornate family tombs that dotted the rural landscape more than sixty years ago are still in evidence on the hillsides, but their numbers are noticeably fewer than in 1945. Many of the tombs were damaged beyond repair during the battle and have been removed and replaced by much smaller burial chambers, partly because of cultural changes and partly because of a great scarcity of usable land. In Naha and other cities, dense development makes residential yards virtually nonexistent, and only residents who can provide proof of adequate off-street parking space are allowed to purchase automobiles. Hence, the average city dweller travels mainly by bus, train, or monorail.

Near Itoman City at the southern end of the island, memories of the war's brutal toll are kept alive in Peace Memorial Park, site of the Okinawa Prefecture Memorial Museum and the huge Cornerstone of Peace monument honoring the battle's civilian and military dead. More than 100 smaller monuments have also been erected in the area, which is near Hill 89, where Generals Ushijima and Cho committed hara-kiri, and the so-called "Suicide Cliffs," where many Okinawans and Japanese leaped to their deaths rather than surrender.

TODAY'S OKINAWA is a land of striking opposites to many who visit there. Despite its wartime ordeal and striking postwar urbanization, the island and its 1.3 million inhabitants also project an amazing sense of stability and sameness. The countryside is still a neat patchwork of cultivated fields and small, tidy farmhouses with white cement-block walls and red tile roofs, where ancient traditions are still honored.

Most natives enjoy remarkably long, healthy lives. In fact, they boast the highest life expectancy rate on Earth, with native-born males living an average of 90.1 years and native-born females an average of 93.2 years. This is attributable to a healthful diet emphasizing fish, pork, and sea vegetables; a temperate climate with a year-round average temperature of seventy-two degrees; and a low-stress, physically active lifestyle.

Farming remains a principal source of livelihood and places Okinawa among the world leaders in the production of sugar cane, pineapples, papayas, and other tropical fruits. The people also continue to excel in the production of pottery, textiles, and glassware.

In addition, many Okinawans have derived a comfortable living from their uninvited American guests, and relations between U.S. military personnel and the native population have generally been cordial. But civilian resentment of the continuing large numbers of U.S. troops and dependents stationed on Okinawa has gradually grown. The feeling is simply that, after sixty-plus years, it's time to reduce—if not eliminate—the American military presence.

Consequently, arrangements were being made in early 2007 to transfer the majority of Okinawa-based Marines to Guam as soon as living quarters can be constructed there—although about 5,000 Marines are expected to remain on Okinawa. A timetable also has been established for turning the busy Port of Naha over to Japanese administration.

EXCEPT FOR BRIEF VISITS, former Marine PFC *Harry Bender* never returned to his native Chicago after the war. The weeks he spent on Okinawa in 1945 were the most agonizing time of Bender's life, but that didn't keep him from falling in love with the Pacific and deciding to settle in Honolulu—where he still makes his home today.

HARRY BENDER

In 1951, Bender became one of a handful of battle veterans who chose to return to Okinawa to live. As a civilian employee of the U.S. Army Corps of Engineers, he found the island vastly changed from the devastated wasteland of six years earlier but still very much a work in progress.

"There was new construction everywhere you looked," he recalled. "The Korean War was going full blast, and Okinawa was the main jumping-off place for our planes, supplies, and combat units bound for the fighting."

Bender lived and worked on the island until 1956, and, during those five years, he saw Okinawa's infrastructure not only rebuilt from the ground up but expanded far beyond anything that prewar Okinawans could have envisioned. "Those muddy trails we traveled in 1945 were transformed into modern four-lane highways," he said, "and towns that had practically been blasted off the map during the battle sprouted into thriving cities."

Since moving back to Honolulu, Bender has returned to Okinawa for periodic visits, most recently in October 2006. On each trip, he marvels anew at the island's transformation.

"Except for the monuments down at the southern end of the island, there's no evidence left of what happened here during the war," he said. "Naha has become a really impressive city with all kinds of high-rise buildings, and when I drive along palm-lined Highway 1, it looks just like a major street in Honolulu."

R..V. BURGIN

FORMER MARINE SERGEANT *R. V. Burgin* has made Texas his permanent home since the war, but he, too, has been drawn back to the Pacific region—especially to Australia, where, as a young recruit in 1943, he met Florence Riseley, a girl from Melbourne who became his wife. The Burgins, who celebrated their sixtieth wedding anniversary in January 2007, have spent large portions of the postwar years in the "Land Down Under," where R.V.'s old K/3/5 buddy, ex-Sergeant *Hank Boyes,* has lived since the late 1940s. The rest of the time, Burgin can be found in or near the Dallas suburb of Lancaster, gardening, fishing, serving as secretary of the K/3/5 veterans organization, and producing its quarterly newsletter.

BILL LEYDEN

Among the recipients of that newsletter is Harry Bender's old buddy from K/3/5's First Platoon, former PFC *Bill Leyden*, who took his two Purple Hearts back to his hometown of Hempstead, Long Island, after the war. He shunned routine employment to travel the country as a professional golfer—despite the fact that he was missing a finger and still carried chunks of Japanese shrapnel in both knees. On Veterans Day 2003, still aggrieved over the loss of his friend and squad leader *Leonard Ahner* on Okinawa, Leyden was honored as Hempstead's "Veteran of the Year."

Former K/3/5 Corporal *Dan Lawler* traded his .30-caliber machine gun for a job with a local baking company in 1946 back at his birthplace of Glens Falls, New York—sometimes known as "Hometown U.S.A."—and reestablished contact with his boyhood friend *Jimmy Butterfield*, who had been blinded in both eyes on Okinawa. A high point of Lawler's postwar life came during his honeymoon in 1950, when he and his new bride

JIMMY BUTTERFIELD

traveled to Washington and called on then-Senator *Paul Douglas* of Illinois, who had served with Lawler on Okinawa as the Marine Corps' oldest private. "He recognized me immediately," Lawler recalled, "and he invited us into his private office ahead of about 200 other people who were waiting to see him. He had to shake hands with his left hand because he couldn't use his wounded right arm at all." In recent years, Lawler, along with Butterfield and several other area WWII veterans, has frequently visited local high schools to tell of battle experiences and show off Lawler's impressive collection of Okinawa souvenirs.

STERLING MACE

After seeing many close friends killed or maimed in combat and undertaking the wrenching task of visiting the mother of a buddy killed at Peleliu when he returned to the States in June 1945, ex-Corporal *Sterling Mace* managed to regain his irrepressible sense of humor. He attended art school and later became manager of the theater at New York's Jones Beach State Park, where he developed friendships with singer Guy Lombardo and many other celebrities. He and his wife, Joyce, now live in retirement in St. Pete Beach, Florida.

Former PFC *Gene Sledge,* the introspective young mortarman of K/3/5, returned to his native Alabama after the war to become a biology professor at the University of Montevallo. His sensitive memoir, *With the Old Breed at Peleliu and Okinawa,* first published in 1981, has become one of the most widely read and acclaimed books of its type to come out of World War II and is often used as a supplementary text for college courses in twenti-

GENE SLEDGE

eth-century history. Because of the book's success, Sledgehammer also appeared in several TV documentaries on Okinawa and Peleliu and frequently served as a spokesman for Marine veterans of these battles. He died of cancer in 2002.

Tank commander *Jack Armstrong* returned to Texas and a job as an apprentice in the pressroom of the *Dallas Morning News* and later owned and managed an automobile service business for thirty-plus years. In 2001, some fifty-eight years after dropping out of high school to join the Marines, Armstrong received his high school diploma at age seventy-six. Two years later, he finally was awarded military disability for damage to his ears suffered while commanding the "Ticket to Tokyo" on Okinawa. He still works every day as a school crossing guard for the Duncanville, Texas, Independent School District and stays in touch with his old buddies from the First Marine Tank Battalion, *Floyd Cockerham* and *Frank Nemec.*

Despite his wartime reputation for attracting trouble like a magnet, Armstrong's fellow Marine tanker, former Private *Howard Towry,* demonstrated both courage and compassion at the end of the Okinawa campaign by rescuing a Japanese doctor and his nurse-wife from almost certain death and taking them to safety in a rear area. (Never mind that he accomplished this good deed in a stolen jeep.) After serving in North China and receiving his discharge, the free-wheeling Towry lived briefly in Dallas, but when the Korean War broke out in 1950, he joined the Air Force and served for seventeen years, retiring as a sergeant and settling in Mississippi. In 1986, the onetime eighth-grade dropout earned a bachelor's degree from the University of Southern Mississippi. He and his wife now own and operate a golf course at Fernwood, south of Jackson.

RAY SCHLINDER

After his courageous, one-man grenade offensive and near-death experience on Sugar Loaf Hill, Corporal *Ray Schlinder* spent nine and a half months in various military hospitals from Guam to Pearl Harbor to San Francisco to Farragut, Idaho. Along the way, he had a couple more brushes with death, and he still carries a piece of Japanese shrapnel embedded in his liver. After his discharge in February 1946, Schlinder returned to his adopted home state of Wisconsin, where he still spends his summers (he moves to Florida in the winter). He has served as president of the Sixth Marine Division Association, and, for most of his life, he maintained close friendships with two of Okinawa's Medal of Honor recipients, Corporal *Dick Bush*, who died in 2004, and Corporal (later Lieutenant General) *Jim Day*, who died in 1999. An unforgettable moment for Schlinder occurred in January 1998, when he and his wife, Margaret, were invited to the White House for President Bill Clinton's presentation of the MOH to General Day. Schlinder had his photo taken with President and Mrs. Clinton, "and I even got a kiss on the cheek from Hillary," he says

DICK BUSH

proudly. Many in his old outfit feel that Schlinder deserves his own medal for "conspicuous gallantry."

Another hero of Sugar Loaf Hill, former 22nd Marines squad leader *Walt Rutkowski,* who was inches away from Major *Henry Courtney* when Courtney was killed by a Japanese shell, returned to his native Chicago after his discharge in February 1946 with only a Purple Heart to show for his bravery. He soon found a job with an oil refinery design company, where he remained for forty-one years. For the past half century, he and his wife have made their home in Mount Prospect, Illinois.

Former PFC *Wendell Majors,* who also accompanied Major Courtney in the charge up Sugar Loaf and saw his Company G, Second Battalion, 22nd Marines, lose 231 of its 238 men before the hill was taken, brought his own Purple Heart home to Searcy, Arkansas, after the war. Within a couple of years, however, he moved to California and bought thirty acres near the town of Reedley, where he still lives. He visited Okinawa in 1987 but found no traces of the hell he experienced there. "I had a guardian angel watching over me," he says of his escape from Sugar Loaf. "Otherwise, I'd never have gotten off that hill alive."

MELVIN GRANT

Marine Corporal *Melvin Grant,* whose brother, Private *Scott Grant,* was killed within a few hundred yards of him during the last stages of the Okinawa campaign, felt the touch of God's hand when he was reunited with his wife, Kate, and his daughter, Laquetta, after the war. He entered the ministry and remained an active pastor for nearly sixty years, serving a total of ten churches in five states and becoming an ordained bishop in the Church of God. But he always remained a Marine as well, wearing his "dress blues" proudly to scores of military functions through the years. As famed author-historian Stephen Ambrose told Melvin during an interview in the late 1990s: "You are one of the only Marines I've ever known who went on to become a pastor. I want to shake your hand and tell you how much we all appreciate what you did." The Reverend Grant and Kate now live in retirement in Moore, Oklahoma.

Following his retirement from the Marine Corps in 1963 as a brigadier general, Melvin Grant's battalion commander, *Spencer Berger,* returned to law school (at age fifty and after a twenty-eight-year hiatus) to complete his degree at the University of Virginia, then devoted most of his attention to raising three daughters. He later became a wheeler-dealer corporate industrialist, buying and operating various companies, including the nation's oldest forging plant (founded in 1828) in Auburn, New York. As the last living U.S. battalion commander in the Peleliu and Okinawa campaigns, Berger observed his ninety-third birthday in December 2006. He currently divides his time between a summer home at Skaneateles, New York, and winter quarters in Savannah, Georgia.

After leading his antitank platoon through four major Pacific campaigns, Tech Sergeant *Porter McLaughlin* was among the first Okinawa veterans to return to civilian life. After his discharge from the Army in October 1945, he went home to Oregon and resumed his prewar occupation as a commercial deep-sea fisherman. But after a few years, he enrolled at the University of Portland, earned a degree in secondary education, and began teaching

PORTER MCLAUGHLIN

government, history, and English in a Portland high school, where his students were invariably impressed when they learned of McLaughlin's wartime experiences. He later moved with his wife and three sons to Salinas, California—a few miles from Fort Ord, where he'd taken basic training in 1942—continuing a thirty-year teaching career that ended with his retirement in 1983. McLaughlin cherishes the two samurai swords he brought home from the Pacific—but not the several pieces of Japanese shrapnel he still carries from Kwajalein—and he stays in close touch with ex-Sergeant *John Knorr,* one of his former squad leaders, who lives in Milwaukee. Their mutual friend and 32nd Infantry comrade, ex-Sergeant *George Murphy,* a Silver Star recipient for gallantry at Attu, died in 2004.

DOUG AITKEN

Doug Aitken, the young radar officer on the kamikaze-killing destroyer *Hugh Hadley,* remained on active duty with the Navy for thirty-one years. After transferring to the Navy Supply Corps in 1947, he served in numerous shipboard and shore-based positions, including deputy commander of the Naval Supply Systems Command. In 1974, after service aboard the U.S.S. *Ranger* during the Vietnam War, Captain Aitken retired from the service but continued to work as a civilian employee of the Navy until 1984. His home in Danville, California, contains a treasure trove of *Hadley* memorabilia, and he serves as official historian for the ship's reunion group. Aitken and his wife, Jeanne Marie, have three grown children and seven grandchildren. Among ex-shipmates with whom they stay in touch is former Lieutenant (j.g.) *Bill Winter,* the only other surviving officer from the *Hadley,* who lives in Boulder, Colorado.

Ben McDonald, who graduated from the University of Texas in January 1945, just in time to serve as a fledgling gunnery officer aboard the cruiser *Wichita* as a brand-new ensign, returned to the UT Law School after his release from active duty in June 1946 and obtained his law degree there in 1949. Since then, he has served as a trial attorney, partner in a law firm, special assistant to the attorney general of Texas, teacher of law and economics at four different colleges, and mayor of Corpus Christi. The author of more than twenty-five articles and books on subjects ranging from oil and gas law to kamikazes, McDonald talks frequently with former *Wichita* shipmate (and fellow great-grandfather) *Les Caffey,* who lives in New Braunfels, Texas.

After the war, Gunner's Mate *Hank Kalinofsky* swapped his Navy whites for the blue uniform of a Washington, D.C., police officer, serving twenty-seven years as a patrolman and working every presidential inaugural parade from Dwight Eisenhower to Gerald Ford. He retired as a desk sergeant in 1976 and now lives in Annapolis, Maryland, not far from the Naval Academy, where the U.S. Navy Memorial bears his picture. Kalinofsky and his wife have three daughters, ten grandchildren, and six great-grandchildren. Turkey remains one of his favorite foods, but he's careful to avoid eating it on Good Friday.

Two decorated veterans of the 96th Deadeye Division—former mortarman *Don Dencker* and ex–tank commander *Bob Green*—have written and published their own memoir-style books about the Pacific war. Dencker, a Minnesota native who now lives in Sun Prairie, Wisconsin, earned a master's degree in engineering after Army service at Leyte, Okinawa, and later Korea. He is the author of *Love Company: Infantry Combat Against the Japanese in World War II*, a 355-page volume published in 2002. Green, a West Texas cattleman and Silver Star recipient who still lives on the ranch founded by his father in 1881, published his hardcover memoir, *Okinawa Odyssey*, in 2004.

Only a handful of men from the 96th Recon Troop, the first U.S. Army unit to locate the outer works of the Japanese defensive system guarding the approaches to Kakazu Ridge, remain alive as this is written. One is former Corporal *Lamont Clark*, an eighty-five-year-old Wisconsin native who earned a Bronze Star and a Purple Heart in the bloody ambush of April 4, 1945, but never received either medal. Another is former PFC *Bill Strain*, who, with a few buddies, fought off hordes of Japanese by listening to their curses when their grenades failed to ignite during a nighttime attack. Strain and his wife make their home in Arkadelphia, Arkansas.

BILL STRAIN

BECAUSE OF THE ENORMITY of the Okinawa campaign, tens of thousands of American veterans who participated in it, on one level or another, are still very much alive as this is written. Yet the youngest of these men are now past eighty, and their numbers dwindle each day.

In numerous cases, close relatives of those who didn't make it back from Okinawa have devoted themselves—and countless hours of effort—to preserving the memory of lost loved ones and making sure that their courage and sacrifices aren't forgotten. Among the most striking examples of this are Frank Niader, younger brother of Marine Private *Bill Niader,* who was killed in action on June 12, 1945, during the fight for Kunishi Ridge. Frank Niader has turned his Clifton, New Jersey, home into a veritable memorial to his brother and has tried to contact every Marine who knew or crossed paths with Bill. As a result, he has established friendships with scores of veterans across the country and has become a leading spokesman for veterans' causes in his area.

QUENTIN "MONK" MEYER

A Brookings, Oregon, woman, Holly Beyer, has performed a similar labor of love in memory of her late uncle, First Lieutenant *Quentin "Monk" Meyer,* whom she never met but who was engaged to Beyer's mother at the time of his death on May 11, 1945, as U.S. forces launched their assaults on the Shuri Line. In an ironic turn of fate after the war, Beyer's mother, Francie Walton, married Monk's younger brother, Marine Corporal *Thomas "Pete" Meyer,* who became Beyer's father. After her parents died several years ago, Beyer discovered a box filled with letters written by Monk to her mother from the Pacific. This triggered a coast-to-coast Internet search for more information on Monk that spanned countless hours and eventually led Beyer to many Marines who had served with her uncle and several who were with him the day he was killed.

⁓

ALTHOUGH OKINAWA received mostly cursory attention from the news media during the fighting, today's typical American adult readily recognizes the name and the fact that a "big battle" took place there. More recently, as the fiftieth and sixtieth anniversaries of the battle and the end of World War II have come and gone, numerous local newspaper and TV reporters have discovered heroic Okinawa veterans in their midst—usually disguised as ordinary senior citizens—and retold their stories.

Still, it seems a safe bet that relatively few Americans fully grasp the scope and ruthlessness of the battle, or its profound impact on the way the war ended and the direction of the peace that followed—much less the vital lessons that Okinawa continues to hold for the citizens of Earth.

As virtually every person who lived through that horrific struggle in the spring of 1945 would attest, these are lessons that civilization can ill afford to disregard. In the shrinking, dangerous world of the twenty-first century, the lessons of Okinawa are as crucial as ever to the survival of humankind. They will almost certainly remain so long after the battle's last warriors have marched off into the mists of history.

On June 23, 2006, to mark the sixty-first anniversary of the battle's end, the governor of Okinawa Prefecture, Keiichi Inamine, stood near the Cornerstone of Peace and spoke of the continuing significance of the monument and the more than 240,000 victims' names engraved on it. "In the world today, we see a repetition of tragedies caused by the vicious chain of violence and retaliation, such as in regional conflicts and terrorism," Inamine said. "It is important for each and every one of us to have a strong will to actively seek peace."

As the final, ultimate struggle of World War II, Okinawa chillingly demonstrated that the human capacity for slaughter, savagery, and chaos is almost limitless. But the monument—and the resurrected Okinawa of the twenty-first century—stand as proof that people's inherent yearning for peace, mercy, and justice can still prevail.

Sources

PROLOGUE

The reconstruction of the incidents of June 10, 1945, is based primarily on the author's interviews with Sergeant Jack Armstrong. The brief summary of the battle incorporates background information from Appleman's *Okinawa: The Last Battle*, Belote's *Typhoon of Steel*, McMillan's *The Old Breed*, and Morison's *History of United States Naval Operations in World War II, Vol. XIV: Victory in the Pacific*.

I. BUILDING AN ICEBERG

Author interviews with PFC Bill Leyden, Sergeant R. V. Burgin, PFC Harry Bender, Seaman Les Caffey, Gunner's Mate Hank Kalinofsky, Sergeant Walt McNeel, and Lieutenant Commander Lewis Lacy help set the scene as the massive U.S. invasion force gathers at Okinawa and prepares to land. Also contributing to the narrative are the collected letters and memorabilia of Lieutenant Quentin "Monk" Meyer and PFC Gene Sledge's memoir, *With the Old Breed at Peleliu and Okinawa*.

Background on the buildup of U.S. forces in the Pacific, the Japanese decision to fortify Okinawa as a final barrier against invasion of the Home Island, and the military commanders involved on both sides is drawn from numerous published sources, including Astor's *Operation Iceberg*, Belote's *Typhoon of Steel*, the Marine Corps monograph *Okinawa: Victory in the Pacific*, Appleman's *Okinawa: The Last Battle*, and Morison's *History of United States Naval Operations in World War II, Vol. XIV*.

Notes

Page 12   *Nimitz knew it was going to be a hard sell:* The interaction among King, Nimitz, Spruance, and Buckner, as well as King's initial opposition to the Okinawa invasion plan, are described in Belote's *Typhoon of Steel* and Leckie's *Okinawa: The Last Battle of World War II.*

II. "LIKE A STROLL IN THE PARK"

The panorama of the unopposed landing by U.S. Army and Marine troops is re-created in eyewitness accounts based on interviews with Armstrong, Bender, Burgin, Corporal Elliott Burnett, Leyden, Sergeant Alex Henson, Corporal Sterling Mace, Corporal Dan Lawler, and Private Howard Towry, all of whom came ashore in the First Marine Division sector.

Glimpses of simultaneous action in the 96th Infantry Division sector are drawn from an interview with Corporal Don Dencker as well as from Dencker's book, *Love Company.* Conditions on the outlying islands of Keise Shima and the Kerama Retto are described in author interviews with Army PFC Ed K. Austin of the 532nd Field Artillery and PFC William Kottas, a 77th Division infantryman. In another author interview, Sergeant Porter McLaughlin recounts action in the sector assigned to the Army's Seventh Division.

The letters of Lieutenant Meyer and an author interview with Private Gil Quintanilla re-create the dilemma of a "lost" unit forced to spend Love Day night on a sea infested with suicidal Japanese frogmen.

Published sources providing additional material include Astor's *Operation Iceberg,* Belote's *Typhoon of Steel,* Leckie's *Okinawa: The Last Battle of World War II,* McMillan's *The Old Breed,* Miller's *D-Days in the Pacific,* Love's *The History of the Seventh Infantry Division in World War II* and *The Deadeyes: History of the 96th Infantry Division,* and Sledge's *With the Old Breed at Peleliu and Okinawa.*

Notes

Page 52   *With the "stroll in the park" continuing:* The statements by Generals del Valle, Shepherd, and Geiger, and Admiral Turner have been quoted in several previously published sources, including Belote's *Typhoon of Steel* and Leckie's *Okinawa: The Last Battle of World War II.*

III. KIDS' GAMES, PONY RIDES, AND BARBECUE

The mostly carefree—but occasionally tragic—scenes across the huge American beachhead on Love Day-plus-1 are re-created in author interviews with Dencker, Grant, Henson, Leyden, Mace, McLaughlin, and Towry.

Additional details are provided by Sledge's memoir, *With the Old Breed at Peleliu and Okinawa,* and Dencker's memoir, *Love Company.* Histories of the First and Sixth Marine Divisions and the Seventh and 96th Infantry Divisions, as well as Appleman's *Okinawa: The Last Battle* and the Marine Corps monograph *Okinawa: Victory in the Pacific,* contribute additional background and overall perspective.

IV. A NASTY SURPRISE ON THE WAY SOUTH

The sudden shock and horror of the invading Americans' first major encounter with Japanese troops in strength is captured in author interviews with 96th Recon Troop veterans Corporal Lamont Clark and PFC Rudy Pizio, who were on the scene, and PFC Bill Strain, who had many close buddies there. Invaluable details are provided by Warrick's *Ghost Troop of the Ryukyus,* which includes a detailed first-person account of the bloody fight near Uchitomari by Corporal John Cain, who was too ill to be interviewed by the author at the time this was written.

Excellent overviews of the battlefield action and the U.S. strategy on April 4 to 9, as the 96th Division launched its costly assaults on the Kakazu ridgeline are included in Belote's *Typhoon of Steel,* Appleman's *Okinawa: The Last Battle,* Dencker's *Love Company,* and Leckie's *Okinawa: The Last Battle of World War II.* Other valuable sources include author interviews with McLaughlin and Sergeant John Knorr and Love's *History of the Seventh Infantry Division.*

V. A DIVINE AND DEADLY WIND

Key details about the events leading to the Japanese decision to launch an all-out campaign of kamikaze attacks against U.S. Navy ships, which reached its apex at Okinawa, are presented from the Japanese perspective in Inoguchi and Nakajima's *The Divine Wind.* As officers in Japan's

Kamikaze Special Attack Corps, both authors possessed unique knowledge of its philosophy and tactics. On the American side, Morison's *History of U.S. Naval Operations, Vol. XIV* offers equally important insights into the American response to the aerial suicide onslaught.

Other published sources contributing important information on the series of "Floating Chrysanthemum" suicide assaults, through which Japan hoped to decimate the giant armada of U.S. warships supporting the Okinawa invasion, include Astor's *Operation Iceberg,* Belote's *Typhoon of Steel,* and Becton's *The Ship That Would Not Die.*

In author interviews, Kalinofsky and Ensign Ben McDonald capture the terror of men aboard targeted U.S. ships; Gunner's Mate Don Brockman recounts the wholesale destruction of enemy suicide boats; and Lieutenant Francis Ferry, one of the Navy fliers who helped sink the super-battleship *Yamato,* gives a moment-by-moment eyewitness account.

NOTES

Page 89   *One early volunteer for the suicide missions:* The pilot's letter is quoted in Inoguchi and Nakajima's *The Divine Wind.*

Page 90   *Admiral Ohnishi was grim-faced:* The admiral's comments are also quoted in *The Divine Wind.*

VI. DEATH IN THE HILLS, DEATH AT HOME

The stark contrast between the costly assaults by Army troops against Kakazu Ridge and the virtual "vacation" being enjoyed at the same time by most of the First Marine Division is illustrated through author interviews with Armstrong, Bender, Burgin, PFC Jerome Connolly, Dencker, PFC Francis Lambert, and McLaughlin. Meanwhile, other author interviews with PFC Paulie deMeis, Grant, Lieutenant Bob Green, PFC Americo Milonni, and PFC Bill Pierce provide eyewitness accounts of the Sixth Marine Division's fierce fighting on the Motobu Peninsula and isolated action by the Seventh Marine Regiment.

Sledge's *With the Old Breed at Peleliu and Okinawa,* plus author interviews with Leyden, Armstrong, and Dencker, offer insights into the reaction by GIs and Marines to the death of President Franklin Roosevelt. Other published sources contributing overviews of the period of April 9 to 24 include Astor's *Operation Iceberg,* McMillan's *The Old Breed,* Dencker's *Love Company,* Green's *Okinawa Odyssey,* Appleman's

Okinawa: The Last Battle, the monograph *Okinawa: Victory in the Pacific,* and the histories of the Sixth Marine Division and the Seventh and 96th Infantry Divisions.

NOTES

Page 116   *General Shepherd knew none of these specifics:* Geiger's underestimate of Japanese strength on Mobuto Peninsula and his subsequent decision to press the attack despite the weariness of his infantry regiments are cited in Belote's *Typhoon of Steel.*

Page 120   *"[I]t was as difficult as I can conceive":* Colonel Shapley is quoted in Belote's *Typhoon of Steel.*

Page 122   *"I'm sending G Company to reinforce you":* Colonel May's message to Colonel King is quoted in *Typhoon of Steel* and Leckie's *Okinawa: The Last Battle of World War II.*

VII. A WALL OF STONE AND FLAME

Author interviews with McLaughlin, along with McLaughlin's collection of letters, capture the irony, incongruity, and bitter humor of this chapter's opening segment. When the scene shifts to the island of Ie Shima and the death of combat correspondent Ernie Pyle, Nichols's *Ernie's War: The Best of Ernie Pyle's World War II Dispatches* offers excellent insights into Pyle's personality and his high regard both by U.S. troops in battle and civilians on the home front. Astor's *Operation Iceberg* and Belote's *Typhoon of Steel* also helped in re-creating the events leading to Pyle's death.

On Okinawa proper, as Army troops advanced south from Kakazu Ridge to the next major Japanese defensive stronghold along the Maeda Escarpment, major Marine units joined the southward push for the first time. Author interviews with Burgin, Mace, and Strain, plus Sledge's *With the Old Breed at Peleliu and Okinawa,* Green's *Okinawa Odyssey,* and Dencker's *Love Company,* illustrate the costly—and increasingly desperate—nature of the campaign.

VIII. MUD, BLOOD, AND MAY-HEM

Even as the war in Europe ended, early May was the worst of times for U.S. combat troops on Okinawa, as author interviews with Armstrong, Corporal Floyd Cockerham, Knorr, McLaughlin, Sergeant George Peto, and Corporal Ray Schlinder illustrate. They reveal the stress and sense of doom that broke men's spirits as incessant rains turned southern Okinawa into a vast corpse-strewn quagmire.

Valuable published sources contributing to this chapter include Appleman's *Okinawa: The Last Battle,* Astor's *Operation Iceberg,* Belote's *Typhoon of Steel,* Benis Frank's *Okinawa: Touchstone to Victory,* McMillan's *The Old Breed,* Sledge's *With the Old Breed at Peleliu and Okinawa,* and the official *History of the Sixth Marine Division.*

IX. BITTER TOLL AT SUGAR LOAF

Letters written in May 1945 by PFC Al Henderson to his wife in Arkansas describe the dismal weather conditions, hint at increasing desperation among American front-line troops on Okinawa, and set the stage for the bloodiest phase of the campaign. Men of the Sixth Marine Division, swept up in the terrible fight for Sugar Loaf Hill—including Corpsman Frank Mack, Private Wendell Majors, Pierce, Sergeant Walt Rutkowski, Schlinder, Sherer, and PFC Dick Whitacre—relive their personal agonies and those of their comrades in author interviews. Particularly valuable are the daily entries in a diary kept by Sergeant Mel Heckt.

Among published sources, Hallas's *Killing Ground on Okinawa,* a book devoted entirely to Sugar Loaf, provides the most detailed account of the Marines' dozen futile attempts to take and hold the hill and their eventual triumph. The Sixth Marine Division's official history also describes the action in great detail. Background is provided by Astor's *Operation Iceberg,* Feifer's *Tennozan: The Battle of Okinawa and the Atomic Bomb,* Lacey's *Stay Off the Skyline: The Sixth Marine Division on Okinawa,* and the Marine Corps monograph *Okinawa: Victory in the Pacific.*

X. THE LIMITS OF HUMAN ENDURANCE

The First Marine Division's late May assaults against Japanese strongholds at Dasheki Ridge, Wana Ridge, and Wana Draw—and their devastating physical and psychological impact—are recounted largely through author interviews. Among the interviewees are Armstrong, Bender, Burgin, Cockerham, Leyden, Mace, Nemec, and Quintanilla. Sledge's memoir *With the*

Old Breed at Peleliu and Okinawa and McMillan's *The Old Breed* contribute important background.

The collected letters and memorabilia of Monk Meyer, along with eyewitness accounts, re-create the scene and circumstances surrounding the young lieutenant's death. A letter by Al Henderson provides a poignant close to the chapter.

XI. DIVINE WIND—PART II

The U.S. Navy's response to Japan's ongoing kamikaze offensive—and that offensive's ultimate collapse—are dramatically illustrated by author interviews with several survivors of those suicide attacks. The story of the kamikaze-killing destroyer *Hugh Hadley*, which forms the centerpiece for this chapter, is graphically told by Captain Doug Aitken, Seamen Fred Hammers, Leo Helling, Don Hile, and Jay Holmes, and Lieutenant Bill Winter.

Previously published sources providing important background include Astor's *Operation Iceberg*, Belote's *Typhoon of Steel*, Inoguchi and Nakajima's *The Divine Wind*, Morison's *History of United States Naval Operation in World War II, Vol. XIV*, the monograph *Okinawa: Victory in the Pacific*, and Sherrod's *History of Marine Aviation in World War II*.

XII. THE CROWDED, ANGRY SKIES

Author interviews with VMF-542(N)'s Sergeant McNeel and Lieutenants Arthur Arceneaux, Herbert Groff, and Frank O'Hara offer close-up views of the air war that raged over and on Okinawa, from dogfights with Japanese planes in pitch-darkness to the airborne commando assault on Yontan airfield.

Important background information on U.S. night-fighter squadrons and their heavy concentration at Okinawa is drawn from Astor's *Operation Iceberg*, Feifer's *Tennozan: The Battle of Okinawa and the Atomic Bomb*, and Sherrod's *History of Marine Corps Aviation in World War II*. General Curtis LeMay's biography, *Mission with LeMay*, offers an excellent overview of the B-29 bombing campaign against Japan and the role it played in the Okinawa campaign. The last gasps of the Kamikaze Special Attack Corps are described in Inoguchi and Nakajima's *The Divine Wind* and Morison's *History of United States Naval Operations in World War II, Vol. XIV*.

XIII. COLLAPSE OF THE SHURI LINE

Author interviews with Bender, Butterfield, Grant, McLaughlin, and PFC Manny Rivas—along with Sledge's *With the Old Breed at Peleliu and Okinawa*—paint a searing portrait of the climactic struggle as the Shuri Defense Zone slowly cracked and disintegrated.

McMillan's *The Old Breed* and the official histories of the Seventh and 96th Infantry Divisions and the Sixth Marine Division provide a panoramic overview of the fall of Shuri and the Japanese retreat southward. Other published sources contributing to this chapter include Appleman's *Okinawa: The Last Battle*, Astor's *Operation Iceberg*, Belote's *Typhoon of Steel*, Feifer's *Tennozan: The Battle of Okinawa and the Atomic Bomb*, Hallas's *Killing Ground on Okinawa*, Sherrod's *History of Marine Aviation in World War II*, and the monograph *Okinawa: Victory in the Pacific*.

NOTES

Page 262   *The news that Sugar Loaf had been secured*: The statements from General Shepherd and Colonel Robb are quoted in Hallas's *Killing Ground on Okinawa*.

Page 267   *Actually, however, the situation wasn't nearly as rosy*: The casualty figures listed here are cited in Belote's *Typhoon of Steel*.

Page 272   *"Although the forces of General Ushijima"*: Colonel Nist is quoted in Belote's *Typhoon of Steel*.

XIV: THE END OF AN ARMY

Author interviews with Armstrong, Lieutenant Colonel Spencer Berger, Corporal Claude Bohn, and Burgin made possible the re-creation of such episodes as Armstrong's final tank mission and Grant's futile search for his brother shortly before the latter's death. An interview with Frank Niader, along with various background materials supplied by Niader, were vital in reconstructing the circumstances surrounding the death of Niader's brother, Private Bill Niader.

Sledge's *With the Old Breed at Peleliu and Okinawa* provides key background on action by the First Marine Division at Kunishi Ridge. Other published sources supplying valuable information for this chapter include Appleman's *Okinawa: The Last Battle*, Belote's *Typhoon of Steel*, Feifer's *Tennozan: The Battle of Okinawa and the Atomic Bomb*, McMillan's *The*

Old Breed, and the official histories of the Sixth Marine Division and the Seventh Infantry Division.

Notes

Page 280   *"The present position will be defended":* Ushijima's order is quoted in Belote's *Typhoon of Steel.*

XV. A CIVILIAN CATASTROPHE

Author interviews with Berger, Dencker, Kottas, and Lawler offer dramatic glimpses of the plight of Okinawa's civilians during the battle and of the steps taken by Americans to prevent their slaughter. Dencker's *Love Company* describes one encounter between U.S. troops and civilians hiding in caves.

Feifer's *Tennozan: The Battle of Okinawa and the Atomic Bomb,* in particular, examines the civilian toll and its long-term effects on Okinawa in extraordinary detail, and Lardner's May 19, 1945, article in *The New Yorker* graphically reveals the attitude of American GIs and Marines toward the Okinawan natives. Other published sources contributing information to this chapter include Belote's *Typhoon of Steel,* Sledge's *With the Old Breed at Peleliu and Okinawa,* and the Sixth Marine Division history.

Notes

Page 310   *The girls at the devastated school in the bombed-out town:* Feifer's *Tennozan* estimates that "up to 100,000 civilians" perished during June but adds that the deaths were too numerous for a "precise count." The above figure represents two-thirds of the total estimated civilian deaths, which, according to Feifer, "final guesses" place at 150,000.

XVI. A SOMBER VICTORY

A number of published sources, including Appleman's *Okinawa: The Last Battle,* Belote's *Typhoon of Steel,* Feifer's *Tennozan: The Battle of Okinawa and the Atomic Bomb,* and the monograph *Okinawa: Victory in the Pacific,* provide details of General Buckner's death. Astor's *Operation Iceberg* includes details about the criticism directed at Buckner by several Stateside journalists, and an author interview with Bohn provides an eyewitness account of the general's death from a nearby ridge.

Among published sources, Belote offers the best overall description of the suicides of Generals Ushijima and Cho, and an author interview with McLaughlin, one of the nearest Americans to the scene at the time of the suicides, focuses on the emotional aftermath.

Additional author interviews with Bender and Peto add drama to the final hours of the battle, as do Sledge's *With the Old Breed at Peleliu and Okinawa* and Dencker's *Love Company.* The official histories of the Seventh Infantry and Sixth Marine Divisions provide overviews and background.

XVII. THE ATOMIC BOMB—AND REPRIEVE

Especially valuable insights into the political and diplomatic maneuverings in Tokyo and Washington that ultimately led to Japan's surrender are drawn from Morison's *History of United States Naval Operations in World War II, Vol. XIV,* Feifer's *Tennozan: The Battle of Okinawa and the Atomic Bomb,* and Allen and Polmar's *Code-Name Downfall: The Secret Plan to Invade Japan—and Why Truman Dropped the Bomb.* The same sources, as well as Belote's *Typhoon of Steel,* also describe U.S. moves to transform Okinawa from a battlefield to the primary staging point for the projected invasion of the Japanese home islands.

Author interviews with Armstrong, Burgin, Caffey, Grant, Kalinofsky, Majors, McDonald, and Towry, plus the published memoirs of Sledge and Dencker, capture the wide spectrum of feelings—gloom, tension, relief, and occasional humor—as Okinawa veterans saw their ordeal finally come to a close.

EPILOGUE: LOVE DAY PLUS SIXTY-TWO YEARS

Much of the portrait of modern-day Okinawa is derived from an author interview with Bender following his most recent return to the island in October 2006, during which he spent three weeks visiting former battle sites and current tourist attractions. Various Internet sources, including the Okinawa Prefecture and U.S. Marine Corps Web sites, Yahoo! Asia News, and Wikipedia, provide other up-to-date information.

The sketches of Okinawa veterans and their postwar activities are based on additional author interviews with Aitken, Armstrong, Berger, Beyer, Burgin, Butterfield, Caffey, Clark, Cockerham, Dencker, Grant, Green, Kalinofsky, Knorr, Lawler, Leyden, Mace, Majors, McDonald, McLaughlin, Niader, Nemec, Rutkowski, Schlinder, Strain, Towry, and Winter.

Bibliography

BOOKS

Allen, Thomas B., and Norman Polmar. *Code-Name Downfall: The Secret Plan to Invade Japan—and Why Truman Dropped the Bomb.* New York: Simon & Schuster, 1995.

Appleman, Roy E. *Okinawa: The Last Battle.* Washington, D.C.: The Center of Military History, U.S. Army, 1948.

Astor, Gerald. *Operation Iceberg: The Invasion and Conquest of Okinawa in World War II—An Oral History.* New York: Donald I. Fine, 1995.

Becton, F. Julian. *The Ship That Would Not Die.* Englewood Cliffs, N.J.: Prentice-Hall, 1980.

Belote, James H. and William M. *Typhoon of Steel: The Battle for Okinawa.* New York: Harper & Row, 1970.

Berger, Carl. *B-29, The Superfortress.* New York: Ballantine Books, 1970.

Birdsall, Steve. *Log of the Liberators.* New York: Doubleday & Company, 1973.

Craig, William. *The Fall of Japan.* New York: Dial Press, 1967.

Deadeyes 96th Infantry Division, The (Second Edition). Paducah, Ky.: Turner Publishing Company, 1998.

Dencker, Donald O. *Love Company: Infantry Combat Against the Japanese, World War II.* Manhattan, Kans.: Sunflower University Press, 2002.

Feifer, George. *Tennozan: The Battle of Okinawa and the Atomic Bomb.* New York: Ticknor & Fields, 1992.

Green, Bob. *Okinawa Odyssey.* Albany, Tex.: Bright Sky Press, 2004.

Frank, Benis M. *Okinawa: Touchstone to Victory.* New York: Ballantine Books, 1969.

Frank, Richard B. *Downfall: The End of the Imperial Japanese Empire.* New York: Penguin Books, 2001.

Hallas, James H. *Killing Ground on Okinawa: The Battle for Sugar Loaf Hill.* Westport, Conn.: Praeger, 1996.

Hersey, John. *Hiroshima*. New York: Alfred A. Knopf, 1946.

History of the Sixth Marine Division. Nashville: Battery Press, 1987.

Inoguchi, Rikihei. *The Divine Wind: Japan's Kamikaze Force in World War II*. New York: Bantam Books, 1978.

Lacey, Laura Homan. *Stay Off the Skyline: The Sixth Marine Division on Okinawa*. Washington: Potomac Books, 2005.

Lambert, Francis J. *Hell I've Been There*. Victoria, B.C., Canada: Trafford Publishing, 2003.

Leckie, Robert. *Okinawa: The Last Battle of World War II*. New York: Viking, 1995.

———. *Strong Men Armed: The United States Marines Against Japan*. New York: Random House, 1962.

LeMay, Curtis E. *Mission with LeMay: My Story*. Garden City, N.Y.: Doubleday & Company, 1965.

Love, Edmund G. *The Hourglass: A History of the 7th Infantry Division in World War II*. Nashville: The Battery Press, 1988.

Manchester, William. *The Glory and the Dream: A Narrative History of America, 1932–1972*. New York: Bantam Books, 1974.

McMillan, George. *The Old Breed: A History of the First Marine Division in World War II*. Washington, D.C.: Infantry Journal Press, 1949.

Miller, Donald I. *D-Days in the Pacific*. New York: Simon & Schuster, 2005.

Morison, Samuel Eliot. *History of United States Naval Operations in World War II, Vol. XIV: Victory in the Pacific*. New York: Little, Brown & Company, 1960.

Morrison, Wilbur H. *Point of No Return: The Story of the 20th Air Force*. New York: Times Books, 1979.

Nichols, Charles S., Jr., and Henry I. Shaw Jr. *Okinawa: Victory in the Pacific*. Washington, D.C.: Historical Branch, U.S. Marine Corps, 1955.

Nichols, David (editor). *Ernie's War: The Best of Ernie Pyle's World War II Dispatches*. New York: Random House, 1986.

Sherrod, Robert. *History of Marine Corps Aviation in World War II*. Washington, D.C.: Combat Forces Press, 1952.

Sledge, E. B. *With the Old Breed at Peleliu and Okinawa*. Novato, Calif.: Presidio Press, 1981.

Smith, Robert E. *A Marine in World War II*. Good Hope, Ill.: Robert E. Smith, 1993.

Thomas, Evan. *Sea of Thunder: Four Commanders and the Last Great Naval Campaign 1941–1945*. New York: Simon & Schuster, 2006.

Warren, James A. *American Spartans: The U.S. Marines: A Combat History from Iwo Jima to Iraq.* New York: Free Press, 2005.

Warrick, Clifford E. *Ghost Troop of the Ryukyus.* Vancouver, Washington.: Clifford Warrick, 2003.

Winton, John. *War in the Pacific: Pearl Harbor to Tokyo Bay.* New York: Mayflower Books, 1978.

PERIODICALS

Alexander, Joseph H. "Rifleman Sledge." *Leatherneck,* July 2001.

Astor, Gerald. "Killing Ground on Okinawa." *World War II* Magazine Presents Victory in the Pacific, Special Collector's Edition, 2005.

Lardner, John. "A Reporter on Okinawa." *The New Yorker,* May 26, 1945.

Leyden, Bill. "A Most Remarkable Marine." *The* (Huntington, Indiana) *Herald Press,* May 30, 2006.

Manchester, William. "The Bloodiest Battle of All." *New York Times Magazine,* June 14, 1987.

McDonald, Ben F. "Ground Zero at Nagasaki Was a Frightful Sight." *Corpus Christi* (Texas) *Caller-Times,* August 7, 2005.

Nordstrand, Dave. "As Courageous as You Can Get." *The* (Salinas) *Californian,* March 17, 2001.

Peto, George. "Worst Days of My Life." *Old Breed News,* October 1998.

Rhodes, Richard. "Living with the Bomb." *National Geographic,* August 2005.

Stebbins, Owen T. "Must Seize at Any Cost." *World War II,* September 1995.

Wendler, Henry O. "It's Over!" *Smithsonian,* August 2005. (Readers share memories of the end of World War II.)

Worden, William L. "The 7th Made It the Hard Way." *The Saturday Evening Post,* September 22, 1945.

AUTHOR INTERVIEWS
(Ranks shown at the time of the Okinawa campaign)

Lieutenant Doug Aitken, November 2005

Lieutenant Arthur Arceneaux, October 2006

Sergeant Jack Armstrong, September 2005, March 2006, August 2006

PFC Ed K. Austin, September 2005

PFC Harry Bender, October 2005, October 2006

Lieutenant Colonel Spencer Berger, October 2006

Holly Beyer, June 2005, August 2005

Corporal Claude Bohn, August 2006

Gunner's Mate Don Brockman, December 2005

Sergeant R. V. Burgin, July 2005, November 2005, April 2006

Corporal Elliott Burnett, October 2005

Corporal Jimmy Butterfield, January 2006

Seaman Les Caffey, October 2005

Corporal Lamont Clark, January 2006

Corporal Floyd Cockerham, March 2006

PFC (Medic) Jerome Connolly, January 2006

PFC W. R. Crow, November 2005

Corpsman Walter L. "Doc" Davidson, January 2006

PFC Paulie deMeis, April 2006

Corporal Don Dencker, September 2005

Lieutenant Francis Ferry, October 2005

Corporal Melvin Grant, February 2006

Lieutenant Bob Green, September 2005

Lieutenant Herbert Groff, October 2005

Seaman Fred Hammers, August 2006

Sergeant Mel Hecht, May 2006

Seaman Leo Helling, May 2006

Sergeant Alex Henson, November 2005

Radioman Irvin Herman, June 2005

Seaman Don Hile, May 2006

Seaman Jay Holmes, May 2006

Gunner's Mate Hank Kalinofsky, July 2006

Sergeant John Knorr, January 2006

PFC William Kottas, September 2005

Lieutenant Commander Lewis Lacy, October 2005

PFC Francis Lambert, September 2005

Corporal Dan Lawler, October 2005, January 2006, September 2006

PFC Bill Leyden, July 2005, October 2005

Corporal Sterling Mace, October 2005

Corpsman Frank Mack, March 2006

PFC Wendell Majors, June 2006

Sergeant Jim Mattern, February 2006

Seaman Bill McCauley, December 2005

Ensign Ben McDonald, October 2006

Tech Sergeant Porter McLaughlin, July 2005, November 2005

Sergeant Walt McNeel, August 2005

PFC Americo "Moe" Milonni, May 2006

PFC J. E. Moore, March 2006

PFC Frank Nemec, October 2005

Frank Niader, August 2006

Corporal Laurence "Buck" Norris, November 2005

Lieutenant Frank O'Hara, September 2005

Sergeant George Peto, October 2006

PFC Bill Pierce, March 2006

PFC Rudy Pizio, January 2006

Seaman Zane Puckett, October 2005

Private Gil Quintanilla, November 2005

PFC Manny Rivas, July 2005

Sergeant Walt Rutkowski, May 2006

Corporal Ray Schlinder, March 2006

Captain Bob Sherer, April 2006

Machinist's Mate Ted Stoval, March 2006

PFC Bill Strain, November 2005

Private Howard Towry, November 2005

Seaman Robert Welch, November 2005

PFC Dick Whitaker, March 2006

Private Jim White, March 2006

Lieutenant Bill Winter, November 2005

Corporal Charles Womack, September 2005

MISCELLANEOUS

PFC Martin L. Allday, Corpsman Bert Cooper, Lieutenant Francis Ferry, Sergeant Trenton Fowler, Gunner's Mate Hank Kalinofsky, Sergeant Raymond Maxwell, Lieutenant James K. Nance, Sergeant Charles Pase, Lieutenant David Straus, Ensign Lyle Tennis, Private Howard Towry. Oral histories (all courtesy National Museum of the Pacific War).

Corporal Richard E. Bush. Medal of Honor citation.

Corporal R. V. Burgin. Filmed interviews (courtesy R. V. Burgin).

PFC Jerome E. Connolly Sr. Unpublished memoir (courtesy Jerome E. Connolly Sr.).

Major Henry A. Courtney Jr. Medal of Honor citation.

D. M. Giangreco. "Operation Downfall: U.S. Plans and Japanese Counter-Measures." Symposium on plans for U.S. invasion of Japan, University of Kansas, February 16, 1998.

PFC Alfred E. Henderson. Collected letters (courtesy Lisa Bess).

Corporal Dan Lawler. Oral history (courtesy Dan Lawler).

PFC Bill Leyden. Filmed interview (courtesy Bill Leyden).

Corporal Sterling Mace. Oral history (courtesy Sterling Mace).

Marine Night Fighter Squadron 542. Yearbook-style memorial tribute and unit history (courtesy Walt McNeel).

Sergeant Porter McLaughlin. Collected letters (courtesy Porter McLaughlin).

Lieutenant Quentin "Monk" Meyer. Collected letters (courtesy Holly Beyer).

William E. Mitchell. Unpublished memoir (courtesy National Museum of the Pacific War).

Sergeant George Peto, "The Hard Luck Kid" and other collected essays (courtesy George Peto).

Internet Web sites:

GlobalSecurity.org

Japan Policy Research Institute (www.jpri.org)

Okinawa Prefecture Official Home Page (www.pref.okinawa.jp/english)

Ryukyu Cultural Archives (http://rca.open.ed)

Harry S. Truman Presidential Library (www.trumanlibrary.org)

U.S. Army Military History Institute (www.usamhi.carlisle.army.mil)

U.S. Marine Corps Official Homepage (www.usmc.mil/)

Wikipedia, the Free Encyclopedia (http://en.wikipedia.org)

Yahoo! Asia News, June 23, 2006

Acknowledgments

SCORES OF PEOPLE helped write *The Ultimate Battle*. They helped as surely as if they'd sat beside me at the word processor, guiding my fingers on the keyboard and stimulating my thought processes, and I'm deeply grateful to each of them.

I owe special thanks for the contributions of the nearly seventy Okinawa veterans who devoted their time and energy to author interviews, some brief and some stretching over many hours. Without their collective memories and insights, this book could never have been completed. Several people who lost loved ones at Okinawa supplied information on long-dead heroes that was unavailable anywhere else. Among them, these individuals shared an incredible number of gripping, tragic, humorous, and unforgettable stories with me—so many that, regrettably, I was unable to fit all of them into the narrative. Thus, along with my gratitude, I offer my apologies for those omissions.

Many of my interviewees became far more than mere sources of information, however. They also became friends—some of the best I've ever had—and I'll cherish their friendship as long as I live. What a joy it was to discover men like Harry Bender, Porter McLaughlin, Doug Aitken, and Melvin Grant, then have the opportunity to travel across the country to meet them face-to-face. It was an equal joy to reestablish contact with some of the veterans I'd met earlier—R. V. Burgin, Bill Leyden, Sterling Mace, and Dan Lawler, to name a few—while working on *Brotherhood of Heroes,* my book on Peleliu.

The staff of the National Museum of the Pacific War at Fredericksburg, Texas, also made tremendous contributions to the book. Both Reagan Grau, the museum's archivist, and Floyd Cox, who supervises its oral history program, opened their files to me, making available priceless battlefield photos and hundred of pages of interviews with Okinawa veterans. The museum's symposium on Okinawa in September 2005 was where my serious research for *The Ultimate Battle* began, and it enabled me to make valuable contacts all over the nation.

As he was during my research on two previous military histories, my good friend Floyd Wood was always willing to draw on his considerable reservoir of World War II knowledge and expertise to answer my questions, however inane they may have been.

The professional contributions of my resourceful agent, Jim Donovan, and my talented editor at Simon & Schuster, Roger Labrie, cannot, of course, be overemphasized.

And finally, I want to thank my wife, Lana Henderson Sloan—a much more prolific writer and better copy editor than I—for her love and support during this project, as well as for the many hours she spent traveling with me to interviews, photographing veterans, marking up my rough drafts, and telling me when she thought something was good—or bad.

My heartfelt appreciation goes out to everyone who had a part in making *The Ultimate Battle* what I hope may be remembered as the ultimate book on Okinawa. Thank you all!

Bill Sloan
Dallas, Texas

Index

Aaron Ward (destroyer), 234

Ahearn, Captain Mike, 180

Ahner, Sergeant Leonard "Hook," 35, 38, 58–60, 113, 357

Air Force, U.S., 13, 353, 358
  see also Army, U.S., Air Force

Aitken, Jeanne Marie, 361

Aitken, Lieutenant Douglas, 217–20, 222, 227, 233–34, 361

Aka Island, 42

Akikawa, General Suichi, 195

Alaska, 18

Aleutian Islands, 10, 18

Allen, PFC George "Bill," 145–46

Ambrose, Stephen, 360

American Expeditionary Forces, 15

Anami, General Korechika, 341, 343

Anderson, Sergeant Beauford T. "Snuffy," 129

Anderson, Lieutenant Julius, 128

Anthony (destroyer), 254

Anzio landings, 148

Appleman, Roy, 282, 317

Arceneaux, Lieutenant Arthur J., 248–49, 251–52

Archer, Commander Robert, 219, 221, 232

Arima, Admiral Masafumi, 89, 92

Arizona (battleship), 120

Arkansas (battleship), 41

Armstrong, Sergeant Jack H., 1–5, 7, 163–68, 274, 327, 358
  on atomic bomb, 340
  at Kunishi Ridge, 1–3, 282–84

in landing on Okinawa, 30–31, 45

on Roosevelt's death, 126

at Wana Draw, 195–97

Army, U.S., 7, 12, 36, 62, 88, 89, 118, 314, 320, 334, 353
  Air Force, 238–40, 244, 253, 339, 343, 347, 351
  armored units, 281
  artillery, 35–37, 143
  Buckner's conduct of battle supported by commanders of, 312–13
  Cho's counteroffensive stopped by, 160–62
  civilians and, 61, 300, 305, 311
  Corps of Engineers, 39, 356
  at Kakazu ridgeline, 132, 134
  in landing on Okinawa, 30, 51, 238
  losses during Okinawa campaign of, 327
  medics, 43–44
  in Operation Olympic, 336
  Q-boats scuttled by, 104–5
  radar devices of, 245
  response to Roosevelt's death in, 127
  and surrender ceremony, 352
  tanks used by, 46, 164
  typical in-action losses of, 215
  see also Seventh Infantry ("Hourglass") Division; Tenth Army; 27th Infantry Division; 77th Infantry Division; 96th Infantry ("Deadeye") Division

Arnold, General Archibald, 83, 264, 274, 288, 318
Arrow fighters, 217
Arthur, Corporal Stanley W., 315
Atomic bomb, 333, 339–41
Attu Island, 10, 18, 81, 125, 235, 263, 361
Augusta (cruiser), 339, 340
Austin, PFC Ed K., 35–37
Australian POWs, 350
Avenger torpedo aircraft, 19, 108
Awacha Pocket, 197, 204

Bache (destroyer), 235
Bair, Lieutenant Dale, 175–76
Baka bombs, 98
Baltimore (cruiser), 253
Barron, Captain Frank, 218, 297–98
Barrow, Sergeant Ted "Tex," 38, 57
Barry (decoy ship), 325
BARs, 40–42, 120–23, 128, 145, 152, 182, 186, 190, 270, 276, 279
Bass, Gunner's Mate D. C., 223
Bataan, 275, 351
    Death March, 348, 350
Bataan (carrier), 110
Battle of the Bulge, 39
Bauman, PFC Roy, 214
Baur, PFC Harman, 163
Beasley, Private Wilburn L., 163
Beasley, Sergeant Chan, 244
Becker, Sergeant Alvin, 120
Becton, Commander Julian, 96
Belleau Wood (carrier), 97
Belman, Lieutenant Dave, 122
Bender, Harry, Sr., 23
Bender, PFC Harry, Jr., 22–23, 35, 113, 157, 210, 261, 315–17, 355–57
Bennington (carrier), 96–97, 99, 108–10, 253
Berger, Colonel Spencer, 281, 306, 360
Betty bombers, 222, 250, 325, 346–48
Beyer, Holly, 363

Bigert, Homer, 312
Biloxi (cruiser), 94
Binyarde, PFC Lloyd, 46
Bishi Gawa, 39
Bishop, PFC Emmitt, 208
Bjork, Colonel Delbert, 80
Black-Widow fighters, 244
Bleasdale, Colonel Victor, 116
Boetai home guard, 280, 298
Bohn, Corporal Claude, 292–93, 313
Borneo, 12
Boyes, Sergeant Hank, 163, 356
Bradley, General James "Jim," 87, 125, 320
Brewer, Sergeant Arvil, 124
Britain, 12, 333, 344
    Nazi bombing of, 245
    launching of Normandy invasion from, 330
    POWs in Japan from, 350
Brockman, Gunner's Mate Don, 105
Bronze Star, 87, 146, 212, 234, 334, 362
Brownlee, Commander Robert M., 220, 228
Bruce, General Andrew D., 138, 139, 147–48, 168, 263
Brugger, Private Edward, 257
B-24 Liberator bombers, 240
B-29 Superfortress bombers, 238–40, 339–41, 343
Buckner, General Simon Bolivar "Buck," Jr., 4, 12–13, 17–18, 131, 156, 164, 174
    at Conical Hill, 206, 262
    death of, 313–15, 319, 336, 347
    division commanders' disagreement with tactics of, 147–48
    final defeat of 32nd Japanese Army by, 294–95
    Ie Shima landing ordered by, 138
    and Japanese withdrawal from Shuri, 271, 274
    military career of, 18

personnel problems of, 147

Sixth Marine Division commendation from, 279

support of high-ranking commanders for conduct of battle by, 312–13

Turner's pressure on, 146, 168

Bunker Hill (carrier), 110, 230–31

Burgin, Florence Riseley, 356

Burgin, Sergeant R. V., 112, 114, 150, 334, 356–57

commissioned officers and, 199–201, 210–11

at end of war, 344–45

at Kunishi Ridge, 290–91

in landing on Okinawa, 31, 33

wounding of, 211–12

Burke, Corporal Jim, 211

Burma, 12, 14

Burnett, Corporal Elliot, 51

Bush, Corporal Richard E. "Dick," 117–19, 359

Bush (destroyer), 99–101, 103

Butterfield, Corporal Jimmy "Butts," 256–58, 357

Byrne, Captain Wilburt, 80

Byrnes, James, 339, 342, 343

"Cactus Air Force," 18

Cactus Ridge, 68, 85–87

Caffey, Seaman Lester, 20–21, 103, 349, 361

Cain, Sergeant John M., 68–74, 76–80, 86–87

Cairo Conference, 12

Campbell, Lieutenant Clark "Bucket," 244

Campbell, Lieutenant William W., 248, 249, 251–52

Cape Gloucester, Battle of, 164, 165, 196, 215, 290

Carney, Major Frank, 350

Carson, Lieutenant William H., 117

Cassidy, Colonel John, 125

Cassin Young (destroyer), 99, 100

Castle Hill, 80, 83, 85, 86

Causeway, Operation, 12

Cavanaugh, Captain Maurice, 287, 288

Chapman, Ensign F.R., 101

Chapman, PFC Harold W. "Chappy," 256–57

Cherry Society, 15

Chiang Kai-shek, 12, 333, 338

China, 12, 333

Chinen Peninsula, 274, 306, 307

Cho, General Isamu, 14–16, 159, 314, 331

counteroffensives of, 128, 129, 155–56, 159, 161–62

suicide of, 322–24, 354

Chocolate Drop, 169

Chulis, Corpsman George, 208

Churchill, PFC George, 40

Churchill, Winston, 12, 333–34, 338

CinCPOA, 12

Civil War, 17

Clark, Admiral J. J. "Jocko," 253

Clark, Corporal LaMont, 67, 76, 77, 80, 87, 362

Clark, Major Prosser, 86

Clay Ridge, 84

Clement, General William T., 178, 275, 350

Clinton, Bill, 359

Clinton, Hillary, 359

Coast Guard, U.S., 118

Cockerham, Corporal Floyd, 164, 167, 358

Colhoun (destroyer), 99–101, 103

Columbia (cruiser), 347

Combat Air Patrol, 220, 225

Condition Red, 56

Congress, U.S., 137–38

Conical Hill, 135, 142, 156, 169, 206, 262, 263

Coolidge, Colonel Joseph, 139–40

Cooper, Gary, 184

Coronet, Operation, 336–37

Corregidor, 275, 346, 351

Corsair fighters, 56, 76, 219, 221–23, 225, 230, 242, 243, 245, 251, 253

Cory, Lieutenant Richard, 109

Courtney, Major Henry A. "Smiley," Jr., 179–83, 186, 191, 193–94, 359

Craft, PFC Clarence B., 269–70

Crouch, PFC James, 77

Curran, Lieutenant Bill, 122

Curtiss (seaplane tender), 325

Dakeshi Ridge, 169, 197, 210

Day, General Jim, 359

Decker, Corporal Don, 65, 66

DeLazier, Lieutenant Amos, 265

Del Valle, General Pedro, 52, 148, 195, 286, 287, 289, 294, 313

De Meis, PFC Paulie, 118–19

Dencker, Corporal Don, 39, 83–84, 127, 132–33, 303–4, 320, 345, 362

Denig, Colonel Robert L., 275, 276

Detore, PFC Shorty, 41–42

Dillow, Lieutenant Rex, 278

Di Stanislao, Radioman Joe, 347

Distinguished Service Cross, 320

Divine Wind, *see* Kamikazes

Divine Wind, The (Inoguchi), 91

Donohoo, Colonel M. O., 171

Doran, Corporal Robert C., 210

Dorsey (minesweeper), 94

Douglas, Paul, 208, 357

Downfall, Operation, 334, 337

Doyle, Private Alexander, 315

Dunfey, Lieutenant Paul, 187

Dusenbury, Captain Julian D., 268

Dutch POWs, 350

Dwyer, Ensign Tom, 234

Easley, General Claudius, 122–25, 142, 146, 319–20

Eighth Army, 336

Eighth Marine Regiment, 294, 313, 319

Eisenhower, Dwight D., 362

Eldorado (cruiser), 131

11th Marine Regiment, 51, 284

Ellington, Lieutenant Charles "Duke," 199

Emmons (destroyer-minesweeper), 103

Engan, Sergeant Alvin, 133

Eniwetok, 148

Enola Gay (B-29 bomber), 339–40

Enright, Sergeant Bill, 170–71, 192

Enterprise (carrier), 231, 236

Epelley, Seaman John M., Jr., 223, 232–33

Ernie Pyle's Story of GI Joe (movie), 140

Essex (carrier), 110

European Theater of Operations, 154

Evans (destroyer), 219–23, 225, 230–32

Fach, Sergeant Don, 288

Farnsworth, Private Vinone "Vern," 192

Feifer, George, 302, 310–11, 314

Ferry, Lieutenant Francis, 108–10

Fifth Fleet, 253

Fifth Marine Regiment, 260, 281, 289, 322

  in Awacha Pocket, 197, 204

  K Company, Third Battalion of, *see* K/3/5

  at Kunishi, 294

  in landing on Okinawa, 33, 37

  losses of, 319

  at Shuri Castle, 268

Fincke, Lieutenant Reginald, 187–89

Finn, Colonel Mickey, 81, 132, 133, 264, 265, 288, 318, 321, 323, 324

First Army, 336

First Marine ("Old Breed") Division, 17, 52–54, 63–65, 112, 114, 147, 148, 150, 205, 272, 274, 319, 328, 329, 358

  in advance on Shuri, 169–70

battle colors of, 269
battle fatigue in, 201–3
end of war celebrated by, 345
at Guadalcanal, 37
at Half Moon Hill, 260
Japanese offensive against, 156,
    160, 162, 163–68
at Kunishi Ridge, 279, 281–84,
    291–92, 294, 313, 326
in landing on Okinawa, 30, 37, 44
and Operation Coronet, 336–37
at Oroku, 281
at Peleliu, 24, 198–99
Pyle and, 138
response to Roosevelt's death in,
    126
at Sugar Loaf, 178
at Wana Ridge and Wana Draw,
    169, 195, 255–58, 271
see also First Marine Regiment;
    First Marine Tank Battalion;
    Fifth Marine Regiment; Seventh
    Marine Regiment
First Marine Regiment, 28, 37, 50,
    157–59, 273, 285, 326
First Marine Tank Battalion, 1–4,
    30–31, 45, 53–54, 164, 195–97,
    274, 327, 335, 340
Fitzpatrick, Captain James A., 84
532nd Field Artillery, 35–37
Flattop Hill, 169
Floating Chrysanthemums cam-
    paign, see Kamikazes
Ford, Gerald, 362
Formosa, 12, 13
Forrestal, James, 312, 333
Foster, Ensign Carl, 97
Fourth Marine Division, 337
Fourth Marine Regiment, 63, 115–20,
    260, 275, 277, 346, 350–51
Fouts, PFC Pete, 58
Fox, PFC Edward "Buzzy," 310
Franklin (carrier), 89, 92–93, 231
Fraught, Machinist's Mate Harold,
    231

Galinsky, Sergeant John, 42
Gaumnitz, Lieutenant Rodney, 178
Gavin, Patrick, 42
Gebhart, Seaman Franklin, 226
Gehres, Captain Leslie, 93
Geiger, General Roy S., 18, 52, 114,
    164, 262, 275, 279, 314, 322
Genghis Khan, 88
Geruma Island, 42
Gillen, Lieutenant L. W., 225
Giretsu commandos, 242–44
Glassman, Lieutenant Bob, 133
Glory and the Dream, The
    (Manchester), 337
Godfrey, Sergeant Steve, 257–58
Goff, Sergeant Stanley A., 346
Golar, Corporal Donald "Rusty,"
    190–91
Grant, Corporal Melvin, 63–64, 130,
    138, 256, 291–92, 340, 360
Grant, Kate, 360
Grant, Laquetta, 360
Grant, PFC Scott, 64, 291–93, 340,
    360
Grasse, Captain Hank, 281
Graybill, Colonel Russell, 124
Green, Colonel Bernard W., 85, 117
Green, Lieutenant Bob, 133, 146, 362
Green, Seaman Charles, 223
Green Hill, 117, 119
Grew, Joseph C., 333
Griner, General George W., 18, 148
Groff, Lieutenant Herbert, 249–50
Grumman Aircraft, 245
Guadalcanal, 17, 18, 65, 199, 249,
    255, 293
Guam, 118, 180, 240, 313, 341, 345,
    346, 355
Gulf War, 353

Hackleback (submarine), 107
Hacksaw Ridge, see Maeda
    Escarpment
Hadley, Commander Hugh W., 218
Haginouchi, Lieutenant Kyoshi, 323

Hagushi beaches, 16, 20, 96, 103, 108,
    110, 131, 138, 143, 154
Haines, Sergeant C. J., 252
Hake, PFC Robert, 133
Haldane, Captain Andy "Ack-Ack,"
    199, 213
Half Moon Hill, 170, 176–78, 180,
    181, 183, 194, 195, 256, 259,
    260–62, 276
Halloran, Colonel Michael, 124
Halsey, Admiral William F. "Bull," 12,
    19, 253, 351
Hammers, Seaman Fred, 224, 229–30
Hammond, PFC Richard, 160
Hara, Colonel Munetatsu, 74, 76,
    120, 123, 124, 134
Hara, Captain Temichi, 107
Hargus, Corporal Whitey, 257–58
Harmon, General Millard F., 13
Harris, Lieutenant R. E., 136–37
Haven (hospital ship), 349, 350
Hawkins, Major Robert O., 248
Hawks, Sergeant Leonard, 68
Hector Hill, 269–70
Heeb, Sergeant John P., 163
Heim, PFC John, 204, 205
Hellcat fighters, 19, 28, 97, 101, 108,
    221, 243–50, 252
Helldiver bombers, 19, 108–10
Helling, Seaman Leo, 223–24, 229,
    232–33
Henderson, PFC Alfred E., 77–78,
    157, 174–75, 215
Henderson, Gladys, 157, 174
Hen Hill, 269–70
Henry, PFC Adrian, 152–53
Henson, Sergeant Alex "Hurricane,"
    48–49, 60–61, 208
Heuer, Sergeant Bob, 133
Higashionna, Tokuyu, 307
Higdon, Sergeant James E., Jr., 278
Higgins boats, 31, 49, 50
Hile, Seaman Don, 227–28
Hill, Seaman Bruce, 229
Hill, Lieutenant Clyde H., 248

Hill 8, 289
Hill 69, 284–85
Hill 89, 272, 295, 314, 317–18,
    321–24, 326, 354
Hill 95, 279, 299, 319
Hill 178, 65, 125, 133, 141
Hill 200, 117, 119
Hilliard, Lieutenant Fred, 248
Hinsdale (transport ship), 47
Hirohito, Emperor of Japan, 154,
    331–32, 341–44, 346
Hiroshima, atomic bombing of, 340,
    341
Hitler, Adolf, 154
Hobbs Victory (transport), 103
Hochmuth, Colonel Bruno, 260
Hodge, General John R., 65, 66, 147,
    270, 272
    Bucker supported by, 312–13
    and Conical Hill, 206
    and Kakazu Ridge, 74, 87, 131
    plans for containing Japanese at
        Shuri, 263, 266, 267
Holmes, Seaman Jay, 221–23, 225–27,
    229
Hongo, Colonel Kikuji, 318, 347
Hoover, Herbert, 337
Hornet (carrier), 97, 101, 109, 253
Horseshoe Hill, 170, 176–78, 187,
    195, 256, 259, 260, 262
Houston, PFC Jack, 185
Hudson, Private Frederick "Junior,"
    214–15
Huff, Seaman Johnny, 229
Huff, Lieutenant John W., 286
Hugh W. Hadley (destroyer), 217–35,
    361
Hutchings, Lieutenant Robert, 178
Hyman (destroyer), 103

Iceberg, Operation, 10, 14, 17, 46
Iegusugu Yama, 139
Ie Shima, 137–40, 234, 240, 251, 253,
    347–48
Igawa, Major Masashi, 138–39

Imperial Combined Fleet, Japanese, 339

Imperial General Staff, Japanese, 14

Imperial Guards, Japanese, 343

Imperial Navy, Japanese, 89

Inamine, Keiichi, 364

Indianapolis (cruiser), 94

Inoguchi, Commander Rikhei, 90–91

Ishikawa Isthmus, 10, 16, 114

Italian campaign, 139, 148

Item Pocket, 142, 148

Ito, Admiral Seiichi, 110

Iwo Jima, 240, 12, 13, 52, 65, 174, 235, 240, 337

J. William Ditter (minelayer), 254

Janick, Sergeant Albert, 40

JASCO units, 24, 49–51, 203–5

Javanese POWs, 350

Jenkins, PFC Oscar, 127

Johnson, Lieutenant Robert, 292

Joint Chiefs of Staff, U.S., 12–13, 337

Jones, Lieutenant Edward A. "Hillbilly," 31, 112, 199

Jordan, Lieutenant Robert, 292

Judy dive-bombers, 92, 97, 99, 217, 220, 225, 230, 231

K/3/5 (K Company, Third Battalion, Fifth Marine Regiment), 9, 64, 112, 154, 320–21, 327–28, 334, 356–58
  at Awacha Pocket, 197
  civilians and, 113, 301, 304–5, 308–10
  at end of war, 344–45, 348
  first Okinawa combat death of, 162–63
  hog butchered and barbecued by, 57–58
  at Kunishi Ridge, 274, 290–91, 294
  in landing on Okinawa, 33–34, 38–39, 47–49
  losses of, 273–74, 315–17, 319

in move toward Shuri, 207–15, 260–61, 263–65
officer problems of, 199–201
at Peleliu, 22–23, 33, 198–99, 212, 213, 215, 328
Pyle and, 138
response to Roosevelt's death in, 127
Southerners in, 268–69
27th Division relieved by, 149–50, 157
at Yontan airfield, 48

Kadena airfield, 16, 107, 128, 131, 221, 240, 253
  in Cho's counteroffensive plan, 156
  kamikaze attacks planned for, 94, 217
  night-fighter squadrons at, 244, 251
  Okinawan conscripts left to defend, 51, 298
  shelling of, 241

Kai, Lieutenant Tomai, 236

Kakazu Ridge—Kakazu West, 66, 68, 84–87, 112, 116, 120–34, 137, 142, 176, 206, 280, 287
  air strikes on, 123, 125
  apartment buildings surrounding, 354
  bombardment of, 132, 143
  casualties on, 120, 122, 123, 125, 127, 131, 169
  counterattacks on, 128–29
  Easley's powerhouse attacks on, 123–25, 319
  enemy dead on, 123, 133
  interconnected subterranean fortifications on, 74, 120–21, 144, 262
  Japanese withdrawal from, 134, 141, 263, 272, 274
  May's assessment of, 73–74, 76
  tanks destroyed or disabled on, 133, 164

Kalinofsky, Gunner's Mate Hank, 26–27, 97–99, 346, 361–62
Kamikazes, 27, 28, 88–111, 168, 216–36, 253–54, 325–26, 343, 348
   air strikes against bases used for, 47, 238–39, 253
   ammunition shortages caused by, 131
   losses to Navy personnel from, 215, 236
   midair collisions of, 220–21
   Okinawa beachhead attacked by, 94, 96–99
   organization of task force of, 91–92
   in Philippines, 89–90, 92
   ships damaged or sunk by, 26, 92, 94, 99–101, 103, 146, 217–20, 225–36, 254, 325
   shooting down of, 102–3, 221, 223, 224, 249, 325, 361
   Yamamoto on mission as, 106–11
Kase, Toshikazu, 332
Kate bombers, 101, 252
Kawabe, General Torashiro, 348
Kawasaki, bombing of, 240–41
Keise Shima, 35–37
Kelley, Lieutenant Maynard, 243
Kellum, Major William C., 249
Kelly, PFC Charles, 159
Kelly, Private Don, 190–91
Kelly, PFC Jack, 243–44
Kelly, Corporal Roy R. "Railroad," 215
Kendall, Ensign Wallace, 233–34
Kennedy, John F., 22
Kerama Retto, 41–43, 53, 234, 235, 347
   civilian casualties in, 60, 297–98
   graveyard of ships at, 47, 103, 231
   suicide boats hidden in, 104–5
Kieman, PFC Ray, 171, 172
Kikusui Operations, 94, 99–104, 106, 111, 216, 217, 221, 235, 236, 253–54, 325
King, Colonel Byron E., 122–24
King, Admiral Ernest J., 12, 13, 19, 337
Kiska Island, 10, 18
Kiyamu Peninsula, 265, 272
Klingman, Lieutenant Robert R., 251
Knorr, Sergeant, John, 91, 153, 361
Kobe, bombing of, 240–41
Kochi Ridge, 142
Kokobu airfield, 220
Konrad, Commander E. G., 109
Korean War, 353, 356, 358
Kottas, PFC William, 41–43, 297
Kramer, Lieutenant William, 68, 69, 72, 77
Kriegsman, Lieutenant John, 104
Kubitz, PFC Charlie, 70, 72, 73, 76, 78
Kublai Khan, 88
Kulp, Sergeant Robert, 124
Kunishi Ridge, 1, 274, 279, 282–95, 313, 318, 340, 347, 363
Kurile Islands, 10
Kwajalein, 10, 81, 125, 263, 361
Kyushu, 10, 107, 216–17, 254, 336–37, 341
   kamikaze flights from, 47, 99, 217, 242, 253, 325
   midair collisions over, 220–21
   raids on airbases on, 231, 238–39

Lacy, Commander Lewis, 21–22
Laffey (destroyer), 94, 96
Lambert, PFC Francis, 125
Land, Bill, 40
Lane, Corporal Eric, 67
Lardner, John, 299–301
LaWear, Gertrude, 91
Lawler, Corporal Dan, 47–49, 138, 304–5, 308–10, 348, 357
Lawrence, David, 312
LCIs (landing craft, infantry), 105
LCVPs (landing craft, vehicles/ personnel), 46–47

Legion of Merit, 234

Leimbach, Lieutenant E. L., 248

LeMay, General Curtis E., 238–40, 339

Leutze (destroyer), 103

Lewis, Seaman Vaughn, 223

Leyden, PFC Bill, 9, 58–60, 162–63, 212–14, 357
  and civilians, 113
  in landing on Okinawa, 31, 35, 38
  on Roosevelt's death, 127

Leyte, 10, 40, 42, 68–69, 90, 92, 235
  Seventh Infantry Division at, 263
  96th Infantry Division at, 70, 84, 144

Lincoln, Abraham, 126

Logan Victory (transport), 103

London blitz, 245

Lombardo, Guy, 358

Loter, Sergeant Tom, 133

Love Company (Dencker), 362

Loveday, Lieutenant George "Shadow," 200–201

Lowe, Private William H., 278

LSM(R) 193 (rocket ship), 219, 232, 234

LSM(R) 197 (rocket ship), 97, 98

LSM(R) 198 (rocket ship), 26–27, 97, 346

LSTs, 44, 47, 49, 50, 94, 103

Luzon, 12, 13, 337

LVTs, 281

Mabie, Captain Howard, 259

Mabuni, 317–18, 321–22

MacArthur, General Douglas, 12, 332, 337, 347, 351–52

Mace, Corporal Sterling, 34, 57–58, 64, 149, 150, 207–9, 357–58

Mace, Joyce, 358

Mack, Pharmacist's Mate Frank, 192–93

Maeda Escarpment, 142–44, 146, 147, 155–56, 159

Magee, Colonel James, 285

Mahoney, Captain J.J., 101–2

Majors, PFC Wendell "Deacon," 183–85, 341, 359–60

Makin, Battle of, 148

Manchester, William, 337–38

Manhattan Project, 349

Manila, Battle of, 332

Mariana Islands, 14, 91

Marine Corps, U.S., 7, 18, 23, 24, 36, 62, 88, 89, 112, 184, 208, 314, 353
  aircraft, 76, 221, 230, 240–41, 253, 266 (*see also* VMF squadrons)
  armored units, 281
  and Buckner's conduct of battle, 312–13
  civilians and, 60–61, 296, 300, 305, 311
  at Guadalcanal, 65
  at Iwo Jima, 65
  in landing on Okinawa, 28–30, 39, 40, 51, 238
  losses during Okinawa campaign of, 327
  oldest private in, 208, 357
  in Operation Olympic, 336
  at Pearl Harbor, 120
  at Peleliu, 9, 24–25, 50, 55, 65
  pontoon bridges built by, 172
  posthumous medals awarded to, 60
  Raiders, 115
  response to Roosevelt's death in, 126–27
  shelling of Kakazu ridgeline by, 132
  and surrender ceremony, 352
  tanks, 46, 164, 167
  at Tarawa, 65
  III Amphibious Corps, 18, 52, 114, 262, 275, 314
  typical in-action losses of, 215
  youngest member of, 118
  see also First Marine Division; Second Marine Division; Sixth Marine Division

Marshall, General George C., 333, 337

Masciale, Sergeant Benjamin, 244

May, Colonel Edwin T. "Eddy," 73–74, 76, 86, 87, 120, 122–23, 206, 262, 320

Maybury, Colonel Daniel C., 86, 161

McCormack, Lieutenant Clement R., 235

McCracken, Lieutenant Richard, 161

McCrae, Lieutenant Harry, 109

McDonald, Ensign Ben, 101–3, 349–50, 361

McDonald, Sergeant Theodore, 133

McGann, Lieutenant Patrick, 234

McKenzie, Lieutenant Robert "Scotty," 199–201, 210, 211

McLaughlin, Sergeant Porter, 81–82, 132, 152–53, 264, 318, 327, 360–61
    at Attu, 10
    and civilians, 62–63, 82–83
    at Conical Hill, 135–36
    in landing on Okinawa, 44–45
    at Shuri after Japanese with-drawal, 269
    at Ushijima's headquarters, 324–25
    visit from "uncle" of, 136–37

McMillan, George, 44, 112, 162, 286

McNeel, Dave, 28

McNeel, Sergeant Walt, 28, 241–43, 252

McNulty (destroyer), 97–98

McQuillan, Captain John J., 45, 137

Medal of Honor, 60, 118, 123, 129, 140, 194, 270, 359

M-8 armored cars, 67–68, 76–79

Meisner, Captain Alan, 259

Messer, Lieutenant Fred, 68–70, 72, 77

Meyer, Cord, 24

Meyer, Corporal Thomas "Pete," 24, 363

Meyer, Lieutenant Quentin "Monk," 24–25, 49–50, 203–5, 363

Meyer, William, 24

Mezado Ridge, 291–95

Miami (cruiser), 253

Midway, 17, 107

Milonni, PFC Americo "Moe," 130–31

Minatoga, 46–47

Missouri (battleship), 348, 351

Mitchell, Lieutenant Willard F. "Hoss," 121–24, 134

Mitscher, Admiral Marc, 108, 230, 231, 235, 236, 313

Mitsubishi, 240

Mongols, 88

Moore, PFC Ellis, 25–26

Mori, General Takeshi, 343

Morison, Samuel Eliot, 17, 106, 332

Morris (destroyer), 103

Moskala, PFC Edward, 123

Motobu Peninsula, 65, 115–20, 131, 345, 351

Mott, PFC Carner W., 208

Mullaney, Captain Baron J. "Joe," 218, 219, 221–25, 227–29, 232, 234

Mullany (destroyer), 103

Murphy, Sergeant George, 44–45, 62, 81, 82, 361

Nagasaki, atomic bombing of, 340, 341, 349–50

Nagoya, bombing of, 240

Naha, 11, 19, 37, 262–65, 271, 275, 320, 353–56

Naha-Shuri-Yonabaru Line, 66, 134

Nakagusuku Castle, 86

Nakmuta, Tetsuo, 323

Nambu machine guns, 117, 194

National Guard, 18, 148

Naval Institute, U.S., 106

Navy Cross, 25, 110, 234

Navy, U.S., 7, 20, 21, 41, 118, 136, 138, 182, 185, 339, 353
    aircraft, 108–10, 351 (see also VMF night-fighter squadrons)

bombardment of Okinawa by, 25–26, 37, 39, 117, 139, 143, 194, 203–5, 266, 289
Buckner's conduct of battle supported by commanders of, 312–13
Cho's offensive stopped by, 160
corpsmen, 43–44, 192
and ground troops before landing, 27–29, 38
hospitals, 59, 130
JASCO reports on enemy locations to, 50
kamikaze attacks on, 88–106, 112, 126, 146, 168, 215–36, 249, 253–54, 325
liberation of POWs from Japan by, 348–50
losses during Okinawa campaign of, 327
mapmakers of, 19
Memorial, 362
Pacific Fleet headquarters, 52
radar devices of, 245
response to Roosevelt's death in, 126–27
Supply Corps, 361
VE Day marked by, 154
see also specific ships
Nazis, 97, 154
Nealon, Lieutenant Robert, 180–82
Nease, Corporal Howard, 162
Needle Rock, 142
Nemec, PFC Frank, 196, 358
Nevada (battleship), 94
New Britain, 31
Newcomb (destroyer), 103
New Mexico (battleship), 94
New Orleans (cruiser), 266
New York (battleship), 123, 266
New Yorker, The, 299
New York Herald-Tribune, 312
New York National Guard, 18, 148
New York Times, 52
Niader, Frank, 363

Niader, Private William V. "Bill," 287–88, 363
Nick fighters, 251
Niemeyer, Captain Tony, 288
Nimitz, Admiral Chester W., 12–13, 17, 19, 52, 146, 238, 239, 312, 313, 351
96th Infantry ("Deadeye") Division, 17, 53, 65, 80, 81, 87, 112, 151, 269, 271, 274, 279, 322, 362
    in advance on Shuri, 168, 169, 205–6
    at Conical Hill, 262, 263
    end of war celebrated by, 345
    Japanese offensives against, 128, 156, 160
    at Kakazu Ridge, 66, 120–29, 131–34, 137, 169, 176, 319
    at Kunishi Ridge, 285, 294
    in landing on Okinawa, 39–40
    at Leyte, 70
    losses during closing days of campaign of, 319–20
    at Maeda Escarpment, 141–47
    shipped out for Philippines, 329
    see also 96th Recon Troop; 381st Infantry Regiment; 382nd Infantry Regiment; 383rd Infantry Regiment
96th Recon Troop, 67–74, 76, 83, 144–46, 157, 174, 215, 362
Nishibaru Ridge, 132, 134
Nist, Colonel Cecil, 272
Nolan, Colonel Daniel, 262
Normandy landings, 21, 139, 330
North Africa campaign, 70, 139
Northwestern University, 22

O'Brien (destroyer), 94
Odenhal, Commander Charles J., 231
O'Hara, Lieutenant Frank, 248
Ohnishi, Admiral Takijiro, 90–92
Oka rocket bombs, 325
Okinawa Odyssey (Green), 362

Okinawa Prefecture Memorial
    Museum, 354
Okum, PFC Ben, 2, 3, 165–67,
    282–84
Old Breed, The (McMillan), 44, 112,
    162, 286, 345
Oldendorf, Admiral Jesse, 347
Olympic, Operation, 336–37
106th Infantry Regiment, 162
184th Infantry Regiment, 80, 81, 83,
    85–86, 161, 168, 264, 268, 322
O'Neill, Captain Robert, 68–70, 72,
    87
Onishi, Admiral Takijiro, 343
Oroku Peninsula, 271, 274–79, 281
Osaka, bombing of, 240
Ota, Admiral Minoru, 275, 276, 278,
    279
Ouki Hill, 132

Pachler, Colonel Francis, 288
Pacific Fleet, U.S., 12, 89, 104, 107,
    249
Parsons, Lieutenant Lloyd J., 246–47
Parsons, Captain William S., 339
Pavuvu, 31, 112, 162, 199, 315, 334
Pearl Harbor, Japanese attack on, 11,
    21, 89, 120, 245, 312, 331, 340
Pearson, Lieutenant Bucky, 163, 210,
    316–17
Peleliu, 16, 18, 38, 65, 170, 205, 249,
    281
    First Marine Tank Battalion at,
        164, 165, 196
    First Marine Regiment at, 28,
        157–58, 256
    JASCO units at, 24, 50
    K/3/5 at, 9, 22–23, 31, 33, 34, 48,
        59, 149, 163, 198–99, 212, 213,
        215, 290, 291, 328, 357, 358
Pennsylvania (battleship), 347
Percival, General Sir Arthur, 351
Perry, Commodore Matthew, 11, 85
Pershing, General John J. "Black
    Jack," 15

Pesely, Lieutenant Ed, 178, 180–81,
    188–89
Peto, Sergeant George, 157–59, 320
Philippines, 12, 14, 18, 54, 89–91,
    235, 345, 348, 351
    see also Leyte
Pick, PFC George, 215
Pinnacle, the, 83, 86
Piper Cub reconnaissance planes, 103
Pisarski, PFC Gene, 72
Pittsburgh (cruiser), 253
Pizio, PFC Rudolph, 68–71, 73, 76
Polidaro, PFC Vincent, 244
Porter, Major Robert, 249
Potsdam Conference, 333–34, 338,
    339
Potsdam Declaration, 338–39,
    341–43, 346
POWs, American and Allied, 348
Presidential Unit Citation, 122, 234
Privateer aircraft, 243
Purple Heart, 87, 196, 234, 357, 359,
    362
Pyle, Ernie, 137–41

Q-boats, 104–6
Quintanilla, Private Gil, 50, 204–5

Radar, 244
Radar Picket Stations, 99–100, 217,
    220, 231, 254
Radford, Admiral A. W., 253
Radio Tokyo, 343
Rall, Sergeant Francis, 86
Randolph (carrier), 236
Ranger (carrier), 361
Redden, Lieutenant James, 40
Redifer, PFC John, 200–201, 211
Reuser, Captain Kenneth, 251
Reuter, Captain Louis, Jr., 143
Revolutionary War, 23
Riley, PFC Kyle C., 72, 77
Rivas, PFC Manuel, 255–56
Rivas, PFC Salvador, 255–56
Robb, Colonel William G., 259, 262

Robbins, Captain Edward S., 160
Roberts, Colonel Harold C., 177, 314
Robertson, Sergeant Alfred C. "Chief," 128–29
Rodman (destroyer-minesweeper), 103
Roe, Lieutenant Jim, 189
Rohrer, Captain Richard, 286
Roosevelt, Franklin D., 11–12, 125–29, 208, 332
Royster, Captain Jack, 122
Rucker, Corporal Henry, 158, 159, 320
Rummell, PFC Raven L., 204–5
Rupp, PFC Christian, 135–36
Russell Islands, 31
Russo-Japanese War, 331
Rutkowski, PFC Walt, 181–83, 186–87, 191, 359
Ryukyu Islands, 10, 14, 92, 327

St. Lo (carrier), 92
Saipan, 13, 14, 18, 148, 174, 240, 332
Sak, PFC Tony, 84
Sally bombers, 242, 243
Samurai tradition, 15, 16, 315, 322
Sanchez, PFC Fred, 193
Santos, PFC Vincent, 211
Sarrett, Corporal George, 31, 33
Sawtooth Ridge, *see* Maeda Escarpment
Schlinder, Corporal Ray, 170–72, 187–93, 203, 359
Schlinder, Margaret, 359
Schneider, Colonel Merlin F., 171
Scoles, Corporal Lloyd, 63
Scripps-Howard News Service, 139
Seabees, 49, 329
Sea Raider Squadrons, Japanese, 42
Second Marine Division, 17, 46–47, 63, 148, 294, 313
Seitz, Captain George A., 231
Seki, Lieutenant Yukio, 91
Sergeant York (movie), 184
Seventh Infantry ("Hourglass")

Division, 17, 53, 65, 80–81, 112, 144, 151–53, 168, 263, 271, 328–29
at Attu, 10
at Conical Hill, 141
failure to cut off Japanese withdrawal by, 267–68
Japanese offensives against, 156, 159–62
at Kakazu Ridge, 120, 125, 128, 131, 137
at Kunishi Ridge, 279, 288–89, 294
in landing on Okinawa, 39, 40
in mop-up operation, 326
at the Pinnacle, 83, 85
Ushijima's and Cho's bodies discovered by, 324
on Yonabaru-Naha highway, 206, 264, 265
see also 17th Infantry Regiment; 32nd Infantry Regiment; 184th Infantry Regiment
Seventh Marine Regiment, 37, 63, 130, 195, 256, 258, 281, 306
at Kunishi Ridge, 285–88, 294
17th Infantry Regiment, 168, 288–89
77th "Statue of Liberty" Infantry Division, 17, 168, 205–6, 271, 274, 319, 329
in advance on Shuri, 169, 263, 274
on Ie Shima, 131, 137–40, 147
Japanese offensive against, 159, 160, 162
on Keise Shima, 36
in Kerama Retto campaign, 60, 104, 105
surrender of Japanese soldiers to, 318–19
see also 305th Infantry Regiment; 306th Infantry Regiment; 307th Infantry Regiment
Shapley, Colonel Alan, 120
Sheetz, General Josef, 132
Sheldrake (minesweeper), 22

Shelton, Corporal Merriel "Snafu,"
    150, 200, 211
Shepherd, General Lemuel, 52,
    114–16, 119, 148, 172, 179, 258,
    262, 279
Sherer, Lieutenant Bob, 194
Sherman, Admiral Forrest, 17, 351
Sherman tanks, 71, 82, 163–65, 172,
    264, 287
    destruction of, 1–4, 78–80, 146,
        165–67, 196–97, 275, 284
    flame-thrower equipped, 163–64,
        196
    at Kakazu Ridge, 133, 164
    at Kunishi Ridge, 282–84
    in landing on Okinawa, 30, 45
    at Sugar Loaf Hill, 175, 259
Sherrod, Robert, 255
Shigemitsu, Japanese Foreign
    Minister, 351
Shimada, Ei, 306
Shimpu Attack Unit, 91
Shimura, Captain Tsuneo, 347
Shofner, Colonel Austin "Shifty,"
    54–55
Sho Operation, 90, 92
Shoumatoff, Elizabeth, 126
Shuikoku, 231
Shuri Castle, 263, 268
    flag raising at, 268–69
    reconstruction of, 354
    ridges around, see Shuri Defense
        Zone
    Ushijima's headquarter's in caves
        beneath, 16, 155, 169, 262,
        265–66
Shuri Defense Zone, 66, 147, 169–70,
    176–77, 197–98, 206–7, 274, 280,
    308, 354
    bombardment of, 131
    Cho's offensive observed from,
        161
    collapse of, 255, 263, 266
    heavy artillery barrages from, 125,
        144, 172, 241, 260–62

Japanese withdrawal from,
    266–68, 272, 305–7
mop-up operation at, 269–71, 273
plan for containing Japanese at,
    263, 266
see also Conical Hill; Half Moon
    Hill; Horseshoe Hill; Kakazu
    Ridge-Kakazu West; Sugar Loaf
    Hill; Wana Ridge—Wana Draw
Shutes, PFC John, 70, 76, 78
Sicily, invasion of, 139
Sieber, Lieutenant Edward, 109–10
Siebert, PFC Donald "Si," 270
Siegel, Colonel William E., 288
Sigler, Captain Wallace E., 249
Silver Star, 25, 28, 50, 87, 120, 129,
    163, 180, 199, 234, 279, 361,
    362
Silverthorne, Lieutenant Spencer V.,
    278–79
Singapore, 351
Sitko Bay (carrier), 249
Sixth Army, 336
Sixth Marine ("New Breed")
    Division, 17, 53, 63–64, 131, 147,
        148, 205, 267, 329
    in advance on Shuri, 168–73
    casualties of, 262, 327
    civilians and, 307
    end of war celebrated by, 345–46
    Japanese offensive against, 156
    KIAs of, 327
    at Kunishi Ridge, 326
    landing in Japan of, 350
    in landing on Okinawa, 30, 38, 52
    at Mezado Ridge, 291–93
    on Motobu Peninsula, 65, 114–20
    and Operation Coronet, 336–37
    at Oroku, 274–75, 279
    Pyle and, 138
    at Sugar Loaf, 176, 178, 181, 182,
        190, 194, 195, 256, 258–60, 262
    see also Fourth Marine Regiment;
        22nd Marine Regiment; 29th
        Marine Regiment

Sixth Marine Division Association, 358

Skylark (minesweeper), 21, 22

Skyline Ridge, 132, 133, 141

Sledge, PFC Gene, 9, 64, 114, 149–50, 162, 163, 268–69, 321, 327–28, 358

   in Awacha Pocket, 197–98

   and civilians, 301

   at end of war, 344

   foot problems of, 273

   at Half Moon Hill, 260–61

   and K/3/5 officers, 199–201, 210, 211

   at Kunishi Ridge, 290–91, 293–94

   in landing on Okinawa, 29, 33, 37–38, 51

   on Nazi surrender, 154

   at Peleliu, 9, 33, 149

   on Roosevelt's death, 127

   at Wana Draw, 263–64

Smith, Colonel Aubrey, 139

Smith, Corporal Stephen, 2, 3, 283

Snedeker, Colonel Edward W., 286

Snyder, Sergeant Walter L., 126

Solace (hospital ship), 43

Solch, PFC Joseph, 121–22

Solomon Islands, 218

Sonan, Shigeko, 302–3

Sonnenberg, Corporal Earl, 84

Soviet Union, 332, 333, 341, 344

Spencer, Commander D. A., 20

Spoerke, Private David, 2, 165–66, 284

Spruance, Admiral Raymond A., 12, 13, 17, 93–94, 253

Stalin, Joseph, 332

Stankovich, Corporal Steve, 181–83

Stanley, Sergeant G. M., 244

Stanley, Lieutenant Thomas "Stumpy," 60, 199, 200, 213

Stare, Colonel Edward, 124

Starling (minesweeper), 20–22

Stebbins, Captain Owen T., 175–76

Steele, PFC Archie, 214

Stephan, Corporal Harlan, 4, 30–31, 165–67

Stilwell, General Joseph W. "Vinegar Joe," 314, 326

Stimson, Henry L., 333

Stonelake, Seaman Robert, 225

Stout, PFC Cecil, 163

Strain, PFC Bill, 145–46, 362

Stuart, Colonel A. J. "Jeb," 4, 45

Sturgeon (submarine), 14

Sugar Hill, 206, 262

Sugar Loaf Hill, 170, 273, 175–95, 262, 280, 287, 341, 351, 359–60

   bombardment of, 179

   casualties on, 175–76, 179, 194, 203, 334

   counterattacks on, 193–94

   Japanese artillery defending, 256, 258

   night assault on, 181–87

   taken by Marines, 259–61

Suicide warfare, *see* Kamikazes

Sumatra, 12

Supreme Council for the Direction of the War (SCDW), Japanese, 331–32, 342

Surigao Strait, 235

Sutherland, General R. K., 351

Suzuki, Baron Kantaro, 331–33, 339, 342, 343

Swallow (minesweeper), 22

Sweeney, Major Charles W., 341

Switzer, Private Harry, 287–88

Tamai, Commander Asaichi, 91–92

Tanabaru Ridge, 132, 134

Tanigawa, Lieutenant Senji, 85

Tarawa, 65, 214

Task Force 38, 253

Task Force 58, 17, 88, 94, 99, 101, 107–8, 168, 217, 218, 221, 230

Taylor, Commander Joe, 93

TEN-Go, 94

Tenbarge, Corporal Alvin, 4, 31, 165–67

Tennessee (battleship), 119, 347

Tennozan (Feifer), 302

Tenth Army, 4, 6, 13, 17–18, 131, 168, 169, 262, 299, 312–14, 322, 326
average yards per day gained by, 255
bombing raids on rear areas of, 156
casualty count of, 175, 215
civilians and, 300, 305
criticism of Buckner's command of, 146, 147
equipment and supplies bogged down behind, 281
failure to cut off Japanese withdrawal by, 263, 265, 268, 271, 272
Ie Shima and, 138
at Kunishi Ridge, 294–95
military intelligence and, 66
mop-up of Okinawa by, 347
naval transport to Okinawa of, 52
and Operation Coronet, 336
surrender ceremony conducted by, 352
at Yaeju Dake-Yuza Dake Escarpment, 279
see also specific Army and Marine divisions

Tesreau, PFC Myron, 273

Texas (battleship), 139

32nd Infantry Regiment, 44, 80–83, 85, 168, 288, 361
at Conical Hill, 135
at Kakazu Ridge, 132, 133
Ushijima's headquarters overrun by, 318, 321–24
Yonabaru to Shuri trek of, 264–65, 269

32nd Japanese Army, 6, 14, 51, 62, 175, 206, 255, 272, 294–95, 331
and Buckner's death, 314
civilians and, 298, 306, 307, 310, 311
defeat of, 297, 317–18, 321–22, 325

destruction of food supplies of, 19
final summary order issued to, 280
holdouts from, 326–27, 347
losses of, 162
reinforcements for, 217, 236–37
Shuri Castle headquarters of, 155
strategy of, 16–17
withdrawal from Shuri of, 265–68

Third Fleet, 347

Thompson sub-machine guns, 36, 60, 204, 244

Threadfin (submarine), 107

305th Infantry Regiment, 42, 139, 140, 263, 271, 297, 319

306th Infantry Regiment, 41, 42, 139, 160

307th Infantry Regiment, 147, 326

381st Infantry Regiment, 39, 83–84, 124–25, 128, 143, 147, 262, 294, 326

382nd Infantry Regiment, 39, 125, 127, 132, 262, 269–70, 294, 303, 320

383rd Infantry Regiment, 39, 67, 73, 74, 78
at Cactus Ridge, 85–87
at Conical Hill, 206
at Kakazu Ridge, 76, 120–24, 128, 129, 206
in landing on Okinawa, 25–26, 39
at Maeda Escarpment, 144, 147

Thunderbolt fighters, 253

Tibbets, Colonel Paul W., 339

Tinian Island, 240, 339–40

Togo, Shigenori, 331–32, 339, 341

Tokashiki Island, 43, 297

Tokyo, bombing of, 240

Tokyo Rose, 243

Tombstone Ridge, 125, 132–33

Tomigusuki Castle, 278

Towry, Private Howard O., 45–46, 53–56, 164, 335–36, 358

Toyama Maru (troopship), 14

Toyoda, Admiral Soemu, 339, 341

Truman, Harry S., 6, 127, 140, 234, 270, 333, 337–41, 343, 344

Turbeville, Lieutenant John G., 319

Turner, Admiral Richmond Kelly, 17, 52, 126, 146, 168, 251, 313

Tuttle, PFC Harry M., 278

22nd Marine Regiment, 114–15, 119, 168, 260, 314
  civilians encountered by, 310
  crossing of Asa Kawa River by, 171–73
  end of war celebrated by, 345–46
  at Oroku, 278
  at Sugar Loaf, 173, 175–94, 359

24th Corps, 74, 87, 131, 141, 147, 206, 263, 272, 313

27th Infantry Division, 17–19, 53, 129, 141, 147–50, 151, 157, 327

29th Marine Regiment, 114–16, 119, 172, 194, 258–60, 275–78, 334

Tyler, PFC William, 315–17

U-boats, 97

Uchiyama, Colonel Yukio, 86

Udo, Colonel Takehido, 115, 116, 119

Ugaki, Admiral Matome, 94, 96, 97, 104, 216–17, 253, 325–26

Uhls, PFC Orlie, 57–58

UNESCO, 354

United Features Syndicate, 139

Urasoe-Mura Escarpment, 65, 73–74, 132, 141

Ushijima, General Mitsuru, 14–16, 18, 66, 128, 169–70, 175, 288, 307, 326
  and Buckner's death, 314–15
  and Cho's counteroffensive, 155–56, 159, 161–62
  and collapse of Shuri line, 255, 259, 262
  Conical Hill defense of, 206
  Dakeshi ordered abandoned by, 195
  defeat of, 315, 317–18, 321–22
  depletion of forces of, 280

  Kakazu ridgeline relinquished by, 134
  Mabuni headquarters of, 278, 295
  and Minatoga mock invasion, 47
  Okinawans conscripted by, 298
  reinforcements for, 217, 236–37
  Shuri stronghold of, 147, 154–55
  suicide of, 322–25, 354
  withdrawal from Shuri of, 263, 265–68, 270–72, 274, 305–6

Utanamori, see Conical Hill

Val dive-bombers, 100, 101, 220–22, 253

Vallina, Machinist's Mate Louis A., 93

Van Vulpen, Captain John, 122

Vargo, PFC Leonard, 293

VE Day, 154

Verga, PFC Harry, 214

Vermeer, PFC Marion, 212–14

Vietnam War, 353, 361

Vissio, Sergeant Louie "Pruneface," 81, 82

VMF (night-fighter) squadrons, 28, 241–52

Von Holle, Captain Alvin E., 39–40

Wainwright, General Jonathan, 351

Wallace, Colonel Clarence, 313

Walton, Francie, 24, 25, 203–5, 363

Wana Ridge—Wana Draw, 169, 195, 196, 208, 255–58, 260, 268, 271, 280

Ward, Corporal August, 70–72, 76–77

War Department, U.S., 300

Warner, Airman Fred, 109

Wasp (carrier), 94

Watanabe, General Masao, 14

Watkins, Lieutenant Richard B., 285

Watt, Lieutenant Ralph, 68, 69

Weaver, Sergeant Marshall W., 121

West Point, U.S. Military Academy at, 18

Westbrook, PFC Marion, 163

Westholm, Commander Rollin, 100
Whaling, Colonel William J., 258, 259
Wheldon, Lieutenant Ned E., 228
Whitaker, PFC Dick, 334
Whitaker, Private Jay W., 163
Whitby, PFC Bob "Pops," 34, 207–8
White, Private Henry, 277
White, Private James S., 276
White, PFC John, 276
White, Private R. R. "Railroad," 277
White, Private Robert S., 276, 277
White, Private W. F., 277
White, Private W. W. "Red," 276–77
Wichita (heavy cruiser), 20–21,
    101–3, 349, 361
Williams, Private Richard L., 315
Wilson, Commander George R., 100,
    101
Winter, Lieutenant Bill, 235, 361
Wishnewski, Corporal John, 315
*With the Old Breed at Peleliu and
    Okinawa* (Sledge), 358
Womack, Corporal Charles "Red," 33
Wood, Commander Hugh, 108–10
Woodhouse, Colonel H. G., Jr.,
    177–81, 187
Word, PFC John D., 42
World War I, 15, 18, 23, 86, 153, 178,
    184, 217, 345

Yaeju Dake, 265, 272, 288–89, 294,
    318
Yaetake, Mount, 115–20, 276
Yahagi (cruiser), 107, 110

Yahara, Colonel Hiromichi, 14–18,
    66, 155, 156, 161, 323
Yale University, 24
Yamato (battleship), 106–11
Yap, Battle of, 249
Yokohama, bombing of, 240
Yokoi, Admiral Toshiyuki, 94, 96
Yokosuka, 350–51
Yonabaru, 11, 206, 262–64, 269
Yonai, Admiral, 343
Yontan airfield, 16, 28, 48–49, 107,
    221, 240, 253, 334
    aerial attacks on, 240–41
    in Cho's counteroffensive plan, 156
    kamikaze attacks planned for, 94,
        217
    night-fighter squadrons at,
        241–44, 246, 252
    Okinawan conscripts left to
        defend, 51, 298
    visibility from Kakazu Ridge of, 85
Yuza Dake, 265, 272, 279, 285, 286,
    289, 294
Yuza Hill, 284–85

Zamami Island, 42, 297–98
Zero ("Zeke") fighters, 49, 51, 56
    in kamikaze attacks, 90, 99–103,
        222, 229–30, 236, 249, 253
    shooting down of, 97, 103, 224,
        249
Zimmer, PFC Ernie, 84, 303
Zinfini, Private Joseph, 160
Ziperski, Private George, 54

Illustration Credits

Numbers in roman type refer to illustrations in the insert; italics refer to book pages.

About the Author

Bill Sloan is an award-winning freelance journalist and the author of nearly a dozen books, the most recent being *Brotherhood of Heroes: The Marines at Peleliu, 1944—The Bloodiest Battle of the Pacific War,* and *Given Up for Dead: America's Heroic Stand at Wake Island.* During his 10 years as an investigative reporter/feature writer for the *Dallas Times Herald,* he covered many of the major events and personalities of the second half of the twentieth century and was nominated for a Pulitzer Prize. He lives in Dallas, Texas.